UNDERSTANDING THE CHINESE MIND
THE PHILOSOPHICAL ROOTS

D0071341

UNDERSTANDING
THE
CHINESE
MIND

THE PHILOSOPHICAL ROOTS

EDITOR
ROBERT E. ALLINSON

CONTRIBUTORS
ROBERT E. ALLINSON   CHUNG-YING CHENG   ANTONIO S. CUA
CHAD HANSEN   CHRISTOPH HARBSMEIER   LAO SZE-KWANG
ROBERT C. NEVILLE   JOHN E. SMITH   KUANG-MING WU

HONG KONG
OXFORD UNIVERSITY PRESS
OXFORD NEW YORK

Oxford University Press

Oxford New York Toronto
Petaling Jaya Singapore Hong Kong Tokyo
Delhi Bombay Calcutta Madras Karachi
Nairobi Dar es Salaam Cape Town
Melbourne Auckland

and associated companies in
Berlin Ibadan

© Oxford University Press 1989

All rights reserved. No part of this publication may be
reproduced, stored in a retrieval system, or transmitted, in any
form or by any means, electronic, mechanical, photocopying,
recording, or otherwise, without the prior permission of
Oxford University Press

'Oxford' is a trade mark of Oxford University Press

First published 1989
Reissued in paperback 1989
Second impression 1990
Published in the United States
by Oxford University Press, Inc., New York

ISBN 0 19 582706 6 (cloth)
ISBN 0 19 585022 X (limp)

British Library Cataloguing in Publication Data
Understanding the Chinese mind: the philosophical
roots.
1. Chinese philosophy
I. Allinson, Robert E. (Robert Elliott)
181'.11
ISBN 0-19-582706-6

Library of Congress Cataloging-in-Publication Data
Understanding the Chinese mind: the philosophical roots/editor,
Robert E. Allinson; contributors, Robert E. Allinson...[et al.].
p.   cm.
Bibliography: p.
Includes index.
ISBN 0-19-582706-6 : $26.00 (U.S. :est.)
1. Philosophy, Chinese. 2. China—Intellectual life.
I. Allinson, Robert E., date
B126. U45   1989
181'.11—dc20   89-9276
CIP

Printed in Hong Kong
Published by Oxford University Press, Warwick House, Hong Kong

Contents

Contributors

Robert E. Allinson
Member, Postgraduate Panel, Department of Philosophy, The Chinese University of Hong Kong, Hong Kong

Chung-ying Cheng
Professor of Philosophy, University of Hawaii at Manoa, Honolulu, Hawaii, USA

Antonio S. Cua
Professor of Philosophy, The Catholic University of America, Washington, D.C., USA

Chad Hansen
Professor of Philosophy, University of Vermont, Burlington, Vermont, USA

Christoph Harbsmeier
Director, Department of East Asian Studies, University of Oslo, Oslo, Norway

Lao Sze-kwang (Lao Yung-wei)
Honorary Senior Fellow (Retired Reader in Philosophy), Institute of Chinese Studies, The Chinese University of Hong Kong, Hong Kong

Robert C. Neville
Dean, School of Theology, Boston University, Boston, Massachusetts, USA

John E. Smith
Clark Professor of Philosophy, Yale University, New Haven, Connecticut, USA

Kuang-ming Wu
Professor, Philosophy Department, University of Wisconsin at Oshkosh, Wisconsin, USA

1 An Overview of the Chinese Mind

ROBERT E. ALLINSON

IN our attempt to understand the Chinese mind, we must agree upon what we mean by 'understanding', by 'the Chinese mind', and by 'philosophy'. While just such answers as these are articulated only towards the end of such a volume as this, it is helpful to formulate some preliminary definitions. To deal with the last question first, why do we choose philosophy as a key to understanding the way of thinking of a culture? This volume is the outcome of a belief that the Chinese mind can be understood through its philosophy. As philosophy is essentially an attempt to understand ourselves and the world around us, we can provisionally understand the philosophy of a culture as a representation of how that culture attempts to understand itself. Thus, we may utilize the attempt at self-understanding (philosophy) as a mirror to reveal what *understanding* means for any particular culture.

This volume is one of the first of its kind to set out to reveal how Chinese philosophy can be understood in the light of techniques and concepts taken from Western philosophy. In this respect, we may expand the mirror image to that of a mirror being looked at through another mirror. Classical Chinese philosophy is investigated with the intention of articulating philosophical terms and key concepts by comparing these terms and concepts with parallel terms and concepts developed in classical and contemporary Western philosophy. It is hoped that by presenting the philosophical roots of the Chinese mind in terms which are familiar to the Western reader that the Western reader can come to a better understanding of the Chinese philosophical tradition which has formed the Chinese mind, and hence to a better understanding of the Chinese mind.

If we have defined philosophy in a preliminary sense as the self-reflection of a culture, then, at the same time, we have come to an understanding of what we understand by 'understanding'. However, we must face the issue of attempting to understand one culture's self-understanding through the self-understanding of another culture. It would be foolish to consider that no problem presented itself in the attempt to cross linguistic and cultural boundaries. By the same token, however, we must not consider the crossing of linguistic and cultural boundaries an impossibility.

As John Smith points out in his chapter on crossing boundaries, even within one's own self, one is constantly changing and consequently a later phase of the same self must *interpret* in order to understand his or her earlier self. The task of crossing boundaries, rather than being something unusual, is something we are doing all the time. In order to cross boundaries, even within ourselves, we have to perform the task of interpretation. Thus, interpretation is an integral part of crossing boundaries.

How does the fact that we are constantly crossing boundaries in order to understand our own selves at earlier times apply to the difficulties of crossing linguistic and cultural boundaries? As John Smith notes, we must not make *too* much out of linguistic barriers. Otherwise, they become a taboo which prevents us from ever making the attempt to understand across cultures. What Smith stresses is that the fact that we refer back to experience in order to interpret across linguistic impasses suggests that there is a corrective to a purely linguistic understanding. To put this another way, there is a dimension of understanding that transcends our linguistic capacities and productions. In fact, as Chung-ying Cheng and Lao Sze-kwang illustrate in different ways in their chapters, it is an integral part of Chinese philosophy that understanding proper rises above linguistic boundaries. If there were not a trans-linguistic understanding, how could we even be aware in the first place that there was something further to understand that transcended our use of language? One must bear in mind that words are *ciphers of experience* and our experience is human which means that it is potentially universal in addition to being cultural and linguistic. We are, first and foremost, human beings and this is what makes possible our bridging of linguistic and cultural barriers.

What of cultural barriers? How much violence might we wreak upon the philosophy of another culture by interpreting it through the philosophy of a Western culture? Are we not forcing interpretations upon a mode of understanding that in many instances might not be there in the first place? Needless to say, cultural barriers are very substantial and form the *raison d'être* of this volume. The very existence of this problem is what makes the attempt to interpret across boundaries an exciting and an important task. It is not a reason to shrink from such a task; it is a reason to proceed with caution and circumspection. To proceed with caution does not mean that there is no hope in understanding when boundaries are crossed. It only means that once we cross boundaries, we may be required to alter our modes of understanding in order to interpret the signs of another culture correctly. The philosophical crossing of cultures becomes itself a philosophical problem within the discipline of philosophy. In addition to the possible rewards we may glean from understanding another culture, we also enlarge the dimension of understanding required within the discipline of philosophy. If we looked upon the problem as imposing an understanding of Chinese philosophy by transposing the categories of Western philosophy upon Chinese philosophy, we would, of course, not only be guilty of cultural imperialism, but we would not further our quest for understanding. But by recognizing that Western philosophy itself can be expanded through its contact with Chinese philosophy, we find that by the end of our study it is not so much a question of interpreting East through West, but of interpreting East through East. What may seem, in the beginning, like an attempt to understand another culture through our own, in the end may result in a shift in our fundamental way of understanding, which is, in the end, the only way to understand across cultures. The difficulty in formulating the problem in the first place by considering that we are imposing Western philosophical categories upon the Chinese mind is to consider that Western philosophy itself is static and impervious to change. In the end, we are not cultural imperialists; we are dancing partners. The only difference is that, in this case, we are inviting our partner to dance.

What of the opposite fear, that instead of understanding too little from this volume we may understand too much? With our philosophical looking glass, will we now be able to see through the mystique of the Chinese mind and will it therefore lose its attraction for us as do the magician's tricks when his sleights of hand are detected by an artful observer? I do not think that we should be afraid of understanding too much, for this fear is based upon the concept of a closed circle of understanding. The closed circle concept is that, after understanding, there is nothing left to understand. All the cards are on the table. There is no more magic to behold. With an open, or creative concept of understanding, after such an act of understanding, there may be more of ourselves to understand rather than less. I think that all of the essays to follow bear eloquent testimony to this.

Will we, as Westerners (and Westernized Chinese) destroy too much of the Chinese tradition by reducing it to Western terms? Again, I do not foresee this result. Cheng's essay, in particular, is encouraging in this regard because it shows that Chinese thought can be *further* developed in Chinese terms and not destroyed in the process of Westernization. What is especially interesting is the role that Western thinking has played in the development of Chinese thought. The current Western interest in the *Yijing (I Ching)* has undoubtedly played a strong role in renewing the Chinese quest into the sources of their own tradition.

Cheng points out that the Chinese tradition is treading a different path from the West. If we follow Cheng further in the direction in which he points, then it is only by a great familiarization with the Chinese tradition that we can hope to retain and maintain both the Chinese mystique and Chinese wisdom. What interests us, in a volume such as this, is that we could never know how Chinese thought differed so much from the West unless we had discovered it under the Western microscope. In fact, what exists is the opposite danger. Rather than understanding too much by our inquiry, without such an inquiry as the present one, by ignoring the uniqueness of the Oriental tradition, there is a real danger that its charm and wisdom may be lost.

There is yet another point here. Cultures, as well as our own individual minds, are capable of change. In fact, there is really no longer a pure "Western" mind any more than there is a pure "Chinese" mind. Perhaps the first result of studying the philosophy of another culture is the realization that there never was a monolithic "Chinese" mind to begin with. Likewise, the concept of a monolithic "Western" mind is a stereotype that overlooks the vast and important differences within the so-called West. For example, in the intra-Western case of the Hebrew language, as John Smith notes, there is no single Hebrew synonym of the word 'sin'. One can only imagine what linguistic and cultural obstacles to understanding exist for one Westerner attempting to understand another Westerner when one considers an example such as this.

As an aside, one may consider the inappositeness and the irony of the use of geographical terms to attempt to portray unities and differences in understanding. Even in "Western" thought, every student of ancient Greek philosophy learns that the cradle of Western science and the beginning of Western philosophy is Ionia which is in Asia minor.

Cultural boundaries have never been pristine, and in this century they are becoming less and less distinct. As a case in point, as Lao Sze-kwang points out, the word 'philosophy' (and here I may add 'religion') is purely of "Western" origin and did not exist even in *translated* forms until as late as Meiji in Japan and thence from Japan into China.[1] However, the equally important fact is that these terms *have existed* for the past one hundred years as translated terms and are now used (in their translated forms) by some as terms to describe ways of thinking which previously were referred to as 'schools of thought' or 'teachings'. For good or ill, the "East" now uses Western labels to describe and thus to understand its own traditions. In these respects, cultural isolationism ended in the Far East over one century ago.

One can question whether one can apply Western categories such as 'philosophy' to the Chinese mind, but the fact is that this is a *fait accompli*. This does not mean that if we do apply such labels we should not do so with caution and qualification. It is part and parcel of a philosophical understanding to question whether applied labels accurately describe what we are attempting to understand. Thus, this discipline, properly understood, contains its own corrective within itself. If there is a real problem of possible misunderstanding created by the category of 'philosophy', then any philosophical understanding worthy of its name should be able to meet such a problem head on.

In the ancient Greek sense of philosophy as 'the love of wisdom', there should be no difficulty at all in attempting to understand the Chinese mind through its philosophy. But, if by philosophy, we mean the art or the practice of systematic argument and the overwhelming reliance upon understanding through the analysis of concepts, we discover that philosophy may mean something quite different to the Chinese mind from what it means to the Western mind. There are two items of great interest that result from this understanding. Firstly, if there is a different orientation in Chinese thought from that line of thinking within Western thought that stresses the importance of logical proof, then our concept of philosophy must expand to include this different orientation as legitimate philosophy, because it may lead us in otherwise unthought-of directions. Secondly, we may discover, by a close analysis of the thought patterns of ancient Chinese thinkers, that conceptual analysis and theoretical understanding were in fact implicit (and sometimes explicit) within the ancient Chinese tradition. Such a result may in fact alter the stereotype (whether this be a self-stereotype or one which is imposed from the West) of Chinese philosophy as not being of the same orientation as Western philosophy. The first of these resultants that is the outcome of our inquiry into the Chinese mind is the perspective proposed by Chad Hansen; the second is the perspective proposed by Christoph Harbsmeier.

Hansen takes the refreshing and eye-opening view that rather than being something alien, formidable, and obscure, Chinese views of language and mind are more plausible and defensible than their Western counterparts. In particular, Hansen argues that Chinese views of language and mind require neither a commitment to obscure and invisible mental objects nor to the psychology of propositional belief. In addition, Hansen stresses the supra-linguistic role that Chinese written language plays among the numerous Chinese oral languages. This supra-linguistic role, in Hansen's view, is the role that is occupied by ideas or concepts in Western theories. It is important to add here that the language that in the West we construe as Chinese with a great number of variant oral dialects, should be more accurately described as a great number of distinct and independently evolved oral languages with their own unique grammatical structures which have all been made to conform to a single written language with its own grammatical structure.

Between the lines, what Hansen is saying is that our difficulties in understanding Chinese philosophy are not created by the obscurities of a more convoluted way of thinking than our own, but that our primary difficulties stem from our own way of thinking that is inherently obscure and convoluted. It is as if we were attempting to examine a biological specimen but insisted upon using a self-distorting lens for our microscope. For Hansen, the Chinese heart-mind does not have the mental counterpart of words and sentences. The fundamental distinction that every student of Western (Aristotelian) logic is taught, the distinction between a sentence and a string of words, does not exist. The syntactic sentence is not central to Chinese language. The Chinese heart-mind, rather than operating through the indirect mediate and abstract medium of words, operates directly and immediately as a source of dispositions and skills. What is of interest to note here is that we have a marvellous example of the use of an outlook of contemporary Western philosophy (the model of behaviourism), to interpret and understand ancient Chinese philosophy. It is entirely possible that ancient Chinese philosophy becomes *more* intelligible (rather than less) by the attempt to understand it through the viewpoints of contemporary Western philosophy. In fact, it may well be that such a model of understanding would make Chinese philosophy more theoretically understandable to the contemporary Chinese mind than it was to its ancient counterpart.

As an aside, we may be struck by Hansen's description of the Chinese mind as heart-mind. This is because in Chinese, the character for 'heart' contains both meanings at once, although in the West we most commonly choose the meaning of 'mind' and leave out the 'heart' connotation altogether. In ancient Chinese pictographic symbols, the character resembles the biological heart, not the brain. The modern character is an abstraction from this ancient pictograph.[2] Hansen's decision to translate by leaving in both connotations reflects an act of philosophical interpretation which to a considerable extent bridges linguistic and cultural barriers. This act, in and of itself, shows a modification of the Western way of understanding in its effort to understand its Chinese counterpart which in turn may expand the Western concept of understanding.

Harbsmeier, in contrast, cites a wealth of classical Chinese sources to support his claim that semantic truth predicates are commonly applied to statements or sentences in classical Chinese by all of the major philosophers, and that occasionally we find nominalized usages that remind us of the abstract notion of truth. He provides evidence for the existence of propositional attitudes such as 'belief' so that Hansen's reduction of 'knowledge' to 'knowing how' is not possible for a range of classical Chinese sentences. Regarding abstraction in ancient China, he shows that the ancient Chinese could speak of such things as the roundness of a circle. And, what is perhaps most interesting of all in a technical sense, he provides a refutation of Hansen's influential claim that classical Chinese nouns are mass nouns, which has been endorsed by such scholars as A.C. Graham. Harbsmeier outlines syntactic criteria for distinguishing between mass nouns, generic nouns, and count nouns.

What do we make of this debate? Perhaps, the most important

consequence of such a debate is its reminder that the Chinese mind is not monolithic and that *Chinese philosophy, rather than being simply a body of doctrines, is a dialogue between philosophers*. It is not so much a matter of choosing 'who is right' as it is a realization that the task of understanding is largely a work of interpretation, and that every act of interpretation that we perform alters and expands the object that we are attempting to understand. The proper result is that the Chinese mind grows under our fingertips as we attempt to understand it. Understanding is not reductionistic; it is expansive. In order to understand we do not need to reduce what is unfamiliar to what is familiar as in the Aristotelian model of understanding. We may expand our repertory of familiarity. Understanding may not only take the form of reductionism, but it may also take the form of growth.

Hansen seems to be joining forces with Lao Sze-kwang in Lao's impressive argument that even the abstract *appearing* form of language *functions* differently for the Chinese mind and thus reveals (in my own words) a different mental functioning. In this, he seems to be joining forces with Chung-ying Cheng as well, who argues that the essential differences between Chinese and Western thought may well be traced to the differences between a phoneme and an ideograph language. For Cheng, the nonpictorial quality of the Greek language lent itself naturally to the development of abstract thought more than the picture image quality of the Chinese language. To enlarge upon Cheng's point, a culture that could learn to function with an alphabet language would both be more theoretically inclined and *ex post facto* conditioned to think abstractly than a culture that was inclined to, and accustomed to, thinking in terms of concrete images. On the other hand, could a culture have developed such a sophisticated argument form as Gongsun Long's White Horse dialogue if it could not practise systematic thinking or analysis by the means of highly abstracted concepts? (This would hold true whether or not one takes the view, as Harbsmeier does, that Gongsun Long's White Horse dialogue is a sophisticated joke.)

With whomever one sides on this issue, the debate itself, and the means taken to resolve it, form the crux of the issues raised by this volume as a whole. For the issue that is being raised is what constitutes the Chinese mind in its essence. It is obvious from the outset that different investigators differ with respect to what they take to be the Chinese mind. If nothing else, this should dispel our illusion that such an entity as the monolithic 'Chinese mind' exists at all. The Hansen–Harbsmeier debate is a debate in which both sides can find the roots of their claims in Chinese culture. And one root, the Harbsmeier root, is a root which we normally associate with the 'Western' mind. Our inquiry, which initially began as a West-East inquiry we find expanding into an East-East debate.

What all of this reflects is that it is not only the subject matter as to what constitutes the Chinese mind that is at issue, but the diversity of means adopted by the various investigators in order to understand the Chinese mind. What counts as a satisfactory explanation from the point of view of Cheng and Hansen is very different from what counts as a satisfactory explanation in the case of Kuang-ming Wu. Instead of proposing an explanation of the difference(s) between the Western and the Chinese mind (as in the case of Cheng or Hansen), Wu invites us to join in understanding the Chinese mind through appreciating its productions. Instead of offering a theoretical distinction between East and West, Wu asks us to *alter* our mode of understanding in order to understand properly the differences between East and West. Wu asks us to *become* a Chinese philosopher in the act of attempting to understand Chinese philosophy. If I may borrow a strategy from R.G. Collingwood's *Idea of History* in order to describe what Wu is proposing, just as a student of Western history must re-enact the way of thinking of the past in order to understand the past, one must re-enact the way of thinking of the ancient Chinese philosopher in order to understand his philosophy. Chinese philosophy cannot be understood as an objective body of data one scrutinizes from the outside. It can only be understood from the inside out. Thus, Wu's *example* (which I have described as a *theoretical proposal*), is at the same time an expansion of our traditional concept of understanding in which we understand across cultures in a way similar to how we understand from present to past within the same culture.

Our investigations, it seems, have borne some unexpected fruit. The investigation into what constitutes the Chinese mind can also yield as a result new *products* of the Chinese mind: new ways of thinking. Our understanding of the Chinese mind is not a mere historical repetition; it is an understanding that can add to the Chinese mind. Interpretation and understanding are inextricably intertwined. We cannot understand without interpreting and our interpretations alter both what we are attempting to understand and our own modes of understanding. There is no neutral body of data that forms the object of our inquiry. What constitutes the Chinese mind is to some extent formed by our modes of investigation and our modes of investigation are in turn altered and expanded by our contacts with the Chinese mind. After reading the essays of Robert C. Neville, or Chung-ying Cheng, or Chad Hansen our idea of the Chinese mind can never be the same again.

We may not be able to totally resolve the Hansen–Harbsmeier debate, although it is not clear that a resolution is really what is needed or desired. The idea that cross-cultural interpretation must yield a resolution of conflicting views is a reductionistic view of the nature of understanding. The fact is that both the object of our study (the 'Chinese mind') and our multi-perspectival approach to our study (our different understandings of what constitutes understanding in the first place) constitute a two-way mirror. Our initial metaphor of looking through one mirror (the self-understanding constituted by one culture's philosophy) into another mirror (the self-understanding constituted by another culture's philosophy) must be expanded to become a two-way mirror in which both the object of our understanding and the mode of our understanding grow and transform to yield a new understanding both of the Chinese mind and of understanding in general. What begins as a study of the Chinese mind ends as a contribution to the study of the hermeneutics of understanding as well.

However, in our endeavours to avoid reductionism, we must also avoid the opposite pitfall of becoming too vague in our attempts to depict the Chinese mind. While it is true that every simplification is an over-simplification, it would be equally inaccurate to say that the Chinese mind had no definable characteristics whatsoever. We must, being aware of the qualifications we have discussed above, venture forth with some essential description (not a definition) of the Chinese mind. Rather than attempting to distill a list of salient characteristics of the Chinese mind *à la* Charles Moore's *The Chinese Mind, Essentials of Chinese Philosophy and Culture*, it may be of interest to attempt to portray the Chinese mind, as distinguished from the Western mind, in its emphasis and consequent development of a single characteristic. In this respect, we could demarcate the Chinese mind in terms of its greater *emphasis* upon, and consequent *development* of, the practical as against the theoretical mind. In this sense, the Chinese mind does not differ from the Western mind in terms of representing a different *kind* of mind but rather a different *degree* of emphasis upon a universal human potential of understanding. The Chinese mind is not a unique and impenetrable way of thinking but a development of a universal human potential in a striking form.

Cheng's and Hansen's analyses of the Chinese language represent ways of attempting to understand the possible origin of the difference in the *directionality* of the Chinese mind. It is a fascinating question whether language influenced the directionality of the Chinese mind or whether the language itself was a reflection of a certain characteristic mode of thought that in turn influenced the creation of a language system that suited its purposes. Either pole of these extremes of conjecture carries with it certain assumptions which are difficult to sustain. If it is a simple case of language influencing thought, the assumption is that a mentality is shaped by its language forms and thus lacks any creative developmental properties of its own. On the other hand, if it is a case that a mentality chooses a language that fits its purposes, then it would appear that a mentality can achieve a sophisticated level of development at a pre-linguistic level. Most likely, the truth lies somewhere in between these two extremes. A mentality, predisposed towards the concrete is likely to manifest its communication form in terms of pictographic and ideographic symbols; these, in turn, would play a strong role in reinforcing these traits. Most likely, the causal arrow between language and thought is a two-way arrow rather than being simply unidirectional. Below, I will offer my own analysis of the origin of the difference in mentality which differs from the linguistic thesis.

Before exploring further the explanation for the difference that we have noted, we may pause for a moment to comment on the nature of the difference. I should like to emphasize the point that whatever difference(s) we discover are not antagonistic differences, but complementary differences. If we see East and West as developing in different degrees and with different potentialities of the human mind, these differences need not be seen as conflicting with each other, but rather as complementing each other to form a more complete whole. This is very much in accord with the view of Chinese philosophy present in the *Yijing*, a text which has attracted much interest in the West. While a very thorough analysis of the *Yijing* awaits the reader in Chung-ying Cheng's chapter, we may note that the primary opposition of the *yin* and *yang* in the *Yijing* is not viewed as one of antagonism but rather as one of complementarity. The *yin* is not complete without the *yang* and vice versa. In fact, it is impossible that one pole exists without the other. If we take this as a metaphor for East-West understanding, then the different modes of understanding of East and West need not be seen as in conflict with each other, but as needing each other in order to form a more perfect and holistic understanding of the human mind. *Yin* and *yang* are not simply differences in kind, but form a continuum of degree where *yin* is in the process of developing into *yang*, and vice-versa. In Cheng's analysis, this continuum is seen in terms of the relationship between the theoretical and the practical, precisely the terms in which we have noted the essential differences between East and West to exist.

Given the *Yijing* as the metaphor which may represent Chinese thinking, I think it is appropriate to borrow Lao Sze-kwang's term 'orientative' (with its built-in unintentional tautological/ostensive pun) to stand for the Chinese directionality of thought. In focusing on directionality rather than content, the idea is not that there exists a difference in the *content* of thought, but that the same mind can manifest itself differently in the direction in which it evolves. This may in turn issue in different *products* of thought, a development to which we shall return shortly.

We may sound one precautionary note before proceeding to propose an analysis of why the Chinese and the Western mind have proceeded in developing in different directions. As some of the chapters depict the Chinese mind as it has existed within a long, historical tradition, we must bear in mind that today, in many ways, the Chinese mind has become Westernized and is rapidly in the process of becoming more and more Westernized. This does not simply mean that Chinese people are now enjoying Western soft drinks and are wearing Western suits. From a philosophical point of view, what this means is that through contact with the West, many Chinese have come to value Western, proof-orientated thinking and, as a result, have lost the roots of their own tradition. What this means is that a Chinese person may need to re-learn the ways of thinking of her or his tradition in the same way as a Westerner must discover the roots of Chinese thought. The 'Chinese mind' that we are investigating may one day be as foreign to all of us as the 'Greek mind' of Athens is to a Westerner today.

Westerners also have the concept of the orientative as a clue to the nature of philosophy, especially in terms of ancient Greek philosophy having a bearing on, and improving, our way of living.

For Plato and Aristotle, if philosophy did not issue forth in making us better human beings, then it was not worth pursuing. Thus, the difference in the Chinese way of thinking is not an absolute differ- ence as we have said before, but a difference in the degree of emphasis placed upon the attainment of this goal. I would now like to propose a basis, rooted in ancient Chinese philosophy, for the difference in this emphasis.

What I would like to suggest is that the development of orientative thinking (in contrast to theoretical thinking) in the Chinese tradition has had to do not only with a difference in language forms (Cheng) or function (Hansen), but also with the absence of a *motive* for developing theoretical thinking at all. In my opinion, the power, scope, and continuity of orientative thinking that was developed in China has drawn its motivation from a more settled vision of the place of man in the world. If man is envisioned as being already in harmony with the cosmos and the world, it is much more likely for a philosophy or philosophies to evolve which point the way to maintaining, enhancing or, if it is lost, recovering that initial harmony with the world. There is absolutely no need, as in the case of Heidegger, for *discovering* man's nature to be in the world (or remembering this) and announcing this as if it were a great insight. This has already been tacitly or explicitly accepted as a long-known fact. And the world is not only the human world of affairs, but the cosmos as a whole. Given the power of this basic underlying presupposition of man as being in harmony with the cosmos, it is difficult, if not impossible, to envision a philosophy like existentialism arising for the Chinese mind in which man is found to be thrown into a world from which he feels alienated.

What follows from this as to the directionality of the Chinese way of thinking? If man does not know himself, or does not feel himself to be at home in the universe, I would suggest that there would then exist a powerful motive for man to quest for the Truth, or, if you like, the ultimate answer to the puzzle of life. In fact, without a clear or settled picture of either the nature of man or his place in the world, there would arise a much greater impetus to evolving special and powerful techniques of proof to demonstrate either what man is or what path is best for him to follow. It has been suggested that it was the belief in a transcendent Deity (and I would add here the transcendent Platonic Ideas) that has provided the motive for evolving theoretical lines of proof in Western philosophy which have carried over to influence the Western mind in the direction of argumentative and logical thinking. As we shall see in the chapter by Robert Neville, however, the notion of transcendence also plays its role in Chinese thought, so that I do not think that this alone could account for the origin and the development of the argumentative tradition in the West.

I think, rather, that the reason why the Chinese mind has not developed strongly in the direction of the construction of theoretical proof structures is that Chinese philosophy has, from the beginning, seen man as being at home in nature. There is no strong drive to find the ultimate answer if one already feels that one has a place and is in that place.[3] Here, the Chinese mind is very different from the Indian mind. While the Indian mind can certainly be said to be very different from a 'Western' mind by its emphasis upon realization and not theoretical inquiry, it is, for all that, very Western in its inventive and subtle devices of argument. And this may come, perhaps, from its not being as much 'at home' in nature as the Chinese mind. An interesting clue to this is to be found in the transmogrification of Buddhism when it is brought to China in which the spectral descriptions of Mahayana are concretized into the earthy descriptions of *Zhan*.[4]

As an illustration of the harmony felt with the world, one may take note of the remarkable homogeneity and continuity that characterizes the Chinese philosophical tradition just as it characterizes the Chinese artistic tradition. While one can hardly expect to find a thriving philosophical school of neo-Platonists in the West, it is not at all surprising to discover that the dominant Chinese philosophical tradition today (as it has been for some time) is neo-Confucianism.[5] This is not simply due to the fact, or perceived fact, that Confucianism discovered the truth and no new traditions are needed, but has more to do with the fact that philosophy which is our mirrored understanding of the world or mental mirror of the world, reflects man in harmony with what is under Heaven. The reflection of a still pond or placid lake where things are settled is a reflection which will not show much change. It is only in the West that our pictures of understanding constantly change to reflect a perceptual world of constant change. One need only think of a seascape by Turner in contrast to a Chinese landscape painting. One mirror reflects the struggle of the elements and man's struggle with them; the other reflects a constant sense of man's feeling of being a part of and not struggling against the powerful forces of nature.

It is natural at this point for the evaluative question to come to mind. Given this attempt to demarcate the Chinese and the Western minds, which is better for the future of civilization? We have already indicated the direction an answer to this evaluative question must take. There is no reason to envision the East-West dichotomy in terms of an exclusive 'either/or'. It is more conducive to the completion of the human mind to consider the contrast between East and West to be a 'both/and'. Having said this, we must ask what has been the contribution of the different halves of the mind. It is evident that the Western unsureness about human nature and its place in the world has led to an ever greater amount of questioning and accumulation of knowledge about the world which has been seen to stand apart from man. At the same time, this has left the Western mind with a great divisiveness of spirit in terms of what should constitute the ultimate spiritual direction for mankind to take. It may be countered that we can also find such spiritual quarrels within the Chinese tradition. We only need to look at the history of Chinese philosophy to find endless bickering between Confucianism, Taoism, and that 'foreign' import, Buddhism, to take the three major traditions as examples. On the other hand, to place these quarrels in an appropriate perspective, we are reminded of the generalized folk saying that every Chinese person is a Confucian, a Taoist, and a Buddhist. He is a Confucian when everything is going well; he is a Taoist when things are falling apart; and he is a Buddhist as he approaches death. While this may have been intended to be taken cynically, it has been taken by some to illustrate a kind of practical wisdom. This kind of practical wisdom is further illustrated in many folk temples in Hong Kong where one can see statues of Kongzi (Confucius), Laozi (Lao Tzu), and the Buddha set up alongside those of traditional Chinese immortals as objects of veneration.[6] Once more, this illustrates the triumph of the practical over the question of theoretical truth.

If, after bearing in mind all of our previous qualifications concerning the follies of simplification and generalization, we allow ourselves to speak freely, we can say that the Chinese mind does not see itself as something apart from nature attempting to understand itself as if it were a foreign 'other'. If one were foreign to oneself (and this is what is meant, I take it, by the simplified reference to the 'mind/body' split we so often hear about that characterizes the West), then, there would be a greater need, I suggest, not only to find an absolute truth by which one can understand oneself, but also to find an infallible (or at least reliable) method for how one can come to this understanding of oneself. If we add into this mixture the thought that not only does Western man not have a settled place in the universe, but that in addition he finds that his own nature is streaked with evil, it is even more critical to come up with modes of proof that whatever understanding we do arrive at is in fact the correct understanding. *For, if we cannot know* ourselves, and what is more, we cannot trust ourselves, this is an additional motivation to finding certain and objectively-testable methods of proof. All of this naturally leads in the direction which is set by Western philosophy, theology, and science.

If, however, one felt at home with oneself and what is more, felt that one's nature was basically good, the idea that one needed a True or a Right way of understanding oneself and an alien world might not arise. Instead, one would only need a gentle reminding of one's ultimate harmony with nature. One would fit into nature just as the houses on the sides of the mountains in Chinese landscape paintings fit into the mountain sides. In the philosophy of Laozi, there is no need of a "proof" of one's being originally in harmony with the universe. The simplest occasional poetic couplet functions as the merest reminder just as the merest shadow of a whip is enough to rouse the wary horse.

In the midst of such a deeply present 'self-in-the-universe' concept, it is natural for a philosophy such as that of Mengzi (Mencius) to evolve, where man is, by nature, good. Of course, the opposite philosophy (as that of Xunzi (Hsün Tzu)) can also arise where man is seen as basically evil. This shows the dangers of generalization. But in keeping with the idea that the Chinese mind is differentiated from the Western in terms of degree and not in kind, we can safely say that there is a great deal more emphasis in Chinese thought on the notion of man's original goodness than on his original evil. In the West, we can count many like Xunzi (Aristotle, Augustine, Aquinas, Hobbes, and Kant to take just a few notable examples), whereas there is no Mengzi. The closest the West comes to Mengzi is with Plato, Locke, and Rousseau.[7] But in Rousseau there is still a tension between man and the world such that (at least in *Émile* and the first *Discourse*) civilization is the cause of the degeneration of man, while in Mengzi and even in Xunzi, proper education and self-cultivation is seen as harmonious with, and even required for, the proper emergence of man's nature (in Mengzi) and to promote goodness (in Xunzi). With Locke, while man is ethical in a state of nature, not all are so and he must be brought into a state of society so that man's natural goodness plays only a minor role in his ultimate development, which for Locke is political.

Plato, in the end, is our best Western example. But between Plato and Chinese philosophy there is still a difference. In Plato, there is still the notion that man must *know* the good before he can be good. In Mengzi, it is completely a matter of *nature*, not of *knowledge*. Of course, for Mengzi, and for Kongzi, one might be removed from one's nature and require education. But the education that is required is one that returns man to his nature ˙ and enables him to develop and refine that nature. There is no need for an insight into a special 'Form of Goodness'. If one takes the myth of the cave seriously, then man's natural condition is one of ignorance. In Mengzi, if we examine the story of the child in the well, one's natural condition is one of the immediate dis- postion to care for one's fellow human beings. One does not first need to be led out of a condition of ignorance, as in Plato. One may be removed from one's nature; but this represents an unnatu- ral condition, a deviation from the norms for Mengzi whereas it is the starting point for Plato. For Mengzi, the man who would not attempt to save the infant who has fallen into a well would be seen as unnatural and inhuman, not simply as ignorant. There is a greater reliance upon human nature in Mengzi than there is in Plato; a greater trust in human nature. For Plato, there is a greater reliance upon and trust in knowledge, not nature. Consider Meng- zi's famous example:

Why I say all men have a sense of commiseration is this: here is a man who suddenly notices a child about to fall into a well. Invariably, he will feel a sense of alarm and compassion. And this is not for the purpose of gaining the favor of the child's parents, or seeking the approbation of his neigh- bors and friends, or for fear of blame should he fail to rescue it.[8]

For Mengzi, human nature is naturally disposed to be good. There is no need for a transformation from ignorance to enlighten- ment. If one is in touch with one's true nature, one will inevitably act towards the good.

For Plato, this is not one's natural condition. In fact, the exam- ples which Plato offers of the natural acts of human beings, as Gyges' speculation as to how he would/could act with his ring of invisibility, and the telling example of our immediate reaction to the sight of dead bodies, are both in striking contrast to Mengzi's tale of the observer of the infant about to fall into the well.

In the case of the ring of Gyges, the story, while related by Glaucon, does not seem to be refuted by Socrates. In fact, Socrates goes directly from this story to the details of the *Republic* as if this is the only answer to the ethical 'problem'. The 'problem' is that if a man possesses a ring of invisibility, he would use it for immoral purposes. How different from Mengzi's example where he never considers if the observer at the well has an audience or not as this would not affect his action one way or the other. In fact, in the above example, it is said that the man at the well acts out of his intrinsic goodness, not for the sake of impressing a potential audience. Contrast this to the story of the ring of invisibility:

No one, it is commonly believed, would have such iron strength of mind as to stand fast in doing right or keep his hands off other men's goods. . .[9]

In Plato's story, one's natural urges, untempered by knowledge, are for self-interest.

And, finally, consider the example of the dead bodies away from the spectacle of which Leontius cannot tear his eyes. Not that this represents any grievous sin, but it is interesting that the example Plato offers of a natural reaction is not one of offering assistance to the helpless, but of doing something against our better nature.[10] There is but a short distance from this to Augustine.

Mengzi does present arguments to counter the argument that human nature is neutral, but that is not the point. It is not that such proofs cannot be given. What is more to the point is that when Mengzi offers the example of the infant and the well, it would probably have been difficult for him to imagine someone in touch with his real nature *not* attempting to save the child.

First, whether or not one agrees with Mengzi, it is clear evidence of his position *vis-à-vis* human nature. In order to refute such positions as unbelievably naïve given the course of human history, it is commonplace to point to the overwhelming historical evidence to the contrary. While this does not, strictly speaking, address Mengzi's point (in a later example he allows how easily human nature can be lost), it does at first seem to blunt it. One can argue that, on this score, Chinese history has no cleaner slate than Western history. Empirical evidence cannot prove one position (human nature as good) to be ethically superior in its empirical consequences to the other (human nature as evil). But Mengzi's reply would be that

that is because men have been distracted from their real natures and so the empirical evidence is not an argument against his original position.

This is not to say that Mengzi is right or that Plato is right or that Augustine is right. All that I am attempting to illustrate is that the tradition of proof and argumentation may not have had as strong a basis for development and nurture if there already existed a strong, built-in tendency to believe that one were at home with one's nature, which was disposed naturally towards the good. If one is at home with one's nature, and that nature tends to the good, then what is the *motus* to prove what the Good is, or even that there is a Good? And without such a powerful *motus*, why would a tradition of proof and argument develop?

One final brief example. In the case of Kongzi, filial piety and the place of the family in general receives a strong emphasis for the development of ethical values. This is re-emphasized in Mengzi and remains constant throughout the Chinese tradition. One has to genuinely search very hard to find any Western analogue to this emphasis upon family relations as the originating source of ethical values. When one finds any Western counterpart, as in the case of Hegel, the emphasis on the family only occurs because of Hegel's systematic need to fit everything together in one organic whole. For the Chinese mind, the value of the family is self-evident. It is not simply an ingredient in an overall proof structure such that the entire world can be seen as fitting into an overall organic whole. What makes for this difference between East and West? If my general thesis of at-homeness is correct, then, for the Chinese mind, the family represents a *natural* extension of oneself. There is no need to prove the priority or the primacy of the family. It is accepted as a given fact.

What I am suggesting is not the rightness or the wrongness of these different forms of ethical valuation, but only that the Chinese did not develop the same degree of emphasis upon, and breadth of development of, argument forms, because there was no felt need for proof of what they took to be themselves or their place in nature. If the views of Chinese philosophers on themselves or their place in the universe were stated as theoretical assumptions, they would then require a logical or at least an empirical proof. But they were not stated as theoretical assumptions; they were stated as descriptions of their own, deeply-felt experience. In a philosophical culture that based itself so strongly (if not self-consciously) on experience, the *importance* (not the existence) of the concept of theoretical 'truth/proof' would not receive as strong an emphasis as a philosophical culture that based itself on the quest for the Absolute.

What can we say is unique about this attempt to understand the Chinese mind that is represented by this particular collection of thinkers who have collaborated to make this volume possible? I notice two tendencies that are present among this group of thinkers. One tendency I would label as an attempt to 'Westernize' the Chinese mind; the other tendency is what I would label as an attempt to 'Sinify' the Western mind. In Antonio Cua's chapter on Confucian morality, we find a tendency towards the Westernization of the Chinese mind. We would have a great deal of difficulty in distinguishing this essay from an analytic philosopher's treatment of the same subject, supposing that he possessed the great familiarity with Confucianism that Cua undoubtedly possesses. What is of interest to note is that Cua treats the Chinese philosophical tradition from a Western point of view in terms of his methodology, and in so doing renders an otherwise obscure (by Western standards) Chinese philosopher accessible to Western minds. If there has been a prejudice against Chinese philosophy as 'not being philosophy', I recommend that the reader of this persuasion turn to this chapter to disabuse himself of this prejudice.

The other direction that is taken in this collection lies in the direction of the Sinification of the Western mind. This is the direction that is taken by Wu in his essay on Chinese aesthetics. Chinese aesthetics offers us a wonderful vantage point from which we can Sinify the Western mind both in terms of expanding our previous concept of the contents of the subject matter of aesthetics and in terms of stylistically altering the Western mode of understanding itself. It is perhaps apposite to focus on Wu's essay in that it is, of all the essays presented, perhaps the most different from what we would expect from a Western philosopher's treatment of aesthetics.

First of all, Wu does not treat aesthetics simply as a discipline which examines our modes of apprehension of special forms which we take to be 'art forms'. Wu presents aesthetics as a special way of viewing the entire universe. Thus, our concept of aesthetics is perforce expanded in the effort to understand Chinese aesthetics. For Wu, we cannot simply take the traditional subject matter that is treated by aesthetics and look for it within the Chinese philo-

sophical tradition. We must expand our initial notion of what constitutes the field of aesthetics in the first place. One example stands
out strongly in our minds since it differs so markedly from Kant's
influential concept of 'disinterested pleasure' that has demarcated
the proper realm of aesthetics for Western philosophers, and that
is the example of the culinary arts. What is required for us, as
Western thinkers, to include the culinary arts, as a valid aesthetic
domain? First of all, it requires a cancellation of the traditional
separation between the fine arts and the practical arts. It requires
an integration of beauty as part of earthly and self-interested enjoyment. We can, of course, attempt to separate the aesthetic
dimension from the satisfaction of appetite in eating, but the
whole point of the example is to show that there is no perfect division between these forms of enjoyment for Chinese aesthetics.
Part of the satisfaction of eating lies in the aesthetics of preparation and presentation; there is an aesthetic dimension which is integral to a self-interested activity. In the West, aesthetics is normally construed as a theory which refers to a special sphere of
experience which is reserved for the corridors of museum walking.
If it is seen as part of the culinary arts, aesthetics can be seen to
apply to our everyday (three times a day) life style. If Westerners
were to admit culinary arts into the aesthetics' academy, this
would constitute a form of Sinification of the Western mind.
Westerners would understand the Chinese mind by themselves
becoming Chinese.

Secondly, and perhaps offering an even more fundamental clue
to understanding the Chinese mind through the Sinification of the
Western mind, is the aesthetic form of Wu's essay itself. Wu's
essay, instead of simply talking about Chinese aesthetics, is an example of Chinese aesthetics in its writing style. It is a presentation,
not simply a representation of aesthetics. The Western mind re-
coils at such a presentation. The Western mind anticipates a
theory of aesthetics, not some literary meanderings. What Wu is
saying/doing, I think, is that the Chinese way of understanding is
more holistic, less divided, and more true of our nature as a whole.
Therefore, if we desire to understand things Chinese, we cannot
do so by insisting upon understanding them with Western precon-
ceptions of the form and the content of the subject matter at hand.

What is meant by a holistic understanding? In holistic understanding, we understand not simply with our analytic minds, but
with all of our senses as well, and therefore with our natures as a

whole. The mind is not divorced from the senses; our aesthetic rapport is the unity of the senses with the mind. Thus, Wu's prose is an attempt to recreate the Chinese, integrative, holistic sense of understanding. If we allow ourselves to experience his prose, we can understand Chinese aesthetics by practise and not from theory alone. This is the second way of understanding the Chinese mind: to become Chinese by adopting the Chinese mode of understanding. We can also say that Wu's essay is a blend of the theoretical and the practical. It is not simply a set of literary meanderings; the literary phrases all have to do with the subject matter of aesthetics. In this sense, Wu's essay can be seen, in its best sense, not as merely Chinese, but as an essay in East-West understanding.

I would like to say a word about Robert Neville's essay and a further word about Cheng's as I think that these two contributions, in particular, point the way towards future development. Robert Neville's chapter is unique in that it represents an attempt to understand the Chinese mind *both* by Sinifying the Western mind *and* by Westernizing the Chinese mind. It Sinifies the Western mind by introducing such concepts as immanence into Western thought. Thus, it secularizes the sacred for the West. By the same token, it Westernizes the Chinese mind by showing how immanence functions as a transcendent concept for Chinese thought. It makes the secular sacred. In this respect, Neville's essay is truly an essay in East-West thought. It is difficult to see where the East leaves off and the West begins and vice-versa. In so doing, it epitomizes where we are today and also points the way towards the future.

Cheng's essay is also unique in that he provides a Western structural framework for understanding the *Yijing* but the content of the structure (the theoretical-practical continuum) is provided by an East-West understanding of Chinese philosophy. While it is difficult to see where the West leaves off and the East begins in his analysis of this difficult Chinese text, it is assuredly an essay both about, and in, Chinese philosophy. The *Yijing* becomes, for Cheng, a model of Chinese philosophy which, rather than attempting to understand the world by minimizing or negating change, attempts to provide a theoretical framework for the understanding of harmony that exists among the elements of a constantly changing world. East and West are combined in such a way that a harmonious structure is seen to emerge from the world rather than being imposed upon it from without.

We are no longer purely Western or purely Eastern. We are all of us hybrids. As the world shrinks both physically through vast advances in telecommunications and transportation and mentally (as we all become more monolithically Western), we must make great attempts not only to understand East and West by attempting to understand the two different thought tendencies as analogous, but we must be careful to preserve the differences. As in the metaphor of the *yin* and the *yang*, East and West require each other for their own existence, and future development depends not on one system of thought replacing the other, but on an integrated growth which maintains and expands both tendencies.

In China today, there is a great accent on the idea of modernization which to a great extent really is translated as Westernization. The danger in this is that a Western way of thinking may supplant a Chinese way of thinking in the stampede towards modernization. It is not that we need to become intellectual Luddites, but we do need to preserve both cultural difference and cultural uniqueness. All too often, in books of this nature, the emphasis is on bridging the supposed gaps between East and West by showing that, at rock bottom, both traditions are standing for the same core set of values. What I would like to suggest is that West and East do not represent different and antagonistic viewpoints, but that we should be as much aware of the differences that do exist as the similarities. Differences need not be antithetical; they can be complementary.

If the following essays illustrate anything at all, they illustrate that differences in interpretations exist as to what constitutes the Chinese mind. And this is a reminder that above all else, an inquiry into truth is dialogical. The dialogue between different thinkers which follows is not only a dialogue *about* Chinese philosophy; it is a dialogue *in* Chinese philosophy. It is a dialogue which not only has its basis in a long standing historical tradition; it is a continuation and a development of that tradition.

Understanding the Chinese mind may take many different forms. We may see what is uniquely Chinese through Western eyes; we may see what is Chinese by altering our Western concept of what is the object of our understanding; we may see what is Chinese by altering our mode of understanding itself; we may adopt a way of understanding that is neither Western nor Chinese but is a hybrid way of understanding which is both Western and Chinese, and is, therefore, something much more.

It is difficult and perhaps undesirable to predict the future course of East-West interrelationships. I dedicate this volume to the cause of keeping all of these various approaches to East-West *rapprochement* open, and, if possible, to suggest new pathways for mutual understanding. For, despite its title, this book reveals something about the Western mind in its efforts to understand the Chinese mind and therefore says as much about the subject as it does about the object of its understanding.

In the end, what does our approach offer in terms of understanding the Chinese mind through traditional Western philosophical categories such as logic, philosophy of language, metaphysics, ethics, philosophy of religion, and aesthetics? Does it offer an understanding of the Chinese mind? I would rather say: our volume does not offer *an* understanding of the Chinese mind, but rather an understanding of the *diverse ways in which we may go about understanding the Chinese mind*. I think that Western philosophical categories will enable us to become more and more aware of the unique and distinctive characteristics of the Chinese mind, so that, at the very least, we can understand *why* it is so difficult to arrive at an understanding.

But this is the least we can hope to gain. At most, we hope to gain much, much more. We hope, through the dialogical encounter between philosophers, to truly understand each other's traditions, and even, if possible, in that very act of understanding, to forge a new tradition which goes beyond our own previous traditions. This is, I very much suspect, the direction of future developments in thinking, and is, in actual fact, the very substance of true understanding.

Notes

1. For a history of the adaptation and translation of the terms 'philosophy' and 'religion' into Japanese, compare with: Tatsuo Hayashi 林達夫 et al., *Tetsugaku jiten* 哲学事典 (Tokyo, Heibonsha, 1971); Shuji Suzuki 鈴木修次 *Nihon kango to Chugoku: Kanji-bunkaken no kindaika* 日本汉语と中国:汉字文化圈の近代化 (Tokyo, Chuokoronsha, 1981); Gino K. Piovesana, *Recent Japanese Philosophical Thought 1862–1962: A Survey* (Tokyo, Enderle, 1963).

2. To see both the ancient pictograph of the heart-mind and its evolution via abstraction into the contemporary character for heart-mind, compare with *Shuowen jiezi zhu*, 說文解字注 , *s.v.*, p. 501.

3. I am not embracing the position espoused by Max Weber that Confucians possessed only an absolute minimum of moral tension. (Compare with Max Weber, *The Religion of China* (Glencoe, The Free Press, 1951), p. 227.) My position has to do with the absence of a motivation for logical or empirical proof construction, not the absence of a motivation for moral development. Here, I would

agree with Metzger's arguments that Weber possessed an inadequate understanding of Confucian morality. (Compare with Thomas A. Metzger, *Escape From Predicament* (New York, Columbia University Press, 1977), p. 4.) Knowing that one's primary task was moral cultivation is to possess some settled knowledge which is perhaps derivative from knowing one's place in nature. In the West, there is no comparable felt assurance that this is man's essential task. In fact, what is man's essential task is an open and debated question in the West. My argument is that it is the lack of a settled vision of man's place in the world that provides the *motus* for the emphasis upon theoretical proof construction in the West.

4. Compare with Robert E. Allinson, 'Taoism in the Light of Zen: An Exercise in Inter-Cultural Hermeneutics', *Zen Buddhism Today*, Kyoto, No. 6, November 1988.

5. In a narrow sense, Neo-Confucianism would refer to the schools of Cheng (1033–1107), Zhu Xi and Lu Jiuyuan (1139–93), and Wang Yangming. Mou Zongsan also distinguishes a third school, that of Cheng Hao (1032–85), Hu Wufeng (1100–55), and Liu Zongzhou (1578–1645). Compare with Metzger, *Escape From Predicament*, p. 52.

6. If you consider Confucianism in imperial China, where it was a state religion, then in the official temples one would have found only symbols of Kongzi and Confucian virtues unlike the syncretic temples of popular religion, where one could find statues of Kongzi, Laozi, and the Buddha arranged side by side. The positioning of the statues even became a point of conflict between the state and popular movements with regard to which was being represented as most central. Compare with C.K. Yang, *Religion in Chinese Society* (Berkeley, The University of California Press), p. 197.

Historically, the conflict between syncretic tendencies and state control is a problem which dates back at least as far as the Song dynasty (960–1279) and possibly earlier. Philosophically, what is of interest is that in the popular mind it is possible for all three religions to co-exist simultaneously. This is in sharp contrast to the 'either-or' mentality of the Western mind. One, for example, would have to be either a Protestant, a Catholic, or a Jew. One could not be all three at once.

7. The case of Nietzsche, while unique, is too complex for an overall comparison and would require a separate discussion on its own. Compare with Robert E. Allinson, 'Evaluation and Trans-Evaluation in Chuang-Tzu and Nietzsche', *Journal of Chinese Philosophy*, Vol. 13, No. 4, December 1986, pp. 429–43.

8. *Mengzi*, II, A:6. Wing-tsit Chan's translation in Wm. Theodore de Bary (ed.), *Sources of Chinese Tradition* (New York, Columbia University Press, 1960), p. 102.

9. *Republic*, II, 360. F.M. Cornford's translation in *The Republic of Plato* (New York, Oxford University Press, 1967), p. 45.

10. *Republic*, 439E–440A.

2   Interpreting across Boundaries

JOHN E. SMITH

WE are involved in communication of some sort at every moment of our waking life. Communication, moreover, has become a major topic of discussion in our age of electronics and computers, and one may wonder whether so much talk *about* communication may not be the expression of an uneasy feeling that our capacity to interpret, to share, and compare experience is eroding. If this is so, we must reorientate ourselves and, instead of concentrating on the devices of communication, return instead to the actual experience of interpreting and expressing what we are trying to communicate. Following the lead of William James, we must reflect on actual interpreting as it takes place in the numerous circumstances and situations of experience. We find ourselves interpreting our own conscious life through memories, hopes, interests, plans, and courses of action and it is through the appreciative understanding of the persons and events in our experience that we come to have a *meaningful* life. Interpreting is called for in all dialogical exchange with others and provides us with the basis for mutual understanding. We interpret the texts that form the treasure-house of our intellectual, cultural, moral, and religious traditions, and thus become part of the living heritage of a people. We interpret, moreover, not only within the boundaries of our own traditions, but across national, ethnic, linguistic, and cultural boundaries in order to enlarge our experience and enter into community with other peoples and with their ways of life.

In attempting to understand the meaning of interpretation, I shall appeal to much that is already known about the topic, but my aim is to keep the discussion closely in touch with the experiential matrix of all meaningful discourse between individuals and communities. Just as many accounts of the logical structure of scientific knowledge fail to take note of the 'flesh and blood' experimenters who do the actual work, so much of what has been written about language, semantics, and semiotics appears to have no relation to the fact that it is individuals and communities attempting to understand each other which is the primary subject of the enquiry.

All communicating, interpreting, and understanding between human beings takes place within the matrix of experience, that which has been encountered, undergone, and done both by individuals and communities. It is well known that experience has been understood in several different senses throughout the history of Western thought. Aristotle's concept of *empeiria*, a combination of acquaintance with situations and some knowledge of how to deal with them, was greatly transformed by Locke and other British empiricists so that experience was conceived as a tissue of sensations and perceptions present to the individual mind and to be used as a touchstone for judging the validity of abstract ideas. That classical view was again transformed by the pragmatists and others and experience came to be understood in far broader terms as the cumulative and funded *meaning* arising from the encounter of the individual with whatever presents itself in society and the world. From this new vantage point, experience was no longer taken to mean the deliverances of the senses since much that we actually experience cannot be construed in those terms. Experience, moreover, was seen as closely related to the formation of habits and as the ability to respond appropriately to situations encountered. In short, experience included not only knowledge of and acquaintance with facts, but 'knowing how' to behave when we are called upon to respond, as well.

Experience, or whatever is directly encountered and received by the experiencing subject, demands *expression*, and the relations between the two have long been the subject of debate among philosophers. Without the use of language and signs of many sorts it would be impossible to determine what has been experienced and what it means. The media of expression enable us to give some stability to experience and to keep it from flowing away in the passage of time. The preoccupation of philosophers with language in recent decades has resulted in an imbalance between experience and expression with the latter assuming a priority as if the analysis of language alone would put us in touch with the substance of our actual encounters with the world. Experience and expression can be distinguished as can be seen from the need to avoid confusing a sign with what it means or with the object to which it refers. The two, however, cannot be separated since they are intertwined so closely that we cannot have one without the other. Experience, nevertheless, must not be subordinated to language since it is to experience that we must continually return in order to assess the

adequacy and accuracy of its expression. In our efforts to understand each other across boundaries we must constantly appeal to a
process of interpretation whereby two individuals come to understand each other's experience through the function of mediating
ideas.

The concrete example of an interpreter at work will serve to
make the basic structure of communication clear. Consider the
situation of two individuals who wish to carry on a conversation
but are unable to do so because neither has command of the language of the other. The most they could hope for under the circumstances is the minimal sort of communication afforded by
pointing and some imitative gestures. In order to converse they
need an interpreter, someone who literally stands between the two
and who has already crossed the boundary that separates them.
The interpreter, that is, understands both languages involved and,
consequently, after receiving a message from one of the parties
and having cast it in the other language, can say to A in A's language: 'What I say to you is what B said to me in his own language'. The distance is overcome solely by virtue of the fact that
the interpreter is in possession of what neither of the distinct individuals has, namely, a command of both languages. The community of understanding thus established between A and B is, of
course, a transient one since it depends entirely on the work of the
interpreter. It can obviously be made more permanent when either
one learns the language of the other, or when each learns the language of the other. As we shall see, however, the foregoing illustration greatly oversimplifies the situation, even if it does make
clear the manner in which two individuals can communicate
through the interpreting activity of a third.

For purposes of ordinary conversation, it may be assumed that
one-to-one equivalents can be found for translating the signs of
one language into those of another. In large scale cultural communication, however, involving long and complex philosophical
and religious traditions, more formidable problems arise and the
boundaries to be crossed are such that we can no longer safely
assume the relatively simple one-to-one meaning equivalents that
are the stock-in-trade of the professional interpreter. One illustration will serve to focus the problem. The work known as the
Septuagint (designated by LXX) is the translation of the Hebrew
Bible or the Old Testament into Greek. Gerhard Kittel, a well
known biblical scholar, raised the question as to whether there is

any counterpart in the Hebrew Bible for the term 'sin' and, in referring to the Septuagint, he writes:

The limitation of the LXX vocabulary here exposed is not due to the translators' method. The reason for it is to be found in a peculiar difficulty in the Hebrew, which obviously has no single word for religious or theological purposes like our word 'sin'.[1]

The limitation pointed out above is but one instance of a problem that stems from fundamental differences in the structure of languages and that, in turn, reflects differences deeply rooted in the cultures from which languages spring. Greek, with its large stock of abstract terms, is admirably suited for the expression of philosophical and theological issues and beliefs. Hebrew, on the other hand, is rich in poetic nuance and vivid images lending themselves to narrative and to history rather than to analytical discourse.

Crossing Cultural Boundaries

In many parts of the world today conflicts abound and therefore it becomes a matter of great urgency to work for the creation of communities of understanding among those of different cultures, philosophical, and religious traditions. Here the boundaries to be crossed are far more complex and imposing than those encountered when we seek to interpret our own lives, or when individuals from the same culture attempt to understand each other. The first obstacle is, of course, language and the great strides that have been made in recent years in the East-West dialogue have been heavily dependent upon the contribution made by Chinese and Japanese scholars in making it possible for so much of that dialogue to take place in English. These scholars have thus been important pioneers in crossing a boundary and in opening up a new world in philosophical and religious thought for those who have no command of the Asian languages. There are, fortunately, signs at present indicating that the dialogue will be enhanced in the future by some reversal in the current and an increase in the number of Western scholars who understand these languages.

In cross-cultural communication three distinct types of encounter present themselves. The first is when we can discern *parallels* and counterparts among two or more cultural systems which make direct comparison possible. In these cases considerable mutual understanding can be achieved on the basis of the experience we already possess. Secondly, there are instances of clear *divergences* in belief and action but which are contained by the fact that these divergences concern the same subject such as the nature of the self or the doctrine of freedom. In those cases, discussion is possible, aimed at discovering whether the differing conceptions exclude each other or whether they may prove to be complementary. Here a greater effort at crossing the boundary is required; if we remain entirely on the ground of our own experience and insight we shall not be able to penetrate the outlook of the other. Thirdly, there are instances of what we may call major *collisions* between established traditions, such as the idea of creation in Western religions and philosophies and either the absence of or rejection of that idea in much of Eastern thought. Here the problems are obviously more difficult to resolve and we shall find ourselves aiming not so much at harmonization or agreement as at gaining some understanding of why we differ.

Let me offer illustrations of these three situations keeping in mind that they are intended to be no more than representative examples indicating how the boundaries might be crossed in each case. The first point to be noticed is that where parallels do exist in different systems of thought and belief, they will have to be discovered and the process of finding them will involve mutual interpretation. Similarities in thought have existed for centuries between, for example, Chinese and Western philosophies, but many of them have come to light only recently as one result of the intensification of the East-West dialogue. The first illustration I wish to consider is philosophical and concerns parallels between some basic ideas in the philosophy of Wang Yangming and the thought of the American pragmatists. Following this comparision will be an illustration from the sphere of religion which shows a remarkable trans-cultural set of parallels among several of the world religions.

Through the work of such scholars as Wing-tsit Chan, Thomé Fang, Julia Ching, and A.S. Cua, I became acquainted with the thought of Wang Yangming, especially as set forth in his *Inquiry* and *Instructions for Practical Living*. I have no intention whatever of turning Wang Yangming into a 'pragmatist', as if the importance of his thought depended on its recasting into some current idiom; it is rather that I could not help but be struck by the parallels I found in his writings to the thought of Peirce, James, and Dewey. There are at least three focal points at which the convergences are most evident. The first is the insistence on an intimate connection between purpose and thought which also embraces values, since all purposive activities are to be understood through the ends to which they are directed. Secondly, there is a strong conviction concerning the transformatory power of ideas; far from being inert, they serve both to orient the life of the individual and they effect changes in the course of events. The third parallel is found in the belief, shared by Wang Yangming and Peirce and James particularly, that human conduct is a sign and a confirmation (or disconfirmation) of the sincerity of what a person professes to believe.

Wang Yangming's fundamental belief is that the attainment of a sincere purpose by the individual represents the highest wisdom and that this purpose is aimed at a form of knowledge which establishes a reasonable order in the mind. The mind, which as Wingtsit Chan has pointed out,[2] meant 'the will' for Wang Yangming, needs to find a definite direction if it is to avoid becoming, in his way of expressing it, fragmented, mixed, and confused. For this reason Wang insisted that we must first attain a guiding purpose before we can proceed to the investigation of things. Actually, as we shall see, the two efforts go hand in hand, but Wang was trying to redress a balance in opposition to those who wanted to give priority to the investigation of things. Without a guiding purpose we could have no idea of what the extension of knowledge means or why we should be engaged in knowing at all. The parallel with the pragmatists is quite clear; they understood the inquiry that aims at overcoming doubt by providing a firm basis for belief as a *purposeful* affair in which thought is guided by what it hopes to accomplish. For Peirce, 'leading principles' direct all scientific inquiry, and, for Dewey, all investigation is a response to the challenge of a problematic situation and we test the outcome by asking whether it fulfills or disappoints the purpose that directed the inquiry at the outset. It might appear that Wang sees purpose only in its moral dimension, but that is not so. For him the investigation of things and the extension of knowledge depend on the initial ordering of the mind and finding the proper direction for all of our activities.

Wang's central doctrine of the unity of knowledge and action expresses not only the intimate connection between the two, but also the dynamic character of ideas. Like the pragmatists, he was not satisfied with the merely contemplative aspect of knowing, but repeatedly emphasized the power of thought in transforming ourselves and the world. In considering the view that knowledge and action must be entirely different from each other because there are those who supposedly 'know' that, for example, parents are to be served with filial piety but are unable to put this knowledge into practice, Wang makes two important points.

The first is that knowledge of what filial piety is cannot be gained without actually practicing it, and the second is that anyone professing to know what filial piety means and either does not or is unable to put it into practice, does not know what it means. Nothing could be closer to what James had in mind when he pointed out that if one wants to know what kindness means, one must first respond to another in a kindly way. Without the experience of that response, kindness could be no more than a word. Peirce and Dewey extended belief in an intimate connection between knowledge and action to the theoretical sphere, maintaining that to know the things of the world we must actively intervene as we do in devising and carrying out experiments. The acquisition of knowledge is not a passive affair. Again, the parallel is clear; like Wang Yangming, the pragmatists were saying that knowledge manifests itself in action and that action is essential in the process that leads to knowledge.

There is yet another important feature in this parallel and it concerns Wang's attack on the belief that we must postpone action until our knowledge is complete. This belief was held by Zhu Xi (Chu Hsi) and has its Western counterpart in the philosophy of Descartes who proposed that we live by a 'provisional morality' until the edifice of knowledge is completed. With arguments remarkably similar to those urged by the pragmatists against Descartes, Wang Yangming insisted that if action can take place only after knowledge is secure and final, we shall never act and, consequently never know.

The third parallel has to do with the idea that appropriate action serves as a sign and confirmation of the reality and sincerity of our belief. Peirce and James were at one in insisting that actually believing in some idea or doctrine involves more than *saying* that one believes, just as actually doubting that something is so is not the same as *saying* that one doubts. The test of believing is found in the performance of deeds dictated by the belief in question; if one really believes in, for example, human equality, then one must treat other people accordingly. Such behaviour, on their view, is a sign or overt evidence for ourselves as well as others of the sincerity of the belief. Wang writes in the same vein when he declares that knowledge of, and belief in, the virtues are to issue in affectionate love of others, and that when this love manifests itself in practice we have evidence that the individual really knows and really believes.

The second illustration of trans-cultural parallels is drawn from a pattern to be found in the world religions. It is too complex to be presented in more than the barest outline, but I believe that will be sufficient for our purposes. William James pointed out some decades ago in his *Varieties of Religious Experience*, that despite the profound and insuperable differences that exist among the major religious traditions there is still to be found one point in which they meet. That point, according to James, is not any one religious belief, but rather a structural pattern manifesting itself in the vantage point of religion itself. Religious insight sets out with a powerful and uneasy sense that there is something *wrong* with us as we naturally stand and that this defect or flaw stands as an obstacle to the fulfilling of our lives. Coupled with this sense is a concern for how this wrongness may be overcome and how we may be *saved* from the defect. Religion has to do with *diagnosis* and *deliverance*; there is first a critical and negative assessment of the human situation, a judgment made by comparing actual human existence with an ideal vision of the perfection of human existence stemming from belief in some form of ultimate Reality. This judgment expresses the nature of the flaw in our being and the reason why the world is out of joint; it is followed by a quest for the deliverer, a power of whatever form that is believed capable of nullifying the deficiency and saving us from the flaw indicated in the diagnosis.

The foregoing pattern is descriptive of the structure ingredient in the major religions and is not imposed from without as the consequence of a theory. On this account, the pattern can serve as a powerful tool for comparison and for crossing boundaries in the face of the bewildering vaiety of belief, ritual, and morality that confronts us when we study the world religions. We can enter into some understanding of religions other than the one in which we were brought up by asking what diagnosis of the human predicament is offered by the Buddhist, Christian, or Hindu traditions in comparison with our own. And we can ask the same question about the conception of the power that is meant to deliver us from what stands in our way. The complaint that there is no agreement _mong the different traditions as to what we need to be saved from or how deliverance is to be brought about, is beside the point. What is important is that the recurring pattern tells us that all the major religious traditions are addressing themselves to the same concerns and are all engaged in presenting their own diagnoses of the wrongness in our being and their strategies for deliverance. We cross the boundary of our own perspective and enter the land of the other when we understand that, when the Hindu tradition speaks of the web of ignorance, the veil of *Maya*, that leads to the misperception of Reality and to the failure to grasp the metaphysical truth that *Brahman* is *Atman*, we are hearing the diagnosis that corresponds to the Christian conception of sin, or human rebelliousness against God and the Buddhist belief that the cause of suffering is to be found in the indiscriminate boundlessness of human desire and its fastening on what is impermanent. These diagnoses are obviously dissonant, but we can understand them across the boundary because they are responses to the same concern. The same holds true with respect to the power of the deliverer; the web of ignorance which, according to the Hindu tradition, prevents us from realizing both our true selves and the nature of Reality, is dispelled by attaining the true metaphysical insight into the identity of *Brahma* and *Atman*. In Buddhist perspective, we are delivered from inordinate and misdirected desire, and hence from suffering, through the Enlightenment of the Buddha and his discovery of the Noble Eightfold Path of discipline whereby the person is transformed. For Christianity, we are delivered from the self-assertiveness that separates us from God and leads us to lose ourselves, through the sacrificial love and humility of Christ. In each case the deliverance is co-ordinated with the particular wrongness about human existence indicated in the diagnosis.

That the three traditions differ greatly from each other is obvious enough and it would be absurd to propose that there is a way of harmonizing them, for that would be to make the basic mistake which says that all religions 'say the same thing'. There are, nevertheless insights to be gained from the comparison and the first is the fact that the pattern of diagnosis and deliverance is transcultural and makes it possible for someone coming from one tradition to gain some understanding of the basic outlook maintained by the other two. In appealing to this pattern, moreover, the adherents of one tradition can consider its diagnosis in the light of the other assessments of the human predicament and see whether these assessments may capture some flaw in human nature that is missing from their own view. In addition, other comparative questions may be raised which may take us further beyond our boundaries. We may ask, for example, to what extent the flaw from which we are to be delivered is seen as intractable and not to be overcome by merely human resources. Theravada Buddhism, with its ideal of the *Arahat*, or 'go-it-alone' saint, believes that an individual can attain Enlightenment through human effort alone, while Christianity, with a different understanding of the flaw in human existence, denies that persons can deliver themselves. The important point is that through these comparisons and questions, our understanding of other traditions is deepened and we gain a clearer grasp of our own.

The threefold pattern illustrated above has further applications and I would suggest that it could illuminate the entire development of Chinese thought especially in view of the fact that there one finds a subtle interweaving of the philosophical and religious dimensions of human life. Chinese scholars throughout the ages have defined the centre of Chinese spirituality in a Humanism properly understood. It is a Humanism, that is to say, not of a reductive sort, that sees no place for a Supreme Power, but rather a Humanism according to which human nature and Heaven are in essential unity. This harmony is both the Ideal and the measure of knowledge and action in the course of individual life and human history. The renowned Sages whose life and thought form the substance of Chinese culture and tradition, despite differences of emphasis and focus, are at one in the belief that the ideal harmony is subject to distortion and even corruption from a variety of sources—selfishness, rebellion, disorder, ignorance, neglect of duty, licentiousness, violence, and many others. The detection of these sources of disharmony together with the continuing debate among Chinese philosophers over whether human nature is basically good or basically evil constitute what was called above a diagnosis of the human situation, an indication of what needs to be overcome or of what obstacles stand in the way of restoring the ideal harmony. The process whereby harmony is restored, the deliverance according to the pattern, is the attainment of Wisdom through discipline of mind and body which leads to the unity of thought and action. Westerners will come to understand Chinese thought and culture very much better than in the past if more attention is paid to the meaning of this recurrent pattern with its obvious parallels with Western philosophy and religion.

Turning now to the second type of cross-cultural comparison previously mentioned, the encounter between clearly divergent beliefs about the same subject, I shall consider but one illustration since it is striking enough to bring home the central point. The Buddhist doctrine of the impermanence of all things and the folly of individual desire in attaching itself to what is impermanent includes the belief that the self is also impermanent, hence the self-regard behind this attachment is likewise vain. The consequent doctrine of no-self (*an-atta*) appears to the Western mind as one of the most puzzling beliefs in Buddhism, largely because of our long tradition in philosophy no less than religion of thinking about the person as unique and enduring, and having an identical centre to which all experience is referred. It appears, then, on the surface at least, that the Buddhists are denying what Western thinkers are affirming and our question is: can there be any crossing of the boundary so that those on each side can come to some understanding of the grounds on which the other view is based? It is understood that, in posing this question, I do not mean to attempt any resolution, but rather to suggest how each position might be *understood* from the other perspective.

Buddhists construe whatever may be called a self in terms of the five aggregates—corporeal sensation, feeling, perception, mental conception, and consciousness—and deny that there is, in addition, any 'soul' or substantial subject. The familiar analogy of the chariot is meant to express the same point; after we have pointed to all the separate parts of the chariot, there is nothing else to be found, hence the chariot is the putting together of its parts. Similarly, when we have pointed to the five aggregates there is nothing further to which we can point and say: that is the self. A Western thinker not already committed to a Cartesian substantial ego can, I believe, understand what the Buddhists have in mind. They are claiming that among the distinguishable contents of consciousness—sensing a colour, feeling a smooth surface, seeing objects, entertaining a specific idea—there is not to be found yet another content that answers to the *self*. The self is no datum of the sort to be found as a unique item in the stream of awareness.

A thinker in the Western tradition may understand and acknowledge the truth of this account, but may, nevertheless, have questions as to whether it can be the whole truth based not only on his or her experience and belief but on other truths claimed by Buddhists. According to the Buddha's example, the overcoming of suffering requires a great effort in the form of rooting out desires attached to what is merely transient, and of commitment to the regimen of the Path. Who or what, it may be asked, is to make this effort and this commitment? The answer is not to be found in any one of the five aggregates but only in their being taken together. Understanding human beings in this way, however, poses the problem that what is said to be true applies universally to everyone who may hear the Buddha's word and seek to follow it. Is there any *one* to whom that word can be addressed? In short, is the unity of the aggregates someone who can be addressed? Another question that arises concerns the positive terms used in the Buddhist literature to describe Nirvana. It is said to be bliss, a holy city, the shore beyond, the harbour of refuge, each of which suggests a destination. If so, how can we avoid asking whether there is anything in the human constitution that can enjoy reaching the goal?

Let us go at once to the other side of the boundary and try to grasp what Buddhists have to say about these questions. The first and most important point is that Western thinkers have been too rash in declaring that Nirvana means annihilation, especially in view of the fact that Buddhists themselves have been emphatic in claiming instead that the goal they seek is one of fulfilment. Buddhists, moreover, have insisted that the no-self doctrine is not to be interpreted as a denial of personality in every sense, but only a denial of the substantial ego and of the self-centredness that it implies. Here, then, is an opening for Western thinkers to re-examine any commitment they may have to that conception of the self. And there is more; Buddhists have often claimed that the fulfilment they seek is not the extinguishing of life itself, but rather the doing away with the limitless and misguided desire which is at the root of all suffering. One might extend this dialectic to include such Buddhist proposals as the Middle Way, which says that the truth is not to be found in either annihilation or permanence because ultimately we do not know. This view has the support of the early tradition where the Buddha is presented as a vigorous opponent of metaphysical speculation and one whose mission is to teach the cause and elimination of suffering and not to answer questions about the inner nature of Nirvana. We must leave the matter there, but from what has been said it should be clear that to the extent that we have succeeded in crossing each other's boundary we shall no longer be satisfied with the view, so plausible at the outset, that the Buddhist doctrine of no-self and Western conceptions of an enduring individual person simply contradict each other.

Finally, I wish to consider the third situation of crossing boundaries where we are involved in what I described as major collisions in belief among several traditions. Two instances will make clear what the problems are and at the same time give some indication of what we may expect in the way of mutual understanding. The first concerns the absence in Buddhism and perhaps Confucianism, although this case is less clear, of any conception of a transcendent Deity as is to be found in the Hebraic, Christian, and Islamic traditions. The second concerns the absence, again clearly in Buddhism but not so obviously in the case of other Chinese philosophies and religions, of the idea of a creation of the world and all finite beings. Obviously these differences in outlook and the lack of parallels and counterparts among the traditions must make it difficult, if not impossible, to cross boundaries. How will those in the Western traditions understand visions of reality where no reference is made to a transcendent Deity or to the idea of cosmic creation? How will those in the Eastern traditions be able to grasp ideas that can only seem alien to them? Posing these questions does not, of course, provide much of a clue about what the answers may be, but I believe that we cannot avoid facing these differences. At least one advantage is to be gained from taking them seriously and that is being led to reassess the meaning and consequences of our own position in the light of the contrast. Buddhists find it difficult to understand how the idea of being a *creature* is compatible with any belief in human freedom. Creation in the Western sense seems to them to imply that whatever or whoever comes into being from a transcendent source is totally controlled by an alien power. Here the challenge is put to the Western religions; why is there no awareness on their part of what seems to others as a blatant inconsistency? The value of the challenge is that it can evoke a salutary response; adherents of the Western religions can take stock of their tradition and come to realize that their major thinkers were well aware of the problem and struggled to find ways of resolving it. Human individuals, they will find their theologians and philosophers saying, were not created whole and entire after the fashion of stars and stones, but were endowed with the capacity of self-consciousness and of responsible choice. Hence not all beings believed to be created are on the same level; there are subjects as well as objects and they may both be creatures without ceasing to be different in nature.

Let us now go over to the other side of the boundary. Adherents of the Western religions will ask why the Eastern traditions accept so readily the belief that the world was always 'there', and will wonder why, if the world might not have been, it nevertheless exists. Or, to put the issue another way, the question will focus on the contingency of finite existence and how the contingent is able to bring itself into being. Creation and transcendent power have always presented themselves to the Western mind as the way of understanding this contingency and of seeing the world as shot through with value and thus as far more than brute existence. As in the previous cases, the aim here is not to join these issues, but to emphasize what may be learned from both sides by a serious consideration of the differences that exist and especially the experiences and motives behind them. To understand where and why we differ in these matters is the most that can be hoped for. The most sincere and determined will to interpret finally comes up against what appears to be an ultimate boundary and barrier at the same time—the fact of the *historical* dimension and those features of religions particularly, and of philosophies to a lesser but still considerable extent, that derive from the insight of founders and sages, prophets and spiritual heroes, whose experience form the substance of all traditions. We cannot, so to speak, go behind these historical deposits and mediate them through a wholly transhistorical rationality. We can, however, cross boundaries and gain understanding even if it is limited to knowledge of the grounds on which our traditions diverge.

In view of the foregoing examples of interpretation at work, we, as philosophers, have the right and even the obligation to raise questions about what there is in the nature of things that makes the process of interpretation possible and provides a rational basis for the crossing of boundaries resulting in successful communication. To initiate the inquiry it is necessary to focus attention on two features of the human world which play an essential role in all forms of communication, including our self-understanding as well as the understanding of others. The first of these is what we may call the reality of *signs*, and the second is the capacity we possess to enlarge, develop, and preserve our experience in the temporal course of life. Since the being of a sign is to be read or interpreted, it follows that a subsequent sign always is required in order to express some part of the meaning of the original sign. The series of signs resulting from the process corresponds to the *temporal* character of experience. This character manifests itself in several ways; there is, first, the unidirectional flow of what has been called the stream of consciousness and we are aware of this flow in our grasp of the difference between the earlier and later parts of an episode. If, for example, we experience the diminishing sound of a train's whistle as it passes, we cannot help but notice the contrast in tones and the fact that the louder sounds were heard *before* the softer ones. Experience is always made up of events spanning time and passing into each other and not of discrete instantaneous moments. It is, however, just this fact of temporal passage throughout experience which makes it necessary for us to employ signs. In order to retain what has literally passed and to endow it with sufficient permanence to become an object for subsequent reflection, we must have recourse to signs expressing the experience.

Signs are thus the conservatories of meaning in that they last and engender an enduring chain of interpretation enabling us to understand the experience, thoughts, and beliefs of minds and civilizations long gone. Time, to be sure, is an order of perishing, but as the philosophers of process have pointed out, time is also what is needed for *lasting* and signs are the medium through which both experience and expression endure. The actual events of experience pass away, but the record of these events and, more important, their significance and value, are preserved in the interpretations, both oral and written, through which individuals and civilizations seek to understand themselves and the world. Memory, of course, plays a vital role in the process, but it, too, cannot function without signs in which are invested the meanings of the past. Memory, moreover, is finite and notoriously fallible; only an omniscient being could write an autobiography without recourse to notes! Signs thus stand athwart the course of perishing and enable us to take the significant past along with us together with innumerable pasts of bygone races and civilizations.

As a framework for further analysis of the meaning of crossing boundaries in interpretation, there is a helpful analogy, first suggested by Josiah Royce, between this process and the process of exchanging currency between two countries. Let us first consider that the value of the currency of a given country is clearly determined for making transactions between individuals and groups *within* the confines of that country. But one currency is involved and it counts as 'legal tender' for all transactions in that country. Suppose now that an individual or group proposes to have dealings with those in another country with its own currency and a different monetary basis. At the point of quite literally crossing the boundary it becomes necessary to determine, in accordance with rules accepted by both countries, the value of one currency in the domain of the other. I cannot simply offer the notes and coins of my currency as legal tender in your country; I must first resort to a system of exchange through which I discover the value of my currency in terms of yours. In conducting transactions I am spending my own currency since I have no other resources, but I must first have had it translated into your currency as the result of crossing the boundary beyond which my currency is no longer legal tender.

The analogy, as is obvious, is between our currencies, on the one hand, and our language, our experience, our traditions and our cultures, on the other. What is the meaning, what is the validity of my means of communication and experience in the realm of your language and culture and, likewise, what is the meaning and validity of your experience in my domain? No analogy can be pushed too far, for there are obvious differences between monetary systems and human languages, religions, philosophies, and cultures, and between exchanging currencies and communicating the substance of our experience. There is, nevertheless, something of importance to be learned from studying the basic experience of crossing a boundary, of passing from one domain to another where we find ourselves in new and strange circumstances confronting novel and unfamiliar ideas, customs, and ways of life. The encounter compels us to attempt to understand the spiritual life of those who dwell in this new domain and at the same time to re-evaluate our own experience and culture in the light of the contrast. What, to take but one example, can the Buddhist doctrine of no-self contribute to the Western traditions in which great emphasis has been placed on the uniqueness and permanence of the individual person? Are the two conceptions incompatible? Are they perhaps complementary in the sense that each grasps some feature or aspect of the self which the other overlooks? The opportunity to wrestle with these and similar questions is one of the important fruits of interpreting across boundaries.

The course of individual life is an unfolding or development in time and, while the experiences, events, and episodes that make up a person's biography are mediated by our relations to others and to the environment, much of the direct experience we undergo stems from the internal dialogue we have with ourselves. Endowed, as we are, with the power of memory and the capacity to anticipate, we find ourselves constantly aware of a present and ongoing self that distinguishes what is past, has been lived through and can be remembered, from what is yet to come and which can, in some of its general features, be anticipated. The temporal character of ongoing life is such that our present selves are continually interpreting our past selves to our future selves. We recall today that yesterday we promised to fulfil some obligation next week. The question is, how does this and similar, but more complex, occasions involve us in crossing boundaries in the sense previously defined? The answer is that since life is a development in time, we inevitably face change and the problem of having to understand ourselves as we grow and discover that our future selves—the joint inheritance of past and present—*may no longer be comprehensible on the basis of past experience*. Oscar Wilde once sought to extricate himself from the awkward predicament of not being able to remember a person who recognized him on the street by saying, 'I'm sorry that I did not recognize you. You see, *I've* changed.' In the course of time we are repeatedly crossing our own boundaries in order to achieve self-knowledge and this is one of the reasons that such knowledge is so difficult to attain. If we recall the example about the promise to be kept, we may discover that the self which made the promise with the full intention of keeping it has inherited a future self no longer as scrupulous in the matter and hence reluctant to honour the commitment.

In his *Confessions*, Augustine, who had a remarkable power of self-understanding, gave us an excellent example of the need to cross boundaries in the interpretation of the significance of his own life. Before his conversion, when he was proud of his learning and exulted in his passions and powers, he tells us that he had a strong sense of his self-sufficiency and of his ability to accomplish whatever he set out to do entirely on his own resources. In the course, however, of his long and anguished spiritual odyssey he came to recognize in himself the will to resist God and when, as he says, he no longer identified himself with the self of which he approved, he found himself with a new consciousness. The experience and vantage point of his former self were no longer sufficient for comprehending his new being; Augustine saw that former self as incapable of interpreting properly the new experience that had come upon him. In reassessing his past, he concluded that he could not in fact have been as self-sufficient as he had supposed, because even then he was being sustained by the divine grace which released his powers and brought them to fruition. The change he records is vivid in the extreme; his later self is as surely convinced that without the help of God he could have accomplished nothing as his earlier self was convinced of its autonomy and independence. A most significant boundary was crossed; the Augustine who came to accept the divine love could then understand the error of his former self, something he could not do when that self was his only guide. Harking back to the currency analogy, the coins of experience possessed by the young Augustine were no longer valid in the domain ruled by his later consciousness; his new relation to God could not have been understood from the earlier vantage point of his self-sufficiency.

The same sort of transformation in experience was pointed out by Hegel in connection with the development of the religious consciousness from youth to age. One and the same person, he says, recites the Creed, first as a child and later as an old person, but there is a world of difference between the two occasions. The child's experience is likely to be dominated by images and pictorial thinking based on what is directly present in ordinary experience. That vantage point allows for no more than a limited understanding of religious beliefs; in order to arrive at a deeper and more sophisticated comprehension the individual would have had to cross the boundary many times. As the religious ideas and their implications become clearer, the inadequacy of the literal and mundane consciousness for understanding them becomes more and more evident. The Creed recited from that standpoint is a Creed limited by the confines of youthful experience. In time a more mature self will emerge, one able to cross the boundary with a wider and deeper understanding. The underlying meaning of growth and maturation lies in the discovery by a person that the boundaries of his or her experience are too limited and need to be enlarged. Much of our conscious life is a continual dialogue with our selves and one that requires a constant effort and a sensitivity to those transitional times when we see the limits of past experience and realize that we must pass beyond them in order to understand the new realm into which we grow. Too often problems of communication are thought to arise only in connection with two different individuals, but, as we have seen they arise as well within the life and experience of one and the same person.

Let us now turn to the situation involving communication between two distinct selves who share a common language and culture. Here what is called for is a mutual crossing of boundaries through the efforts of both persons to enter into the thought and experience of the other. It is of the utmost importance to avoid the common mistake of supposing that each individual has an *intuitive* grasp of his or her own ideas and meanings, and that the task is that of *inferring* the ideas and meanings of the other person. As we have seen, self-understanding in every case requires a dialogical process and therefore it will not do to draw a sharp distinction between the two situations as if self-understanding were wholly intuitive and understanding between two distinct selves totally inferential. Inference, in any case, is the wrong mode since it is interpretation that is involved; we seek to understand both ourselves and the other through the interpreting of signs. The major difference between the two situations is not that one is intuitive and the other mediated, since both are mediated. It is rather that each of us has an acquaintance and an intimacy with his or her domain of experience that we lack in relation to the experience of the other person. Hence, the need for interpretation if the boundary separating the two fields of experience is to be crossed. Each must be willing and able to understand experience other than his or her own. The mutual sharing and comparing of experience where each has some grasp of what the other thinks and means is a matter of interpretation not inference; the latter is a logical transition to what is not present as when I infer that the door has another side hidden from my view, whereas interpretation is the process of determining the meaning of signs—words, gestures, facial expressions, tone of voice—that are present and directly encountered.

In every dialogue between two persons, each is present to the other not merely in the immediate sense of manifest bodies and hidden minds, but rather as two integral persons each of whom is a dynamic complex unified by a definite course of experience and by a centre of intention. In the mutual recognition of each other, we are establishing a context wherein each takes the other to be a structured self intending to express itself through ideas and experiences couched in the form of signs. As an illustration, let us suppose that I am asked a question by a student to whom I am trying to explain what interpretation means. I assume immediately that the student has a particular problem or perplexity in mind and my task is to discover what that person is, as we say, 'driving at'. My belief that the student has such an aim in putting the question stands in the background in my mind and provides a unity for the ensuing conversation. I try to understand the question, perhaps by rephrasing it and then asking, 'Is that what you meant?' My aim is to enter the domain of the other in such a way that the two of us will ultimately have some basis for believing that we have the same meaning before us. Two purposes guide and focus our conversation; there is my purpose which is to explain the meaning of interpretation and there is the student's purpose which is to get an answer to a question about interpretation. Each of us must be motivated by the common aim of crossing the boundary of our experience, and, in this case, since I am the one who is to answer, I must include within my own experience the meaning that the student meant to convey.

The actual process of communication is thoroughly dialogical. It involves questions and answers, clarification of terms, the use of examples, descriptions of experiences, and the like. In order to understand the student's questions, I must avail myself of all the resources I have in my own experience and these may well prove inadequate. It may well be that the student's difficulty points to a problem I had not thought of before so that I cannot answer the question satisfactorily. This possibility, however, can be discovered only in the course of the conversation and the clues we give each other to make clear what we mean. It frequently happens that we can test how well we have communicated when one party crosses the boundary of the other's experience by expressing a point in a new form of words and says, 'When you say. . . , do you mean . . . ?' and then follows another formulation which the speaker grasps on the basis of his or her experience and which is meant to express the same meaning expressed by the first speaker. It is only through the persistent process of sharing and comparing that we can ever achieve mutual understanding.

If one were now to consider the general bearing of all that has previously been said about interpretatation and communication on the development of Chinese philosophy over the centuries, one feature stands out above all others and that is the essentially *dialogical* character of the history of Chinese thought. Perhaps I should add that this character may appear more striking to someone who looks upon that history from a Western perspective than to those who participate in the internal development of Chinese philosophy. In any case, the dialogical development is clearly present and it has significant implications for the entire enterprise of seeking understanding across cultural lines. For if the major thinkers of a culture have developed their own thought through the medium of an internal dialectic, they should be all the more prepared to enter into a cross-cultural effort aimed at mutual understanding. Here a brief comparison will make the point more perspicuous. Hegel, above all Western philosophers, viewed the history of philosophy as a vast dialectical exchange of philosophical positions and doctrines. And, as he pointed out, this history is not to be seen as a simple succession of points of view in which each succeeding philosophy merely cancels what went before. On the contrary, Hegel saw a process of genuine development in which the strengths and weaknesses of various positions are brought to light as the result of a critical exchange. We need not pass judgment upon his particular conception of how the process leads to a culmination in his own system; the important point is the cogency with which he brought different and opposed positions together to confront each other with the hope that inadequacy and error might be eliminated and truth be made to triumph. Not all Western thinkers viewed philosophy in this way, but is is safe to say that much of the development that took place was due to mutual exchange and criticism of ideas. Aristotle made his commentary on certain doctrines of Plato, the medieval thinkers carried on dialogues with each other and with both Plato and Aristotle, the British empiricists stood in judgment on the doctrines of the great rationalists of the seventeenth century, Kant sought to reconcile the two positions and he was, in turn, the object of criticism at the hands of Hegel. The exchange has, of course, continued to the present day.

If, however, we turn to the development of Chinese philosophy in this respect, it seems that the dialogue to be found there is both more intense and more finely focused than that which we find in Western philosophy. This is no doubt due in large measure to the homogeneity of Chinese thought and culture in comparison with Western thought that embraces such diversity as the ancient Graeco-Roman world, the development of medieval theology and philosophy, and ultimately the thinkers representative of the European nations and the Anglo-American traditions. Whatever the explanation, an internal dialogue of mutual interpretation and criticism is unmistakably present in the panorama of Chinese thought. This dialogue is manifested in two ways; on the one hand, there is the question and answer form of exchange between individual thinkers focusing on particular issues and topics, and, on the other, there is the long record of interactions of Chinese thinkers with both the Classics and the enduring religious and philosophical themes. Kongzi (Confucius) and Mengzi (Mencius) commence the dialogue with Mengzi confirming the ideas of his predecessor upon which he was obviously dependent, but also advancing the discussion with his bold belief in the original goodness of human nature, a view that was to be the object of discussion for centuries to come. This same sort of dialogue was to be carried on many times in the history of Chinese thought and one thinks of the interchange, separated by almost two centuries to be sure, between Zhu Xi and Wang Yangming on the question of the priority of the sincerity of the mind (will) over the investigation of things. Even more important to the continuing dialogue was the fact of a work like *The Great Learning* that served as a focal point to which all thinkers had to respond. This small work and others like it served as a sort of interpreter or third mind constantly mediating between all the minds engaged in plumbing their depths and insights. The importance of constant and recurring themes moreover, added to the coherence of the dialogue. Each thinker found himself addressing the Doctrine of the Mean, Human Nature, Universal Love, Heaven, the Nature of *Dao*, Harmony and the Doctrine of Change, Humanity and the Non-existence of the Self, to name but a few of the central concerns of the entire tradition. Thinkers participating in such a long and unified dialogue must find themselves admirably equipped to engage in the currently emerging endeavour to achieve intercultural understanding.

Notes

1. Quell and others, 'Sin', in Coates (1951), p. 4.
2. Wing Tsit-chan (1963a), p.655.

3   The Chinese Case in a Philosophy of World Religions

ROBERT C. NEVILLE

THE intention of this chapter is to suggest how to test an hypothesis about philosophy of religion against some aspects of Chinese religious philosophy. The first section will review briefly the history of the development of philosophy of religion in the West, including its present orientation toward world religions. It will also present at greater length a conception of the discipline I believe viable, methodologically sound, and interesting. Part of that conception is a role for systematic philosophical categories in terms of which alternate religious rituals and practices, conceptualities, and paths of spiritual development can be expressed, contrasted, and compared.[1] The second section will put forward a set of these categories, emphasizing especially creation and the specification of creativity in chaos, order, actualization, and the lure of the spiritual path. These categories obviously have a Western origin, and it is an open question whether they are fruitful or distortive in expressing non-Western material. The third section will consider this question with regard to certain important elements of Chinese religious philosophy: theism/non-theism, immanence/transcendence, symmetry/asymmetry in causation, temporal/eternal creativity, primitive/sophisticated religion, the ontological context of sagehood, moral metaphysics, principle/material force, practice and self-cultivation, and related issues in Confucian, Daoist, Chinese Buddhist, and Neo-Confucian thought. My conclusion will be that Chinese religions express and can develop a spirituality of ontological creativity devoid of the difficulties of the Western theism/mysticism split. This plan addresses the purpose of the present volume, namely, to bring Western philosophical techniques to the service of developing the contributions of Chinese philosophy.

Philosophy of Religion

Philosophy of religion is an invention of modern Western philosophy. The modern period opened with the theme of deep scepticism. Instead of asking the medieval question of whether God's existence can be *proved*, without doubting for a moment the divine existence, the early modern philosophers sought to prove God precisely because they doubted. Philosophy of religion arose with the assumption that philosophy needs an integrity of its own irrespective of the outcome of reflections about God.[2] The sceptical roots of philosophy of religion in Western modernity have been transformed since the nineteenth century, however. Philosophy of religion now requires an empirical base, has a nearly universal scope of world religions regarding its topic, and has interwoven religious pluralism into the self-reflexive problem of the philosopher's own identification of religiousness. The question no longer is whether (this) religion is true, but rather what various and unusual truths are expressed or embodied in the diverse religions of the world. Although there tends to be a non-historical mentality in the practice of many of the world's religions, the scholarly study of them treats them in an historical manner, with the question of 'truth' often finding ironic and paradoxical applications. For better or worse, philosophy of religion does not begin with definitions of religion but, instead, finds itself to be an intellectual practice for understanding religious matters as they develop. The 'religions' thus are traditions and living inheritances in the midst of which we live, and philosophy of religion is among the disciplines that offer some guidance as to how to respond.

The methodological conception of philosophy of religion that I propose arises from the observation that, like any activity, religious activity is selective. This is one crucial meaning of the Confucian notion of *li* or ritual propriety. In a given situation, a religious community or person does not make all possible responses, or even an all-inclusive response, but a selective one. There are many grounds for the selections, among them conformity to traditional lore, stories, scriptures, ritual practices, social habits, and relevant ideals, as well as rejection, non-conformity to, or modification of, any of the above. Intellectual life helps to lift up and articulate the selective principles or occasions in existentially relevant ways, and, of course, in doing so makes the selective activity all the more complicated and focused. As in other areas of life, there is no guarantee that the selective principles are consistent with one another or even responsibly acceptable when formulated at a higher level of abstraction.

Whenever a reponse is selective, it treats some aspects of the situation as important and worth carrying on, and it treats other aspects as unimportant and not worth responding to. Selectivity, thus, is evaluative.[3] This characterization of selectivity as evaluative is extremely abstract, for I intend it to apply to all aspects of religions, including the Chinese. A ritual dance, for instance, moves one way rather than another. Religious institutions have one organization rather than another, with certain kinds of legitimation rather than others. Responses of communities or leaders to significant events are selective. The development of religious language and literature is selective. The influences of religion on social structures, politics, law, the arts, and culture are selective. The articulation of religious problems, tasks, crises, and opportunities is selective. In each of these and many other domains, scholarly disciplines can articulate the issues regarding selection, and what principles are employed, or are misapplied, or ought to be applied. Even if history is not an important dimension to the discipline identifying a particular element of religious selectiveness, by focusing on the phenomenon as selective its historical particularity is expressed.

Philosophy of religion, I suggest, is the critical reflection on what is gained and what is lost in any and all selective responses in religion. By critical reflection I mean not just the identification of what is gained and lost—indeed other disciplines might do that far better than philosophy—but the analysis also of what might be gained and lost with alternate responses, and a comparison of the alternatives. Another, perhaps more traditional, way of putting it is that philosophy of religion looks at the relative worth of the selective principles involved, and at their alternatives.

In its Western history, philosophy of religion has focused mainly on religious conceptualities, the belief structure of religions. This of course is too narrow, but nevertheless an important focus. Given the neurological structure of the human organism, people are guided most efficiently by ideas, and their selective principles not only are embodied in their ideas but their ideas in turn become selective principles. Philosophy of religion thus can analyse the development of the high-level abstractions that find expression in religious literature, doctrines, and philosophy. At the same time, philosophy of religion engages in critical reflection about the selective principles covering all the scholarly disciplines that study religion, not only philosophy itself but also theology, history, comparative studies, social science studies, philology, scriptural exegesis, and others. Especially in our time, there is an interaction and mutual influencing of the selective responses in religious life and the disciplines by which those responses are understood. Philosophy of religion itself, whatever intrinsic value it has as a kind of understanding, is one of the more useful tools for the development of intelligent religious life.

I should stress that philosophy of religion, on this conception, relates to other disciplines in the field of religion as a partner, depending on their findings and supplying its own kinds of interpretation. There is no sharp line between intellectual life within religion and the practices of the disciplines studying religion. Philosophy of religion thus is participatory. This view stands in contrast to the imperial role once claimed for it, as if philosophy of religion were in charge of determining what is true and good in the field. Truth claims and moral claims are among the selective responses evaluated by philosophy of religion, and in this sense the discipline presses those questions. But the sense in which philosophy of religion presses those questions is by evaluating what is lost and gained by the abstract affirmations at issue. The context in which the philosophy of religion is practised is that of the multifaceted study of religion.

In order to compare alternate selective responses, such as alternate conceptions of the goal of religious practice—sanctification, visionary experience, sageliness—it is necessary to represent the alternatives as diverse specifications of a vaguely open opportunity. It must be possible to represent the situation as vague in the sense that all the alternatives are possible responses. In dealing with the conceptions of religious responses, it must be possible to represent the alternate conceptions as specifications of an inclusive vague category. 'Goal of religious practice' is extremely vague and allows of many different specifications of the nature of 'goal', of 'religious', and of 'practice'. But perhaps it is not vague enough. Perhaps it cannot recognize those religions that downplay goal-oriented behaviour, or that reject the whole notion of 'religion' as an organizing idea. The only way to determine whether it is properly vague is to turn philosophy's tables and ask what is gained and lost by using that philosophical abstraction rather than alternatives. This of course is to engage in systematic philosophy, for those questions are exactly the ones pursued by systematic philosophy in the development and criticism of a system of categories. The vague categories need to be sharp enough to exclude their own alternatives as determined dialectically from within. At the same time they must be vague enough to carry along what is worthwhile in any of their possible specifications and to avoid losing what should not be lost at that high level of abstraction. Philosophy of religion thus includes as a proper part the practice of systematic philosophy, or a critical borrowing from it, in order to make its evaluative comparisons. Of course at the most abstract level of a philosophical system, it is impossible to state and compare the alternatives without an even more abstract ground, except from within the dialectic of one's own intellectual procedure. The critical tests for sytematic philosophy include a careful consideration of alternatives to any system of categories. One's system can be put forward, not as a final, critically established truth, but as an hypothesis that embodies these gains and those losses. Other systems have different virtues and vices, and religion looks a little different from their standpoint. Philosophy of religion is enriched rather than impoverished by a plurality of systems, each of which provides grounds for comparison and contrast.[4]

The importance of the vague categories of systematic philosophy is that they provide the grounds for recognizing and articulating differences. Because different religions, say Christianity and Islam, have alternate specifications of the vague concept of God, it is possible to see with some precision where they are congruent, where different, where mutually irrelevant, and what kinds of realities are articulated with gain and loss by each specification. Because Christianity and Buddhism do not have explicitly alternate specifications of a common vague concept like God, it is far more problematic to determine how they relate to one another. One must abstract even more to ask, for instance, how they alternately account for the causes of the appearances of the world, and then must inquire whether the alternate conceptions of those causes have similar religious significance in both traditions. No *a priori* guarantee can be given that there must be universal vague categories. In this sense, the development of a philosophical system adequate to a philosophy of religion for world religions is an empirical project. The worth of any system depends on how well it gives expression to the important things in the world, and this can be seen only be examining piecemeal what is gained and lost by virtue of its abstractions.

The capacity to practice philosophy of religion for world religions depends in part on the viability of the project of speculating

a system of categories in terms of which their connections, discon-
nections, similarities, and differences can be registered. Not to
attempt such a synoptic vague view is to leave the understanding of
world religions in a disarray of parochial viewpoints, with no conceptual instrument with which to internalize such viewpoints one
within another. However much certain religions might prize their
particularity, including ignorance of other religions or of segments
of their own religion, or reject the fact that there are alternatives,
a philosophical understanding of any religion requires seeing it in
relation to others.

Comparative Categories

My purpose in this section is to sketch certain vague philosophical categories that I propose for the comparison and contrast
of world religions. In the final section these categories will be employed to interpret certain phenomena of Chinese religious philosophy as a partial test case.

The first philosophical category, which I call ontological creativity, is approached through the question of being. What is it to be?
The categorical answer to this is complex. To be a determinate
thing is to have essential features of one's own and conditional
features by virtue of which one is determinate with respect to other
things. To be is to be a harmony of essential and conditional
features.[5] This is a straightforward metaphysical claim that can be
defended on its own. It contrasts with atomism, which neglects the
conditional features, and with idealism, which neglects the essential ones.

If we further press the question of being, however, we note that
there need to be two or more things in the world if there is one
determinate thing, because to be determinate requires conditional
features relative to the other things with respect to which the thing
is determinate. Therefore the question becomes, what is it to be a
plurality of determinate things? The categorical answer I suggest
to this is that to be a plurality is to be the contingent product of a
unified ontological creative act. The reason for this is the following. Suppose there are two things, each determinate with respect
to the other and each with appropriate conditional features and
also essential features. The cosmos of their relations is constituted
by the interplay of their conditional features. Each thing, however, is a *harmony* of its conditional and essential features; neither

could even have its conditional features unless it had the essential features defining its own position. How then are the respective essential features of the two things related? Not by their cosmological connections. Rather, by being in a deeper ontological context of mutual relevance. Existing in that context is wholly and absolutely contingent: things are simply made to be together with ontologically related essential features and cosmologically related conditional ones. At least this is my hypothesis, defended at length elsewhere.

The question of being, then, is to be answered vaguely by acknowledging the contingent existence or being-createdness of the plurality of existents. The contingency cannot depend on an ab-original primal stuff, for that would have to be minimally determinate, and an even prior context of mutual relevance would be required. So the contingency depends on creation *ex nihilo*, to use the old phrase.

At this vague level, one cannot say that there is a determinate creator apart from the activity of creating. So there is no literal determinate God affirmed in the conception of creation *ex nihilo*. The character of the creator consists only in the creating of the contingent world. If one reads the contingent world as having the form of a person's act, a story-like structure, then one can specify the creator on the model of an individual agent, as Western religions have done. If, on the other hand, one reads the world as having a different structure, then non-theistic models will be used for specification. To speak of 'the' creator is to bias the vague category of 'creation of the world' in favour of an individual agent creator. If properly qualified as a specification, that theistic view supports the ontological creation hypothesis by giving it at least one family of concrete specifications that are vital in some major religions. The important question is whether this understanding of creation and the contingency of the world can be given specification in non-theistic traditions without serious distortion. I shall return to this question in the next section with regard to certain aspects of Confucianism and Daoism.

To take ontological creativity as the way into philosophy of religion may be to give too great a priority to causation, and it may reflect the Western bias toward creativity. One might instead take the idea of the religious path as the best way to a comparative standpoint. I would argue, however, that in at least most religions, the conception of the religious path is dependent on a more basic

conception of how and why things are.[6] In the next basic category
to be discussed, the religious path emerges as one way of responding to ontological creativity.

The second basic category arises from the suggestion that ontological creativity must manifest itself in all of the primary categories of existence. Let us call those categories a 'primary cosmology'.
The categories of course are determinate, and as such they are
products of the ontological creative act. But because they are
primary with respect to the world they are the elementary expressions of creativity. When seeking to attend to ontological creativity,
my hypothesis is that cultures identify it in one or several of the
elements of the primary cosmology presupposed in the culture.
Primary cosmologies receive many expressions, from the mythic to
the philosophical, and in a living culture these reinforce one
another. Philosophical expressions of a primary cosmology are
highly selective, and there may be several philosophies, mutually
incongruent, which each attempt to express what the culture supposes as its primary cosmology. In China, for instance, the ancient
ideas of *yin* and *yang* were developed in many ways, connected
with ideas of Heaven, Earth, and Humanity, with moral speculations in Mengzi (Mencius), with physical speculations in the
medieval Daoists, and with systemic concerns in the writings of
Zhou Dunyi and succeeding Neo-Confucianists. In the West,
Aristotle proposed a primary cosmology in the categories of the
Metaphysics and the *Physics*, categories developed in diverse ways
through the civilizations of Europe and the Muslim world, cul-
minating in the great system of Hegel. More recently Peirce and
Whitehead have provided serious alternatives to that multifarious
tradition.

Regarding the religious use of primary cosmology, my hypothesis is that sanctity, the *mysterium tremendum et fascinans* is defined around the categories of the cosmology. In order to illustrate
this, I shall give a brief exposition of the cosmology articulated in
Plato's *Philebus*. On independent grounds, I believe this cosmology
is the most promising for philosophical purposes. Furthermore, it
is my empirical hypothesis that it collects together many of the
most important phenomena of religion in appropriately vague
abstraction.

Plato's suggestion was that there are four basic categories: the
unlimited, limit, the mixture of these two, and the cause of mixture. The unlimited, or unformed, or indefinite, or chaos, was a

category already ancient in Plato's time and well-fleshed both in myth and Ionic philosophy. The unlimited stands in contrast to limit, or order, or form, structure, pattern, or law, word, or speech. The things of our world, Plato said, are mixtures of the unlimited and limit.

He never said that either exists as an independent entity. Pure unlimitedness is inconceivable; it would be like thinking of absolutely nothing. Rather, we see that the mixed things of our world always have a plurality within them, and the items in the plurality have something of a life of their own irrespective of the mixture; moreover, each of the items in the plurality is itself a plurality, and so on. Finally, there is a kind of intrinsic dynamism to the plurality or unlimited that makes mixtures unstable and constantly creates new situations. The unlimited is restless, if rest is defined as abiding in a formed structure. The unlimited is a principle of plenitude, overflowing any finite formed mixture. Depending on the formed mixture that constitutes the reference point, the dynamism of the unlimited can be destructive or constructive. From the side of the unlimited itself, there is no normative reference point, and the process of pluralization is fundamentally amoral. To be sure, there is no 'side of the unlimited itself', so the unlimited manifests itself always with the forms of the microprocesses of the mixtures on the human scale. The unlimited appears with the inexorability of the passage of seasons: incipience, growth, flourishing, and decay; it is the blind power of the sea, the storm, the volcanic fireball, the nuclear reaction.

Limit, too, is never pure, but is always some determinate structure of a real or imagined plurality. In the Platonic scheme the limits are always patterns that might enter into the world in order to bring things into relation and integrate them: larger than, double, the measures of change and motion, relations like the virtues among the parts of the soul, relations such as courage and friendship among people, social structures. Limit takes its determinate structure from the plurality it is to measure, yet it is not reducible to the actual structures things have. We can always conceive of a limit as a possible way of integrating its plurality, and we can conceive of alternate limits for a given plurality. For Plato, the limit is normative for its plurality in the sense that by integrating things the way it does, the limit achieves in the mixture the value of having those things together. In his many dialogues, especially the early and middle ones, Plato analysed forms of things by imaginatively varying the components of a potential mixture and the ways of relating them, showing that different worths result from different combinations. The fundamental meaning of limit is measure, whether applied to physical things as in a cosmological structure or to social things as in law, or legislative and judicial speech, or to policy as in the will of the ruler.

The mixtures of existence are the concrete processes for which the unlimited and limit are the stuff and measure respectively. The essence of mixture, over and above the unlimited and limit mixed, is whatever is involved in existential concreteness. A mixture is an actualization of a possible limit in a plurality that has potential for being so limited. Actualization individuates the potential mixture and gives it definite position in the existential matrix relative to other mixtures. Mixture as actualization is to be distinguished from an external mixer, as Plato imagined it in the likely story of the *Timaeas* or Aristotle discussed in connection with efficient causes of artificial things. Mixture is simply the existential actualization of a complex process involving limit and the relative unlimited.

Plato characterized the cause of mixture as balance, proportion, due measure, and the like. The cause of mixture is not the limit as measure, for limit merely achieves the value to be obtained in the particular mixture. Rather, the cause of mixture is the measure of getting the right limit on the relevant plurality in the right place relative to all the other mixtures, pluralities, and possible limits. Whereas in the *Republic* Plato conflated the value in forms with the value of having the right form in the right place, in the later *Philebus* he distinguished them. The later distinction recognizes the importance of a kind of general ecological balance that gives any specific thing its harmonious (or disharmonious) centrality in the whole continuous process; it also recognizes the individuality of finite stretches of process. The cause of mixture causes by virtue of the appropriateness of the finite mixture in the larger whole. There are, of course, also causes in the sense of regularities of nature, but these are structural limits to be embodied when the right potential pluralities are there.

The religious applicability of this primary cosmology is obvious on the superficial level. The unlimited is the central focus of the worship of the Great Mother, emphasizing fecundity, with the danger of birth out of season. The limit is the focus of the worship of the male deity imposing order on the female chaos, the religion of social order and kingship. Each of these needs subordinate aspects of the other in order to acknowledge the insistent realities of life. Many religions, especially those of India, ancient Greece, and China, enjoy a pantheon of male and female deities, frequently in subordination to more fundamental cosmic forces or processes that they symbolize. The fundamental cosmic forces are the inner life of concrete mixtures, however their existential quality is conceived. Many Indian religions take consciousness or some analogue as the model of actualization; Western religions emphasize the occupation of space and time; Chinese religions emphasize position in a web of social and natural relations. The great monotheistic religions combine the unlimited, limit, and mixture elements by subordinating the first to the second and construing the second as the mode of operation of a transcendent ground of actualization; that is, the male principle conquers the female unruliness of chaos with the imposition of order; the creative actualization of the world is the work of order-imposing. The mystical underbelly of the monotheistic religions denies the determinateness of the creator-God and reverses the male-female order: the deeper religious experience is to transcend the merely arbitrary order of the world to the abyss of neutral chaos, seen as the creative expression of the utterly empty actualizing principle. In all the religions, or at least the major religious cultures that have created civilizations, there is recognized a need for attunement with the universe and its ground, a process of sanctification, of living out the religious life, perfecting oneself or one's community in terms of measures far broader than self-interest; the path of spiritual perfection is the search for attunment with the cause of mixture.

This quick set of obvious correlations is indeed superficial and requires many qualifications and nuances. Indeed, it suggests a massive empirical project of examining various religious practices to see how they relate, if at all, to the categories of the primary cosmology. Undoubtedly, such a research project would quickly call for the reformulation of the primary cosmology. I make the correlations here, however, in order to establish a kind of initial plausibility to the ontological category and the primary cosmology that I intend now to relate in considerable detail to certain aspects of Chinese religious culture.

The Chinese Case

The long history and extraordinary complexity of Chinese religions make any generalizations about them simplistic. For my purpose it is sufficient to delineate the matter under test in pragmatic ways. Western scholarship is only beginning to gather data on the rituals and social customs of the practice of religions in China, and much empirical work needs to be done to overcome the stereotyping of the rather ahistorical categories of 'Daoism', 'Confucianism', and 'Buddhism'. Therefore I shall prescind from the personal and social practices of Chinese religions in most respects and concentrate on that end of the spectrum that can be called religious philosophy, or philosophical religion, as embodied in classical texts. The great texts are in their own ways selective representations of the far richer concrete life of religion, but I shall not attempt to assess in just what ways they are selective, how they represent particular social classes, and the like. Moreover, in the present discussion I shall arbitrarily disregard Chinese Buddhism because it needs to be understood within the history of Buddhism that took place so much outside China.[7] My intent is to discuss how certain ideas developed through Chinese intellectual history that relate to the categories of ontological creativity and the primary cosmology.

Never in China did the idea of creation *ex nihilo* develop in ways comparable to its theistic use in Europe. In an earlier paper I examined how both classical Daoism and classical Confucianism embodied elements of ontological creativity without embracing the entire concept, and argued that a perception of the entire concept helps explain certain of the respects in which Daoism and Confucianism have needed one another as correctives. That discussion will not be rehearsed here.[8] Rather I want to focus on a related issue.

Perhaps the reason creation *ex nihilo* never struck a spark in Chinese religious philosophy is that it seems to require a conception of a transcendent creator. That is, Western theism has supposed that God is an independent entity creating the world out of nothing; this contrasts with Western mysticism that supposes that God is not an entity but the formless abyss out of which the world is created. Chinese tradition has had no taste for anything transcendent of the world. Nor has it had much of a sense of the world as a product of an external creative act. Rather there is, in Chinese tradition, a deep appreciation of the immanent definition of things,.that is, the definition of things in terms of their relations with one another, often dynamically interpreted as interactions of *yin* and *yang*. To be sure, in pre-Confucian times there was wide-spread belief in gods and goddesses and, like the ancient Meso-potamian religions, the king was viewed as a mirror-surrogate for a male, heavenly, ruling deity. But this imperial god of heaven was not ontologized into a transcendent world creator, but always re-mained a part of the world. With the passage of time he was neut-ralized into a co-operative divine principle with Earth, as in the *Yijing* hexagrams; this is an example of immanent definition.

David Hall and Roger Ames argue that immanent definition is the essential character of Chinese thought whereas transcendent definition is essential for Western thought.[9] There may be some truth to this, but the issue depends on what is meant by 'transcen-dent'. If what transcends is a determinate being, like a god, then the main burden of Chinese thought is immanent whereas the theistic, though not the mystical, strains of Western thought are transcendent. There is a much deeper issue than this way of dis-tinguishing the transcendent from immanent definitions of things, however. According to the category of ontological creativity, all definitions of things are immanent in the sense of being harmonies of relational conditional features and integral essential ones; no definition of a thing makes relational reference to a transcendent creator. At the same time, there is an asymmetry in the existential status of things. The things together are dependent on ontological creation for their very being, although what they are depends on their immanent context. The ontological ground has no character in itself, except the created character of being the creator of this world. The ontological creative act thus expresses the asymmetry of the *ex nihilo* creativity that is undefined, unconstrained, and unreal apart from creating, and is defined, constrained by the char-acter of the norms created, and real in the act of creating. The asymmetry is not the cosmological asymmetry of time, although the march of time may be asymmetrical in its own way. Temporal causes are among the many kinds of immanent definition. The whole complex array of temporal modes, and the timeliness of things in time, are among the things created. Rather the asym-metry is the ontological directedness of the move from nothing to the complex of somethings.

If there is some universal point to the category of ontological

creativity, then irrespective of whether there is a transcendent determinate creator, there still is the asymmetry of the creative move
from non-reality to definite reality. If one infers back from the
contingency of the world to the creativity grounding it, then the
undefined, unconstrained, and unreal ground can be called 'transcendent' of the limits of the world. Indeed, by the arguments
above it must be so transcendent because to be in the world is to be
determinate and anything determinate requires a prior context of
mutual relevance, namely the ontological creative act. But in this
sense, the order of knowing that allows the term 'transcendence' is
different from the order of being that moves from unreality
through creativity to the created world.

The Western traditions, both mystical and theistic, illustrate
ontological asymmetry clearly. The mystical traditions of Boehme
and Eckhardt express it in the terms used here. The theistic traditions over-express it perhaps in the insistence that the transcendent sources have a determinate character. I believe, however, that
in the complex dialectic of theistic symbolism, the determinate
characters ascribed to God are meant symbolically, that is, not
literally; they describe instead some aspect of ontological creativity expressed in the primary cosmology, for example lawgiver or
lover. The medieval attempt to say the transcendent God is simple was a recognition of the logic of creation *ex nihilo*, as was the
use of the analogy of proper proportionality. The Western philo-
sophic tradition also often recognized ontological asymmetry without determinate transcendence. Plato's Form of the Good in the
Republic for instance is indeterminate in itself and not an object
of knowledge, but is creative of the knowable and the knowing.
Aristotle's Prime Mover is pure act, without potentiality and
hence without the limits that would give determinate distinction
from anything else; Thomas Aquinas used this as a model of divine
simplicity. For Descartes, God creates both the principle of non-
contradiction and the norms of goodness, and hence is not *a priori*
determined by them himself. Spinoza's God is infinitely complex,
but determinate only in the creative product of *natura naturata*.
There are of course many examples of transcendent determinate
theism, but those I have cited would agree that there is asymmetry
in ontological status and that the definition of determinate things is
wholly immanent.

The question is whether in the Chinese tradition, admitting the
principle of immanent definition, there is significant illustration of

the asymmetry in ontological status. I believe there is, though not in forms closely analogous to Western forms. The Chinese forms follow what I call the 'way of incipience'. This way involves taking a stand with some immanently defined state of affairs in order to refer to an ontologically more basic state in which the former was incipient. The latter state I call the ontological ground of the former. It has no character except the incipience of, or readiness to, give rise to the immanently defined state. Although the Chinese tradition rarely connotes an ontological ground actively creating the immanently defined state of affairs, it does note an assymmetrical relation between the determinate state and the indeterminate state in which it is incipient. The ontological ground is not temporally antecedent to what emerges from it, although in some cases temporal metaphors are used to explain it. Western philosophy has also found temporal metaphors almost unavoidable in talking about the 'priority' of the creative ground.

The first illustration of the point is of course the famous beginning of the *Daodejing*.

The Tao that can be told of is not the eternal Tao;
The name that can be named is not the eternal name.
The Nameless is the origin of Heaven and Earth;
The Named is the mother of all things.
Therefore let there always be non-being so we may see their subtlety,
And let there always be being so we may see their out-come.
The two are the same,
But after they are produced, they have different names.
They both may be called deep and profound.
Deeper and more profound,
The door of all subtleties![10]

I take it that 'the Tao that can be told of' is the primary cosmology, the fundamental structure of the world that is the mother of all determinate things. This is the *dao* of movement and time, of the interchange of *yin* and *yang*, of the ten thousand things, of Heaven and Earth. The eternal, nameless *dao* is the source of this. The 'subtlety' of non-being is the incipience of the named *dao* in the eternal; the 'outcome' is the expression of the *dao* brought to being. There are not numerically two *dao*s, since the eternal has no being or determinateness separate from the named *dao*. Rather, there is one *dao* with the internally asymmetrical structure: world-being-created. From the standpoint of the determinate named *dao*, there are two names ('Nameless' is a name) to indicate the productiveness or creativity in the asymmetry. There is no standpoint for the eternal *dao*, because it is the eternal creating of the determinate temporal structure of the path of the world. This is an exact specification of the category of ontological creativity.

Laozi's (Lao Tzu's) writing is extraordinarily sophisticated. What about the more primitive background elements in the Daoist or pre-Daoist tradition? Norman Girardot has produced a wonderful compilation and interpretation of those early sources.[11] He traces many metaphors of 'origin': from the primeval soup, or sea, to the lump from which the primal couple arises, to the gourd in which they float, to further and further differentiation. The round gourds, bloated self-contained bodies, people without anuses, all call attention to the elementary undifferentiated and indeterminate state that is incipient with determination but not yet determinate. The myths Girardot types express the asymmetry of development in temporal, if not historical, terms. That is not a reference to a chronological past, but to the non-chronological 'moment' of *illa tempore*. He rightly points out that the 'redemption' theme of Daoism insists upon this point. The Daoists did not advocate repealing civilization to return to a neolithic society, despite the call for small villages and primitive ways. Rather, the Daoists urged a recovery of the depths of primitiveness in a life determinately formed by civilization. The evil of civilization is not in its determinate structure but in the fact that people have lost contact with the ontological depths in which it rests. Therefore there needs to be a ritualistic and emotional recovery of the uncivilized spontaneity, the soupiness, the unformed ready fecundity of the ontological depths of existence. I shall return to the salvation theme shortly, but now call attention to the non-temporal asymmetrical relation between the primitive state that is all incipience and the civilized state.

Classical Confucians did not engage in much metaphysical metaphorizing like their Daoist contemporaries. That they did not feel the need to do so may have come in part from their appreciation of the Daoist formulation of the common Chinese heritage; but it also came from their immanent concerns with social and personal life, as Hall and Ames rightly emphasize. Nevertheless, like the Daoists, the Confucians assumed an ontological asymmetry of genesis as a vertical dimension within the horizontal dimension of time. As to time, the Confucians were extraordinarily subtle in their theories of education and character development;

moreover, they understood units of passage of time on the model of the paradigmatic changes in the *Yijing*. But at any moment of time there operates a vertical asymmetry uniting the incipience of affairs with the co-temporal outcome. Confucius argued, for instance, that it takes a long while to learn the rules of propriety. But 'humanity', that which gives authenticity to proper actions, can be touched in the depths of the situation at any moment. Even more directly, Mengzi illustrated the ontological asymmetry in his remarks about the 'Four Beginnings'. Each of the beginnings is an incipience of a virtue that can be expressed in the proper medium, or inhibited in its expression. The beginning has no special shape of its own, but is known by its unfolded expressions. In the example of the start of alarm and distress caused by the sight of a child about to fall into a well, Mengzi was not speaking about a baby's condition, but a condition that permanently remains with people throughout their lives, however much they may cover it over and block its expression with selfishness. The point of his moral claim that human nature is innately good is that the ontological underpinnings of overt action, no matter how evil, corrupted, or depraved, include the incipiently virtuous responses of the four beginnings.

Later Chinese thinkers found various ways of expressing the non-temporal asymmetry of ontological creativity. The third century philosopher, Wang Bi, a Confucian in social theory, wrote, in his commentary on Laozi,

All things in the world came from being, and the origin of being is based on non-being. In order to have being in total, it is necessary to return to non-being.[12]

In the same treatise he formulated the distinction between substance and function, a distinction with more ancient roots. A thing's inner essence is its substance, but this expresses itself with regard to other things so as to achieve definition as the thing's function. Unlike my own distinction above between essential and conditional features, both of which are determinate with regard to one another, the Chinese distinction is between a thing's ontological depths, indeterminate if cut off from function, and its worldly expressed character that is immanently defined. Wang Bi's point with regard to moral life is that one's overt functioning in the world ought to recover the depths of non-being in its substance.

Zhou Dunyi in the eleventh century wrote:

The Ultimate of Non-being and also the Great Ultimate (*T'ai-chi*)! The Great Ultimate through movement generates *yang*. When its activity reaches its limit, it becomes tranquil. Through tranquillity the Great Ultimate generates *yin*. When tranquillity reaches its limit, activity begins again. So movement and tranqillity alternate and become the root of each other, giving rise to the distinction of *yin* and *yang*, and the two modes are thus established.

By the transformations of *yang* and its union with *yin*, the Five Agents of Water, Fire, Wood, Metal, and Earth arise. When these five material forces (*ch'i*) are distributed in harmonious order, the four seasons run their course.

The Five Agents constitute one system of *yin* and *yang*, and *yin* and *yang* constitute one Great Ultimate. The Great Ultimate is fundamentally the Non-ultimate. The Five Agents arise, each with its specific nature.[13]

The juxtaposition of the Ultimate of Non-being with the Great Ultimate I take to be a basic statement of the asymmetry of onto-logical creation *ex nihilo* with the sytem of being. Furthermore, the movement begun by the Great Ultimate, generating *yin* and *yang*, is not a chronological or historical movement, but a primary level of movement. Given that level of movement there can be the combinations of *yin* and *yang* that give the level of the basic elements, which level in turn enables the movement of the seasons and natural changes. From the standpoint of any of the more specific movements, there is an enabling level of movement that transcends it, down to the Great Ultimate that is transcended by the Ultimate of Non-being. But of course the lower levels are nothing except insofar as they enable the higher. Zhou did not suggest that Non-being could 'be' by itself, or that there could be the Great Ultimate without its moving *yin* and *yang*, or indiscriminate *yin-yang* movements that aren't formed as the basic elements. The intrinsic nature of the lower levels is to create or enable the higher ones.

Finally, to illustrate the continued power of concepts of ontological creation in Chinese thought, I want to call attention to Zhu Xi's 'Treatise on *Ren*'. Two qualifications must be mentioned first. One is that the topic of his discussion is moral virtue, not metaphysics; this is a continued development of the classical Confucian tendency, and is compatible with the fact that Zhu Xi also was interested in metaphysics. The second is that his discussion is explicitly oriented to what I called primary cosmology, namely, to the categories of Heaven and Earth. Even with these qualifications, note the importance of ontological creation.

The moral qualities of the mind of Heaven and Earth are four: origination, flourish, advantages, and firmness. And the principle of origination unites and controls them all. In their operation they constitute the course of the four seasons, and the vital force of spring permeates all. Therefore in the mind of man there are also four moral qualities—namely, *jen*, righteousness, propriety, and wisdom—and *jen* embraces them all. In their emanation and function, they constitute the feeling of love, respect, being right, and discrimination between right and wrong—and the feeling of commiseration pervades them all. Therefore in discussing the mind of Heaven and Earth, it is said, 'Great is *ch'ien* (Heaven), the originator!' and 'Great is *k'un* (Earth), the originator.' Both substance and function of the four moral qualities are thus fully implied without enumerating them. In discussing the excellence of man's mind, it is said, '*Jen* is man's mind.' Both substance and function of the four moral qualities are thus fully presented without mentioning them. For *jen* as constituting the Way (Tao) consists of the fact that the mind of Heaven and Earth to produce things is present in everything. Before feelings are aroused this substance is already existent in its completeness. After feelings are aroused, its function is infinite. If we can truly practice love and preserve it, then we have in it the spring of all virtues and the root of all good deeds. This is why in the teachings of the Confucian school, the student is always urged to exert anxious and unceasing effort in the pursuit of *jen*. In the teachings (of Confucius) it is said, 'Master oneself and return to propriety.' This means that if we can overcome and eliminate selfishness and return to the Principle of Nature, (*T'ien-li*, Principle of Heaven), then the substance of this mind (that is, *jen*) will be present everywhere and its function will always be operative.[14]

This passage incorporates most of what has been developed above, save for the point about the absolute indeterminateness of non-being, in its expression of the vertical asymmetry of ontological creativity, or, in reverse, the vertical asymmetry of transcendence. The emphasis on the controlling and pervasive power of origination as such, not antecedent causes but generativity, indicates a powerful commitment to ontological asymmetry as a dimension running obliquely through immanent definition.

Hall and Ames admit that transcendence themes entered Chinese thought after Kongzi (Confucius), and claim that these themes have obscured the interpretation, even translation, of Kongzi.[15] My comment on this is that their case may hold as far as Confucius is concerned, as he seems to have been somewhat uninterested in the kinds of topic where the issues of ontology would be raised. As soon as Confucians did become interested in those topics, for instance regarding the issue whether human nature is innately good or bad, I claim that they employed thought patterns of ontological creativity. I suspect, though am not prepared to prove, that Kongzi's collected sayings are expressions of a fundamentally oral/aural, not literate, sensibility. As Eric A. Havelock has argued, in the oral/aural culture it is difficult if not impossible to frame issues in abstract terms; abstractions need words you can distance yourself from and look at, as on the written page.[16] Laozi and Zhuangzi (Chuang Tzu), by contrast, were highly literary writers, immersed in a literate culture using symbols and myths as symbols and myths, and adept at finding metaphors for abstractions. The same was true for Mengzi, Xunzi (Hsün Tzu), and the later writers to whom I have referred. Thus it was easier for them than for Kongzi to relate to ontological matters. Moreover, the Daoist tales discussed by Girardot from periods prior to the literary expressions of Laozi and Zhuangzi, although by no means abstract, presented a sensibility at home with the asymmetry of ontological creativity. Therefore, I would conclude that if Kongzi had been put in the right cultural frame of mind to consider the right topics, he would not have dissented from the sensibilities of his antecedents, contemporaries, and successors in the respects discussed.

As defined above, ontological creativity is not merely vertical asymmetry of generation running through levels of determinate organization, but the original creation *ex nihilo*. This is found in Laozi and several others quoted, but not in Kongzi, and only barely in Zhu Xi. There is a pervasive difference from the Daoists affirmed by many of the Confucians consisting in a hostility to recognition of the Ultimate of Nonbeing, as Zhou put it, or the Unnamed Eternal *Dao*. The issue here, I believe, is not so much a metaphysical disagreement but a practical one: does one return to ontological depths by finding quietude and tranquillity, or by a special stance in the midst of action? The Daoists have tended in the former and the Confucians in the latter direction; or at least this is the way the Confucians have perceived the disagreement. My own sense is this: the Confucians agree with the Daoists that authentic life requires returning to and recovering the depths of nature, and they variously disagree among themselves only with regard to how far down those depths reach. Zhou Dunyi, a Confucian, was comfortable with the Daoist idea of the Ultimate of Non-being. Kongzi himself advocated a return to propriety, interpreted in terms of the original harmony of Heaven and Earth; for him, that harmony was the fundamental origin of all specifics, the principle of combination of the elements of the *Yijing*. Zhu Xi, after Zhou, gave a profoundly ontological rendition of the harmony or Mind of Heaven and Earth.

With that reference to the ontology of Heaven and Earth, it is necessary to turn from testing the category of ontological creativity to testing the primary cosmology, the expressions of creativity in the unlimited, limit, mixture, and cause of mixture. The initial correlations are obvious: Earth, the material force or *qi* is the unlimited; Heaven, principle or *li* is limit; their determinate interaction, or harmony, or *dao*, or Humanity as their joint expression, is the mixture; and the integration of daily life with authentic attunement to the deep harmonies of the world, the goal of the great man or sage, is the cause of mixture. In my view, the integral mix of Chinese Confucianism and Daoism, and Sinicized Buddhism, express these four basic categories of the primary cosmology with greater balance, clarity, self-consciousness, and harmony than any other major tradition, though all traditions give some recognition to the categories. I want to comment briefly on how the primary cosmology throws light on the Neo-Confucian controversies about principle and material force, and then to focus on the soteriological issues concerning the cause of mixture.

Like the Greek, the ancient Chinese tradition appears to have recognized a partnership of heaven and earth, male and female, *yin* and *yang*, from the earliest times. If the primary cosmology picks out some important features of the universe, the partnership of Heaven and Earth is the necessary co-implication of limit and the unlimited in mixture. Heaven, the limit, determines the nature of things, and Earth provides the things with the potential to bear that nature. Chinese tradition interestingly interprets movement as the relative ascendency of some limit on some plurality, or vice versa. The unit of change is not the substitution of one limit for another, as in Aristotle's theory of contraries, but rather the relative ingression and egression of a limit. Indeed, the more basic Heavenly orders or principles are those that determine the process of ingression of particular limits, the patterns of *yin-yang* vibrations.

When the schools of Zhu Xi and Wang Yangming debated the relation between principle and material force, the issue had achieved abstract metaphysical expression. Both schools recognized that neither has a determinate character without the other, and the presence of one entails the presence of the other. Zhu Xi's school emphasized that neither can be reduced to the other. Limit without the unlimited to measure is inconceivable; so is the unlimited without the articulation of limits. Therefore their separate characters of functions must be borne in mind when analysing the mixtures. Precisely in their interactions does the truly divine Mind appear that is the ontological origin of the universe, as in the quotation above from Zhu Xi.

On the other hand, Wang's school recognized the integrity of the mixture itself, with respect to which both principle and material force are abstractions. In the inmost heart of the individual singular existent is to be found the real operation of principle, uniting this nature normatively to its expression in all other natures. Furthermore, this real operation of principle is material action: there is no true separation of knowledge and action for Wang, because the individual existence of the mixture is the operative locus of both principle and material force. That Wang's school fell into the metaphors of mind and seemed to some to reduce material force to mental principle was an accidental misreading, I believe. Wang did not prefer principle to material force, but rather the existential centre of the mixture to the dualism of either. To return to the heart-mind is idealism of a different sort from a preference for mentalistic principle over material. More than most in the Confucian tradition, Wang and his school emphasized the cultivation of heart-mind in action rather than quiet sitting; the locus of the operation of Heaven and Earth is in active, struggling, civilized human life.

My conclusion about the principle-material force controversy, polemical though it has been, is that it is not a real disagreement. All parties recognize principle, material force, and their mixture or harmony, and all base their moral theories on straightening out one's relation to these three. Zhu Xi's school drew out the metaphysical implications of the necessary co-implication of limit and unlimited. Wang's school focused on the existential priority of the mixture over the others in abstraction. To follow out this debate yields a gratifying enrichment of the Western categories, far more sensitive in many respects than the Western discussion.

It is with respect to soteriology, however, that the Chinese tradition makes its most distinctive contribution. Philosophers of religion are reminded by all traditions that salvation, redemption, spiritual perfection, or whatever the practical path of religion is called, is the controlling focus of religious life. Metaphysical considerations may undergird and shape practice, but the practice is the point. Nowhere has this been clearer than in the Chinese tradition. Confucianism, Daoism, and Chinese Buddhism, have given priority to the spiritual or cultural quest for perfection, and have engaged in metaphysics only where that was believed to be helpful to practice (beliefs about this differed).

The cause of mixture is the ideal harmony of all elements justifying any one. The religious significance of this is that it is possible for the harmony to be distorted in actual fact, so that the justifying cause of mixture is only ideal. The Daoists and Confucians had slightly different conceptions of the religious problem from which salvation is necessary, and therefore slightly different conceptions of the cause of mixture.

For the Daoist tradition, the religious (or cultural) problem is that our civilized life becomes detached from and out of harmony with the *dao*. In terms of our analysis this means that civilized life does not adequately acknowledge and express its roots in the relation between the eternal and named *dao*, in the originating impulse of incipient non-being. The Daoist path thus is a celebration of emptiness, of nothingness, of relaxation into a womb-like unactive readiness. This rarely if ever has meant a pursuit of mystical fusion and bliss, of *samadhi*. Rather, the emptiness is to be recognized in the fullness of practical life, in the space between the spokes, in the hollow of the bowl. The esoteric Daoist cultivation of immortality in the form of the primeval infant is not a search for a transcendent, non-temporal blissful union with the *dao*, but a continuation of individual life reinforced and reorganized by the originating incipiency of infancy. In the practical life of philosophical Daoism, the search for the simple is not a yearning for ancient times, but an attitude shift about present life, a letting go of striving, a welcoming of the spontaneous impulses grounded ontologically in the eternal *dao*.[17] The cause of mixture is conceived in Daoism as a vertical harmony among the various horizontal levels of reality, a harmony such that the more specific levels are given their truest operation by letting them express the creativity of the lower levels. The Daoist butcher did not gain expertise by ever more advanced courses in bovine anatomy. Rather, he learned to let the placing of the blade and the shove of his shoulder be in tune with the nothingness, the hollows and spaces, that pervade the ox as much as himself.

For the Confucian, the religious problem is not so much to realign the layers of one's being as it is to cleanse oneself from the selfishness that blocks the right operation of one's responsiveness to the harmonies of Heaven and Earth. Like the Puritans, the Confucians see the religious problem to be a positive evil in individuals (the Confucians disagree among themselves about the origin of selfishness, and about whether an unselfish person would do right naturally or would need education).[18] I believe the Confucian soteriological path has three roughly distinguishable elements. The first is that individuals are defined by their relations to other things, principally to other people, and that these relations are given social structure. The first element of the cause of mixture then is a proper harmony of the individual with the cosmos, especially with its social components. The second element comes from the ancient recognition that true social harmony is different from faked codified harmony that in reality can involve oppression and hide selfishness. The emphasis on humanity, *ren*, from Kongzi through Neo-Confucianism, is aimed to give authenticity, life, and spontaneity to the pursuit of social harmony. The rules of propriety are not the norms for social behavior; the norm rather is the authentic human spirit that inhabits them. It was for this reason that Kongzi was willing to wear the economical silk cap rather than the ostentatious linen one, but was not willing to short cut respect for ancestors by eliminating the bow outside the temple (*Analects* 9:3). The third element is that the way to achieve harmony with the cosmos is through personal cultivation. Whereas the philosophical Daoist would be wary of making a project out of self-development, the Confucian believes that constant effort is required to identify and eliminate the pockets of selfishness blocking the way to harmony.

The nature of Confucian self-cultivation is not personal nitpicking of the sort so typical of seventeenth- and eighteenth-century Puritan lives. Rather it is the discipline of meditation designed to open the person to substance, the inner pool of tranquil incipience before feelings are activated. But instead of waiting for some mystical experience of this, the Confucian discipline is to integrate the attention to tranquillity with the activities of everyday life so that the tracks from incipient feeling to actual response to particulars can be followed and straightened out. Sincerity is the

Confucian virtue whereby there is clear, unselfish passage from the inner substance of incipient function to its outward expression. The payoff is in the outward expression. But that expression is false, and worse than valueless, if it does not arise from the sincere soul. From the early *Doctrine of the Mean* to the contemporary writings of Du Weiming and Zheng Zhongying, this conception of self-cultivation, of the path of the sage, was at the centre of the most creative Confucian thinking.

To summarize the contrast between Daoism and Confucianism regarding the cause of mixture or the goal of spiritual life (with apologies for the sweep of the generalization), the former focuses on the harmony of the world with its ground, particularly on the expressions of the primary cosmology with the creative act *ex nihilo* itself. The latter focuses on the harmonies among the elements of the primary cosmology, and cites attunement with the ontological creative act as the means to achieve that harmony. There are different stresses of values held in common in the Chinese tradition.

My argument has been that both the category of ontological creativity and the categories of the primary cosmology are illustrated by the Chinese philosophico-religious tradition. They are illustrated perhaps even more clearly than in the Western traditions that gave rise to my terminology. In several instances I have shown how various expressions of Chinese thought have provided specifications of the vague categories employed to frame the comparative aspects of philosophy of religion.

Let me conclude by reversing the argument. What can the Chinese tradition contribute to philosophy of world religions? It can contribute precisely these versions of ontological creativity, devoid of the difficulties of the theism-mysticism split characteristic of the West, and of the categories of the primary cosmology. Whereas the authority of the primary cosmology, such as it is, might indicate that the categories of Heaven, Earth, and their harmony are fundamental and not curious anthropocentrisms, the reverse of this point is that the authority of the Chinese categories legitimates that part of the primary cosmology.

Or to put the matter more realistically, having attempted to relate basic Chinese ideas to the category of ontological creativity and to the categories of the primary cosmology, we are now in a position to ask whether the richness of the Chinese tradition would find abstract, valuable expression in the categories proposed for the philosophy of world religions. To answer that question, we would have to ask what, in the Chinese tradition, does not receive expression in the proposed categories, and to assess the loss that involves. My remarks have been intended only to indicate the direction the discussion might follow. The next step is for systematic and empirical analyses to determine what is gained and lost in specific cases. I cannot suppress my delight at the irony of my preliminary findings, however, namely, that Chinese thought gives a more inclusive and balanced expression to the genius of creation *ex nihilo* and a Platonic cosmology than the West has been able to achieve.

Notes

1. The division of religious affairs into ritual and other tradition-borne practices, conceptualities and their expressions, and personal and corporate disciplines of spiritual development was put forward in my *Soldier, Sage, Saint* (New York, Fordham University Press, 1978). There are, of course, many ways to divide the phenomena. The selective approach of the present essay concentrates on Chinese conceptualities about what should be understood in order to orient spiritual discipline. For a more detailed experiential approach to religious phenomena see John E. Smith's *Experience and God* (New York, Oxford University Press, 1968).

2. John Locke's *Reasonableness of Christianity* and Leibniz's writings, especially about theodicy, were transitional from rational apologetics for religion to the critical independent stance of philosophy. Spinoza's *Theologico-Political Treatise*, David Hume's *Dialogues Concerning Natural Religion*, and Immanuel Kant's *Religion within the Limits of Reason Alone* were the first truly great works in philosophy of religion. Hegel's lectures on philosophy of religion, Emerson's essays about the Oversoul, Nietzsche's critique of the culture of Christianity, Royce's philosophical reconstruction of a religious metaphysics, and John Dewey's magnificent *A Common Faith* are among the outstanding landmarks in the development of the discipline.

3. This theory of selectivity as evaluative is developed at length in my *The Puritan Smile* (Albany, State University of New York Press, 1987).

4. The conception of philosophical categories as vague was invented by Charles Peirce. I have developed it at length in *Reconstruction of Thinking* (Albany, State University of New York Press, 1981), Chapter 2.

5. This claim is given detailed examination and defence in my *God the Creator* (Chicago, University of Chicago Press, 1968). I have also discussed it at length in *The Tao and the Daimon* (Albany, State University of New York Press, 1982), especially Chapter 3.

6. In this argument I follow John E. Smith who analyses religion in terms of the ground and goal of human existence, with the religious 'problem' intervening.

7. I have discussed Chinese Buddhism with reference to ontological creativity in some detail in *The Tao and the Daimon*, Chapters 9–11.

8. See 'From Nothing to Being: The Notion of Creation in Chinese and Western Thought', in *Philosophy East and West*, vol. 30, no. 1 (January 1980), pp. 21–34. This essay formed the basis of Chapter 7 of *The Tao and the Daimon*.

9. See their *Thinking Through Confucius* (Albany, State University of New York Press, 1987).

10. Wing-tsit Chan's translation in his *Source Book in Chinese Philosophy* (Princeton, Princeton University Press, 1963), p. 139.

11. See his *Myth and Meaning in Early Taoism: The Theme of Chaos (hun-tun)* (Berkeley, University of California Press, 1983).

12. Chan, p. 323, see note 10.

13. Chan, p. 463, see note 10.

14. Chan, p. 594, see note 10.

15. See Hall and Ames, note 9 above.

16. See his *Preface to Plato* (Cambridge, Harvard University Press, 1963); see also Walter J. Ong's *Orality and Literacy: The Technologizing of the Word* (London, Methuen, 1982).

17. See Wu Kuang-ming's marvellous *Chuang Tzu: World Philosopher at Play* (New York, Crossroad, 1982).

18. On the similarities between Confucianism and Puritanism, see my *The Puritan Smile*, Chapter 2.

4 Language in the Heart-mind

CHAD HANSEN

Introduction

Chinese philosophy allegedly deals with what language cannot describe, define, or otherwise capture. The paradigm is the mystical *dao*—the orthodox Neo-Confucian view of Daoism is that Daoist theory entails that language cannot express the *dao*.[1] Because of this, Daoist theory requires two component theories: a theory of *dao* and a theory of language. If the Neo-Confucian interpretation is accurate, Daoist theory of *dao* could not have much content. However, orthodox accounts of Chinese thought struggle to explain this notoriously incoherent notion of *dao*. They pay too little attention to the part of Daoist theory which might be lucid—the theory of language. I propose to turn our attention to the theory of language component. I will argue that it gives us a way to make the theory of *dao* clear. I will propose a new account of the paradoxes that discussing *dao* allegedly generates.

Traditional neglect of the theory of language has led scholars to stereotype Chinese philosophy as strong in ethics and weak in analytic philosophy. This is misleading. Chinese normative ethics is embarrassingly weak. Its main strength lies in a novel moral psychology (novel, that is, from the Western point of view). However, that moral psychology (the theory of human nature) is based on a theory of heart-mind. I will argue that the interesting aspects of the Chinese theory of the heart-mind are intimately related to contrasting features of their theory of language. The preoccupations of modern analytic philosophy are precisely where Chinese philosophers make some of their most interesting contributions. The results of their theory of language and mind, furthermore, profoundly influence Chinese normative ethical dialogue and their view of education. The Chinese theory of language is the key to understanding Chinese philosophy in general.

I will discuss some celebrated and some relatively unknown contrasts between classical philosophical Chinese and modern English. These contrasts help explain how classical theories of language worked and what phenomena motivated those theories. I will also discuss a neglected but key contrast between Western folk psychology[2] and the classical Chinese theory of the heart-mind. Finally, I will outline the historical development of these theories through the classical period. The sketch will, of necessity, be brief.

Theory

Contrasts: Language and Theory of Language

I find the following perplexing. We speculate frequently (usually paradoxically) about how Chinese logic may be different from Western logic. Then we react sceptically to the suggestion that their theory of language or their psycholinguistic theory might differ from those of eighteenth-century British empiricists. We ought easily to appreciate that a particular culture's common-sense theory of language might differ from ours. Philosophers from a particular culture tend to take their own language's traits as essential characteristics of all languages.

Western theories, for example, tend to generalize across Indo-European languages. We theorize mainly about languages with phonemic writing systems, inflectional sentential syntax, clear structural distinctions between descriptive and prescriptive forms, and required subject/predicate structure.

Chinese theories of language differ in part because the language they explain differs. Their theories account for a pictographic[3] written language with a grammar that relies almost exclusively on word order for grammatical role-marking. There are no part-of-speech inflections to draw attention to formal properties of sentences. The prescriptive sentence has at least as good a claim to be the basic sentence as does the descriptive sentence. (All too frequently, distinguishing the two moods is a matter of interpretation rather than grammar.)[4]

Not all the differences in language will result in differences in theory of language and not all differences in theory are best explained by differences in language. Certain differences in theory are particularly striking. Some concepts in the theory of language are so basic to the enterprise of philosophy that their absence calls for explanation. Western theories of language centrally employ philosophical concepts such as truth, belief, meaning, and propositional knowledge. The Chinese theory of language has no formally adequate counterparts of 'true', 'believes', 'knows that', or 'idea'[5]. Western theory treats the function of language as descriptive or representative. Chinese theory treats the function of language as socializing, regulating, and co-ordinating behaviour.

The Structure of Language

Western theories of language, from Aristotle to Chomsky, fix on syntax. Syntax, until the last decade, typically dealt with sentences and the sentential structure of language. I intend a broader sense of structure for this discussion, however. I am interested in the structure of *language* in the sense of a theory of its constituent parts. What subdivisions of language are important and why? What parts make up other parts? What kind of structural system is language—a written structure—a spoken structure? Is sign language language? Is body language language?

Of course, Chinese theorists do not have answers to these specific questions. These are simply the kinds of question that will remind us how the notion of a structural theory is more general than the familiar notion of a syntactical theory. Let me list the structural features of language that would draw the attention of Chinese philosophers.

Written versus Spoken   Chinese philosophers wrote using Chinese characters, not a phonemic alphabet. They tended to assume (probably correctly) that characters developed from pictures. Most characters are made up of one or more units of basic meaning which we call radicals. Radicals tend to be used as semantic categories even in constructing otherwise phonemic characters—the most frequent composite character type. For example, the phonetic *ma* with the 'earth' radical means dust, with a 'hand' radical means touch, and with a 'stone' radical means grind. (In phonemic characters, one of the units contributes a phonetic hint as well as some meaning.)[6]

Pre-Han writers wrote characters vertically on bamboo strips or on silk. They used no punctuation and thought of strings of characters as precisely that—strings. In theory there seemed to be no notion of words playing generalizable syntactic roles in some specifiable string structure—for example a sentence. The character's grammatical role, in fact, depends almost entirely on word order and context. In general, no inflectional markings for sentential roles were preserved in the writing system.[7]

Other cultures on the periphery of China adapted Chinese characters as their own written language. The process was not significantly different from the adaption of characters by the various Chinese languages. The differences were matters of degree. Where these other native languages were inflected, they developed modified writing forms. In Japan this involved putting the inflections (written in a phonemic alphabet) between the characters. These characters served and still serve as a common writing medium for several Chinese languages and Japanese. Speakers of each different Chinese language pronounce the characters differently. In principle, we could use Chinese characters to write English or any other human language.[8]

The point here is not specifically about the pictographic nature of the writing system, but about its inter-language character. Our attention is drawn to the character as a basic unit because it is common to many languages. If we consider character as equivalent to words, then words are individuated in the written, not the spoken, language. We would have good reason to treat language as a written system that is spoken—rather than as a spoken system that is written.

A Chinese philosopher, thus, would have little reason to insist that written language is merely a recording of verbal language. Obviously, the literate Chinese faces a greater challenge in learning how to write after knowing how to speak than, for example, literate Germans. He is not merely acquiring spelling rules.[9] The written language is clearly independent of any *particular* spoken language. We would reasonably regard it as a more universal medium of communication than we do spoken language.

With one written form for up to forty languages, we would rationally individuate these languages in a different way than we typically do in the West. The tendency to refer to Chinese languages as dialects suggests we are individuating by written form. We have only fragmentary evidence of the degree to which the written language diverged in grammatical structure from the various ancient spoken Chinese languages. There appear to have been different Chinese languages in ancient times as in modern times. It is plausible to suppose that, like modern Cantonese and Mandarin, they had significant differences in grammar.

The various spoken languages no doubt influenced both new structures and new characters introduced into the written language.[10] Aside from our cultural assumption that written language is totally parasitic on spoken language, however, we have no reason to exclude the possibility that the written language developed partly independently. Writing was a related but distinct and more widely based social practice than speaking.

Chinese written language has less lexical ambiguity than any of the modern spoken Chinese languages—which have a high number of homophones. We can presume that the ancient written language also specified more than spoken languages. Some characters were probably invented solely to capture a theoretically important distinction that spoken language did not mark. An example is *bian* 'distinction' which has the same structure as *bian* 'divide'. They differ in that, between the two vertical units being divided, the former has a *yan* 'language' radical where the latter has a *dao* 'knife' radical. Presumably, this marks the awareness of the distinction making character of language. We see evidence that the Moist (Mohist) language theorists invented characters with parallel motivations.[11]

Our own tradition individuates words by languages (which would correspond to dialects of Chinese). To be a translation in one language of a word from another language is not to be the same word, but to have the same meaning.[12] Thus, our theory of word individuation is part of our reason for postulating an interlinguistic meaning for different words in different languages. Given the difference between written and spoken language, an ancient Chinese linguist would have equally good reason to individuate words by their written form. He would then say different Chinese languages simply pronounced the words differently. Prior to encountering Sanskrit or Japanese, he would have little reason for a theory of translation or interlinguistic meaning. The character itself would serve the relevant interlinguistic role.

Sound and Pictures We sometimes describe Chinese characters as pictographs or ideographs. There are some ideographs in English—Arabic numbers.[13] Briefly, that a character is an ideograph entails that its written shape be partly or largely a function of the meaning of the character. In pictographs, a spatio-temporal isomorphism explains the relation between the written word and the parts of the world it picks out.[14] In purely phonemic languages, the written shape of a word is (or, at some point in linguistic history, was) primarily a function of its sound.

Written Chinese was standardized at the end of the classical period of philosophy. Before this standardization, Chinese characters were relatively more varied and more pictographic. They were more intuitively recognizable as pictures. The Han characters are, in turn, relatively more pictographic than the simplified characters promoted in modern China.

The Western common-sense model of language and mind reflects the phonemic character of Western written languages. We typically (and incorrectly) assume that the word *is a sound*. The sound has meaning by virtue of the mental association between the sound and some mental item—the idea. Explaining what an idea is has been a long-standing challenge to Western philosophers. We can conveniently understand it using Chinese as a model. The idea is a pictograph in an inner private language. Let us call this language 'mentalese'[15]—the transcultural language of the mind.

Ideas are to words in language as characters are to sounds. Ideas are strung together in the mind to form mental sentences or beliefs. These mental sentences correspond to different sentences in each of our conventional spoken languages. In communication the speaker translates the mentalese into sounds and the listener translates the sounds into mentalese.

Westerners (and modern Chinese who have learned this theory of communication) take this picture seriously. I do not. Western common sense regards this view of language and mind as obvious and inescapable to any conscious language user. We end up insisting that the ancient Chinese philosopher of language must implicitly agree with us even if he never directly talks of such things. Given what a Chinese philosopher reasonably believes about language, however, it would be irrational for him to agree with us.

Classical Chinese philosophers do not formulate any mental language theory.[16] Our uncritical acceptance of the theory makes us claim that Laozi (Lao Tzu) was implicitly committed to it. Laozi's theory of language, however, treated language as a system of distinctions—not ideas or pictures. Knowing a word was analogous to mastering a skill. The writing or verbal skill combined with an ability to make a distinction. This ability to discriminate is also a learned, socially defined skill. The test for mastery or knowledge of that skill is irreducibly social or conventional.

Chinese theorists did not embellish this pragmatic theory with a theory of *meaning, concepts, belief*, or *ideas*. Were they even to regard their characters as pictures, they would have intuitively recognized the crucial flaw in Western common-sense theory of language. Pictures (ideographs) stand in need of interpretation as much as do sounds. Learning a language requires an ability to recognize shapes or patterns. If we have that ability it explains equally our ability to learn written language and to learn how to recognize a word's extension. If we do not have that ability or skill, then we could never learn to read even our own inner language—we would never be able to associate the items of mentalese with sounds. Consequently, the theory of mentalese cannot be an explanation of our ability to make distinctions—it presupposes it.

Pictographs, conventional or mental, require interpretation just as phonemic written words and sounds do. Had Chinese thinkers invented a 'mental picture' view of how the mind learns language, it would have seemed redundant to them. It would never have seemed to them to have solved any important issue about language. They would have seen that it provided neither an explanation of how we learn words nor an explanation of how words mark distinctions.

Western mentalese theory has another important consequence that contrasts with the Chinese philosophy of language. The mental inner language was not social or conventional. It arose as a pure interaction between reason and the world. The process was one of abstraction from private sense experience. Each of us individually abstracts from a different inner experience. We rationally select a class of objects and with no social guidance we select the common features of our sensible experience of things in the class. This inner process of concept formation is commonly regarded as a preliminary and necessary step to learning a language. We cannot learn any word for something until we have derived from our private experience a corresponding mentalese concept.

Chinese philosophers, by contrast, all regard language as essentially social. We are taught to make certain distinctions with certain words. The central question in the Chinese philosophy of language focused on whether historical tradition or nature governed the use of the word and the distinctions we make in the world using the word. There were two kinds of anti-traditional or natural answer. One was that the distinctions existed in nature. The other was that the human propensities to make those distinctions were natural (innate). The traditionalist answer led to relativism. The distinctions in language are correct if they are those treated as appropriate by a community. Different linguistic communities may adopt radically different sets of distinctions. The mental picture theory was not one of the available options.

Functional Parts of Speech   We use traditional Western grammar to analyse Chinese word order. This presumes the sentence is the pivotal structural unit. The sentence is vital for meaning theory. Sentences may be true or false. Words are not. So we understand a word's meaning as the contribution it makes to the truth of a sentence. Thus we divide words into classes according to the functional roles they play in a sentence.

The way of describing Western languages treats different words as playing different roles. Words are, that is, role-specialized. We regard 'nation', 'national', and 'nationalize' as different words.[17] A word root, on the other hand, is what undergoes role specialization. Adding an inflection to a word root makes a word. We could say that '-ity', '-tion', '-ly', '-s', '-ize', and so forth provide the word *roots* with syntactic mobility. Given these role-marking inflections, most English roots can play a variety of different sentential structural roles.

Classical Chinese philosophers' theories about their own language, by contrast, fix on the word as the basic unit. They think of a word as having a scope—the part of reality it selects. They pursue an interest in how stringing or combining words affects this scope.[18] This interest leads them to study compound terms and some phrases and sentences. However they do not pick the sentence out as a distinctly structured string. It is a string and their theories are generalized to phrase strings. They never specifically identified sentence strings as truth-bearing strings.[19]

Chinese characters work as English roots do except that no *part-of-speech* inflections turn characters into role-specialized words. The natural position for a Chinese philosopher of language is that characters are *words* and *words* are syntactically mobile. We string words together. What do we form? We form compound words and phrases.

What happens when we combine these into bigger clusters of language? There are many ways to describe the language hierarchy from this point. Our Western textbook theories would typically list something like sentences, paragraphs, chapters, books, life works, literary movements, and literary traditions. Philosophers might list sentences, arguments, and theories. Ancient Chinese language theorists listed *shuo* 'explanations' as the next level. The top of the language structural pyramid, I shall argue, was *dao* 'prescriptive discourse'.

I usually translate *ming* following the accepted practice as 'name', but 'word' might be more appropriate. Adjectives, verbs, and even quantifiers count among *ming*. Part of the reason sino-logists regard 'name' as an acceptable translation of *ming* lies in the implicit semantics for this view. Given that *ming* covers such a variety of word types, the only semantic feature shared is scope. A typical *ming* is individuated by what parts of reality it picks out. It includes some and excludes the rest.

This semantic point motivates the contrast theory of language. That theory is a distinctive trait of classical theories of language. Learning any term inherently involves learning its complement or converse. To know a term's scope, one must be able to distinguish what does and does not fall within that scope. This is the semantic side of the pragmatic claim that learning names consists of acquiring skill at making distinctions.

English common *count* nouns have two other semantic prop-erties in addition to scope—identity and unit selection. In knowing a noun such as 'cow', we know what counts as the same cattle *and* what counts as *one* cow. English mass nouns have only the first of these, identity. That means that semantically we know what counts as *the same* x—the same water, the same rice. Mass nouns do not have a principle for determining what counts as *one* water or rice. We choose different individuators in different contexts—a bucket of water and a cup of rice. Adjectives (and one-place verbs) have only the property of scope. We do not (normally) think of 'red' as a substance. We do not say the very same *red* can occur here and there. (Note that the same paint can—and it may not be the same *shade of* red.)

Since all Chinese nouns are mass nouns, we can explain why scope would become the major focus of Chinese semantic theories. Chinese philosophers recognized no basic distinctions among *ming* except those associated with scope. We could also predict that they would tend to adopt a substantive reading of adjectives. They would interpret 'hard' and 'white' as substantives with spatial and temporal locations since mass nouns and adjec-tives function in basically the same way. Thus we can explain the tendency to use *ming* ('name') even for feature-placing terms like adjectives.

Imperative versus Declarative   Classical Chinese makes no regular grammatical distinction between imperative and declarative sentences. Both may lack a subject (for that matter, both may have subjects). Some particles and terms help translators decide which English mood to use, but we mainly rely on context and sense. We distinguish interrogative mood more reliably because of the use of question *ming*. Interrogative word order, except for the interrogative *ming* and the final question particles conforms closely to the imperative/declarative word order.

Pragmatic versus Semantic   Western folk theory of language not only focuses on the sentence, it focuses on the declarative sentence. We treat the declarative sentence as the complete and standard form. The interrogative form appears to be inverted and the imperative form to be 'lacking a subject'. Western folk semantics treats imperative sentences as parasitic on declarative sentences. We follow or obey an imperative sentence if we bring about the state of affairs represented in its declarative form. To make it true is to obey. This focus informs our view of the function of language in general. We say that we use language to communicate information about the world. We assume that the basic role of language is the role of the basic sentence—representing or describing facts. The sentence states a truth or a falsehood.

It would be inaccurate to insist that the imperative sentence is primary in Chinese for two reasons: (a) as we have noted above, the sentence itself is not a central focus of their theory and (b) we do not have a clear distinction between imperative and declarative mood. However, the prescriptive function of language informs the Chinese view of language as the descriptive function informs ours. The base of prescription is the *ming*—not the sentence. (*Ming* 'command' is the usual verbal form of *ming* 'name'.)

No clear distinction between fact and value typifies Chinese theory of language. The role of language lies primarily in shaping behaviour and picturing the way things are as a means to accomplishing that role. In guiding behaviour, language must connect with the world in which we act. The important point is that the descriptive role is subordinate.

Our folk theory of language interacts with our folk psychology. For Western theorists, the mind's function mirrors that of language—representation. Language conveys facts by conveying ideas—mental pictures of facts. The mind manipulates and stores those mental representational items. The meaning of a bit of language is a representational item in our mind. Our theory of consciousness and sense experience both mesh with our theory of language in the same way. Experience leads to the internal conscious states we call beliefs and we translate these into the sentences of our respective languages. Conscious beliefs are constructed from ideas or concepts just as sentences are constructed from words.

The counterpart theories in China mesh equally well. The Chinese concept of mind more resembles the Western 'will'. Their heart-mind directs the body. Its function is guidance and its content is derived from language or practical intuition, not abstractions from conscious experience.

The essential function of language is to guide behaviour. Bodies of language do so constitute a *dao* 'way'. Humans internalize the guiding discourse and the heart-mind implements the internalized code in guiding our action in the real world. As we act, feedback from the world must be sorted or distinguished before we can continue to follow the internalized code.

To evaluate our feedback, we need to have skill at making distinctions for each *ming* contrast in the code. We make evaluations for and against by discriminating among responses in relation to learned *ming*. This skill at discriminating or distinguishing is the functional counterpart of Western concepts. Our patterns of discriminating or distinguishing are the internal measures of the ranges or scopes of terms.

In general, then, we understand Chinese philosophy best as being based on pragmatics rather than semantics. The pragmatic function of language is not describing or representing reality, not stating truths, but guiding actions and co-ordinating social interaction. Language is a social convention which undergirds other social conventions. Humans are social animals, but we are social animals in whom historically evolved conventions rather than instinct govern social behaviour.

As I noted above, one could see the descriptive function as subordinate to the prescriptive function. We can derive the fact-stating function of language from the pragmatic function. We translate knowledge of the truth of the sentences into the ability to construct 'strings of language.' In the place of a representational theory of mind, Chinese theories tend towards a linguistic skill theory. The mind programs itself by internalizing language. The language guides behaviour. Chinese theories did not appeal to beliefs or other 'content states' to explain how language fulfilled its function.

We understand language. In Western folk theory, this claim would be elaborated in the following way: the mind translates sounds of a language into the mind's language of ideas. In Chinese theory, the elaboration moves directly to practice: heart-mind guides our behaviour using the formulae in language.[20] We may wonder how the heart-mind does this. This basic answer is that the heart-mind makes a distinction in situation based on inputs from the world. How speakers make the distinction will differ for different pairs of terms. We must usually take our ability to make distinctions as a primitive notion. Some people can never learn to make left/right distinctions. That is not a distinction based on any specific sense or internal data. It is a skill at following a kind of guiding discourse. If someone simply fails to understand the clues we normally give in teaching this distinction, it is hard to imagine how to teach such a person.[21]

We can appreciate how different our cultural perspectives are by noting the differences between standard examples. Western theories focus on concepts of sense—colour or extension. Chinese theory worries about how we learn up/down, before/after, or here/there. Western theory seeks to explain the ability to distinguish by postulating the inner pictographs. Chinese theory takes 'learns to distinguish' as primitive. We often read this aspect of Chinese theory as intuitionist.

Western folk theory (WFT) demands an explanation of our ability to distinguish in response to a name. Most adherents assume that the mentalese theory *is* the explanation. Reason (rational abstraction) replaces intuition. We make distinctions by matching objects in the world to our ideas. We arrive at the ideas by abstracting from our experience. We learn language by associating words with ideas. If the object in the world 'matches up' with the idea, then we use the word associated with the idea to classify it.

The relation of the idea to the world is pictographic—an individualized character of the mind. Viewed like this, we see that WFT begs the question it purports to solve. We interpret one language by translating it into another. It does not explain how we interpret language *simpliciter*. Instead of answering this primitive question, WFT gives us a picture of translating our ordinary social languages into private ones. We have not eliminated the problem; we need to interpret mental ideas just as we need to interpret char-

acters. The problem has not been solved but pushed off to a mysterious medium. We gloss over this circularity in WFT because the
ideas are in our minds where (a) we fail to notice how mysterious
and magical they are and where (b) our *privileged closeness* helps
us forget that the relation between the ideas and the world is
language-like. Since the ideas are *ours* we assume that they constitute a base language. WFT explains understanding as translation
into this private language.

To see the circularity in Western folk theory's explanation of
how we make distinctions, consider colours. WFT says we learn
'red' by associating with a mental red item. We see lots of red and
abstract the shape and solidity, motion, and even the shades and
hues. When we get a sufficiently abstract idea of red, we are ready
to learn the English word. Then, when we obey commands employing red, we do so by comparing the idea the word calls to mind
with external objects. Thus we differentiate between red and blue.

The problem is that we have also acquired ideas of blue and
green. How do I manage to 'pick out' my idea of red from the
other ideas when I hear the word 'red'. We have to be able to
discriminate among colours before we can employ the process
which should explain how we discriminate among colours. The feel
of a solution comes from the fact that we do the discrimination
'off-stage' where we do not see the trick. The mystical connection
takes place in the depths of our minds—rather than right out there
in the public, social world.

The crucial difference between these two traditional theories of
language lies in the social/individual contrast. Western popular
theory presents the ideas as a psycholinguistic theory. They are a
non-social language into which we translate whatever language we
acquire. Chinese characters are social and learned. Chinese theory
treats learning language as acquiring the ability to follow socially-
shared discrimination patterns.

Socialization and Co-operation

Their contrasting theories of language and of mind betoken deep
differences between Chinese and Western attitudes towards the
individual and society. A language is always the language of a
community. The sounds do not represent pictures in our subjectivity. If sounds correspond to anything, they correspond to the characters or graphs of a shared and unifying system of conventional

pictures. Language is social. It is the key way in which we socialize with other humans. In the absence of theories of a private mental semantics, Chinese ethical theories start from radically different views of human nature and mind.

Philosophy and Relativism

The central elements linking the theory of language, theory of mind, *and ethics* are the *ming*. The scope of a term corresponds to the skill of dividing things. We are all similarly trained to discriminate in guiding behaviour. However, each situation in which we guide our action by codes made up of *ming* is unique. We inevitably extrapolate from the circumstances in which we learned the word to a circumstance in which we apply it. In this sense, the scope of a term is never fixed by our training.

People can, therefore, learn different *dao* made up of the same *ming*. They discriminate between X and non-X differently. What we would call their disagreement in moral attitude is understood as rival sub-dialects. The Moist pattern of behaviour guidance differs from the Confucian. Both are learned patterns characterized by differences in language—specifically stressing different terms and making different distinctions. They both call their guidance systems *dao*. The sceptical question that prods Chinese philosophy into analysis is whether there can be any constant, non-relative standard for *dao*. Can the distinctions taught with the names in each action guiding *dao* be fixed in a non-question begging way? Are there, in other words, constant *ming*? If there are no constant *ming*, there can be no constant *dao* constructed from *ming*.[22]

The relativity of language to social convention and the absence of a theory of sentences and truth made the argument for relativism intuitively compelling.[23] Plato's studied concentration on truth, knowledge, and common meaning made the argument for realism intuitively compelling. Classical Chinese philosophers worked from a pragmatic rather than semantic model. They had a heightened appreciation of the relation of language to language users. They studied language in its social dimension first and then tried to apply the analysis to the relation to reality. They ran into exactly the problems they should have—indexicality, the historical theory (without the help of causal metaphors or natural-kinds metaphysics), and scepticism of whether we can fix what counts as following a rule. There is no cosmic axis from which to fix classification conventions.

Mozi (Mo Tzu) started the philosophical dialectic by prescribing that society modify the conventional system of distinctions. He thought that general utility was an appropriate gauge for linguistic revision. Linguistic reform would result in a psychological change which would result in an ethical advance. We should *make constant* that system of word contrasts which best promotes human co-operation in our common interests and survival.

However, Chinese relativists note two things. Firstly: any attempt to *fix* a constant way takes a value norm for granted. Any norm would involve a term contrast (say 'benefit' and 'harm'). Secondly: any norm which distinguishes among possible *dao* must itself be applied in particular situations. No situation would be exactly like the model situation in which the normative contrast was exemplified. Hence, nothing would make an application of the norm correct. No amount of learning fixes the way in which a chosen pattern will be applied in unique situations.

If the norm is intuitive, then it will usually be a conventional norm. From the point of view of conventional, orthodox morality, utilitarianism is immoral. This attack on utilitarianism is common to Kantians and Confucians (although their theories have little else in common). If we test a theory by its coincidence with our intuitions, we will tend to justify our existing moral practices.[24] If one tries to revise standards, one needs to postulate a standard by which to judge the revision.

Mozi's utilitarian criterion looks like an anti-traditionalist universal standard. That standard justifies a different guiding discourse in each tradition. But how can we show that the *li* 'benefit' standard is the correct one? Any system for evaluating systems has to evaluate itself. In general, all actual competitors *shi* 'approve of' themselves and *fei* 'reject' rivals. In this competition, a neutral way to choose the criterion without taking it for granted appears impossible. Such, at least, is Zhuangzi's (Chuang Tzu's) argument.[25]

There is a second constancy problem about *dao*. Even if we accept some standard, given the particularity of conditions of action, no system can make a population's classifications constant. A culture might realize the hope of getting people to change, but not the hope of a perfectly uniform pattern of making discriminations.

It is not that they would deviate, but that there could be no way of determining which pattern was a deviation and which was a faithful following of any given *dao*. Social practices cannot reliably control the mystical or intuitive component of discriminating in guiding action.

Concepts

'Conceptual scheme' is a rough synonym for *language*. 'Perspective' normally suggests spatial or visual angles of view. I will use the term 'conceptual perspective' (C-perspective) to present this feature of Chinese thought. By that I mean the practice of guiding perspective which is enshrined in a language as defined by its pattern of word contrasts and distinctions. I propose we do an intercultural thought experiment. How would we theorize from a classical Chinese C-perspective? I will use 'see' figuratively with this sense of theorize. I do not mean that Chinese literally 'see' a different world. To see things from a C-perspective is to understand how we would theorize and act from that perspective. Now I want to set out the C-perspective of the classical Chinese theory of language.

Dao: *Guiding Discourse and its Interpretation in Space-time*

Given its recent cultist uses, philosophers may consider *dao* the central enigma in the morass of obscure Eastern thinking. In fact, *dao* causes less translation controversy than most other philosophical terms. Almost everyone uses *way*.[26] However, although *way* is a relatively 'plain' word, even a frequent term in philosophy, its use is usually offhand and non-theoretical. Western philosophy has paid little attention to this venerable all-purpose word.[27] Unlike *knowledge*, *good*, *true*, *idea*, and so on, our philosophical tradition has not accumulated analytic theories of the term 'way'.

Way is, however, a perfectly respectable, common-sense term in English. I shall offer here an analysis of features which *way* shares with *dao* but also warn of some important structural properties separating the two terms.

Way comes close to being a primitive concept of ordinary English. A *way* answers a *how* question. It's partial synonyms include *course*, *path*, *custom*, *habit*, *manner*, *practice*, *method*, *process*, *direction*, *means*, *style*, *mode*, *fashion*, and *mechanism*. However, it is hard to find a genus of which *way* is the species. In the traditional sense of *definition*, then, *way* no more has a definition in English than *dao* does in Chinese.

Fortunately, philosophers no longer care about traditional genus/species definitions! We usually accept replacement formulae and for *way* there are many candidates. The sense of *way* that intuitively most closely parallels that of *dao* is 'course of action'. X is a *way* $=_{df}$ some subject (S) can follow X to get from Y to Z. The subject need not be a person. Even rocks have a way of rolling down hills. The question of what counts as following a way raises familiar questions.

The English word 'way' conceals a type/token distinction. We may regard all the ways (tokens) the dancers danced that dance as examples of the way (type) to dance it. I do not have any adequate account of what makes a way-token belong to a way-type. I suspect that is because whether one is following a way raises the kinds of questions Wittgenstein raised about following a rule.[28] There may be no fact of the matter of what constitutes following a way-type.

A way-token, on the other hand, is a segment of world history. The actual string of events, the course of events is one sense of way. That historically actual way may be a guiding model only if we take it as marking a way-type. Which way-type it marks is not fixed, of course, for the same Wittgensteinian reason.

However, there are other ways to point to ways. Typically, we express a way in language—let us say we 'linguify' a way. The advantage of language for the human species is that it allows the accumulating and transmitting of ways. Language has storage and transmission efficiency as compared with demonstration or direct transmission from master to apprentice.

Notice the essential vagueness in how a language expresses a *way*. We do not use the notion of rules, imperatives, or the general distinction between describing and prescribing. Any language game that guides action constitutes a way-type. To regard a way as consisting of rules of imperatives is to shift our focus from the *ming* (which, remember, may be names or commands) to sentences. The non-sentential structure marks an important difference between 'way' and *dao*.

Let us see how 'way' works in translation and start to get a sense of the Chinese use of *dao*. We start by surveying predicates and modifiers which Kongzi (Confucius) used with *dao*. In *The*

Analects, Kongzi treats a *dao* as a communicable thing. A *dao* can be heard (4 : 8), spoken, studied (6 : 12), corrected (1 : 4), modelled, walked (5 : 7), or wasted, present or absent (3 : 24). A *dao* can be born and grow (1 : 2), be strengthened (15 : 29), be small or great (19 : 4). One can master a *dao*. *Dao*s guide the skills (16 : 5), including the skill of speaking (17 : 12). A *dao* performance is a source of pleasure (13 : 25, 1 : 1, 16 : 5). Different people interpret *dao*s differently in their performances and attitudes (17 : 3).

Distinguishing *dao* types and tokens in Chinese raises another interesting contrast with English. All Chinese nouns function largely as English mass nouns do. We can count with them in diverse ways. The implicit metaphysics is part/whole, not type/token. Like mass nouns, Chinese nouns do not have an intrinsic principle of individuation.[29]

Dao operates like a mass noun. If X is *dao* and Y is *dao*, then the sum of X and Y are *dao*. This mass-like behavior of *dao* gives it the generality of 'being', the Western philosophical concept most confused with *dao*. *Dao*, however, is practical not metaphysical. The interpretation of *dao* as metaphysical is one of the key mistakes of the ruling interpretive theory.

In Chinese, *dao* is a 'general' mass term. It is not a proper name. The distinction in Chinese is more subtle than in English. Since all nouns are mass nouns, they can be regarded as logically singular. But a mass noun can be modified so as to narrow its extension. Normally, we cannot modify a proper name.

Chinese writers (including Daoists) modify *dao* regularly. They modify *dao* using the names of specific historical individuals (4 : 15). Your father has a *dao*; Kongzi has a *dao*; the former kings had a *dao*; villages have a *dao*. You can regard Heaven's or nature's *dao* (*tiandao*) as a specific deity's prescriptions or as the sum of all *dao* that occur in nature. We can also distinguish different *dao* by periods of history (3 : 16), or by reference to specific skills (4 : 5), or normative systems (16 : 11). There are ways to do all manner of things and there is the straight and narrow way. *Dao*s have parts (8 : 4) but we can view them as one even when they seem disparate.

We may be tempted to think of *dao*s as theories.[30] Theories, particularly normative theories, guide behaviour. People at times have different theories and there are theories of how to do almost anything. Normative theories are particularly apt candidates as ways. We interpret them. The problem with 'theory' as a translation of *dao* is that it is *too* theory-laden. Theories have a particular kind of internal proof structure—they consist of some sentences and some rules for generating other sentences. Ways, however, need not come in theoretical form. 'Truth' is an integral concept to theories but not a concern of philosophers in this period.[31] Furthermore, like 'way', 'theory' individuates too precisely.

Dao is closest to the English mass noun 'discourse.' The inner structure of 'discourse' is appropriately indeterminate. We can sum across different specific discourses as we may sum across *dao*s. Your discourse and my discourse make our discourse. This properly leaves open the mechanics of how discourse guides action. For the time being, we should resist temptation to a belief-desire or practical syllogistic account of human action.

Roger Ames (among others) has suggested an aesthetic model for understanding the relation between *dao* and action.[32] Think of the relation between guiding discourse and action on the model of a musical score and a performance. The concept of interpretation bridges the worlds of art and semantics. The artistic interpretation does not render one symbol system into another. It executes a symbolic programme and yields a performance. Interpretation takes a type into a token.

The important relation is that between a guiding discourse and behaviour. Consider what interpretation has in common where it consists of following rules and reading poetry. A *dao* can equally be a code of behaviour, a musical score, a poem (for recitation), or assembly instructions. Belief/desire and reasons for action analysis seem strangely beside the point when we focus on this wider notion of guiding discourse.

So as an initial anaylsis, *dao* is guiding or prescriptive discourse. A 'way' is a way *to do* something. Consider an instruction set or programme as an example. This instruction set may range from, say, the rules of a game to a computer programme. We learn the way to do something by studying the instructions and by running the programme we have internalized. An instruction set, like a computer programme, may need debugging during the practice. The programmer 'debugs' the computer. Our teachers 'debug' us.

As I noted above, we can learn how to do things without discourse. We can learn by imitation and by trial and error. We can continue to regard *dao* as discourse if we generalize discourse to include the language of modelling (body language). Any imitation might be treated as a case of following guiding discourse. The *dao* token expresses a *dao* type. We try to execute another token of that type.

In English, 'literature' shares with 'discourse' the possibility of generalization beyond verbal language. Plays, dances, and dowsing can be considered parts of literature. We speak comfortably of musical literature, for example. Kongzi uses *li yue* 'ritual-music' as a compound term in *The Analects*. Both are transmitted *dao*. Both guide performance. We best understand Kongzi as urging the study of guiding literature to be the study of *dao*.

These literature forms—music, ritual and poetery—share this: we interpret them in performance. We practice and learn these different *dao*. We take delight in performing them. (The character for *yue* 'music' may also be read as *le* 'pleasure'.)

The Chinese concept of literature has a similar breadth, but slightly different motivation and implications. The Chinese character *wen* 'literature' or 'language' originally referred to the decoration or embellishment on bronze or pottery artifacts—the artistic designs. By extension, it has come to encompass all *cultural* embellishments or decorative refinement. Humans refine themselves through *wen* 'literature'. Such decorative refining constitutes civilization—translated as *wenhua* 'literature-changed'.

I have proposed a theoretical framework to explain some features of the use of terms in philosophical Chinese. I argue that Chinese thinkers have a unique view of language, some of it motivated by the unique features of the Chinese language. That view, in turn, motivates certain assumptions about the heart-mind and human nature. Different theories of language and mind motivate, in turn, different ethical theories. Chinese theory of language stresses language's customary nature and behaviour-guiding essence. Its theory of heart-mind stresses how discriminating among objects guides behaviour.[33] Language is linked with social practices such as ritual and music. Together they reinforce a social conception of human nature and give a powerful explanatory framework for a role ethic.

The apparatus that underwrites a Kantian ethic, autonomous reason, is similarly linked to Western views of language and mind. Western theory of language treats language as more parasitic on an individual, rational process of abstraction from experience. It treats language as a much more private thing—at least at its base.

Conventional languages work by translating an inner, subjective, and inherently private mental code. We postulate the faculty of reason motivated in part by a search for a supra-cultural and extra-linguistic basis for action. This forms a different explanatory framework. Ethical individualism, the dignity of each rational being, the supreme value of a faculty of reason, all fit more neatly with this subjective theory of language.

The ordinary usage of *dao* in Chinese differs from 'way' in English in one final way. Classical Chinese uses *dao* as a verb. The most common translation of this verbal use is straightforwardly linguistic—'to speak'. Thinking of the nominal use as 'discourse' helps explain the otherwise ad hoc connection between the verbal and nominal use. However, 'to speak' seems at once too broad and too narrow. Too broad because not just any speech is *dao*-ing. Only speech which guides behaviour counts. This caution would not be necessary if we assumed that all language, all discourse, guides behaviour. I have argued that Chinese philosophers from the Pre-Han period shared this assumption.[34] However, 'speech' is also too narrow. We can guide behaviour by gesture, example, and literature as well as by speech. This caution, too, would not be necessary if we would think of language broadly, namely, as we do when we speak of 'body language' and the language of dance, of music, and so forth. Sometimes translators render this verbal use of *dao* as 'guide.' Between the two translations, 'speak' and 'guide', lies a verbal concept that almost perfectly parallels the nominal interpretation, 'prescriptive discourse'.

Xin: *Philosophy of Mind*

Given these differences in philosophy of language, we should resist the temptation to assume that Chinese philosophers shared the Greek theory of the psyche. That theory, inherited by Western common sense, informs modern folk psychology (WFT). In familiar versions, WFT treats the mind as a repository of representations. The representations derive from stored sense/data—experiences. The mental representations coincide for all sentient creatures and any human language must express them.

Beliefs, as mental representational content, picture facts. Beliefs are like mental sentences made up of concepts rather than words. Translated into a conventional language, they are sentences. Thus Western folk psychology meshes with Western theory of language.

I propose a shock. To understand the Chinese theory of mind, we should make full use of the computer analogy. I do not argue that Chinese thinkers had concepts of computer cybernetics. The point is that the computer analogy allows us a way of talking about the mind that avoids Western folk psychology. It should help us avoid exporting Western folk psychology to ancient China. Let us dispense with the rococo theory of beliefs, desires, truth, correspondence between mental items, inner consciousness, and experienced data. We start with the plain notions of input and output, and a processing unit. We will leave the nature of the processing unit undetermined for the moment. Our interest is in how to programme it to appropriate social behaviour.

The input is what Hayakawa calls 'the niagara of words'.[35] The output is a human performance—a course of action or *dao*-token. *Dao* is the sum of all discourse inputs. The paradigm Confucian form of *dao* is a ritual text or book of etiquette. It tacitly includes, however, parental instruction, television advertisements, university lectures, musical scores, and examples. Any activity designed to influence our behaviour counts, although linguistic activity is the central case. The output is behaviour. Instruction givers usually decide if their *dao* has appropriately guided the student's output.

The type/token ambiguity of 'way' corresponds to the input/output ambiguity with *dao*. An output is a *dao* token, an actual course of action. We can think of the input as a regulative 'programming-to-follow' a possible course-type. Construe the output as realizing (making actual) that course-type.

We can also think of the course-type as a set of possible course-tokens. This gives us a non-linguistic sense of *dao*. That possible cluster of courses is the intended output of our prescriptive discourse. In that case, following *dao* is making a possible course of action actual.

This conception of the interface between language and action reminds us that *dao* does not consist of information—at least not initially. Our computer is not an information processor, but an exercise in artificial robotics. A *dao* is a programme which may include data statements but need not. The *xin* is the central processing unit (CPU). It reads and executes the programme—the linguistic *dao*.[36] It interprets the possible course of action intended in the discourse and guides the body in performing it. The behaviour-guiding programme requires programme-branching—we will call the branches *shi-fei* (see below). The branching consists of the *xin* making an evaluation and then executing a bit of *dao*. The idea of sensory input fits into the Chinese theory of mind at this point. Its role is not giving a picture of reality. The senses also make *shi-fei* evaluations which the heart-mind uses in its *shi-fei* branching control. The programme checks for any branching condition which requires the evaluation from sensory parallel processors. The *xin* receives the evaluation sensory results and returns its own *shi-fei* (this/not this, pro/con, yes/no, is/is not, true/false, or assent/dissent). This *shi-fei* output is a form of the *xin*'s contribution to the deluge of *dao*. The outward behaviour may be an utterance, 'Good!', or a behaviour which models a *dao* for the *shi-fei* situation. In sum, the human heart-mind is an action-oriented *dao*-interpreter.

We use 'heart-mind' to translate *xin*. This is because the philosophical psychology of ancient China did not use a cognitive/affective contrast in their talk of well-honed human performance. It does not mean that Chinese philosophers were poor at physiology. 'Heart' and 'mind' denote faculties, not organs. It is an empirical matter whether the mind is the brain. (It is.) Similarly, it is an empirical matter whether the heart is the heart. (It is not). We understand the *faculty* of *xin* best as the faculty that guides the body's behaviour.[37] Beyond that, we are safer with the computer analysis than with a belief-and-desire analysis.

Thus, we should not model the *xin*'s functioning in terms of a practical syllogism, or calculative faculties. It is not *reasoning* from beliefs and desires. Chinese theories do not generate any counterpart to the faculty of reason—or sentential information processing, argument, axiomatics, or deductive form. Practical functioning does not start with realising desires given certain beliefs. It starts with an instruction set—from outside or inside. The *xin* is the CPU and, aside from its *shi-fei* branching evaluations employing sensory input, we may regard it as a 'black box'.

De: 'Virtue', 'Power', or 'Dao Within a Person'

The *xin* takes in the discourse, the programme, the instruction set. 'Hold the brush in the right hand.' The programming language is a human language. We may come equipped with a hard-wired programme for acquiring the programming language dominant in our environment. Of course, no one comes programmed with a specific language. Learning a language consists of learning to follow the *dao* that are spoken or coded using that language. Learning a language is internalising a *dao*. As we learn a language, society programmes our *xin* as a compiler-interpreter enabling us to use the community's language in the heart-mind's guidance functioning.

The heart-mind must, accordingly, have some innate behavioural dispositions to guide it in internalizing a human language. Since it is a pre-linguistic guiding, it seems that there must be an unspoken *dao*—some hard-wired programme. Do not regard this hard-wiring as 'innate knowledge' of rules or definitions, or propositions. The hard wiring is a behaviour-guiding programme that aids our reading-in and executing the cultural, behaviour-guiding programme. We can regard *de*, *qua* guiding programme, as an internal or innate *dao*. The natural human tendencies to respond to smiles, to babble, to mimic, to be affected by dispproval, to acquire conventional behaviour in general, and to enjoy showing off mastery of any acquired recognized skill all figure in our accumulating language. They are arguably more vital than hypothetical innate data about possible human languages.

Translators decode *de* as 'virtue'—another ambiguous English term. It is not troublesome for the same reason 'way' is. 'Virtue' has acquired *too many* connotations. Its Greek predecessor, *arete*, had the non-moral sense of excellence. As Donald Munro has argued, this is the most plausible counterpart of *de*.[38] *De* should not be understood as priggish moralism but as excellence or skill. We can treat Arthur Waley's translation, 'power', as an attempt to avoid the moral connotations. Virtue consists in the character and inclination to exercise skills—among them moral skills. The core skill, nevertheless, is interpreting discourse into action. Derived skills are those conveyed by discourse—skills at ritual performance, music, and the arts (fine and martial).

Returning to the computer analogy, then, we can locate *de* at two different levels—the innate and the acquired *de*. The innate *de* is the hard wiring that enables us to acquire cultural programming—to internalize *dao*. This gives us an elegant way to understand a traditional Chinese formulation for *de*: a natural *dao* 'within'.

Employing our 'language acquisition device', we internalize a cultural *dao*.[39] The effect on our *xin* is natural and physical. It is neither hardwiring, nor is it a perfect mirror of the *dao*—the public discourse. Our translator gives us an internal *realisation* of the publicly available linguistic programming. Although this new state is not innate, it is a state, not a bit of language. It is a potential state of the heart-mind—a disposition that corresponds to the *dao* expressed using language. It is a state that will result in a specific *dao*-token in some situation. If that *dao*-token is one of the set of possible courses intended by the *dao*-type which programmed us, then we have learned that *dao* successfully. Thus, this acquired-state potential can be understood as '*dao* within' us. It constitutes our ability and inclination to act on the *dao* we have internalised.

One difference between us and computers is this: we load a programme in a computer all at once and then run it. The programmer, herself, however, typically has an intermediate task—debugging the programme. As social computers, we are more or less constantly being debugged—at least until we become a Sage. At that point, we can debug others.

There is never a simple stage of wholesale 'reading in'. We get bits of social programming and act on them. We then get *shi-fei* responses from our programmers (parents, older siblings, teachers, playmates, friends, and colleagues). Our *de* is constantly being adjusted by social responses. The 'niagara of discourse' (the cultural *dao*) includes these responses. Their effect on us is to alter our internal dispositional programme state—our *de*.

Part of our programming is to programme others. Thus Kongzi says 'It is only by establishing others that we establish ourselves.'

Shi-fei: *'This/that'*, *'Is/is not'*, *'Yes/no'*, *'True/false'*, *'Pro/con'*, and *'Assent/dissent'*

The senses, as noted, are important in this Chinese theory of language and *xin* but in an unfamiliar way. Rather than thinking of the senses as presenting us with data or information, we should think of the *xin* as consulting them for feedback evaluations to be used in programme branching. They help the *xin* decide whether the conditions exist to run parts of the programme. They provide the test input for programme control—branching or conditional commands. The heart-mind's overall *shi-fei* evaluation, based on the *shi-fei* results from the senses, lies at the root of guidance. They guide the output of complex, situation-sensitive programmes.

As we noted above, a minimally intelligent programme branches for different situations. To follow the sidewalk to school, the *xin* must monitor the senses and decide if this is the sidewalk or not the sidewalk, if this is or is not a cairn, broken twig, or turn right sign. Our teachers hone this skill at dividing input conditions to discriminate which *ming* applies so we can follow language-based social programming. Interpretation requires this constant *shi-fei* activity. Knowledge of a language consists in this ability to link action/output to the discourse in a reliable or appropriate way. Otherwise we fail to follow the intended *dao*.

Shi-fei thus also plays a role in debugging us. Others, teachers and other social 'superiors', evaluate whether we have run a programme correctly. We get *shi-fei* auditory feedback from other people in response to our performance. A *fei* response triggers some change in our internal *de*. *Shi-fei* thus represents the basic form of assent/dissent response. This explains why they are traditionally translated as right/wrong when, as Graham has argued, they are grammatically indexicals—'this' and 'not-this'.[40] We can also internalise this evaluation. Our own *xin* faculty can evaluate whether it has executed a command or run a programme based on its feedback.

Ming: 'Name', 'Terms', and 'Words'

We programme a *xin* to make *shi-fei* decisions in executing *dao* by teaching *ming*—names. Our computer programmes check for a 'true/false' condition in a sentence or formula in branching and programme control. A computer model mirroring the Pre-Han theory of mind will test for applicability of a name. Thus, as Graham suggests, we may think of *shi-fei* as 'is or is not the thing in question'. The burden of guidance comes from the *ming* 'name'. *Shi* and *fei* are the 'logically proper names' of this *practical* theory.

Learning names involves learning both what is and what is not in a name's scope. Only if we know both, can we use a name effectively in guiding discourse—in a *dao*. Classical theories of language, I have argued, are contrast theories. For a name to have any guiding function in discourse, there must both be that which it does and does not pick out. For it to have a scope is for some things to lie outside its scope. Names form the basis of a guiding *dao*. They provide the occasion for the *xin* to test what procedure to run and when one has run it properly. A *ming* is a basic unit of a regulative system. *Ming* are the nuclei of *dao*. The basic distinction between humans and animals lies in having the hard wiring to acquire names and thus to be able to internalize and execute *dao*. Thus we use father/son, before/after, left/right distinctions in a sea of discourse to guide behaviour.

Bian: 'Make a Distinction'

The *xin* discriminates or makes distinctions, *bian*. *Bian* is the core linguistic behaviour—the key to being able to use names in guidance. As I explained above, two closely related characters are pronounced *bian*. The philosophers use the character with the language radical. Mozi and the Neo-Moists (Neo-Mohists) both rely heavily on *bian* in their theory of language. (The Neo-Moist analytic texts are sometimes referred to as *Mobian*.) Their point, however, has been widely misinterpreted.

The misinterpretation arises because ancient Chinese philosophers not only used *bian* to explain how words guide behaviour. Their justified view is that all philosophical disagreement rests on *bian*. Translators, ignoring the ambiguity of 'argument', thus translated *bian* as 'argument' and supposed the Moists were dealing with logic and argument structure. The point, rather, is this: different philosophical schools carve the world at different places. Their *shi-fei* judgments differ. They differ either because the schools use or stress different *ming* or they use the same *ming* (have internalized the same public *dao*) but have different *de* 'internal realizations'. They disagree because each discerns differently what a *ming*'s range includes and excludes.

Remember that the interpretive counterparts of words are distinctions, neither a particular object nor members of sets of objects. The objects in the system are mereological objects. Mozi does not explain mastering a *ming* as knowing the meaning or recognising the object. On the contrary, he explained it as being able to discriminate—to find the edges of the mass object. When we do this, we *shi-fei*—using the name in executing requests. *Shi-fei* activity is choosing and rejecting. In relation to names, it consists in indexical choosing of this and not-this. Disagreement is difference in C-perspective. Chinese philosophers do not understand it as holding different beliefs, theories, or assumptions. Disagreements come because we *bian* in conflicting ways.

Zhi: 'Guidance Wisdom': Programmes and Know-to

The modern compound term for knowledge is *zhidao*. The object of *zhi* is a prescriptive discourse—a *dao*. Knowing, in other words, is skill at executing *dao*. Knowing is knowing the way to do something (knowing how). Alternately, (to do justice to both the inclination and character involved in having *de*) we may interpret it as knowing *to* do something. Initially, we come to know an encoded *dao* by 'reading in' the strings of words in the discourse. Nature programmes us with some natural capacity (*de*) and, given that *de*, our community programmes us with *dao*.

Knowledge of *dao* comes together with knowledge of *ming*—knowing how to *bian*. To know a *ming* is to know how to guide action with it. Mozi talks of the blind man who does not know black/white—does not know how to use them to sort out things in front of him. The blind man does know black/white in a different sense, however. He knows (how) to construct phrases with them, such as coal is black and snow is white.

These *dao*, these bodies of prescriptive discourse, *create* the distinction between *zhi* 'knowledge' and ignorance.[41] To study is to study a *dao*; to know is to know a *dao*, to be ignorant is to be ignorant of a *dao*. The epistemology of classical Chinese does not track metaphysical reality. It tracks *dao*. Thus, translators of *The Analects* especially, sensing this practical focus on knowing, frequently translate *zhi* as 'cleverness'. *Zhi* refers to skilled performance, not information processing. (Information processing may, of course, be a component in a performance).[42]

Zhi, unlike 'knowledge', does not take a propositional context. That is, *zhi* takes either a noun phrase or verb phrase as its object. 'Know', in English, takes full sentences (or propositions—'that'-phrases) as its object. What this means is that when Locke talks in general philosophical terms about knowledge, he generally intends knowledge that something is the case. Zhuangzi would be talking about knowing to (or how to) respond in some situation. The response might be a linguistic one—knowing to 'bravo' the performance or knowing to 'close (it)' the door.

Wei: 'Deeming' or 'Regarding'

Zhi is still usually a 'success verb' in Chinese. To talk of someone's knowing to do something is to *shi* the *dao* he follows in doing it. Chinese has non-endorsing structures as well. When he does not endorse the *dao* someone follows in responding, Laozi would say they 'good' the book. Alternately, he may say that, *yi* 'with regard to' the book, they *wei* 'deem (it)' 'good'. This *yi-wei* structure is as close as one gets in Chinese to 'believes'. Careful translators prefer 'deem to be' or 'regard as' in translating *yi-wei*. Like *zhi*, *yi-wei* does not take a propositional context. It may be thought of as 'term-belief'. To *yi-wei* is to have the inner disposition (the *de*) to assign a *ming* to objects. *Zhi* is *wei*-ing correctly.

Ke: 'Admissible', 'Assertable', or 'Acceptable'

Rather than a semantic notion of truth, most of the Chinese philosophical discussion of language uses the pragmatic concept *ke* 'acceptable'. Outside the theory of language, *ke* simply means permitted or acceptable action. Arguably, considering speech performances as actions, using *ke* of language hardly extends the meaning. It simply underscores the social nature of language use and the standards of language correctness.

Ke applies to words when we use them appropriately, pronounce them correctly, and sort things acceptably using them. *Ke* applied to longer strings sometimes signals only that a string of language *might have* an appropriate use. Thus, writers frequently allege that strings that are apparently not true could be *ke*. There *might be* contexts in which using them would be correct.[43]

Chang: 'Constant'

Chang is the main concept of Chinese meta-criticism of language and *dao*. *Chang* plays a counterpart of the role played by 'truth' in the Western tradition except in a pragmatic context. It gives a certain reliability to *ke*. A constant *dao* is one that never needs revising. Mozi proposes revising any language that does not lead to the greatest overall utility. He thus states his moral theory in its most general fashion. We should make language that does promote utility constant.[44] Two kinds of consideration might require us to revise our *dao*.

Reflective Instability   First, given human nature and hard wiring, the prescriptive discourse might never result in the intended output. Different *xin* might read in the same *li* 'ritual' or other linguistic *dao* and produce different *xing* 'conduct'. The translation or realization of *dao* internally, the altered *de*, might be different for different *xin*. This is the worry implicit in Kongzi's theory of the Rectification of Names.[45] The Rectification of Names is a public debugging procedure designed to produce *dao*-tokens that coincide with the *dao*-type.

The second concern raises a more familiar skeptical query. The first question reminds us of Wittgenstein's linguistic scepticism. How can we be sure we are following a rule or using a word correctly? This is an interpretive question, 'has an instruction set been followed by a given output?' The second question asks a prior question, 'which instruction set is correct?' In ancient China, this became the question, 'which linguistic discourse is the correct one to read in?' It would be one that is constant—the constant *dao*.

We might understand both reflective questions using the computer analogy. Given our compiler's hard wiring and the world, could we generate/find a *dao* that would never need change? Could we generate one that would never be misinterpreted? Rather than asking if a *dao* is *true* or *objectively correct*, Laozi asks if it can be constant.[46]

Practice Instability   If the command set were consistently (presumably correctly) interpreted and executed by our *xin*, it might still result in an outcome that would be unstable. It might lead to social upheavals that would bring about changes in *dao*. It would not support a stable homeostasis, balance, or equilibrium in society. Or, as Mozi argued with respect to Confucian family-based morality, it may be a self-defeating *dao*. It may fail to lead to its own goal or get there less efficiently than some alternative *dao* would. Any *dao* that is unstable in this sense is not a constant *dao*.

The Daoist slogan is that any *dao* which can be spoken is not a constant *dao*. That leaves one to wonder if an unspoken *dao* might be constant. We may wonder what conduct we would follow if there were no linguistic *dao*. What if we followed only the course of nature or our hard-wired *dao* in the heart—the innate *de*? A common interpretation of Daoism is that only this hard-wired *dao* is constant. All spoken *dao*, on the contrary, are inconstant in one of the above senses. Either it would be subject to vagaries of interpretation or it would be subject to revision. I argue that Daoists only commit themselves to scepticism that any spoken *dao* can be constant. That natural programming is constant does not follow—and some Daoists, at least, are aware that it does not follow.[47]

Old Perennial Problems: Permanence and Change   This analysis of classical Chinese philosophy of language has an interesting corollary: we need not considers Daoists to be proponents of metaphysical flux. That is not to deny that Daoists regard things as changing, but to deny that they think metaphysical change is either an interesting or important philosophical problem. There is neither a Chinese Heraclitus nor a Parmenides.

Change *is* a problem in Greek and Indian thought. Both focus semantically on the relation of names to particular objects. This focus makes it appear important that the particulars remain the same. Otherwise we could not account for re-identification over time. Thus it seems a problem that physical objects undergo constant change. In China, classical philosophers focused on the relation of names and a scope or thing/kind. That particular objects included within the scope undergo continued change does not provoke very much philosophical concern. Constancy seems a quite pragmatic matter. Does the scope change over time because of the way *we use* the word?

A word may change its scope in two ways. One is that the object moves and changes so the line of demarcation no longer encompasses it. The other is that people start using the word differently, or use it inconsistently. Then we will choose a different use for the word. The problem of flux in China is the problem of flux in language not in things. *Whatever is going on in the world*, language is not attached to things in a consistent way. Social practices of marking distinctions are always changing.

Zhuangzi formulates the strongest version of this Daoist scepticism. He supports his scepticism by drawing attention to the behaviour of indexicals. Here change is a problem, but obviously not the problem of the object in front of us changing. The reference of the indexical does change but that reveals something about the indexical, not the object. His favourite example is *shi-bi* 'this-that'. Since the same *shi* is used in *shi-fei*, he generalizes that pair with all its implications. *Shi-fei* activity in choosing things using names is an indexical activity. No discourse, therefore, can assure constancy.

The theory that things have to stand still for names to catch them belongs to Greek and Indian philosophy. Chinese philosophers worried that the names themselves do not stand still. The objects in question, furthermore, were not medium-sized physical objects, but scattered stuffs. The word translated as 'thing' (*wu*) is more appropriately translated as 'thing-kind.'

Summary: *Dao* is a Guiding C-perspective

We should think of *dao*, then, as a programme for guiding action. At one level, a *dao* is the discourse that humans learn—roughly equivalent to a language. We learn the *ming* in the discourse by acquiring an ability to make *shi-fei* reactions based on sensory feed-back. *Shi* equals 'it is the thing in question.' *Fei* equals 'it is not the thing in question.'

I suggested that we call the set of *ming* which we acquire and use in guiding our behaviour 'our concept perspective' (C-perspective). The C-perspective guides our use of sensory feed-back in guiding our action. We should not, otherwise, think of it as a picture of reality. The perspective is not a window of view nor does it consist of obedience to rules—prescriptive sententials. It is a *way* of operating in the world with conceptual resources and distinctions. Classical philosophers' accounts of discourse stress the conceptual contrasts and slight the sentential content.

I have used the computer analogy to avoid letting either mind/ body or conceptualist assumptions sneak into the account. There are two levels of internal programming or *de*. Firstly, there must be some natural inclination and ability to acquire the social *dao*. Secondly, there is the internal state that results (which may be different for each individual) when we 'read in' a *dao*. Perhaps, due to differences in the innate *de*, the programmes run differently with different people.

Names guide us—not sentences or rules. They guide feed-back distinctions in a branching programme. Thus the ordinary role of reason—argument evaluation—plays a minimal role in this account of human action.

Chinese philosophy of language, then, concentrates on the different ways language may handle classification. Scepticism centres on how schools might classify differently, not on individual subjectivity. Chinese theories of language concentrate on permissibility rather than 'truth'. A constant concern is conformity and harmony in language application and in language-guided behaviour. Classical Chinese philosophers seldom discuss purely semantic questions. When they do, they deal with the semantics of terms and compound terms rather than sentences. Chinese philosophers note that different C-perspectives are possible. In general the closest early formulation of the objective point of view is a deistic one. Confucianism moves from the view that heaven's *dao* is the conventionally written *dao* (Kongzi) to the view that it is all hard-wiring (Mengzi (Mencius)) then back to the view that it is conventionally linguistic (Xunzi (Hsün Tzu)). Mozi holds that there is a linguistic formulation preferred by heaven—but not the existing conventional *dao*.

Daoism emerges with the concept of a natural *dao*—which might not be identical to the heavenly *dao*. Daoists moved from a natural constitution view of *dao* to a relativist one. Schools may prescribe many different world paths. Choosing (*shi*-ing) any C-prespective presupposes a C-perspective—a school's preferred discourse. Zhuangzi explains the disagreements about things as based on different ways of sorting things. His was a relativism of conceptual structure not beliefs.

Finally, a crucial ambiguity mars the mass notion of *dao*. On the one hand, given the mass-like character of the term, *dao* is one in a straightforward and trivial sense. We can sum the *dao* of each thing-kind into the *dao* of the whole—the *dao* of the universe. This *dao* is a numerical or metaphysical unity in a rather trivial sense. However, this mere summing of *dao* does not capture what is important to orthodox Confucians. Their *dao* must be an organic unity in which each partial *dao* plays a harmonious and proper role. That approach allows *dao* to play the role of an absolute prescriptive.

Theory of Language and Mind—a Historical Sweep

Understanding the theory of language gives us a distinctive perspective on the chief figures and schools in Chinese philosophy. We cease to treat Chinese philosophy as obscure and rationally incomprehensible. Theory of language is a central concern informing the theories of the pivotal theorists of the period. It gives us a novel and natural way to subdivide the period to replace the schools approach.

The Constructive Period

The first stirring of the philosophical impulse in China focuses on naturalistic, social theories of education or enculturation. The constructive philosophers embrace the regulative view of language and a constructive social theory of education. Essentially, in this period, the questions are: 'In which linguistic *dao* should we cultivate skill? Which forms of language use should we make constant?' The two positions are traditional and utilitarian. Early Confucians limited their concern to how to use existing literature as the guide to behaviour. Mozi then raised the sceptical question about these traditional standards. He wanted to substitute another *dao*. Doing that, he saw, involved substituting new language forms for old ones. This meant changing the instruction set and instilling in people a new pattern of internal action guidance.

Traditionalism: Early Confucianism   Kongzi never clearly raised the reflective question about social conventions and tradition. When we are trained to perform according to the accepted conventions we alter our nature. Confucians view such altering as a positive and fulfilling natural process. Being programmed in this way is being humanized. We are cultivating our *ren* 'humanity'. Kongzi implicitly accepts a plain and straightforwardly naturalistic theory of how this happens. As we practice performing a social form (ritual, music, poetry) we modify our nature so that gradually we perform easily and well. Acquiring skills through practice in this way is deeply fulfilling for us. Indeed, it is our nature.

The philosophical problem that did occur to early Confucians concerned interpretation. It became unmistakably clear to them that a gap lay between the text and the performance. We see different performances of the same play, same musical score, same ritual or rules of etiquette. This fact seemed significant to Kongzi's disciples because they wanted to divide the ritual performances, especially, into good and bad. We cannot appeal to the literature to settle such disagreements since it is the interpretation of the literature that is in question.

Confucians knew that the interpretation of linguistic discourse into action raised difficulties. Two important concepts resulted. One was the Rectification of Names. Confucians intended it to provide a social-authority solution to the linguistic scepticism. By setting examples of name use in action, political/social leaders can influence how others guide behaviour using the codified tradition.

For Confucians this amounts to extending the application of model emulation in educational theory to include language. The second concept was a mysterious one—*ren* 'humanity'. It plays both the role of a goal of character-building education and that of a solution to the interpretation problem. The goal of *ren* (see above) relates closely to the concept of 'human'. Confucian theory treats the educational outcome as natural despite its arising from practicing conventions. Paradoxically, *ren* also plays the role of guiding the interpretation of the literature of discourse into behaviour. This essentially human virtue is the ability to 'catch on and continue' in interpreting human conventions.

Utilitarianism   Mozi repudiated the traditional literature and discourse that Confucians practice as their *dao*. He asked the philosophically reflective question: 'Should we follow our accepted social practices?' He advocated evaluating customs and practices by a utilitarian standard. We should *chang* 'constant' those practices and customs, hence those ways of speaking which tend to the well-being of all in the greater social whole.[48]

In remarkably many ways, Mozi seems to agree with the Confucians. Both Mozi and Kongzi urge using models (social/political leaders) to exemplify, teach, and enforce correct usage—to regularize language use. Uniformity in language use leads to co-ordination of behaviour and social order.

In advocating a reformer's view of social conventions, he knowingly urges reforming human character. He focuses on language more clearly than Confucius did and sees changing language as an integral part of changing humanity. In socially promoting a utilitarian way of using *ming* and making *bian*, we change people's dispositions towards behaviour. Although Mozi agrees with Confucians that language is conventional, he proposes an ideally *constant* language as the constant *dao*.

What makes language ideal, however, is not its semantics, but its pragmatics. Mozi counsels making constant those language practices that have the effect of optimising human behaviour. He does not claim that the ideal language corresponds with an external reality (except possibly Heaven's will).

Confucians and Moists advocated teaching and practicing different *dao*s. Their arguments and justifications produced no agreement. Moists observed that following their *dao* leads to greater good where good amounts to greater utility. Confucians claimed that the Moist *dao* leads to immorality—from a conventional point of view. The question-begging nature of their attempts to state the disagreement led to Zhuangzi's relativism.

The Anti-language Period

We normally associate an anti-language impulse with Daoism. Actually, Mengzi, a Confucian, formulates the earliest robust form of this tendency. The essence of his position is opposition to that which both early Confucians and Moists agreed on. Mengzi rejects linguistic *dao*.[49]

Innatism   Mengzi formulates an anti-language version of Confucianism. His motivation is to secure Confucianism against the Moist attack and simultaneously to evade the Confucian problem of interpreting *dao* into behaviour. Anti-language innatism enables him to respond to Mozi's reflective challenge. Following the Proto-Daoist, Yang Zhu, he treats natural constitution as the basis of *dao*.

However, Mengzi's account of our natural constitution is much more elaborate than Yang Zhu's. For Mengzi our natural make-up includes the moral *xin* complete with its capacity to *shi-fei*. The *xin*, in Mengzi's view, does not require programming through education. Nature programmes it with all the moral behaviour it needs.

This programming emerges as a potential—as seeds of virtues. Only the seeds are present at birth. The potential matures naturally over time given suitable conditions of growth. The mature *xin* then issues *shi-fei* decisions using its innate programming. As the Lu-Wang school slogan has it, Mengzi holds that all the traditional conventions of Confucianism are 'footnotes in my heart-mind'.

Practical wisdom consists in the ability to apply *shi-fei* correctly in each unique situation. This is an acquired, practical intuition. It requires no external programming. Having no use for language, Mengzi simply ignores the interpretive problem. He does not have to worry about how to get from *li* to behaviour. He never even mentions the Confucian theory of Rectification of Names. The correct *dao* is hard-wired in our *xin*.

Mengzi allows that language can do what Kongzi and Mozi thought it could do—it can affect behaviour. Thus Mengzi must oppose it. If it affects the heart-mind, then it is either redundant or destructive of the natural programming of the *xin*. The only way to secure proper development of the natural guide is to avoid any *forcing.* So, not only is development of a linguistic *dao* unnecessary, it is destructive. Language disrupts natural instinct. Language garbles, stunts, and warps the natural impulses. In a world in which the Moists and Daoists were silenced, Mengzi would not have used language at all.[50]

Primitivism   The traditional Neo-Confucian interpretation commits Daoism to the generalized Mencian point of view. The difference lies in the richness of content of the innate programming. The primitivist version of Daoism is the Daoism of Laozi. Laozi assumes that innate programming funds only primitive, village-level human behaviour. Daoist primitivism[51] judges only that pre-linguistic level of behaviour as natural and acceptable.

The Daoists' anti-social, anti-conventional ends motivate this anti-language theory. Laozi formulates the connection between language and *dao* most clearly. In Laozi's theory, Daoist political anarchism follows from linguistic anarchism. When society teaches us its language, it encourages the disposition to discriminate in rigid (and socially approved) ways. The tendency and ability to sort things into kinds drags traits of conduct in its wake. The traits may be simple. (We always prefer good to bad.) Or they may be more complex and contextual. (We guide behaviour with black and white—but no fixed bent toward either.) Even in the complex case, our social practices cause us to follow socially-uniform ways of acting. We prefer black to white in cases where society condones it.

Thus, with a different motive, Laozi also suggests that natural behaviour requires abandoning language. Unlike Mengzi, he regards this as a radical step. It requires that we abandon distinctions, desires, and deliberate, concept-guided action.

The Daoist anti-language theory of *wu-wei* 'no deeming' explains in what sense it is non-action. Laozi opposes action based on language and names. Like Mengzi, he accepts 'natural' action—behaviour generated by our natural constitution. Mengzi and Laozi disagree on how rich and extensive these natural dispositions are. They do agree in championing guiding behaviour using these rather than a linguistic *dao.*

The primitivist argument goes as follows. Names presuppose social conventions for classifying and separating things. Acquiring *ming* affects our natural inclinations to discriminating behavior. It reshapes our desires in accord with socially-governed performance criteria. Knowledge or wisdom consists in embracing these orthodox word contrasts. Knowledge is, therefore, a species of social constraint on our natural spontaneity. From a Western perspective, Daoist opposition to knowledge is a paradox in itself. Knowledge (see above), however, does not consist of descriptively grasping the way things are. It consists of internalizing a guiding process. The process manipulates language to manage our conduct. Hence, to preserve natural behavior, we must reject all conventions—and that includes language.

The paradox arises when we look at the Daoists' own language. It constitutes a constructivist *dao*. They teach us to discriminate between natural and conventional behaviour. They further teach us to guide our behaviour using these terms. We are to *shi* natural behaviour and *fei* conventional behaviour. Thus our actions in following Daoism constitute deeming and would violate the *wu-wei* slogan.

The Analytical Period

In the constructive and anti-language periods, theory of language and theory of mind were part of a general theory of education. Now the focus on language becomes the exclusive interest of a group of philosophers. We know them as the School of *Ming*.

I divide this school into three factions based on their differing practical interests in language. The first faction wants to change language behaviour to achieve some kind of ideal language. The second represents the development of realism in theory of language. Like Mozi, the realists suppose the world and the real differences among natural kinds to provide the underpinning to correct language. The third type of theory of language generates an anti-realist theory. It holds that the distinctions marked by language are arbitrary; it might sort things into kinds in widely divergent ways.

Ideal Isomorphism   Gongsun Long is an example of idealism in theory of language. He claims to be supporting a Confucian principle of language use: one *ming*, one thing (kind). His claim of intellectual affiliation is plausible despite orthodox Confucian distaste for his style.

Consider what rectification of *ming* requires for success in guiding action using an instruction set. To know how to apply a string of *ming* in a specific case, we need to know if the types in this case are the types named in the string. One string may guide us with regard to an X. A potentially conflicting string may give different counsel about Y. Implicitly, if we decide the thing in the situation is an X, then we cannot consider it also to be a Y. To decide on which string to apply, we tacitly judge the object an X and not a Y. Relative to the *dao* in question, there must be one-*ming*, one-kind.

Now this conflicts with common usage because, typically, we use different names to pick out the same things. I am both a son, a father, a husband, a teacher, a male, a human, a primate, a mammal, an animal, and a thing. Ordinary *ming*, that is, have overlapping structures. I do not want people to use the canons directing demeanour toward animals to command conduct toward me. Thus I say, 'I am a man, not an animal.'

Gongsun Long advocated abandoning this overlapping in the system of *ming* to clarify language. This amounted to a systematic proposal to eliminate general terms and describe each thing-kind with the most specific name possible. He makes this point in a series of difficult dialogues concerning 'white horse', 'hard-white', 'left-right', and 'designation-name'. The proper interpretation of these dialogues is still the subject of debate.

Ordinary Language Realism   The richest source of analytic theory of language comes from a group known as Neo-Moists. Later Moists may have split into groups with quite different specializations.[52] The *Mozi* incorporated an assortment of definitions and propositions from this analytic group in a garbled form. They were preserved (with more than the usual textual corruption) down to the nineteenth century. Then scholars began to unravel the secret of their organization. A.C. Graham recently completed that work. The result is the single most important step in this century towards understanding Chinese philosophy.

We do not have the space to examine the Neo-Moist theories in detail. In general they championed two conflicting ideas. Firstly, they tried to understand how ordinary language worked. They did not approve, in general, of Gongsun Long's search for an idealized language. Overlapping of terms is a natural language trait and we need make no attempt to eliminate it.

Secondly, they thought terms in language had the scopes they did because there were objective differences between things. The real differences could serve as a check on language use. When we use a *ming* of a thing, we do so by virtue of a real difference in the world. The problem of *bian* is deciding which differences should count. The Moists were sure that some did—those that did not they called 'wild pickings out'.[53] However, Moists offered no general causal theory of similarity and difference. They based their reasoning on intuitive similarity and difference.

In the absence of an adequate realistic basis for a theory of distinctions, the Neo-Moists turned their attention to showing the incoherence of the anti-language position. To claim that all language is inherently inadequate or perverse is to do something inherently inadequate or perverse. To deny distinctions is incoherent—not assertable. Distinctions basically fix what is *shi* 'the thing in question'[54] and *fei* 'not the thing in question'. To *fei* 'object to' distinctions is to *fei fei*. 'To *fei fei*', 'to object to finding something outside the range' the Moists tell us, 'is *fei* "wrong"'.[55]

The Moists also drafted a term-based version of the law of excluded middle. For any *ming* 'name', any thing is either *shi* or *fei*—either is or is not the thing in question. So whenever people dispute about whether something falls within or without a division, one of the parties must be correct. (Canon B35) This is the strongest statement in the tradition of semantic realism in the theory of language. The collection shows that the position that most have taken to be the essence of Daoism was clearly refuted by these arguments. Daoists who were philosophically up to date in ancient China would not have been tempted by it.

The Neo-Moists also do some near logic—the study of inference relations.[56] The early and exploratory study is in glaring contrast with Western logic. Traditional Western logic writings tended to overstate logical and rational power. Western rationalism experienced traumatic disenchantment when faced with the observation that (deductive) logic could not lead to new knowledge. Moists began with the modest goal of finding reliable (but merely syntactic) regularities in language conventions.

Even in that limited project, they were disappointed. They concluded that ordinary language had no reliable syntactic forms that could preserve assertability. They did not try to reform the feature away but accepted it as an inescapable (and unobjectionable) ordinary language trait. They appeared ready to accept the Daoist claim that language could not be constant. A certain amount of vagueness in language is pragmatically necessary.

The study of inference forms illustrates an important (but still controversial) point. Either the Moists never discovered the sentence or it was the 'last and most difficult' of their linguistic discoveries.[57] That they could discuss—or appear to discuss—inference without either semantic concepts like truth or a clear notion of a sentence is testimony to their philosophical resourcefulness.

The Neo-Moists rejected the ideal language tendencies of the Rectification of Names. They reached a conclusion which was either a reaction to Gongsun Long or to the formal principle he represented. This result was as follows: certain compound *ming* in Chinese 'pick out' a larger scope than either of their component *ming*. Other compounds 'pick out' a smaller scope than either of their component *ming*. Again, the tone of the discovery was one of simple acceptance of the arbitrary and inconstant way language works. Unlike Gongsun Long, the Moists proposed no general theory to unify these divergent patterns of word use.

Relativist Mysticism Despite their acceptance of some ordinary language arbitrariness and erratic uses, the Moists maintained their realist faith. The way the world is limits how we should use language. Appropriateness of language use was not *merely* a conventional matter; however, they did not offer an explanation-based (scientific) account of natural-kind distinctions. They regard straightforward similarity and difference as the only basis for linguistic distinction-making. The problem is that the standards of similarity and difference are no more fixed than are the standards of tall and short. The paradoxes of Hui Shi formulate this problem for Chinese realism.

We classify Hui Shi as a member of the school of *ming*. We also know him as the *bian* 'distinguishing' companion of Zhuangzi—the great Daoist philosopher. Just as Gongsun Long's technical results were to support Confucianism, Hui Shi's bolster Daoism. Hui Shi devised ten paradoxical propositions. They assert the relativity of spatial and temporal *ming* to a context, that 'tall' and 'short' depend on where you stand.

The *Zhuangzi*—especially in the 'Autumn Floods' chapter—extends many of Hui Shi's insights. The single most important result is Hui Shi's comment concerning similarity and difference in general. He argues that between any two things, no matter how alike, some difference exists. Between any two things, no matter how different, there is some similarity. This attacks the weak point

in Neo-Moist realism about the separation of kinds. His conclusion—stated as the tenth thesis—is a combination of Daoist
Monism and Moist ethics. The world is one body; love all things
equally.

The Relativist Period

The pragmatic focus of all theorising about language makes even
the Moist realists accept some relativism. Language is, after all, a
convention and conventions could always be different. If that were
not so, Mozi's original proposal for altering language would be
worthless. Moreover, they have a weak link in their attempts to
defend realism against the Daoist tide. They failed to answer Hui
Shi's scepticism. We could accept the reality of similarities and
differences and still justify drawing unorthodox distinctions. We
shall always be able to find a similarity or difference to justify any
chosen atypical contrast. This scepticism leads to the consummate
philosophy of the period—and the most seriously misunderstood.

Scepticism: Zhuangzi Zhuangzi mourned the death of Hui Shi as
his loss of someone to sharpen his wits on. They shared the scepticism that similarity/difference would give a constant basis for *ming*
and *dao*. Otherwise there were great differences. None is more
notable than style. Hui Shi only authored ten terse paradoxical
propositions. Zhuangzi was a literary giant. He exploited Chinese
philosophy's refreshing lack of Platonic bias against poetry and
fantasy. His masterpiece blends image and argument as no other
work in philosophy, East or West, has done.

Zhuangzi appreciated the Moist point that the anti-language
position was self-condemning. He also saw what might have been
Gongsun Long's point: no *ming* can have everything in its scope.
Monism was inherently inexpressible. So he did not accept Hui
Shi's monistic Daoism. He made no absurd claims about the existence of some incommensurable object or any blanket rejection
of language or distinctions. Zhuangzi does not contrast 'natural'
with 'linguistic' or 'conventional.' Internalizing language is as
natural as eating.

Realists' attempts to show that distinctions come from *tian*
'heaven' or 'nature' do not fail. They succeed—but all too easily.
No one fails to express a natural *dao*. All actual *dao* are naturally
occurring *dao*. So each must share their 'success' with all their

rivals. They get their victory, but not their opponents' defeat. Nature equally 'dictates' all actual ways of dividing things into kinds—both Mengzi's and Mozi's.

Nature, no doubt, will dictate a potentially inexhaustible set of alternative ways of marking distinctions among things. Each will have advantages from some point of view (typically the outlook of those committed to the classifying system). Each will have disadvantages according to some conflicting C-perspective. We cannot coherently formulate an account of an absolute standpoint. We cannot define the realists' faith that we should make a single ideal language constant.

To formulate an absolute C-perspective would be to *shi* one system of distinctions and *fei* others. All *shi*-ing, however, is from a perspective which presupposes another *shi*. Mengzi's *xin* theory, for example, cannot stand without the assumption that we should follow the guidance of the *xin* rather than our other organs and tastes. Each organ may have different *shi-fei* reactions. Even if we could imagine an 'axis of *daos*', it would represent only the infinite possibilities of *shi-fei* distinction making—not some absolute perspective from which we can judge and sort *daos*.

Zhuangzi concludes that our genuine nature as easily allows that we follow conventional distinctions as that we abandon them. Pragmatic benefits surely follow from using language as others do. On the other hand, he shows an inclination to the Confucian inference that we must follow a *particular* historical convention. His fantasies show a consistent willingness to imagine how diverse classification systems might work. He calls this openness to alternative possibility 'enlightenment'. Who knows what benefits would come of adopting some other basis for assigning things to types?

Consider one practice Zhuangzi did not conceive of—that we might adopt a causal-explanatory, deductively-structured way of defining our distinctions. Perhaps a culture that adopted that mode of assigning names to things would be able to fly, go to the moon, and work all kinds of wonders. Science is pragmatically superb. Other C-perspectives may be possible which are as much an improvement on science as science is on traditional perspectives.

Nature herself does not choose a system of this-ing and that-ing that preserves our species. Nor does she reject one that might result in our self-annihilation. There must be points of view (say that of other large mammals) which would *shi* the death of the human species.

Pragmatic Confucianism: Xunzi (Hsün Tzu)   Xunzi's approach differs from Zhuangzi's primarily in treating Zhuangzi's light-hearted flirting with a 'death is preferable to life' point of view as frivolous and irrelevant. We start out assuming that we want survival and dominion over other animals. (We require no justification for this.) Then we ask what linguistic conventions best contribute to this. Zhuangzi presumably would object that Xunzi begs the question in preferring species survival. Xunzi's reply is 'So I beg a question. . . Now lets get on with some real issues.'

The bald acceptance of this pragmatic goal gives Xunzi's system, theoretically relativist, a misleadingly absolutist tone. His position resembles that of a more sophisticated Mozi. He is aware both that language cannot bypass conventionality and that selective reform of linguistic conventions is hard. Moist reforms in language and conventions may disrupt social life in ways we cannot foresee. Argument by authority (brilliantly intuitive sage kings invented it), its long history, and successful practice make interfering with these conventions unwise. Xunzi would ban any further speculative 'disordering of *ming*' If we go on with these attempts to experiment with alternatives, we run the risk of anarchy.[58]

One way, one *dao*, of rectifying names and guiding conduct effectively guarantees human success—the traditional one. This does not follow from some real counterpart of the traditional *dao* in nature. *Dao* arises pragmatically from a real context, but is still a human response to the *tian* 'natural' *dao*.

Xunzi spelled out much of the theory outlined in the concepts section. He argued that human sensory organs register distinctions in similar ways, and that species-similitude yields a basis for shared conventions of word use.[59] This makes social co-ordination of action—morality—possible. We may not be able to prove from some absolute, natural point of view that our way of dividing and discriminating between things is really correct. Nevertheless, we can establish shared conventions. These conventions provide the only germane standard of evaluation.

This process admittedly requires authorities. Human social nature does depend on linguistic authorities. We need teachers and scholars to model an acceptable use of language. The scholarly authority-structure provides the continuity and uniformity of linguistic conventions which underwrite our lives together.

Xunzi's students were instrumental in setting up China's first legalist dynasty and ending the anarchy of many *daos*—and the fertile period of Chinese classical philosophy.

Conclusion

The classical Chinese theory of language and *dao* is accessible to rational insight. It is neither mystical, irrational, unintelligible, nor otherwise unattainable to Western minds. It is radically different from traditional Western theories of language. It shows neither semantic nor sentential focus. The difference permeates the theory of mind. Chinese thinkers treat mind as an action guide which uses language as a guide. It does this by making feedback judgments of *shi-fei* in carrying out a *dao*.

Theory of mind, in turn, anchors theory of human nature and inspires, therefore, ethics and political theory. Subjectivism in theory of language—the theory that language is tied to internal, private, conceptual, or mental states—yields subjectivism in theory of mind. If the mind works in robust aloofness from society, this fact affects ethical and political theory. Individualism, in its strictest versions, may be intelligible only if we reject the classical Chinese theories. Awareness of the social nature of language and mind may undermine Western ethics.

Chinese theory of language and mind shows a realistic appreciation of the effect of society on the *xin*'s functioning. The social nature of language and the importance of language in the heart-mind may help explain the non-individualist formulation of ethical questions. Mozi, for example, does not ask how *I* should govern *my* action, but how *we* (society) should govern *ours*. His reflective doubt of convention thus differs from Socrates' scepticism.

Despite the alien context, the enchanting differences in the language, and the remoteness of their peripheral concerns, the ancient Chinese theory of language has a 'modern' ring. It addresses the perennial problem of realism/relativism and does so in an ethical context. It addresses the issues of language and mind while making neither Platonic nor Lockean assumptions.

These assumptions still shape and govern Western discussions— even those sceptical of the Platonic tradition. While Chinese theories do not solve all the problems, they offer a rich lode of material for the philosophical imagination. Some may serve as correctives for several supposed universals concerning mind and language.

Research into Chinese theories of language and mind has barely begun. How to extend it to include sentences and argument is not clear. For that matter, it is not clear that such an elaboration is necessary. The same is true for the apparently missing distinction between declarative and imperative functions of language. We may even doubt that an intelligent, rational philosopher working in the ancient conceptual scheme has any reason to postulate consciousness or sensations. Chinese theory of language and mind challenges us to rethink our deepest assumptions about ourselves.

Notes

1. See Raymond M. Smullyan, *The Tao is Silent* (New York, Harper and Row, 1977) for one of the few intelligible statements of this claim.
2. I borrow this term from Stephen Stitch, *From Folk Psychology to Cognitive Science: The Case against Belief* (Cambridge, MIT Press, 1983).
3. I should perhaps substitute here 'what they took to be a pictographic language' to avoid begging the question against those who think it is important to characterize Chinese as logographic rather than pictographic or ideographic.
4. Writers routinely omit subjects from sentences in both moods. Subjects may be present in both.
5. See my 'Chinese Language, Chinese Philosophy and "Truth"', in *The Journal of Asian Studies*, May 1985, hereafter: Hansen 'Truth'.
6. I say 'hint' because the characters work for all the Chinese spoken languages through time. This means that for any specific language (modern or ancient) it may be a perfect match and may be the barest hint for another. I assume this was true of the characters when they were created. In modern simplified characters, the phonemic element is usually more purely phonemic.
7. Some ancient uses of characters suggest that there may have been an inflection structure in some ancient spoken languages.
8. They could be used for 'inhuman' languages as well. One could do the first order predicate calculus in Chinese, programme in Chinese (though it requires mastering a typing convention), and 'sign' in Chinese.
9. The slogan that written language is just a copy of speech seems to me to be false even for English. Written language is not simply a copy of speech. In English the rules of written and spoken language are more similar than for Chinese, but they are, none the less, notoriously different. The history of writing indicates that not only Chinese, but all written languages, are designed to represent morphemes. We preserve the morpheme 'arch' in words where it is pronounced '-ark-', for example. Consider archbishop and archangel. As our written stylists always tell us, much more is involved in writing than merely learning to spell and reproduce the alphabet. The rhythms, rules, and vocabulary are different in English written and spoken language. The amount of difference in each language is a matter of degree. In Chinese, modern written Chinese (Mandarin) diverges less from the acceptable spoken Mandarin than literary Chinese does. Modern written Chinese diverges a great deal from Cantonese. Cantonese students learn to write quite competently without ever becoming Mandarin speakers. They learn a written grammar. The

theory that written language is just a record of speech faces difficulties long before it has to confront the Chinese characters.

10. For example, Chinese writers frequently refer to a character's having been 'borrowed'—used in the place of some character with the same sound in the writer's language. We theorize that alternate 'borrowed' forms may have emerged in this way when writers from different regions filled gaps in the written language in their separate ways.

11. See A.C. Graham, *Later Mohist Logic, Ethics and Science* (Hong Kong and London, Chinese University Press, 1978), pp. 76–81.

12. Notice that we still individuate words by the writing conventions for putting spaces in written strings. It can be hard to justify these points of individuation for spoken language.

13. Sinologists sometimes object to either description. They argue that characters ought to be described as 'logographic'. This is because the great majority of characters are of the phonemic combination type—they consist of a meaning category radical and a phonemic hint. See the above discussion.

14. I use 'world' in Wittgenstein's sense, not as an object, but all that is the case. Thus, the isomorphism is spatio-temporal rather than merely spatial. Pictographs of objects will be purely spatial, but verbal terms can 'picture' events or actions in space-time.

15. I borrow this term from David Lewis. See his 'General Semantics' in *Synthese*, 27 (1974).

16. Interpreters frequently use the framework of folk theory of language in their explications. Graham (1978, pp. 30–40) understands that Chinese theorists are not Platonic realists, but still understands them as conceptualists, employing our familiar notions of meaning and ideas, definitions, and *a priori* truths.

17. Linguists, as noted above, would focus on the morpheme, which is a constant in these inflectional forms.

18. Modern Chinese words consist mostly of two or more characters. The characters are more appropriately thought of, therefore, as morphemes than as words. But in classical Chinese, they usually functioned as independent words.

19. See the discussion below of analytic ordinary language and realism. Graham has argued that the Neo-Moists did 'discover the sentence' though he acknowledges that it was the 'last and most difficult' of their linguistic discoveries. Graham, see note 11, p. 25. I doubt that we can conclude that they ever made so specific a discovery when they continue to talk about sentences and phrases using the same Chinese term—*ci* 'phrase'. To have made the discovery is to have made a distinction between strings of words which are not sentences and those that are. To have made such a distinction and then continued to use a more general term for the new, more specific intention with no explicit explanation is, at best, atypically obscure for a school with an appetite for precision.

20. Technically, the Chinese view requires that the mind be a syntactic state machine—it must compute and react to structures in language with a structured pattern of action. Chinese theories do not include much syntax and their theory of heart-mind is not yet that of a computer parsing commands.

21. Clinically, I understand, they give a complex set of alternate 'mnemonics' for various normal situations. Dyslexia may be a mild form of this same syndrome.

22. The first line of the *Daodejing* expresses this sceptical challenge in its most succinct form. 'No *dao* which can be a guide is constant. No name which can name is constant.'

23. Notice that the prevalence of relativism does not correspond to a prevalence of subjectivism. A term's scope is relative to a social, historical context but not to an inner subjectivity. Each person's process of distinction-making may differ—we do speak idiolects. But the inner world of sense or ideas is neither the only variable

nor even the key one. My process of distinction making (my idiolect) may differ over time, and all kinds of physical and social conditions. The individual subjectivity is not the locus of scepticism. It is context sensitivity.

24. Changes are possible. As John Dewey argued, the tradition can be trained in a kind of self-criticism that tends to greater and greater rational coherence. Dewey thought it an open question whether that process repeated between radically different moral traditions would tend toward convergence.

25. See my 'A Tao of Tao in Chuang Tzu', in Mair (ed.), *Experimental Essays on Chuang Tzu* (Honolulu, University of Hawaii Press, 1983).

26. The most notable exception is Carus, who translates it as 'reason.' See his *The Canon of Reason and its Virtue* (Chicago, Open Court, 1913). It plays a role in Chinese philosophy *as central as* 'reason' is in Western philosophy. But *dao* is as different from 'reason' as Chinese philosophy is from Western philosophy.

27. I am tempted to think that the Scholastic concern with 'mode' is closest to a philosophical counterpart of way. It has fallen into disuse, eschewed as too obscure.

28. See Saul A. Kripke, *Wittgenstein On Rules and Private Language* (Cambridge, Harvard University Press, 1982). .

29. See Hansen, *Language and Logic in Ancient China* (Ann Arbor, University of Michigan Press, 1983), pp. 30–55.

30. See Wing-tsit Chan, *A Source Book in Chinese Philosophy* (Princeton, Princeton University Press, 1963), p. 136.

31. See Hansen, 'Truth' and Munro, *The Concept of Man in Ancient China* (Stanford, Stanford University Press, 1969).

32. See Roger Ames and David Hall, *Thinking Through Confucius* (New York, Syracuse, SUNY Press, 1986).

33. Confucian theorists are divided on whether heart-mind function depends on internalizing language distinctions. Mengzi represents the view that the *shi-fei* 'this/ not this' distinctions are innate. Xunzi treats them as trained in language—though the language is based on conventions which are responsive both to our sense apparatus and an external reality.

34. See my *Language and Logic in Ancient China* (Ann Arbor, University of Michigan Press, 1983), ch. 1.

35. S.I. Hayakawa, *Language in Thought and Action* (New York, Harcourt, Brace and World, 1939), p. 15.

36. Mozi, *Harvard-Yenching Institute Sinological Index Series* (Taipei, Chinese Materials and Service Center, Inc.), 1973, 66/40/17. Hereafter all references will be to this series and abbreviated HY.

37. It is true that early Chinese philosophers thought it identical with the physical heart.

38. Munro, see note 31, especially the appendix for this argument and a discussion of Waley's translation.

39. Or is it our morality acquisition device? Actually it is a conventional guidance/acceptance device.

40. A.C. Graham, *Chuang Tzu: The Inner Chapters* (London, George Allen & Unwin, 1981), p. 52n.

41. *Analects*, 5 : 21.

42. *Zhi* is also used in the acquaintance sense. There, however, it creates no danger of misunderstanding for us.

43. I take the 'White Horse Dialogue' of Gongsun Long to be a prime example, along with the 'Ox-horse' fragments of the Moist Canon. See Hansen, note 29 above.

44. Mozi, HY 82/47/18. The three standards of language also presupposes a similar view, but is not stated in terms of *chang* 'constancy'.

45. *Analects*, 13 : 3.
46. Confucian apologists now celebrate the flexibility inherent in interpretation. Its force in classical China was precisely the opposite—as a base of scepticism and relativism. The Confucian Rectification of Names arose as an attempt to *limit* interpretive flexibility and provide a *chang dao*; it signalled an awareness of the gap between *any* dao and action. It was not a doctrine intended to enhance individual flexibility, but one designed to respond to the perception of such flexibility using a political means to control it.
47. The best attack on the view that what is natural is correct is found in *Zhuangzi* Chapter 2. See especially A.C. Graham, *Chuang Tzu: The Inner Chapters* (London, George Allen & Unwin, 1981) pp. 51–2.
48. Mozi refers to the well-being of the *guo*. Despite the translation as 'state' we must not think of Mozi's theory as nationalism rather than universalism. He clearly thought of the state as embracing all manking.
49. The inspiration for Mengzi's argument, however, is a proto-Daoist. Yang Zhu first developed the strategy of deriving guidance from something other than language. See A.C. Graham, 'The Background of the Mencian Theory of Human Nature', *Tsing Hua Journal of Chinese Studies*, 6/1, 2 (1967), pp. 215–74. Yang Zhu argued that some aspect of our natural constitution should guide us—in particular, our *qi* 'material force'. Yang Zhu, reacted against the constructivism of both Kongzi and Mozi. He reacted against accepting social conformity as a basis of action and appealed to the authority of heaven in justifying his anti-social attitudes. We see little evidence that Yang Zhu developed his view in an explicitly anti-language form. Thus Mengzi was first with that.
50. *Mengzi* 3B : 9.
51. I borrow this handy classification from Graham, *Chuang Tzu*, part four.
52. Graham, 1978, p. 3.
53. Mohist Canon, B 66. Graham (1978), p. 437.
54. For the various philosophically interlocked uses of *shi*, see Graham (1978), pp. 120–3 and (1984) p. 52.
55. Or perhaps they are telling us to *fei fei*ing *fei*.
56. This study is found in the 'Xiao Qu' translated in Graham (1978), pp. 469–94 as 'Name and Object.'
57. Graham argues that they *did* discover the sentence in Graham (1978) section 2/5 and page 25. I argued that no such conclusion was warranted, in Hansen 'Truth'.
58. *Xunzi*, HY 84/22/30–5.
59. *Xunzi*, HY 83/22/16–20.

Glossary

辯	bian	distinction	是	shi	approve of
常	chang	constant	是彼	shi-bi	this-that
道	dao	way	是非	shi-fei	This/not-this
德	de	virtue	說	shuo	explanations
刀	dou	knife	天	tian	heaven
非	fei	reject	為	wei	deeming
以	yi	with regard to	文	wen	literature
可	ke	admissible	文化	wen hua	literature changed
利	li	benefit	無為	wu-wei	no deeming
礼	li	ritual	心	xin	heart, mind
礼樂	li yue	ritual music	行	xing	conduct
樂	le	pleasure	言	yan	language
命	ming	command	樂	yue	music
名	ming	names	知	zhi	Guidance Wisdom
仁	ren	humanity			

5 Marginalia Sino-logica[1]

CHRISTOPH HARBSMEIER

Satyam eva jayate.[2]
'Truth' will prevail.

This is an exploratory essay in the anthropology of logic. I shall begin with a study of the concept of truth in ancient China, and I shall then proceed to an investigation of some ancient Chinese attempts to construct logically sound arguments. In the process of the discussion I shall also comment on some recent literature on the subject. I shall raise questions such as the following:

Did the ancient Chinese have a semantic concept of truth? Why exactly should we be entitled to assume that they did? How, for example can we be sure that the ancient Chinese did not have a pragmatic way of looking at truth in terms of appropriateness and social usefulness of utterances?

Did the ancient Chinese stress the importance of truthfulness or good faith?

Did the ancient Chinese have a concept of a sentence? What exactly is the evidence that they did? Why can we not say that they simply had names which they applied to objects?

Did the ancient Chinese have attitudes such as belief towards statements? If so, how exactly do we know that they did? And, for example, how can we be sure that when we ascribe to them the belief that 'Socrates smokes' is true, all they do is that they treat Socrates as if he were smoking. In other words: they entertain no attitude towards any proposition, only towards an individual, Socrates.

Did the ancient Chinese have a concept of knowledge? What exactly is our evidence that they did? For example, how can we be sure that when we understand them as knowing that Socrates smokes they successfully treat Socrates as smoking?

Did the ancient Chinese words like 'red' mark a quality, or could it be that Chinese 'adjectives' work quite differently so that the Chinese for 'red' in fact refers to an abstract object consisting of all red objects everywhere, past and present.

Did the ancient Chinese have a concept of a property or quality, or did they manage without such abstract notions?

We need to ask whether the logical workings of the Chinese mind and the grammatical workings of Chinese sentences might not be quite radically different from those our European translations tempt us to make them out to be. Moreover, it is quite conceivable that the nature of the Chinese language may have channelled Chinese thinking in certain ways that Indo-European languages have not channelled Indo-European thinking.

My point of departure will be a detailed discussion of the concept of truth in ancient China.

The Concept of Semantic Truth in Ancient China

The Semantic Concept 'Is True' Versus the Abstract Concept 'Truth'

There is a crucial distinction between the question of whether the ancient Chinese did or did not apply semantic truth predicates like 'is true' to sentences on the one hand, and on the other hand, whether they developed, defined, or discussed a theoretical concept of truth. I intend to investigate these two questions separately.

It is far from clear why every culture should have an abstract and theoretical 'hypostatised' concept of truth. Such a theoretical construct is philosophically highly problematic, vastly more problematic than ordinary predicates such as 'is true' which I expect all sorts of cultures to have.

The Semantic Concept of Truth

To remove some possible doubts, let me briefly indicate as best I can what I take to be the notion of semantic truth. I call a sentence 'p' true exactly if p. I say the sentence 'Snow is white' is true if, and only if, snow is white. This is not a definition of truth, but at least it is a criterion for my use of the expression 'is true' as applied to sentences. There is nothing original about this way of giving a satisfactory criterion for the use of the concept 'is true'. I am simply following a well-known seminal article by Alfred Tarski entitled *Der Wahrheitsbegriff in den formalisierten Sprachen* (1935).

I want to ask whether the ancient Chinese have constructions or expressions that allow them to apply a properly understood semantic concept of truth to their sentences.

Some Preliminary Remarks on the Concept of Semantic Truth in Ancient China

At the outset, some rather obvious remarks may be necessary to avoid misunderstandings. Evidently, the ancient Chinese did not have the English noun 'truth'. Nor did they have a word entirely synonymous with the English 'true'.

Further, the ancient Chinese language certainly does not provide one central and standard technical term for truth like the English 'truth' or the Greek *alêtheia*. This is indeed an interesting fact. The ancient Chinese did apparently only have many ways of calling something 'true' with various additional nuances. This, I hasten to add, does not necessarily mean they were not interested in truth. I submit that it would be a little insensitive to accuse Eskimo thinkers of not having a concept of snow, or of taking little interest in snow, because they happen to have so many specific terms to cover the semantic area of snow.

I do believe that the ancient Chinese assigned a place in their scheme of things to the notion of factual truth of sentences which differs in significant respects from what we are used to. The general intellectual climate in ancient China was such that Wang Chong's[a] (AD 27–100) concern for truth for truth's sake, of which we will hear a little more below, was untypical. It was more typical of dominant trends in classical Greek civilisation, and of the later scientific and technological Chinese literature.

Similarly, Later Moist (Mohist) scientific preoccupation with the truth of theoretical statements, for example in optics, was less than typical of the mainstream of ancient Chinese literature that has come down to us, although it certainly bears witness to a high degree of sustained concern with the truth of theoretical statements.

There is no single towering and crucial concept in Chinese that is equivalent to the central Greek concept *alêtheia*. Factual truth (*ran*[b], *dang*[c], and so on, Sanskrit *satya*) was not in China lumped together with moral truth (Chinese *dao*[d], Sanskrit *dharma*) into one nomimalized and then hypostatised concept like *alêtheia*, Truth with a capital T, or *Wahrheit*. There is a profound difference of emphasis between Western and Chinese notions of truth. The Chinese thinkers were preoccupied with the right way (*dao*[d]) of doing things, whereas Western philosophers were more preoccupied with what is true of things. Consider Aristotle's abstract definition:

Thus a person has got it right (*alêtheuei*) who considers that things which are separate are separate and that things which belong together belong together. (*Metaphysics*, 1051, b 3)

A very important question is whether we have statements of this plain theoretical sort in ancient China. Examine, for example:

We call it 'being straight' to declare something 'this (or, right)' if it is this (or, right), and to declare something 'not-this (or, wrong)' if it is not-this (or, wrong) (*shi wei shi, fei wei fei yue zhi*[e]). (Xunzi (Hsün Tzu) 2.12, compare with H. Köster (1967), p. 12)

This passage from Xunzi is difficult. I want to stress two important contrasts with Aristotle here: (a) Aristotle is interested in a formal definition of what it is to be right, whereas Xunzi defines what it is to tell the truth, and (b) Aristotle thinks of the subject term and the predicate term being separate or belonging together whereas Xunzi thinks of a predicate applying or not applying to a thing. Both are profound differences.

For Aristotle the question is one of the theoretical definition of *alêtheuein* 'being right', whereas for Xunzi the problem is the more social definition of *zhi*[f] 'being straight, telling the truth'. For Aristotle the paradigm of a statement is a general statement of the 'All philosophers are humans' or 'All humans are mortal' variety: his paradigm of a proposition essentially relates two terms. For Xunzi, as for all other early Chinese philosophers of language, the main concern is not in this way essentially tied up with a relation between two terms. Chinese philosophers of language were mainly concerned with the relation between names and things.

Comparisons of this kind require detailed philological study of the original classical Greek and the original classical Chinese texts. They do not require any basically adequate philosophical theory of Latin or Greek.[3] They do require that one looks at Greek and Chinese texts from a philosophical perspective.

The relevant texts, however, are not just the strictly 'philosophical' ones (whatever that term would mean in a Chinese context). Consider a narrative passage:

'If she succeeds in this matter you will control the land and have the people as your children. If she does not succeed, then I fear you will lose your life. If you want her to succeed, why don't you see me?' Yin Chi's father kowtowed and replied: 'It is just as you say (*zheng ru jun yan*[g] lit.: GENUINE BE-LIKE YOU WORD). . . .'. *Zhanguoce*, no. 494, ed. Chu Tsu-keng, p. 1724)

Yin Ji agrees with Sima Xi's (Ssu-ma Hsi) two conditional statements. His way of speaking suggests that a relation called *ru*[h], 'be like' can obtain between words and the facts. But this, of course, is far from being a theoretical or 'philosophical' statement.

In an only slightly more 'philosophical' vein we have passages like this:

Kongzi (Confucius) knew that the Way is easy to put into practice, and he said: 'The Book of Songs says: "The enlightenment of the people is very easy." These are not empty words (*fei xu ci ye*[i]).' (*Han Shi Waizhuan*, 5.16; compare with J.R. Hightower, 1951, p. 176)

Does the 'not empty words' not come close to their being true? We shall have to closely investigate matters of this sort.

For the time being, I shall leave aside the Greek (and English) evidence as well as the comparative problems. I shall turn to a detailed study of Chinese thinkers' use of what may appear to be predicates of semantic truth.

Some Classical Chinese Terms Connected with the Notion of Semantic Truth

What, then, were the classical Chinese words that came closest to the semantic concept of 'truth'? As a first orientation I shall simply list these words and try to indicate roughly and in a preliminary way their semantic nuances.

(a) *shi*[j]: be this, be it, be right
(b) *fei*[k]: not be this, not be it, be wrong
(c) *shi*[l]: be solid, be real
(d) *xu*[m]: be empty, be tenuous, be unreal
(e) *ran*[b]: be so, be the case
(f) *fou*[n]: be not so, not be the case
(g) *you*[o]: have, exist, there is such a state of affairs
(h) *wu*[p]: lack, not exist, there is no such state of affairs
(i) *cheng*[q]: be honest, be sincere, be genuinely so
(j) *xin*[r]: believe, be loyal, be trustworthy, be reliably so
(k) *wei*[s]: to fake, create artificially, be fake
(l) *dang*[c]: to fit, to fit the facts

(m) *guo*[t]: to go beyond, to not fit, to not fit the facts
(n) *zhen*[u]: be genuine, be genuinely so
(o) *qing*[v]: inherent state, essence, genuine state of affairs
(p) *ke*[w]: be able to, be admissible, be logically acceptable
None of these terms corresponds perfectly or exactly with the concept of semantic truth. But then neither does the English word 'true'. (Compare this with 'a true friend'. It is a sobering reflection that 'true' etymologically is related to German *treu* and is thus very much like *xin*[r] and far from being a purely logical term.) We neither expect words in any natural language to be unambiguous, nor do we expect them to correspond exactly to words in a different natural language. None of these words represents 'the concept of truth in ancient China'. But in what follows we shall try to investigate how some of these words were used by Chinese thinkers.

The Notion of Semantic Truth among
Ancient Chinese Thinkers

In the following sections we shall consider some ancient Chinese thinkers and schools of thought. We shall ask ourselves to what extent these thinkers had occasion to employ semantic truth predicates.

Did Kongzi Have a Concept of Truth? Kongzi comments:

The Master said: 'After a state has been ruled for a hundred years by good men it is possible to get the better of cruelty and to do away with killing. How genuinely adequate (*cheng*[q]) is this saying (*yan*[fa])!' (*Lunyu* 13.10, compare with Lau (1983), p. 125. Compare also *Lunyu*, 17.4)

Kongzi quotes a sentence, and he commends the sentence by calling it *cheng*[q]. The old commentary says: 'This saying is an old one and Kongzi believed in it (or: held it to be trustworthy) (*xin zhi*[x]).'[4] (Here we have a belief context with a pronominalized sentential object.)

Kongzi commented: 'Is it not so (*ran*[b]) that talent is difficult to find?' (*Lunyu* 8.20, compare with D.C. Lau (1983), p. 75)

I submit that there is a good *prima facie* case to be made for D.C. Lau's translation: 'How true it is that talent is difficult to find.'
From later sources (*c.* 200 BC) we have the following story about

Kongzi which I quote because it illustrates how semantic truth predicates are commonly ascribed in classical Chinese:

[Yanzi said:] 'When one's entourage is good then each of the officials will find their proper places and good and evil will be properly differentiated.' When Kongzi heard of this he said: 'These words are trustworthy (*ci yan ye xin yi*^y)!. . .' (*Yanzi Chunqiu* 3, ed. Wu Tse-yü, p. 239 and *Shuoyuan*, 7.37, ed. Chao Shan-i, p. 197)

Suppose I say 'I submit that the claim that classical Chinese had no concept of 'truth' is not trustworthy, that is, it is not to be believed, it is to be rejected, it is to be dismissed. This is not so. The facts are otherwise.' I state this without using the concept 'truth', one might insist. (Although I am certainly mentioning it.) But would this mean I do not here show, by speaking the way I do, that I do have a concept of truth? It seems to me that I do express the notion of semantic truth. I just happen to express the notion of semantic truth in slightly different ways, that is all. The Chinese, it seems, had such different ways of expressing that a sentence was true. Just as Plato sometimes has *orthôs legeis* 'you speak correctly' and at other times *alêthê legeis* and various other locutions which all critically involve a semantic concept of truth. It is the different Chinese locutions that we are exploring in what follows.

Did the Book *Mozi* (*Mo Tzu*) Employ a Concept of Semantic Truth?

Looking at it from the point of view of what you are saying, what everybody calls 'acceptable (*ke*^w)' need not necessarily obtain (*ran*^b). (*Mozi* 49.24, compare with Mei (1929), p. 246)

Here the speaker, a ruler, attributes to the listener, Mozi, what one is tempted to construe as a distinction between 'is (subjectively) acceptable (*ke*^w)', and 'is (objectively) so (*ran*^b)'. Note that what everybody calls 'acceptable' (*ke*^w) is a form of words, sentence, or a claim. And that same thing is said to be not necessarily *ran*^b 'objectively so'. I therefore maintain that *ran*^b in this passage is pointedly used as a semantic truth predicate.

Did the Early Daoists Have a Concept of Semantic Truth? In the *Laozi* (*Lao Tzu*) we read:

What the ancients said: 'If one bends one is preserved intact' is surely no empty saying (*xu yu*^z). (*Laozi*, 22, compare with Lau (1963), p. 35)

Heshang Gong's commentary elaborates:

These are correct words (*zheng yan*[aa]) and not empty words (*xu yan*[ab]). (Compare with E. Erkes (1950), p. 49)

Perhaps 'being not empty' could mean 'has its point', but Heshang Gong's commentary does not take it that way. Calling words 'not empty' is a classical Chinese way of calling them true.[5]

Trustworthy (*xin*[r]) words are not beautiful. Beautiful words are not truthful (*xin*[r]). (*Laozi*, B1, tr. D.C. Lau (1982), p. 117)

Heshang Gong's fascinating commentary leaves little doubt as to how he understands Laozi at this point:

'Truthful words' correspond to the reality concerned (*xin yan zhe ru qi shi ye*[ac]). (Compare with E. Erkes (1950), p. 134)

Do we have an incipient ancient Chinese correspondence theory of truth here? Or did our early commentary radically misunderstand Laozi? Does it present us with a Buddhist interpretation totally alien to the indigenously Chinese ancient tradition and insensitively introduce the old text through Heshang Gong's commentary?[6]

The *Zhuangzi* (*Chuang Tzu*) states a philosophical thesis and then asks whether it corresponds to the facts.

The disputers of this world all say: 'The finest substance has no form. The greatest thing cannot be encompassed'. Is that the reliably real state of affairs (*shi xin qing hu*[ad])? (*Zhuangzi*, 17.21, compare A.C. Graham (1981), p. 146)

Here we certainly have a text which is explicitly concerned with the truth of a general statement.

Did the Later Confucians Have a Concept of Semantic Truth?   In the *Mengzi* (*Mencius*) a certain Xian Qiumeng retells a story which he introduces by *yu yun*[ae] 'the story goes', and then goes on to complain:

I do not know[7] whether this story (*ci yu*[af]) is genuinely so (*cheng ran*[ag]). (*Mengzi*, 5A4, compare with D.C. Lau (1984), p. 185)[8]

I would therefore translate this as 'is genuinely true'.

In the *Mengzi* a similar question is applied to an explicit philosophical thesis:

'All men can become Yao or Shun. Is there such a state of affairs (*you zhu*[ah])?' Mengzi replied: 'It is so (*ran*[b]).' (*Mengzi*, 6B2, compare D.C. Lau (1984), p. 243)

Book 5A contains an extended series of queries whether certain claims which are explicitly quoted are true or untrue. This series provides crucial and positive evidence on the question of whether the ancient Chinese had a semantic notion of truth. Xunzi's essay entitled Discourse on Corrections (*Zheng Lun*[ai]) consists of another extended series of enquiries whether certain stated claims are true or not. Here is a sample:

The common people who make up theories (*shuo*[aj]) claim: 'Jie and Zhou were in charge of the world. Tang and Wu usurped the throne.' This is not so (*shi bu ran*[ak]). If one thinks that Jie and Zhou once held the formal position of an emperor, that they personally occupied this position, that is so (*ran*[b]). If one says of the world that was in the hands of Jie and Zhou, that is not so (*bu ran*[al]). (*Xunzi*, 18.11, compare Köster (1967), p. 225)

Shi[j] 'this' refers to the statement or claim which Xunzi has just quoted. The phrase *shi bu ran*[am] 'such a claim is not true' after a quotation recurs eight times in that chapter alone. In any case, in this passage Xunzi quotes certain claims and rejects them. He even goes on to consider more specific alternative formulations. One of these he finds true, the other untrue. In another place Xunzi addresses the question of whether human nature is good, as follows:

Mencius says: 'Human nature is good.' (I) say: 'This is not the case (*jan*[b]).' (*Xunzi*, 23.36, compare Köster (1967), p. 307)

'This (*shi*[j])' must refer to Mengzi's claim which has just been quoted. In this very chapter Mengzi is quoted four times, and his claims are explicitly rejected (as untrue) four times.

The historical work *Zhanguoce* explicitly ascribes truth to words:

Zhang Yi said: '. . . Chen Zhen will leave Qin and go to Chu. . . .' The king said to Chen Zhen: 'I have heard that you wish to leave Qin and go to Chu. Is this true (*Xin hu*[an])?' Chen Zhen replied: 'That is so (*ran*[b]).' 'Then Zhang Yi's words were actually trustworthy (*Yi zhi yan guo xin ye*[ao])?' (*Zhanguoce*, ed. Chu Tsu-keng, p. 201; compare J.I. Crump (1970), p. 63)

The fascinating chapter 58 of the *Dadai Liji* is difficult to date with confidence (the book stabilised around AD 100 but contains much earlier material). It contains the following passage:

Dan Juli asked Zengzi: 'As for "Heaven is round and Earth is square", is there truly such a state of affairs (*tian yuan er di fang zhe, cheng you zhi hu*[ap])?' Zengzi replied: 'Li, have you heard that this is so?' Dan Juli said: 'I, your disciple, have not investigated the matter. That is why I presume to ask.' (*Dadai Liji*, 58, ed. Kao Ming (1975), p. 207)

We need not go into the rest of Zengzi's interesting reply. It suffices to say that we have here a scientific/philosophical thesis the truth of which is queried in an eminently Confucian text. The observation that no one word corresponds exactly to the English 'true' in this passage is inconsequential. In any case, here is a passage where we do have such a word:

Kongzi said: '. . . You are not the right person.' Zai Wo replied: 'That I am not good enough is genuinely so (*cheng ye*[aq]). I respectfully accept orders.' (*Dadai Liji*, 62, ed. Kao Ming (1975), p. 244)

How Did Han Feizi (Han Fei Tzu) Look upon Truth?   Han Feizi focussed on the distinction between truth and belief. He made a distinction between the factual truth of words on the one hand and psychological attitudes (for example, of belief) on the other.

It is in the nature of words that they are taken to be trustworthy (*xin*[r]) when many people advocate them. Take a thing that is not so (*bu ran zhi wu*[ar]). When ten people maintain it, one has one's doubts. When one hundred people maintain it one thinks it is probably so (*ran*[b]). When one thousand people maintain it, it is incontrovertible. (*Han Feizi*, 48.6.6, compare W.K. Liao (1959), vol. 2, p. 269)[9]

What is this 'thing' (*wu*[as]) that is 'not so'? One cannot maintain facts as such. If one could only maintain facts, one could most certainly never be wrong! The 'thing' must be something like a statement or a claim.

The two master's (Wu Qi and the Lord of Shang) words were fully[10] fitting-the-facts (*yi dang yi*[at]), but Wu Qi was dismembered and the Lord of Shang was pulled to pieces between carts. (*Han Feizi*, 42.2.13, compare W.K. Liao (1959), p. 210. There is a close parallel in *Han Feizi*, 13.3.25.)

Finally, we may mention one of the cases where Han Feizi explicitly rejects an opponent's thesis as untrue:

When the opponent says: 'One has to depend on a sage, then there will be good order', then that is not so (*bu ran yi*[au]). (*Han Feizi*, 40.5.3, compare with W.K. Liao (1959), p. 203)

Did the Lüshi Chunqiu (Lü Shih Ch'un Ch'iu) Employ a Notion of Semantic Truth? The *Lushi Chunqiu* distinguishes factual truth from explanatory truth:

Every thing's being so must necessarily have a reason (*ku*[av]). And when one does not know the reason, then even though what one says fits-the-facts (*dang*[c]), this is the same as ignorance. (*Lüshi Chunqiu*, 9.4, compare R. Wilhelm (1928), p. 111)

This text commonly asks whether a stated claim is true or not:

'When I was the heir apparent I heard that the former kings said: "To be a sage is easy." Is there such a state of affairs (*you zhi hu*[aw])?' 'That is so (*jan*[b]).' (*Lüshi Chunqiu*, 18.1, compare Wilhelm (1928), p. 291)

The alternation of *ran*[b] 'it is so' with *you zhi hu*[aw] 'is there such a state of affairs?' is important because it indicates that *you*[o] asks about a claim, not a thing or fact. In this case, the claim is a general 'philosophical' one.

But of course semantic truth is not necessarily a philosophical matter at all:

Many words look as if they were not right (*fei*[k]) but turn out to be right (*shi*[j]). Many others look as if they are right (*shi*[j]) but turn out to be not right (*fei*[k]). (*Lüshi Chunqiu*, 22.6, compare R. Wilhelm (1928), p. 401)

The spirit of scientific inquiry in our text is aptly expressed in the following passage:

When you get hold of words you must investigate these. (*Lüshi Chunqiu*, 22.6, compare R. Wilhelm (1928), p. 399)

Did the Later Moists Have a Technical Term for Semantic Truth? The Later Moists made a technical term of the very word *dang*[c] which was commonly used for the adequacy or truth of sentences in other early texts. Consider now a typical use of *dang*[c];

To say 'There is no one who gets it right (*wu sheng*[ax]) in disputation' necessarily does not fit the facts (*dang*[c]). (A.C. Graham (1978), B 35)

Here the Moist quotes a claim ('no one gets it right in disputation') and quite properly he finds this claim necessarily factually untrue, since disputation is about contradictions, one of which must be true. A.C. Graham (1978) has shown satisfactorily that Later Moist concerns are neither sociological nor political in this context. Their concern turns out to be, in some fairly modern sense, logical.

The technical Moist term *dang*[c] is carefully distinguished from *ke*[w] 'acceptable, admissible'. Like our 'right' and 'wrong' *ke*[w] may apply both to utterances and to actions, and it is a multivalent term. It so happens that the Moists are concerned with *ke*[w] 'acceptable' as applied to utterances within a logical context.[11] The distinction between 'assertible' and 'acceptable' is logically crucial. There is no evidence to suggest that the Later Moists were ever guilty of an elementary confusion between these two different notions.[12]

Did Gongsun Long (Kung-sun Lung) Have a Concept of Logical Truth?

Consider now Gongsun Long's famous question:

Is 'A white horse is not a horse' acceptable (*bai ma fei ma ke hu*[ay])? (*Gongsun Longzi*, ch. 2, ed. Luan Hsing (1982), p. 15)

The question is not whether one can assert this sentence. (Of course one can! Gongsun Long is just asserting it!) The question is whether thus asserting it would be acceptable or not. The question is not whether it is morally acceptable, or whether it is socially acceptable (good form), or whether it is pragmatically appropriate to utter such a sentence, although these meanings could be expressed by *ke*[w]. The question is whether it is logically acceptable, whether one can make a logical case for it. The rest of the famous dialogue is indeed about this latter question.

Acceptability (*ke*[w]) is not the same as fitting the facts (*dang*[c]). Something is *ke*[w] 'acceptable, admissible' because it conforms to rules of debate. Something is *dang*[c] 'true, fitting the facts' if it conforms to the reality it describes.

What Was Wang Chong's (Wang Ch'ung's) Attitude to Truth?

Wang Chong (AD 27–100) explains the purpose of his great work *Lun Heng* as follows:

Again, I was distressed that in fake books and vulgar writings there was so much that was not based on fact and genuine (*bu shi cheng*[ba]). Therefore I wrote the *Lun Heng*. (*Lun Heng*, ch. 85, ed. Zhonghua Shuju (1979), p. 1683, compare Forke (1962), vol. 1, p. 70)

In his afterword, Wang Chong makes it quite explicit that his purpose in writing *Lun Heng* is none other than to refute untrue sentences which he quotes, and to promote truth. Wang Chong is a living refutation of the view that pre-Buddhist Chinese philosophers did not have, or did not place central emphasis on, the notion of the objective truth of sentences. He says:

Explanation and discourse argue about what is so and what is not so (*bian ran fou*bb). . . . One discards what is ungenuine (*wei*s) and retains what is genuine (*zhen*u). (*Lun Heng*, ch. 85, ed. Zhonghua Shuju (1979), p. 1690)

*Ran fou*bc 'be so, not be so' is an expression that comes close to an abstract notion of truth. When Wang Chong argues about *ran fou*bc 'whether it is so or not' it seems to me he is quite precisely arguing about semantic truth. Wang Chong speaks of *zhen*u 'genuine' and *wei*s 'fake' as applying to claims, statements, or sentences. In any case there would be no such things as ungenuine or untruthful facts to reject. If there is no fact, there is nothing (no fact) to reject. One can only reject sentences or statements as untrue, not facts. Are we to assume that by asking whether claims were justified or not, Wang Chong radically departed from pre-Han philosophical tradition? He is indeed a special case. But as we have seen in one sense he seems to continue an earlier line of philosophers as prominent as Mengzi, Xunzi, and Han Feizi. Moreover he was singularly important in the history of science in China.

Does the *Yinwenzi* Have a Notion of Semantic Truth?   The *Yinwenzi* is a work of some importance for the history of Chinese logic which dates from the beginning of the third century AD. It shows no traces of Buddhist influence. In it we find the following passage:

An old saying goes like this: 'Not knowing is compatible with being a gentleman. Knowledge does not make someone any less of an insignificant person. That a workman is incapable (of things other than those he specializes in) is not incompatible with being skillful. That the gentleman is not knowledgeable is not incompatible with his governing well." This is true (*ci xin yi*bd). (*Yinwenzi*, ed. Li Shixi (1977), p. 14.)

Nominal Notions of Truth in Ancient Chinese Texts

The nominalized concept of truth is an abstraction from the verbal use. Before we specifically investigate the question whether the Chinese had an abstract notion of truth, we must ask whether they were capable of abstraction, or more specifically whether they had such concepts as that of a quality, a property, or of an attribute.

Did the Ancient Chinese Have a Concept of a Property?   It is important to realise that the notion of a property may be present even when there is neither a technical term for 'property', nor a morphemical marker (like Greek *–otês* English *–ness*) of the term used to refer to a property. Consider the following Later Moist theoretical statement:

The circularity of a small circle is the same as the circularity of a large circle. (A.C. Graham (1978), p. 474)

The classical Chinese for 'circle' and for 'circularity' is the same: *yuan*[be]. But it is very clear that if the ancient Chinese understood this sentence at all they must have been able to distinguish between a circle and circularity. (The Later Moist could surely not be taken to refer to the character *yuan*[be] being present in both phrases.)

But let us look for technical terms for 'property' in classical Chinese. In one of the most remarkable documents of early Daoist theorising, the chapter *Jielao* 'Explaining Laozi' from the book *Han Feizi* (third century BC), the concept of *li*[bf] is extensively used and discussed as a technical term[13], but as often happens the key term turns out to be impossible to translate satisfactorily. I shall risk the translation 'attribute' for *li*[bf] in its technical usage in the *Jielao*:

Being short or being long, being large or being small, being square or being round, being strong or being brittle, being light or being heavy, being bright or being dark, these are called attributes (*duan chang, da xiao, fang yuan, jian cui, qing zhong, bai hei zhi wei li*[bg]). (*Han Feizi*, 20.34.16)

Generally, attributes (*li*[bf]) are an apportioning of being square or being round, of being short or being long, of being coarse or being fine, of being strong or being brittle. (*Han Feizi*, 20.29.2; compare A.C. Graham (1978), p. 429)

We note that *duan chang*[bh] literally: 'being short or being long', or 'length', cannot here refer to short and long things. Neither does *duan chang*[bh] refer to the alternative whether a thing is long or short. *Duan chang*[bh] indicates a dimension.

Moreover, these pairs of concepts are not just arbitrary illustrations or examples of *li*[bf]. They seem deliberately lined up to indicate a range of dimensions or parameters along which physical objects may be said to have attributes: one-dimensional length, three-dimensional size, shape, elasticity/strength, granulation, weight, pigmentation. It is interesting that smell and taste, for example, are omitted. On the other hand, Han Feizi provides some further examples of attributes (li^{bf}) of a different type:

Among the fixed attributes (*ding li*) there are (those of) being persistent or perishing, being dead or living, flourishing or declining. (*Han Feizi*, 20.29.4)

These attributes (li^{bf}) of things combine to form one *gestalt*:

Out of the flow and flux things were brought forth. When the things came about they brought forth attributes (li^{bf}), and these were called the *gestalt* (*xing*). (*Zhuangzi*, 12.39, compare B. Watson (1969), p. 131)

From the *Lüshi Chunqiu* we have an interesting definition of *li* which in the light of the *Jielao* we might try to translate as follows:

Therefore if distinctions do not fit the attributes (*li*) they are false. If knowledge does not fit the attributes (li^{bf}) it is misleading/fraudulent. Misleading or false people were executed by the former kings. Attributes (li^{bf}) of things are the ultimate source of being right or being wrong (*shi fei*[bj]). (*Lüshi Chunqiu* 18.4, ed. Ch'en Ch'i-yu p. 1178)[15]

We can paraphrase this as follows: we are right in calling a horse white on the ultimate basis that the attribute 'is white' is present in the horse. Knowledge as well as disputation must be measured against this ultimate standard.

Here is how Han Feizi explains li^{bf}: 'As for the attributes (li^{bf}) they bring about the patterning of things.'[15] Han Feizi states the obvious in the theoretical manner of a logician: 'Things have attributes (li^{bf}).'[17] Again he specifies the obvious in the manner of a logician: 'The ten thousand things each have their different attributes (*wan wu ge yi li*[bk]).'[18]

We have seen that Han Feizi speaks of the 'fixed attributes (*ding li*[ti])'. We now need to inquire what he means by *ding*[bl] 'fixed' in such contexts. Han Feizi says: 'When the attributes (li^{bf}) are fixed/distinct it is easy to divide things up (into classes (*lei*[gn])).'[19] It is only when attributes (li^{bf}) are fixed that we can distinguish between things, since we must use the attributes (li^{bf}) of things as our criteria.[20]

It is tempting indeed to maintain that Han Feizi (if indeed he is the author of the *Jielao*) was developing something like the theoretical notion of an attribute or a property. The fact remains significant that this conceptual innovation, if that is what it was, was not taken up by others later. The Chinese could speak of properties when they wished, but usually they did not.

Did the Ancient Chinese Have an Abstract Notion of Truth?   The problem of nominal concepts of semantic truth is complicated by the fact that there is often little obvious difference between 'truth' as the 'property' of a sentence that makes it true, and 'reality, the facts of the matter'. A recently discovered manuscript from the Mawangdui tomb provides neat evidence of the place the Chinese accorded to truth in their scheme of things:

Only after understanding the correspondence between names and objects, only after exhaustively understanding what is real and what is fake (*qing wei*[br]) and being free of confusion, can one complete the Way of the emperors and kings. (*Jingfa*, 1976, p. 29.)

As the abstract notion of size is expressed by the pair *da xiao*[bs] 'large/small' in classical Chinese, so the abstract notion of truth is expressed by pairs like *qing fou*[bt] 'what is real and what is fake'. In the text I have just quoted, attaining Truth is described as being dependent upon obtaining truth.

The problem of *shi fei*[bj] 'whether something is right or not' is an important one in ancient Chinese philosophy, just as for Epicurus the *krisis tou orthôs ê mê orthôs* 'the distinction (*bian*[bu]) between what is correct (*shi*[j]) and not correct (*fei*[k])' is an important one.[21]

Considering a matter as certain, for Han Feizi, is considering it as certainly true. Throughout his book he emphasizes the need to check the reliability or certainty of what one hears. He speaks of 'deciding the genuine facts of a matter (*cheng*[q]) by checking and comparing'.[22] Han Feizi talks about '. . . trying to find the genuine facts of a matter (*qiu qi cheng*[bv])',[23] and recommends 'listening to others' words and trying to find what fits the fact (*qiu qi dang*[bw])',[24] as well as 'comparing and checking words in order to understand the genuine facts of a matter (*zhi qi cheng*[bx])'.[25]

The nominal concept of *cheng*[q] 'genuine facts' is not always purely factual, for Han Feizi can also ask:

Whom could one ask to decide the real facts of the case (*cheng*[q]) of the Moists and Confucians? (*Han Feizi* 50.1.31, compare W.K. Liao (1959), vol. 2, p. 298)

Here the question of *cheng*[q] 'genuine facts' clearly involves both factual and moral issues, just as it does in the case of Western concepts of truth.

The importance of semantic truth can be brought out without actually using a noun for 'truth'.

When one gets hold of words one must investigate the truth (*cha*[by]) of these. . . . Hearing something and investigating (*shen*[bz]) it brings good fortune. Hearing something without investigating it is even worse than not hearing it at all. . . . Whenever one hears words one must carefully appraise the person (from whom they come), and one must test (*yan*[ca]) them according to the principles of things (*li*[bf]). (*Lüshi Chunqiu* 22.6, compare R. Wilhelm (1928), p. 399)

What more splendid evidence of the scientific spirit and interest in tested truth during pre-Han times can one look for than such programmatic statements?

In Han times *shi*[1] 'solid, real' was commonly nominalized and came to mean something like 'the solid facts of a matter'. Wang Chong, the great philosopher and scientist, writes programmatically:

In scientific discourse (*lun*[cb]) what matters are the solid facts of a matter *shi*[1]). (*Lun Heng*, ch. 85, tr. A. Forke (1962), vol. 1, p. 73)

I repeat, in his afterword, Wang Chong makes it quite explicit that his purpose in writing the *Lun Heng* is none other than to refute claims that are untrue and thereby to promote truth. He is a living refutation of the view that Chinese philosophers would not place central emphasis on the notion of scientific objective truth.

Concluding Remarks on the Concept of Truth

I have presented a sampling of the ample philological evidence which suggests that the ancient Chinese philosophers had notions close to that of semantic truth, and that they commonly applied predicates of semantic truth to sentences. My translations may, of course, all be taken to beg the question. But I suggest they should rather be taken to demand a clear answer: how are we to understand the passages I quote without ascribing to the Chinese notions of semantic truth, without offending against what is known about ancient Chinese philology?

An Alternative Account of Semantic Truth   Professor Hansen argues: 'Chinese philosophy has no concept of truth.' (C. Hansen (1985), p. 492). If I understand him at all, he means by 'concept of truth' just the kind of semantic concept of truth which Tarski has propounded. But having no such concept of truth—far from being taken as a disadvantage, this is described as a mark of ingenious and wise pragmatism. The pre-Buddhist Chinese are credited with a subtle and workable 'pragmatic' alternative to Western 'Platonic' and 'semantic' approaches to truth.

The (hypo)thesis that 'Chinese philosophy has no concept of truth' is resumed, somewhat surprisingly, as follows: 'The hypothesis that Chinese philosophy seldom employs semantic concepts such as truth, as distinct from pragmatic concepts such as appropriateness of utterance. . .'[26] In short, we are invited to consider the thesis that the Chinese philosophers seldom used a concept which they did not have!

We read: 'I shall argue that given the structure of doctrines in the philosophical texts of the period, a pragmatic interpretation of classical Chinese is a more explanatorily coherent theory than a semantic (truth-based) alternative.'[27] Unfortunately no clear picture begins to emerge of what exactly this pragmatic interpretation might be like. We are told that 'Chinese philosophers discourse about language in a pragmatic, Confucian way, focusing on social-psychological techniques for shaping inclinations and feelings that direct behaviour in accord with a moral way.'[28] In short: we are asked to believe that pre-Han philosophers generally (also anti-Confucians) talked about language in a 'Confucian way'.

But neither Gongsun Long nor the Later Moists, to name but some opponents of Confucianism, did talk (or 'discourse') about language, focusing on social-psychological techniques, and so on, in a 'Confucian way'. Gongsun Long's frivolous paradoxes and the Later Moists' formalistic arguments (both of which we shall briefly discuss below) had little to do with 'social-psychological techniques'. Contemporary Confucians found these logicians profoundly un-Confucian in their lack of concern for the social and ethical significance of their either frivolous or fruitlessly over-sophisticated theories.

Hansen concedes: 'Of course, for Chinese (philosophers and laymen) the truth of a doctrine did make a difference, and, in general, Chinese [sic] did de re reject false propositions and adopt true ones. However, they did not "use a concept of truth" in philosophizing about what they were doing. Chinese philosophical theories about how to evaluate doctrines do not depend on a distinction that matches our familiar true/false dichotomy.'[29] So the Chinese did, after all, reject false 'propositions' and accept true ones. How, under such circumstances, they can be said to have no concept of truth remains entirely unclear. The solution is supposed to lie in the addition 'de re'.

The de re/de dicto *Distinction*   The distinction between *de re* and *de dicto* is not made clear in Hansen's paper. However, it is easy enough to illustrate in a rough way that is sufficient for our present purposes. Suppose I say 'I am looking for a black cat', then I am either looking for a certain cat (a case of speaking *de re* of a black cat), or I am just looking for anything that satisfies the description 'black cat' (a case of *de dicto*). The opposition disappears when I change the verb in such a sentence. 'Statement' in 'they rejected the statement' does not have both a *de re* and a *de dicto* reading. (As Quine and others are fond of pointing out, assent and dissent are not essentially linked to propositional attitudes.) Only a *de dicto* reading of this sentence is conceivable. The opposition arises only with certain intensional verbs like 'look for' and is basically plain enough. When applied to a highly sensitive philosophical term like 'proposition', and in logically very different contexts as after a verb like 'reject', the distinction *de re/de dicto* becomes highly problematic, to put the matter very mildly. It is far from clear what one would have to do in order to reject a proposition (or statement) *de re* but not *de dicto*.

The Concept of a Proposition   By rejecting false propositions and adopting true ones, the Chinese would have demonstrated that in a logically crucial sense they did have an operative concept of the predicate 'is true'. Understanding the predicate 'is true' is logically more crucial than understanding the philosophically most problematic nominal construction 'truth'.

Moreover, in expressing judgments on this matter in language, one is inclined to think the ancient Chinese would have employed a way of articulating the notion of truth. For how can the truth of a doctrine make a difference to them, if they 'have no concept or idea of truth at all'?

The matter is not made less complicated by the fact that a 'proposition' is an abstract theoretical concept which the Chinese never came anywhere near to using, let alone defining. By contrast, the notion of a proposition was achieved and carefully defined by the Stoics: *axiôma lekton autoteles apophanton hoson eph' hautôi* 'a proposition is a complete thing that is expressed which is assertoric by itself'.[29] The proposition is conceived very subtly by the ancient Stoics, and generally by philosophers of language in modern times, not as a form of words but as a semantic content that may be expressed by a form of words in certain contexts.

The Concept of a Propositional Attitude   Intimately connected with the notion of a proposition is that of propositional attitudes like that of belief. We are told 'No single character or conventional string of ancient Chinese corresponds in a straightforward way to "believes that" or "belief that". No string or structure is equivalent to the word "believe" or "belief" in the formal sense that it takes sentences or propositions as its object.'[30] We need not dwell on, but certainly need to point out, the extraordinary conceptual and categorial confusion concerning the term 'proposition' here. A proposition, not being a form of words, never ever could be the object of a verb (though it could be an object of thought), a fine point which—as we have seen—was already quite plain to the ancient Stoics well before the Christian era, and that is absolutely basic in philosophical logic. In the context of the philosophy of language we are not free to use terms like 'proposition' in its loose non-technical sense. The Stoics have defined the term precisely in order to avoid such conceptual vagueness in the context of philosophy.

But let us not do away with logic. Let us, instead, and from a logical point of view, take a philo-logical look at some pertinent ancient evidence which Hansen does not discuss or mention:

There were some who believed that there had not yet begun to be things (*you yi wei wei shi you wu zhe*[cc]). (*Zhuangzi*, 2.40; compare with A.C. Graham (1983), p. 54)

One might be tempted to interpret the common formula *yi X wei Y*[cd] as 'treat X as a Y'. But examples like the present one are not amenable to such an interpretation. What would the people here referred to be treating as what? Hansen needs to show in detail why we are not entitled to take Zhuangzi to be ascribing a belief to certain people in this particular sentence, and in particular, how we can manage to do so.

There is other evidence:

Then his friends believed that he was ashamed to become Official Recorder (*xin qi xiu wei shi ye*[ce]). (*Lüshi Chunqiu*, 26.6, compare with R. Wilhelm (1928), p. 449. Compare also *Mo Tzu*, 31.5)

The crucial question is this: how are we to take *xin*[r] in this pattern or *xin zhi*[cf] 'believes it'? Hansen nowhere shows that he is aware of sentences of this sort. He needs to show how and why *xin*[r] in these contexts is not what it certainly appears to be to all translators: an ancient Chinese word for 'believe that'. Until he comes up with a better argued philological solution one is inclined to take xin^r here as a verb such as 'believes that' with a sentential object. If xin^r had as its object a fact, one could never not believe something (*bu xin zhi*[cg]) or not consider something as so (*fu ran*[ch], or *bu yi wei ran*[ci])?[31] For justified non-belief would then be an attitude to a non-existent fact, an attitude towards strictly nothing. If belief had facts as its object, then there could not be any beliefs that are not based on facts. Belief must be about statements or claims. It is closely connected with the notion of a sentence.

Having heard about this, Confucius said: 'From this point of view people will describe (*wei*[cj]) Zi Chan as inhumane, but I do not believe this (*wu bu xin ye*[ck]).' (*Zuozhuan*, Duke Xiang, 31, *fu* vii, ed. Yang Po-chün, p. 1192, compare Couvreur (1951), vol. 2, p. 578)

What Kongzi has no faith in, here, is explicitly people's description (*wei*[cj]) of Zi Chan as inhumane. Sometimes one is even tempted to take *wei* as a psychological verb meaning 'consider as', as in:

The superior man will maintain Yang Zhen to be less than a man (*Junzi wei Yang Zhen fei ren ye*[cl]). (*Zuozhuan*, Duke Xuan, 2.1, ed. Yang Po-chün, p. 652, compare with S. Couvreur (1951), vol. 1, p. 565)

The disposition to say of Yang Zhen that he is less than a man is closely connected to the belief that Yang Zhen is less than a man. In any case *wei*[cj] came to mean 'imagine that' quite regularly in early colloquial Chinese of the fifth century AD, for example in the *Baiyujing*.

The Theoretical Concept of a Sentence as Opposed to the Practical Ability to Distinguish Sentences from Non-Sentences   Without some operative notion of a declarative sentence or a statement, how could the Chinese (*de re* or otherwise) possibly reject false statements or accept them? If they knew what one might reject or not reject, they surely could tell statements from other things. Otherwise we should have to conclude that they quite literally never knew what they were talking about. They might make such mistakes as rejecting any non-sentential string.

The question whether the ancient Chinese had a technical term for 'sentence' is totally different from the question whether they had sentences. The question whether the ancient Chinese had a technical term for 'sentence' has to do not with Chinese grammatical practice but with Chinese theoretical linguistic conceptualisations. A.C. Graham (1978), pp. 480–483 and elsewhere, has argued persuasively that the Later Moists did develop such a technical term, cǐ (misleadingly translated by Graham as 'proposition', a translation which he has since regretted).[32] We read: 'Thus, Chinese does not so much obscure sentence relations as omit to signal them overtly.'[33] However, a student of Chinese grammar, for example, of nominalization or sentence connectives, must certainly study exactly the ways in which sentence relations were signalled overtly in that language through word order, grammatical particles, and lexical specialization of words. Word order and the occurrence of particles, surely, are overt signals.

We are told: 'Chinese theories of language did not concentrate on sentences because, simply, classical Chinese sentencehood is not syntactically important.'[34] But on the contrary, the modal particle yi[cm] and the ordinary final particle yi[cn], er yi[co], and er[cp] as well as er[cr] and so on, show the crucial syntactic importance of the sentence in Chinese. They only occur after strings that happen to constitute sentences. To the extent that certain particles are restricted to sentence-final positions they do presuppose an operative notion of the sentence among the writers of classical Chinese. Wang Chong (AD 27–100) writes:

When written characters express a thought (yi[cs]) they make up a sentence (ju[ct]). When there are a certain number of sentences (ju[ct]) we string together paragraphs (zhang[cu]) by means of them. When paragraphs have a certain coherent structure we make chapters (pian[cv]) by means of them. (Lun Heng, ed. Chunghua shuchü, 1979, p. 1589; compare with Forke (1962), vol. 1, p. 451)

The most common word for sentence in Chinese—as the current ancient Greek logos—was rather vague and could refer to all sorts of linguistic entities. The technical term for a sentence as used by the logicians won little general acceptance among writers of classical Chinese. Thus in general the ancient Chinese writers were faced with a range of rather vague terms for 'sentence', but upon reflection they were able to identify and define the concept reasonably well.

In the later philological tradition, He Xiu (129–182) refers to the parsing or punctuation of sentences as ju du[cw] in the preface to his edition of the Gongyang Commentary. The ju[ct], I prefer to think, marks off a sentence, and the du a smaller unit.

Gao Yu (*floruit* 205–212) tells us that he learnt to 'put commata and stops (*ju du*^(cw)) and to chant' when he was young.[35] Liu Xie (465–562) makes a sequence *zi* 'character, word', *ju*^(ct) 'sentence', *zhang*^(cu) 'paragraph' and *pian*^(cv) 'chapter'.

When men write literature they make sentences (*ju*^(ct)) on the basis of characters (*zi*^(cx)), they put together sentences to make paragraphs (*zhang*^(cu)), and they put together paragraphs to make chapters (*pian*^(cv)). (*Wenxin Diaolong*, ch. 34, ed. Lu K'an-ju and Mou Shih-chin (1981), vol. 2, p. 177. Compare with Vincent Shih (1959), p. 186.)

Yan Zhitui (531–590+) obliges us by describing the function of the (mostly sentence-final) particle *ye*^(cy) as follows:

Ye^(cy) is a word that finishes a sentence and aids punctuation (*zhu ju*^(cz)). (*Yanshi Jiaxun*, ch. 17, compare with Teng Ssu-yü (1968), p. 161)

Exactly: that is just what *ye*^(cy) does most of the time. And that is why *ye*^(cy) is such a useful and ubiquitous particle in classical and literary Chinese.

The Concept of Truthfulness or Good Faith

The concept of semantic truth which we have discussed so far is entirely different from that of truthfulness or good faith. The idea that the Chinese have their own special notions of truth and truthfulness is not a new one. Some time ago I came across a poem from the journal *Punch* dated 10 April 1858. The song is called *A Chanson for Canton*, and it begins as follows:

> JOHN CHINAMAN a rogue is born,
> The laws of truth he holds is scorn;
> About as great a brute as can
> Encumber the Earth is JOHN CHINAMAN.

Now I read in the *Journal of Asian Studies* dated May 1985 the following intellectually more ambitious formulation: 'Truth-telling and promise-keeping are central elements in a Judeo-Christian-Kantian moral structure.'[36] And further: '. . . "telling the truth" and "keeping promises" are not salient examples of morality in Chinese philosophy.'[37] This is something more than a poetic insult; it is an extremely serious claim about truthfulness or good faith in ancient China. One is surprised to hear such claims about a culture which cultivates such sayings as *yan er wu xin fei junzi*^(da) 'if one speaks without good faith one is not a gentleman'. In any case, I propose to briefly present some of the abundant philological facts that prove that the ancient Chinese thinkers, like most of us, valued truthfulness and good faith. Kongzi, for one, said:

'I do not see how an untrustworthy (*xin*ʳ) man can be acceptable. When a pin is missing in the yoke-bar of a large cart or in the collar-bar of a small cart, how can the cart be expected to go?' (*Lunyu*, 2.22, compare with D.C. Lau (1983), p. 17)

Philology, the science of textual interpretation, is the yoke-bar and the collar-bar of any enquiry into the question of whether the ancient Chinese valued good faith as a salient example of morality or not. Does the ubiquitous and cardinal Confucian virtue of *xin*ʳ involve truthfulness and good faith or is it just a matter of faithfulness and loyalty? The answer to this question depends on a close examination of the ancient Chinese texts in which the virtue *xin*ʳ is discussed or mentioned, like this one recommending the formula *yan zhong xin*ᵈᵇ which has since become canonical as describing the Confucian ideal of verbal behaviour:

Zi Zhang asked about proper action (*xing*ᵈᶜ). The Master said: 'If in word you are loyal and trustworthy (*yan zhong xin*ᵈᵇ) and in deed single-minded and reverent, then even in the lands of the barabarians you will act effectively. But if you fail to be conscientious and trustworthy in word or to be single-minded and reverent in deed, then can you be sure of acting effectively even in your own neighbourhood?' (*Lunyu*, 15.6, compare with D.C. Lau (1983), p. 149)

Is *zhong xin*ᵈᵈ 'loyalty trustworthiness' a synonym compound? We must look for definitions of *xin*ʳ. Here is an early definition:

Xin (good faith/trustworthiness) is the words agreeing with the thought. (*Mozi*, I quote the translation in A.C. Graham (1978), p. 276)

Of course, the concept of *yi*ᶜˢ 'thought', here, is not unproblematic. Moreover, the dialectical chapters of the *Mozi* are perhaps not representative enough for early Chinese culture. How about the mainstream Confucian Jia Yi (Chia I) (200–168 BC):

If one's promises are effective and one's words correct that is called *xin*ʳ (trustworthiness). Xin Shu (*Hsin Shu*), ch. 8, Dao Shu (*Tao Shu*), compare with Ch'i Yü-chang (1974), p. 928.)[38]

From the earliest times of the codification of Confucian conduct the concept of *xin* has played an important part: in addition to *zhong*ᵈᵉ 'faithfulness, loyalty' it was (by the earliest commentator) taken to be one of the *wu xing*[df] 'five forms of conduct' in *Xunzi*, and it was most certainly one of the educationally all-important *wu chang*[dg] 'five constants' that became the focus of attention in early Han times.

The realist philosopher Han Feizi (died 233 BC) did take the notion of good faith seriously enough to declare the following (in what was to become the opening paragraph of his book):

Any minister, if not loyal, must be condemned to death. If what he says be not true (dang[c]), he must be condemned to death, too. (*Han Feizi* 1.1.6, I quote the translation in W.K. Liao (1939), vol. 1, p. 1)

Han Feizi is using the term *dang*[c] 'fit the facts' to express an idea that I believe Liao's translation captures well enough. Han Feizi speaks of the importance of telling the truth.[39]

The importance of telling the truth is the subject of innumerable stories. Here is one that is of independent special interest. The state of Sung is besieged by Chu. A certain Hua Yuan of Sung admits to Zi Fan, a spy from Chu, that the situation in Sung is extremely precarious:

'Therefore I am telling you the real situation (*shi yi gao qing yu zi*[dh])' (*Gong Yang Zhuan*, Duke Xuan, 15)

By telling the truth Hua Yuan wins over Zi Fan, who in turn tells the truth about the situation in Chu. One version of this story comments:

The gentleman will approve their making peace. Hua Yuan told Zi Fan the genuine-situation/truth (*yi cheng gao Zi Fan*[di]) . . . The gentleman will approve their telling each other the genuine-situation/truth (*junzi shan qi yi cheng xiang gao*[dj]). (*Hanshi Waizhuan*, 2.1)

There is good philological evidence that good faith and promise-keeping was a 'salient' feature in Chinese thinking. The Neo-Confucian Chen Xiang (1159–1223) in his *dictionnaire philosophique* entitled *Beixi Ziyi* (ed. Xinhua shuju, Beijing, 1983) pp. 26–8, clearly distinguishes between *xin*[r] meaning 'be trustworthy, that is in good faith', and *xin*[r] meaning 'be trustworthy, that is undoubtably true'.

Argumentation in Ancient China

We have seen that the ancient Chinese had words for semantic truth and for good faith. But did they ever provide arguments that were intended to logically prove the truth of a conclusion? Do we find strict logical argumentation in ancient China?

As examples of incisive and ingenious argumentation I shall first introduce and explain some remarkable Later Moist arguments which I shall compare with some Chinese Buddhist arguments of the seventh century. Thereafter I shall discuss the 'sophist' Gongsun Long's famous White Horse Dialogue, concentrating on the social and logical background of the dialogue and some problems of methodology in the interpretation of the text.

Some Late Moist Arguments on Scepticism and Relativism[40]

The Later Moists defined logical analysis as follows:

Logical analysis (*bian*[bu]) is contending over claims which are the contradictories of each other (*zheng fan*[dk]). Explanation one calling it 'an ox' and the other calling it 'not an ox', that amounts to contending over claims which are the contradictories of each other. (Compare with A.C. Graham (1978), A40)

Contradictories (*fan*) are what cannot be both regarded as unacceptable at the same time. (A.C. Graham (1978), A73)

If one maintains a sentence, one is thereby committed to denying the negation (or rejecting the denial) of what one says. Consequently, refusing to deny any sentences, as the Daoists are fond of doing, simply turns out to be inconsistent:

Canon: To reject denial is inconsistent.
Explained by: he does not reject it.
Explanation: If he does not reject the denial (of his own thesis that denial is to be rejected) then he does not reject denial. No matter whether the rejection is to be rejected or not, this amounts to not rejecting the denial. (A.C. Graham (1978), B79)

Suppose someone maintains that one should reject denial. Then, if he means what he says, the thesis that one should not reject denial should be denied. But if one admits that that thesis should indeed be denied, then one is not really maintaining that one should reject denial: in at least one instance (that is, the thesis in which one rejects denial) one fails to reject denial. One's position is therefore inconsistent.

Let us rephrase the matter more along our usual lines of thinking: suppose someone (the Relativist) maintains the statement P ('For all propositions s: s is true'). He is then maintaining that 'P is true'. Now by substituting non-P for s in this formula we get 'non-P is true' as a consequence of P. Thus the Relativist is committed to two statements: (a) P is true, and (b) non-P is true. In other words: this special substitution demonstrates that the Relativist is contradicting himself.

Maintaining P implies denying non-P. But denying non-P violates the principle that no sentence is to be denied. Therefore maintaining P is self-contradictory. If he maintains that no statements are to be denied, the Relativist is committed to denying the statement that not all statements are to be denied. He is therefore contradicting himself.

The argument is subtle and incisive, and in this particular instance the text is quite clear and the interpretation seems straightforward.

With stunning persistence the Moist goes on to claim that it makes no difference whether the Relativist is right or wrong in refusing denial. It is not a question of whether the Relativist is right or wrong. The point is whether the Relativist position is self-contradictory or not.

The Moists make an almost identical proof against considering all saying as contradictory:

Canon: To claim that all saying contradicts itself is self-contradictory.
Explained by: his saying (this).
Explanation: To be self-contradictory is to be inadmissible. If these words of the man are admissible, then this is not self-contradictory, and consequently in some cases saying is acceptable. If this man's words are not admissible, then to suppose that it fits the facts is necessarily ill-considered. (A.C. Graham (1978), B71)

The crux in this argument is again the application of a thesis about all statements to that thesis itself. If the Relativist declares his own thesis to be included among the incoherent or contradictory theses which are to be rejected, then he both maintains and rejects his thesis and therefore contradicts himself.

If, on the other hand, he does not include his thesis among the theses which are incoherent and to be rejected, then there is at least one thesis which is coherent and not to be rejected so that the Relativist is again contradicting himself.

Whoever constructed arguments of this sort, we may safely conclude, was a thinker of considerable logical sophistication. He represents an early but advanced logical and scientific subculture of which, unfortunately, all too few traces have been thought worth handing down in the Chinese tradition.

Gongsun Long's White Horse Dialogue

Gongsun Long was widely considered as flippant by contemporaries like Xunzi. Already Han Feizi has the story, surely inspired by Gongsun Long's stunt of demonstrating that a white horse was not a horse, about a certain 'sophist' Ni Yue:

Ni Yue was a man of Song, and he was the sort of person who was good at disputation. He maintained that *bai ma fei ma ye*[dl] 'WHITE HORSE IS-NOT HORSE' and he belonged to the disputers of the Jixia Academy in Qi. Riding a white horse he passed a customs point and he had to pay his horse-tax. (*Han Feizi* 32.13)

At this point I simply wish to outline the argumentative nature of Gongsun Long's text as I see it. As I see it Gongsun Long was not so intellectually advanced that he could pre-empt Lesniewski, but he was perfectly capable of presenting a series of sustained arguments. He was, as his contemporaries were quick to point out, a rather frivolous figure. For he liked to argue for the logical acceptability of a sentence which was plainly untrue, namely that *bai ma fei ma*[dm] 'WHITE HORSE IS-NOT HORSE', a sentence ordinarily understood to mean that white horses were not horses.

As we have seen, people were quick to poke fun at this by imagining someone arguing this point with a customs officer who levies duty on horses. Would Gongsun Long be able to convince such a customs officer? Of course not! But then Gongsun Long only liked to argue his point in a sort of logical game. He was a 'stunt-man of logic'. He said: 'Here is a thesis *bai ma fei ma*. You try to refute it, and I shall defend it.'

How, then, could Gongsun Long defend such a plainly untrue thesis? This is the crucial question, and for once I do have a clear answer. He defended it by using a peculiarity of the ancient Chinese language which makes the sentence *bai ma fei ma*[dm] ambiguous between two interpretations: (a) A white horse is not a horse, and (b) 'White horse' is not (the same as) 'horse'. While the opponent would be furiously attacking the statement on interpretation (a) Gongsun Long would quietly persist in defending his statement under the interpretation (b). That was his trick. It was a simple trick, but it seems to have worked and to have had its comic effect. After all, Gongsun Long could appear to successfully defend a thesis which was totally outrageous. This is how the (late) first chapter of the *Gongsun Long Zi* introduces the issue:

Gongsun Long and Kong Quan once met in Zhao at the palace of the Lord of Pingyuan. Kong Quan said: 'I have long heard about your noble conduct, and I have wanted to become your disciple. However, I cannot accept your thesis that a white horse is not a horse. Please reject this thesis, and I will beg to become your disciple.'

Gongsun Long replied: 'Your words are self-contradictory. The reason I have made a name for myself is none other than this discourse on the white horse. If you now make me abandon this discourse I have nothing to teach. Moreover, if one wishes to make someone one's master, this is because one's wisdom and learning is not up to his. If now you make me abandon my thesis, this would be first teaching me and then making me your master. First teaching someone and then making him into one's master is self-contradictory. Moreover, that "white horse" is not "horse" is precisely a thesis which Kongzi advocated. I have heard it said that the King of Chu was once wielding his bow Fan-ruo with his (famous) Wang-gui arrows. He was shooting at crocodile and rhinoceros in his (legendary) Yunmeng Park, when he lost an arrow. His ministers were scrambling to collect the arrow, but the King replied: "That is not worthwhile. The King of Chu has lost his bow, and a man from Chu (*Churen*dn) will find it. Why go and look for it?"

'When Kongzi heard about this he commented: "The King of Chu may be humane and just, but he is not perfect yet. Surely he should simply have said: 'A man (*ren*do) has lost the bow and a man (*ren*do) will find it.' What reason is there to bring in the 'Chu'?" In this way Kongzi made a distinction between *Churen*dn "a man of Chu" and *ren*do "a man".

'Now to approve Kongzi's distinguishing between *Churen*dn "man of Chu" and *ren*do "man" but to disapprove of my distinguishing *bai ma*dp "white horse" from *ma*dr "horse" is self-contradictory.' (*Gongsun Lung Zi*, ch. 1, (ed.) Luan Hsing (1982), p. 5)

Kongzi suggests that the King should have said *ren*do instead of *Churen*dn. There is, so far as I can see, no suggestion that he denies that a Chu man is a man. What the text focuses on is the distinction between *Churen*dn and *ren*do. *Churen*dn and *ren*do are not the same. There can be occasions where one should use one rather than the other. That is the issue as it is understood in our text.

On my interpretation, the White Horse Dialogue turns out to contain very subtle reasoning. Take the following example:

If someone is looking for a horse, you can offer him a brown or a black horse. If (on the other hand) he is looking for a white horse, you cannot offer him a brown or a black horse. Supposing (now) that 'white horse' was nothing other than 'horse'. Then what he would be looking for would be the same thing. And if what he is looking for was the same thing, then the white one would not be different from 'a horse'. But if what he is looking for (in those two cases of 'white horse' versus 'horse') was the same, why should it be that the brown and black horses were acceptable in one case but not in the other? It is evident that the admissible and the inadmissible are not the same as each other. Therefore, since a black or brown horse remains the same, but since one can answer that there is 'horse' and cannot answer that there is 'white horse' this means that the thesis that a white horse is not a horse is conclusively demonstrated to be true.

There is a logical technique in the sophist's arguments which is of special interest to the historian of logic: he seems to apply something like Leibnitz' law of identity which says that if X and Y are identical then one must be able to substitute them for each other in any sentence, *salva veritate*, without this affecting the truth or otherwise of the sentence involved. Thus the sophist reasons that if 'white horse' was the same as 'horse' then 'I am looking for a white horse' should be true under exactly the same circumstances as 'I am looking for a horse'. But this is not so. Therefore, 'white horse' and 'horse' cannot be the same.

Why does the sophist change the example from 'having a white horse' to 'seeking a white horse'? Here again, it does look as if something logically quite subtle may be going on. For 'have an X' counts as what analytical philosophers call an 'extensional context', whereas 'seek an X' creates an intensional context in the relevant sense. The relevant basic idea behind this distinction between extensional and intensional contexts is not hard to explain. If I have a certain horse, and without my knowing about it this horse is deaf, then in every sense of the word I do 'have a deaf horse'. If, on the other hand, I am looking for a certain horse, and without my knowing it this horse happens to be deaf, then—in one psychological sense of 'look for'—I am not looking for a deaf horse, that is, my mental attitude is not towards a horse under the description 'deaf horse'. After all I do not know that the horse is deaf. 'Looking for white horses' is no more 'looking for horses' than 'looking for black swans' is 'looking for swans'. On the other hand it is perfectly true that 'having a white swan' is indeed 'having a swan'. When the sophist changes the example from 'having a white horse' to 'seeking a white horse', I cannot help feeling that he had a perception of this subtle logical difference between 'having' and 'seeking'.

This, in simple outline, is the logical core of the White Horse Dialogue as I understand it. It is not very logically exciting to a reader familiar with modern philosophy. On the other hand: would one expect anything very logically sophisticated to be propounded at the court of the Duke of Pingyuan?

Professor C. Hansen on the White Horse Dialogue   I believe Gongsun Long was more congenially and much more adequately understood by men like Xunzi and Han Feizi than by some of his modern interpreters. Consider this modern interpretation:

Then the question, 'Of what is ma^{dr} "horse" the name?' has a natural answer: the mereological set of horses. 'Horse-stuff' is thus as object (substance or thing-kind) scattered in space-time. . . . As a result, Chinese theories of language tend to treat adjectives as terms denoting mass substantives; for example, red is the stuff that covers apples and the sky at sunset. (C. Hansen (1983), p. 35)

W.V.O. Quine happens to write in one of the most famous chapters of his most famous book:

A further alternative likewise compatible with the same old stimulus meaning (of the word 'gavagai' C.H.) is to take 'gavagai' as a singular term naming the fusion, in Goodman's sense, of all rabbits: that single though discontinuous portion of the spatiotemporal world that consists of rabbits. Thus even the distinction between general and singular terms is independent of stimulus meaning. (W.V.O. Quine (1960), p. 52)

We are asked to believe that by a curious historical coincidence Gongsun Long happened to assume that 'horse' refers to just the sort of spatio-temporally discontinuous abstract object consisting of all horses past, present, and future, scattered through space and time, which Quine mentioned.[41]

The object referred to by the Chinese word ma^{dr} 'horse' is in Hansen's preliminary formulation called a 'mereological set'. This is a very advanced technical term in mathematics.[42]

Mereology is a subtle and abstract mathematical theory introduced to avoid such notoriously paradoxical logical constructions of sets as the book catalogue of all book catalogues which do not mention themselves. Such a construct, if acceptable, is logically troublesome. One only has to ask oneself whether such a book catalogue which mentions all book catalogues that do not mention themselves, should or should not mention itself. . .

Lesniewski designed a part/whole formalism which he called mereology (after Greek *meros*, root *mere-*) in which such sets would come out as syntactically ill-formed. In this way he did bypass an important set-theoretical problem. For this he is justly famous.

All this is interesting, but it seems to me to have nothing whatever to do with Gongsun Long's thought, unless we find that Gongsun Long (or his contemporaries) speak of discontinuous horse-parts scattered through space and time which they most certainly do not. Even less do they speak of objects consisting of such proper parts as apples and sunsets scattered through space and time or whatever is the 'mereological set' specified to the Chinese mind by *bai*[dq] 'white'.

Our interpretation of Gongsun Long's views must start, we all agree, neither from Quine nor from Goodman or Lesniewski, but from the genuine parts of the *Gongsun Longzi* text as it has come down to us. I find the use of terminology like 'mereology' thoroughly uncongenial because if we are to take it seriously its use would constitute a bizarre case of interpretative anachronism. But if we are not supposed to take it seriously in its technical meaning then the term is misapplied: 'mereological set' is a technical term which has only a technical meaning. Loose use of such a technical term is misuse.

Until I find, in pre-Han literature, clear references to anything like mereological sets or to discontinuous objects scattered through space and time I shall consider this concept a very distinctly twentieth-century mathematical construct, not an implicit third century BC idea.

Perhaps it is unreasonable and unfair to focus so much on just one passage in which Hansen introduces his central ideas. Let us now turn to a much more charitable development of Hansen's ideas, that by Professor A.C. Graham.

Professor A.C. Graham on the White Horse Dialogue   A.C. Graham writes:

Chad Hansen in his *Language and Logic in Ancient China* has opened the first radically new approach to the 'White Horse'. It is an application of his hypothesis that Classical Chinese nouns function like mass nouns rather than the count nouns of Indo-European languages. (A.C. Graham (1986), p. 196)

We start from one of Hansen's crucial insights, that thinking with mass nouns is in terms of whole and part, of which what for us are class and member are only one variety. (A.C. Graham (1986), p. 199)

We note that A.C. Graham declares the mass noun hypothesis the crucial inspiration for his new interpretation. But for all his enthusiasm he wisely avoids the term 'object' or 'mereological set' for the overall horsy mass. He very appropriately avoids using the concept of 'mereology' at all in interpreting ancient Chinese thought:

But if he (Gongsun Long) is thinking of horse as a mass with discontinuous parts similar in shape, and of white as a mass of discontinuous patches of colour, then for him a white horse is indeed a part of the former mass combined with part of the latter. (A.C. Graham (1986), p. 197f)

Following Hansen, A.C. Graham claims that ma^{dr} is a mass term. However, ma^{dr} 'horse' behaves syntactically quite differently from mass nouns like $shui^{ds}$ 'water' and again from generic nouns like $sheng^{dt}$ 'domestic animal', not to speak of abstract nouns like ren^{du} 'benevolence', proper nouns like $Zhongni^{dv}$ and pronouns like ci^{dw} 'this item'. Before one can decide whether ma^{dr} is a mass noun, one surely has to study closely the question of whether there is a distinction between count nouns, generic nouns, and mass nouns among classical Chinese common nouns. Graham nowhere begins to address this problem which is so crucial to his (and Hansen's) case. If classical Chinese does make a distinction between mass nouns and other nouns, then it becomes an empirical and researchable question as to whether ma is a mass noun or not. It is only when the mass noun hypothesis is formulated in a specific way so that it can be effectively tested against the facts of classical Chinese, that I begin to be seriously interested in it. In this I follow Thomas Aquinas' advice to the infidels: *Disciplinati autem hominis est tantum de unoquoque fidem capere tentare, quantum natura rei permittit.*[43]

Let me identify some of the diagnostic syntactic conditions that might clarify ancient Chinese distinctions between count nouns, generic nouns, and mass nouns.[44]

Count Nouns Count nouns may be quantified not only by *duo*[dx] 'many, much' and *shao*[dy] 'few, little', but also by *shu*[dz] 'a number of', *ge*[ea] 'each', and *jian*[eb] 'each of the objects'. A count noun refers to items that can be counted by numbers immediately preceding the count noun, for example, *san ren*[ec] 'three persons', not 'three kinds of people'. Mass nouns and generic nouns are never quantified by *shu*[dz], *ge*[ea], or *jian*[eb], and as we shall see below they behave differently when counted. We have *bu guo shu ren*[ed] 'no more than a few people'[45], *ci shu zi*[ej] 'these several men'[46], *zhi shu wu*[ek] 'these several things'[47], *ci shu jie*[el] 'these several accomplishments'[48], *shi shu guo*[em] 'these several states'[49], *shu kou zhi jia*[en] 'a home of a number of persons'[50], *shu shi*[eo] 'a number of generations'[51]. Of course, units of time and other measurements of all sorts are commonly counted with *shu*[dz], and they are never counted with classifiers.

Some nouns are used both as mass nouns and as count nouns. Thus we have *shu jin*[ep] 'a number of units of money'[52] in spite of the fact that *jin*[eq] is also often used as a mass noun meaning 'metal'. This, I think, is simply a case of lexical ambiguity or possible textual corruption.

Classifiers are count nouns, since we do have *de che shu sheng*[er] GET CART A-NUMBER-OF ITEMS 'get a number of carts'[53]. We can also count them in the same way as ordinary count nouns with a classifier: *ge che san bai liang*[es] WAR-CHARIOTS THREE HUNDRED VEHICULAR-ITEMS, 'three hundred war chariots',[54] not: *san bai liang ge che*[et]. One might at first sight suspect that the complexity of the phrase may be a motive for the choice of this construction. However, it is also possible to find examples such as *che yi sheng*[eu] VEHICLE ONE VEHICULAR OBJECT, 'one chariot'.[55]

With count nouns like *ma*[dr] we find a construction like *ma san pi*[ev] HORSE THREE ITEMS 'three horses'[56] but never *san pi ma*[ew], THREE ITEM HORSE. We have *ge zhong er si*[ex], MUSICAL BELL TWO SET, 'two sets of musical bells'[57], but never *er si ge zhong*[ey].[58]

Some count nouns are never counted with classifiers in our literature, and we suspect that they could not be either: classifier nouns belong to this group, as well as *ren*[du] 'man' (which may turn out to be a classifier noun: *Shun you chen wu ren*[ez] 'Shun had five ministers'[59] and *yan*[fa] 'word, sentence' (contrast the more general *yu*[fb], 'talking, speech').

Generic Nouns   Consider the following pairs of classical Chinese words:

1. *ma*[dr] (count noun) 'horse' versus *sheng*[fc] (generic noun) and *chu*[fd] (generic noun) domestic animal.
2. *ren*[du] (count noun) 'man' versus *min*[fe] (generic noun) 'people'.

Unlike count nouns, generic nouns are never modified by *shu*[dz] 'a number of', *ge*[ea] 'each', *jian*[eb] 'each of the objects'. Like count nouns, but unlike mass nouns, generic nouns can be modified by *qun*[ff] 'the whole flock/crowd/lot of', *zhu*[fg] 'the various', *zhong*[fh] 'all the many', *wan*[fi] 'the ten thousand, all', *bai*[fj], the hundred, all'.

Generic nouns are never counted with classifiers in the manner of mass nouns (*yi bei shui*[fk] 'one cup of water')[60] or in the manner of count nouns (*ma san pi*[ev] 'three horses'). They thus constitute a proper subcategory of nouns in their own right.

The semantics of counting is different in generic nouns and in count nouns. *Liu ma*[fl] will normally mean 'six horses', whereas *wu sheng*[fm] must mean '(the) five kinds of domestic animals' and *liu chu*[fn] must mean 'six kinds of domestic animals'.[61]

Wu ren[fo] will always mean 'five men', whereas *wu di*[fp] has to mean 'the five barbarians'.[62] *Wu min*[fr] are 'five kinds of people'[63] and certainly not five individuals of lower rank. Indeed, *min*[fs] are never counted as such, except by unspecific numbers such as *wan*[fi] 'the ten thousand'.[64] *Ci liu ren zhe*[ft] means 'these six individuals (or people)'[65], whereas a little further on in the same text *ci liu min zhe*[fu] means 'these six kinds of people'.[66] *Min*[fs] 'people' and *ren*[du] 'man' are both very common. The functional and semantic contrast between them is surprisingly sharp and clear in a large body of pre-Han texts. I used to think that *min*[fs] 'people' may occasionally be used as a count noun, but as I have perused the indexes to find instances of this, I have come to change my mind. I would be interested to see pre-Han examples involving *min* as a count noun.

Ren[du], *min*[fs], and *di*[gc] refer to humans. But they refer to humans in radically different ways. *Di*[gc], 'barbarian', and *min*[fs], 'people', are generic nouns; *ren*[do] is a count noun.

The distinction between count nouns and generic nouns is, of course, not absolute in Chinese any more than in English. For example, we have the English count noun 'flower', and 'five flowers' would normally be interpreted as 'five individual flowers'. However, if a florist says that he stocks 'five flowers' one naturally concludes from the context that he means kinds of flower. Similarly, in the very special context of the *Zhouli*, I found a fascinating similar case involving even our *ma* 'horse', when it speaks of an official *bian liu ma zhi shu*[gd] 'distinguishing between those who belong to the six kinds of horse'.[67]

One such isolated (and probably late) example does not force us to abandon the general observation that *ma* 'horse' is a count noun. It does cause us to reflect that the distinction between count nouns and mass nouns (in English as in classical Chinese) is not an absolute one even in the fairly clear cases. But the crucial point in our present context is that there is no evidence whatever that *ma*[dr] is a mass noun.

Mass Nouns   Compare the following pairs:
1. *dan*[gc] (count noun) 'basket' versus *shi*[gf] (mass noun) 'food'.
2. *shu*[gg] (count noun) 'tree' versus *xin*[gh] (mass noun) 'firewood'.
3. *fu*[gi] (count noun) 'axe' versus *tie*[gj] (mass noun) 'iron'.

With mass nouns we regularly find constructions like *yi bei shui*[fk] ONE CUP WATER 'one cup of water'[68], *yi dan shi*[gk] ONE BASKET FOOD 'one basket-ful of food'[69], *yi che xin*[gl] ONE CART FIREWOOD 'one cart-load of firewood'[70], *yi gu tie*[gm] ONE GU-MEASURE IRON 'one *gu* of iron'[71]. We have:

He takes one plate of meat (*yi dou rou*[gn]) and feeds the knights with the rest. (*Han Feizi*, 34.7.24, compare with W.K. Liao (1959), vol. 2, p. 90)
Shu Guyang took a beaker of wine (*yi shang jiu*[go]) and offered it up. (*Han Feizi*, 10.2.7, compare with W.K. Liao (1939), vol. 1, p. 70)

There may be no explicit number in this sort of construction:

If you leave goblets of wine and platters of meat (*zhi jiu dou jou*[gp]) in the inner court. . . (*Han Feizi*, 34.29.3, compare with W.K. Liao (1959), vol. 2, p. 113)

The distinction between count nouns, generic nouns, and mass nouns needs much further investigation and refinement. I shall explain it in greater detail in my forthcoming contribution to Joseph Needham's *Science and Civilisation in China*. My preliminary conclusion at this point is that classical Chinese count nouns do not seem to behave like classical Chinese mass nouns. By inherent classical Chinese grammatical criteria *ma*[dr] would appear to be a count noun, capable, perhaps, of functioning as a generic noun under special circumstances, but certainly not as a mass noun.

Final Methodological Reflections   In principle, of course, we can construe all English references to a horse as references to 'time-slices' of 'horse-stuff'. And as Quine has shown, we would not risk ever being definitively refuted by any linguistic behaviour of the speakers of English. The indeterminacy of translation applies not only to translation from Chinese into English. It also applies to homophonous 'translation' of a sentence into the same sentence by the same speaker. And as Quine has recently[72] confirmed to me in conversation, the case of an imagined aboriginal language is only a (perhaps ultimately misleading) expository device. The imaginary aboriginal word *gavagai* is quite marginal to Quine's philosophical purpose. The English 'rabbit' raises exactly the same problems for English speakers, only less palpably. Similarly, there is no need to go to classical Chinese in order to demonstrate that those who appear to speak of horses may be construed to be thinking of mereological sets or objects. The English case is good enough to prove this point, and indeed the point has been made many times.

One can refuse to accept any of the ancient Chinese evidence that suggests that the ancient Chinese people entertained such things as mental representations of sentences or sentence meanings (as Hansen appears to do): it will always be possible to say that they just happen to speak or write as if they had such representations.

W.V.O. Quine's remark on translation and 'logicality' may be worth pondering at this point: 'Wanton translation can make natives sound as queer as one pleases. Better translation imposes our logic upon them, and would beg the question of prelogicality if there were a question to beg.'[73]

But instead of ending on this hard-headed and uncompromising note, I prefer to close with some lines attributed to Lucian which I came across as I worked on this conclusion. Here, then, is the last distichon of the epigram *Eis tên heautou biblon* 'On his own book':

> *Ouden en anthrôpoisi dikridon esti noêma*
> *All 'ho sy thaumazeis, touth' heteroisi qelôs.*[74]

I hope the gentle reader will not take this quotation as expressing the present writer's sympathy for a philosophical position of relativism. It is just that such is life!

Notes

1. I should like to thank Professor Nathan Sivin for singularly helpful and incisive criticisms of an earlier draft of this paper. I am also grateful to Professor Chad Hansen for useful hints and comments.

2. *Upanishads* 3.1.6, compare with S. Radhakrishnan (1962), p. 688. The adaptation of the translation is my own.

3. If that were required, no one would be entitled to speak of English sentences until a satisfactory theory of English is forthcoming.

4. Compare with *Lunyu*, ed. Liu Pao-nan, vol. 3, p. 89.

5. Conversely, calling a sentence *xu yan*[ab] was a way of indicating that the sentence was false. Compare with *Xunzi*, 18.71.

6. For the dating of Heshang Gong's commentary see Gu Fang (1982), who argues for the third or fourth century AD; and Jin Chunfeng (1983) who provides strong and detailed evidence in support of a Han date.

7. It seems quite impossible to take this sort of *zhi* 'know' to have anything other than a propositional object.

8. For examples of questions concerning truth *you zhu*[ah]? 'is there such a state of affairs?' in *Mengzi* compare with 1B2, 1B8, 2B1, 2B8, 2B9, 5A5, 5A6, 5A7, 5A8, and 6B2.

9. Compare with *Han Feizi*, 30.17, Liao (1939), vol. 1, p. 291 and *Zhanguoce* No. 302, Crump (1970), p. 377.

10. For a systematic treatment of *yi* in early texts see Harbsmeier (1986).

11. Hansen (1985), p. 506 translates *ke*[w] as 'assertible'. This distorts the very precise logical force of *ke*[w]: The Mohist insists that it is *bu ke*[az] to make contradictory statements. (A.C. Graham (1978), p. 71) But as we have seen one can unfortunately very easily make self-contradictory claims. Self-contradictory claims are assertible. The point is that such assertible statements are unacceptable.

12. Such confusion as there is on this point in C. Hansen (1985), p. 506, is not due to the Moists.

13. I count no less than 22 occurrences of *li*[bf] in the *Jielao*.

14. For our interpretation see Liang Chhi-Hsiung (1982), vol. 1, p. 159 and also D.C. Lau, 'Taoist Metaphysics in the *Chieh Lao* and Plato's Theory of Forms', *Wen Lin*, 2.

15. Compare R. Wilhelm (1982), p. 301 and A.C. Graham (1978), p. 192 for alternative interpretations of this important definition.

16. *Han Feizi*, 20.27.4. The phrase *cheng wu zhi wen*[bm] is grammatically ambiguous. We could also translate: 'is the pattern which brings about things'. This difference is inconsequential for our present purposes.

17. *Han Feizi*, 20.27.11.

18. *Han Feizi*, 20.27.15. Compare with *Zhuangzi* 25.63.

19. *Han Feizi*, 20.34.17.

20. C. Hansen (1983), p. 31, contrasts Chinese and Western conceptual schemes concerning objects as follows: 'The mind is not regarded as an internal picturing mechanism which represents the individual objects in the world, but as a faculty that discriminates the boundaries of substances or stuffs referred to by names. This "cutting up things" view contrasts strongly with the traditional Platonic philosophical picture of objects which are understood as individuals or particulars which instantiate or "have" properties (universals).' Neither the crucial book *Han Feizi* nor any of the crucial concepts *xing*[cn], *qing*[v], *mao*[bo], *zhuang*[bp], *li*[bf] figure in the index of that book. A more systematic discussion of all of these concepts will be found in C. Harbsmeier (forthcoming), subsection 1.4.8, 'The concept of a property'. The concept of subsumption will be discussed in 1.4.9 of the same work.

21. Compare Diogenes Laertius, *Vitae philosophorum*, X.147, ed. Loeb, vol. 2, p. 670.

22. *Han Feizi*, 47.2.31, contrast the translation in Liao (1959), vol. 2, p. 250.

23. *Han Feizi*, 32.2.20, compare with W.K. Liao (1959), vol. 2, p. 27.

24. *Han Feizi*, 46.6.12, compare with W.K. Liao (1959), vol. 2, p. 247.

25. *Han Feizi*, 48.4.21, compare with W.K. Liao (1959), vol. 2, p. 266.

26. Hansen (1985), p. 514.

27. Hansen (1985), p. 493.

28. Hansen (1985), p. 495.

29. Hansen (1985), p. 491.

29. For a lucid discussion of the concept of a proposition in Stoic logic see Benson Mates, *Stoic Logic* (Berkeley, University of California Press, 1961), pp. 27–33.

30. Hansen (1985), p. 500.

31. Similar observations apply to negative epistemic contexts: if knowledge did not have statements as its objects but was a way of treating facts, as we are asked to believe (Hansen (1983), pp. 500f), then how could one not know whether something were true. Not knowing something would then be a way of treating a non-fact, nothing. If knowledge in ancient Chinese was a skill, then a sentence saying that I do not know X in Chinese would have to be taken to presuppose that the X was true and assert that the speaker has not the skill to reliably recognize this. Compare with Hansen (1983), p. 65.

32. I have not seen any convincing counterarguments to A.C. Graham's account.

33. Hansen (1985), p. 497.

34. Hansen (1985), p. 500.

35. Preface to *Huainanzi*, ed. Liu Wendian, p. 2a.

36. Hansen (1985), p. 515.

37. See note 36. I hasten to confess that I do not have a very precise idea what exactly a 'Judaeo-Christian-Kantian moral structure' might be.

38. For a more detailed survey of this important but hitherto unstudied list of 55 definitions of pairs of opposite ethical terms see Needham's vol. 7, part 3 of *Science and Civilisation in China*, section 1.2.4: 'The art of definition in traditional China.'

39. Compare Hansen (1985), p. 515, who declares: '. . . Chinese treat utterances as actions with behavioural consequences, not as conveying information for use in a rational decision process.'

40. My account here is heavily indebted to the monumental and quite indispensable book by A.C. Graham (1978). Though I am in essential agreement with Professor Graham's interpretation, we differ on some significant details.

41. Compare with, incidentally, the remark 'How amusing that Socrates should invent Hare's prescriptive analysis of evaluative discourse.' (Compare with *Times Literary Supplement*, 15 August 1985, p. 881, review of Iris Murdoch, *Acastos*, by Martha Nussbaum.)

42. One might be excused for thinking we should have to read the classical account of mereology by the Polish logician Stanislaw Lesniewski (1886–1939) in E.C. Luschei *The Logical Systems of Lesniewski* (1962), in order to learn what Gongsun Long had in mind. A glance through the simplified account of mereology in *Encyclopaedia Britannica*, 15th ed., vol. 11, pp. 36–7, by Nicholas Rescher will convince most people that this would not be a slight task. Presumably P.M. Simons (1982) offers some welcome extra help.

43. 'A disciplined person will [only!] seek such certainty in each thing as the nature of that thing permits.' *Summa Contra Gentiles*, book 1, ch. 3, (ed.), Biblioteca de Autores Cristianos, Madrid (1967), p. 99. Compare with Aristotle, *Ethica Nichomachea*, 1094b.

44. Already Zhang Shizhao (1907) distinguishes between 1. *guyou mingci*[ee],

proper nouns', 2. *putong mingci*[ef] 'generic nouns', 3. *jihe mingci*[eg] 'collective nouns', 4. *wuzhi mingci*[eh] 'material nouns', and 5. *chouxiang mingci*[ei] 'abstract nouns'. Our present task is to see whether we can establish objective syntactic criteria for setting up a classification of this sort for Classical Chinese.

45. *Zuozhuan*, Duke Ai 12, ed. Legge, p. 836, line 10.

46. *Zhuangzi*, 8.21.

47. *Zhuangzi*, 23.14.

48. *Xunzi*, 7.9, ed. Liang Qixiong, p. 69.

49. *Xunzi*, 15.36.

50. *Mengzi*, 1A3.

51. *Zuozhuan*, Duke Xiang 13, ed. Legge, p. 456, line 7, and Duke Xiang 31, Xi 33, ed. Legge, p. 222, line 12.

52. *Zhuangzi*, 1.39.

53. *Zhuangzi*, 32.23, compare with B. Watson (1968), p. 356 'four or five carriages'.

54. *Mengzi*, 7B4, see also 3B4 and 7B34.

55. *Zuozhuan*, Duke Cheng 18.2, compare with S. Couvreur (1951), vol. 2, p. 167.

56. *Zuozhuan*, Duke Zhuang, 18.

57. *Zuozhuan*, Duke Xiang, 11.10, compare with S. Couvreur (1951), vol. 2, p. 274.

58. For details see Wang Li (1980), p. 240ff as well as J.S. Cikoski (1970), p. 101ff.

59. *Lunyu*, 8.20.

60. For the use of measures with mass nouns see the treatment of mass nouns below.

61. *Han Feizi*, 37.13.45. See also 'Take the shit of the five domestic animals (*wu sheng*[fm]) and wash yourself in it.' (*Han Feizi*, 31.13.39)

62. *Liji*, ed. S. Couvreur (1913), vol. 1, p. 725f, where there are several other relevant examples.

63. *Shang Jun Shu*, ch. 6, ed. Gao Heng, p. 66.

64. The case of *chen*[fr] (count noun) 'minister' versus *li*[fw] (generic noun) 'official' is especially interesting and puzzling. *Ci wu chen zhe*[fx] means 'these five ministers' *Zhanguoce*, no. 185, ed. Zhu Zugeng, p. 770), whereas *wu li*[fy] means 'five kinds of officials'. (*Zuozhuan*, Duke Xiang, 25) However, I have found one isolated instance where in fact *li*[fw] is used as a count noun. In *Lüshi Chunqiu*, 18.8 we find two officials first mentioned as *li er ren*[fz], OFFICIALS TWO MEN, and then in the end we hear that *er li*[ga] 'the two officials ' made a report. One needs to study whether *li*[fw] is really ambiguous between a generic noun and a count noun reading, or whether this instance is just a stray case motivated by the special context. In any case *wu chen*[gb] apparently never has that generic reading.

65. *Han Feizi*, 44.2.7 and 44.4.2.

66. *Han Feizi*, 46.1.19 and 46.1.39.

67. *Zhou Li*, ed. Lin Yin, p. 339.

68. *Mengzi* 6A18.

69. *Lunyu* 6.11.

70. *Mengzi* 6A18. For further examples see J.S. Cikoski (1970), p. 101ff.

71. *Zuozhuan*, Duke Zhao 29, *fu* 5, compare with S. Couvreur (1951), vol. 3, p. 456.

72. 14 April 1987.

73. W.V.O. Quine (1960), p. 58.

74. Translated as:

> No single thought that men embrace
> Can merit have, or pride of place.

For what seems wonderful to thee
Others deride with mockery.
(*Lucian*, vol. 8, tr. M.D. McLeod, Loeb Classical Library, p. 526.)

Key to Characters

a	王充	*aj*	說	*bs*	大小	*db*	言忠信
b	然	*ak*	是不然	*bt*	情否	*dc*	行
c	當	*al*	不然	*bu*	辯	*dd*	忠信
d	道	*am*	是不然	*bv*	求其誠	*de*	忠
e	是謂是、非謂	*an*	信乎	*bw*	求其當	*df*	五行
	非曰直	*ao*	儀之言果信也	*bx*	知其誠	*dg*	五常
f	直	*ap*	天圓而地方者	*by*	察	*dh*	是以告情於子
g	誠如君言		誠有之乎	*bz*	審	*di*	以誠告子反
h	如	*aq*	誠也	*ca*	驗	*dj*	君子善其
i	非應辭也	*ar*	不然之物	*cb*	論		以誠相告
j	是	*as*	物	*cc*	有以爲未始	*dk*	正反
k	非	*at*	已當矣		有物者	*dl*	白馬非馬也
l	實	*au*	不然矣	*cd*	以X爲Y	*dm*	白馬非馬
m	虛	*av*	故	*ce*	信其羞为史也	*dn*	楚人
n	否	*aw*	有之乎	*cf*	信之	*do*	人
o	有	*ax*	無勝	*cg*	不信之	*dp*	白馬
p	無	*ay*	白馬非馬可乎	*ch*	弗然	*dq*	白
q	誠	*az*	不可	*ci*	不以爲然	*dr*	馬
r	信	*ba*	不實誠	*cj*	謂	*ds*	水
s	僞	*bb*	辯然否	*ck*	吾不信也	*dt*	牲
t	過	*bc*	然否	*cl*	君子謂羊	*du*	仁
u	真	*bd*	此信矣		斟非人也	*dv*	仲尼
v	情	*be*	圜	*cm*	已	*dw*	此
w	可	*bf*	理	*cn*	矣	*dx*	多
x	信之	*bg*	短長、大小、方	*co*	而已	*dy*	少
y	此言也信矣		圓、堅脆、輕重、	*cp*	耳	*dz*	數
z	虛語		白黑之謂理	*cr*	爾	*ea*	各
aa	正言	*bh*	短長	*cs*	意	*eb*	兼
ab	虛言	*bi*	定理	*ct*	句	*ec*	三人
ac	信言者如其實	*bj*	是非	*cu*	章	*ed*	不過數人
	也	*bk*	萬物各異理	*cv*	篇	*ee*	固有名詞
ad	是信情乎	*bl*	定	*cw*	句讀	*ef*	普通名詞
ae	語云	*bm*	成物之文	*cx*	字	*eg*	集合名詞
af	此語	*bn*	性	*cy*	也	*eh*	物質名詞
ag	誠然	*bo*	貌	*cz*	助句	*ei*	抽象名詞
ah	有諸	*bp*	狀	*da*	言而無信非君	*ej*	此数子
ai	正論	*br*	情僞		子	*ek*	之数物

el	此数節	*ez*	爵有臣五人	*fn*	六畜	*gc*	狄
em	是数国	*fa*	言	*fo*	五人	*gd*	辨六馬之属
en	数口之家	*fb*	語	*fp*	五狄	*ge*	簞
eo	数世	*fc*	牲	*fr*	五民	*gf*	食
ep	数金	*fd*	畜	*fs*	民	*gg*	树
eq	金	*fe*	民	*ft*	此六人者	*gh*	薪
er	得車数乘	*ff*	群	*fu*	此六民者	*gi*	斧
es	革車三百两	*fg*	諸	*fv*	臣	*gj*	鉄
et	三百两革車	*fh*	衆	*fw*	吏	*gk*	一簞食
eu	車一乘	*fi*	萬	*fx*	此五臣	*gl*	一車薪
ev	馬三匹	*fj*	百	*fy*	五吏	*gm*	一鼓鉄
ew	三匹馬	*fk*	一杯水	*fz*	吏二人	*gn*	一豆肉
ex	歌鐘二肆	*fl*	六馬	*ga*	二吏	*go*	一觴酒
ey	二肆歌鐘	*fm*	五牲	*gb*	五臣	*gp*	卮酒豆肉

6 Chinese Metaphysics as Non-metaphysics: Confucian and Taoist Insights into the Nature of Reality

CHUNG-YING CHENG

As an ultimate conceptual orientation and as a comprehensive explanatory scheme, Western metaphysics originates from a quest for ontological being represented as early as Pythagoras and Parmenides in ancient Greece and as late as Whitehead and Heidegger in modern times.[1] What functions as the mediation for such a quest for ontological being which gives rise to all major metaphysical systems in the Western philosophical tradition has been always an intriguing and challenging question. If we compare and contrast the Greek quest for ontological being (called *einai*) in Western philosophy with the Chinese search for cosmological becoming (called the *dao*) in Chinese philosophy, one important answer derives from the nature of the language in use. Both as a vehicle of thinking and as a form of life, language both represents and makes the initial difference. As a phonetic language, the Greek language is auditorily orientated and tends to present a world of meanings in separation from a world of concrete things. For there is nothing in the phonetic symbols of the Greek language to suggest the presence of sensible objects. This easily leads to conceptual abstractions, certainly more easily than would an image-language such as the Chinese language. The separation of the sensible from the non-sensible can thus become an inherent tendency in the use of a phonetic language just as the cohesion of the sensible with the non-sensible can become an fundamental feature of the use of an image-language. This contrast should highlight the difference between the metaphysical orientation of the Greek quest for ontological being and the metaphysical orientation of the Chinese search for cosmological becoming. This contrast should also explain why Chinese metaphysics is the least metaphysical of all metaphysics or is non-metaphysical in the sense in which Greek, and hence Western metaphysics, is metaphysical, since what is metaphysical in the Western sense is predicated upon the separation of the sensible from the nonsensible, the practical from the transcendental.

The Chinese search for cosmological becoming in the Chinese philosophical tradition is presented and preserved in the two primary texts, the *Yijing* and the *Daodejing*, each being a work with a cosmological outlook which is not confined to cosmology but covers both ethics and philosophical anthropology.

Although we do not know precisely who composed these texts, their creation is historic and historically significant, providing insights into both the minds which composed them, and the collective wisdom of the Chinese experience of reality as a whole. The historical origins and forms of presentation of these two texts differ markedly. To see these differences and also to see how these two texts are related will enable us to recognize how metaphysical thinking became orientated and established in the Chinese philosophical tradition.

The origins of the *Yijing* date back perhaps to the beginning of the Xia Dynasty around the eighteenth century BC. The Zhou people began to use the *Yijing* symbolism for divination in the twelfth century BC and the texts, as we know them, gradually came into being. There are two important issues of dispute regarding the formulation of the text of the *Yijing*. Firstly, what kind of text was formed when the *Yijing* symbolism came to be used for divination. Secondly, how the *Yijing* symbolism was used for divination. These two questions are in a certain sense interrelated, for the symbolism of the *Yijing* must have first developed in such a way that it was *logically* sufficient for divination. And only when the nature of divination was well understood, could the text be developed to suit the purpose.

Very often when scholars assume that the *Yijing* was used for divination, it is assumed that it had no philosophical import, whereas an examination of the symbolism and the text reveals that there must be a cosmological philosophy of reality in change before any divination can be made. Furthermore, an analysis of the divination process as well as the interpretative context also shows that divination is for *getting* practical advice on the basis of the hidden correct identification of a certain situation through the symbolism of the *Yijing*. This is not to deny that the future is subject to change and that human beings are capable of making a choice. It is to make the best possible advice available in the face of an identifiable situation. Divination therefore combines both the process of generating knowledge of the future based on the generated knowledge of the present relative to an understanding of the totality of the world, and the practical provision of a guide for action in the light of this knowledge. One may therefore see divination as a problem-solving or conflict-resolving process, or a process directed towards problem solving and conflict resolving *based* on rational and moral considerations.

In lieu of actual knowledge, divination is devised and seen as a rational process of producing knowledge. There are also the following elements related to the divination process.

(a) The knowledge of a present situation is a holistic or organismic type of knowledge which applies to all single elements in the whole situation.

(b) It contains knowledge of elements and their relationships which are contained in the knowledge of a large whole.

With this understanding of divination we can see that there is a logic in divination (the foretelling of the future and one's necessary action) just as there is a logic in the organization and structuring of the *Yijing*'s picture of the world. We may term the action of divination as one of *totalistic projection into the future of the present situation of the world for the purpose of the orientation of individual action.* In fact we must recognize that there is cosmological thinking in the organization of the *Yijing* symbolism and that there is epistemological thinking as well as practical moral thinking in the practice of divination and of the interpretation of the *symbolism* of divination, when divination is understood correctly in the above sense. One can see that the original texts of the *Yijing* originated as a consequence of the process of this metaphysical, epistemological, and practical thinking.

In order explicitly to articulate and reconstruct the *Yijing*'s cosmological thinking in the formulation of the symbolism of the *Yijing*, and of the *Yijing* epistemological thinking and practical or ethical thinking in the interpretation of the *Yijing* divination, we have to trace the *Yijing* way of thinking to the primordial existential situation of a human person when he finds himself in a network of relationships.

A human person in such a network finds that he is related to other persons and things in the world, to nature (heaven and earth) and to the world as a *whole* (including things he may not understand), and furthermore, that he is related to things in the past as well as to things in the future. The difference between past events and future events is that he may not change things in the past, but he may act to change the future; he can have control of some part of things in the world and in time, whereas he is controlled by other parts of things in the world and in time. He also finds that his own self-understanding and understanding of the purposes of life sometimes make a difference to his life. He finds that his life has potentiality and that he can cultivate himself to fulfil this potentiality.

On the other hand, the human person has many limitations, some of which he may overcome, but some of which he can only accept. In other words, man in his primordial existential situation can establish an understanding of his existential situation containing elements of chance, open possibilities, and restrictions. In Heidegger's language, man finds himself to be a being-in-the-world, and as a being-in-the-world he can awaken to his knowledge of his being a being-in-the-world through self-reflection and historical reflection. His knowledge of this can make a difference to his being-in-the-world for he can make a difference to himself and the world.

In light of what is said above regarding the primordial existential situation of a human person, we may suggest that there are three phases of development of metaphysical thinking in the *Yijing* philosophy: (a) the existential phase, (b) the cosmological phase, and (c) the practical phase. In what follows we will make corresponding analyses of these three phases.

Existential Analysis of the Existential Phase

(a) Man in his existence comes to experience the existence of the whole world of things and to experience his being as a part of the whole world (the principle of man as being-in-the-world).

(b) Man in his existence also experiences changes and transformations of things and hence the change and transformation of time. For him time consists in the change in, and transformation of, things in the world and time is real (the principle of being-in-change or being-in-time).

(c) Man in his existence experiences an openness to the world and time and a correlative or corresponding sense of uncertainty of the self in relation to this openness to the world and time. This sense of uncertainty gives rise to human anxiety, misgiving, and worrying about the world and time (the principle of being-in-misgiving or *youhuan* as indicated in the Appendix of the *Yijing*).

(d) Man in his existence experiences an urge to project himself (his will and his efforts) into the world and time so that he only participates in the world and time in order to make a *change* in, and a transformation of, the world and time (the principle of being-in-projection or of totalistic futurization).

Cosmological Analysis of the Cosmological Phases

(a) All things in the world are interrelated and the interrelationships constitute a context or field in which everything becomes defined and positioned (the principle of totality).

(b) All things change and transform according to their relationships to each other, their positions in the world, and their relationships to the whole world (the principle of universal change).

(c) Change and transformation originate from the inner reality of things and point to a common source internal to all things in the world which is unlimited in space and time and inexhaustible in energy and power (the principle of comprehensive creativity).

Practical Analysis of the Practical Phases

(a) In experiencing the world man can achieve limited knowledge of things and their interrelationships to things in the world, and he can recognize that such knowledge is essential to his efforts to achieve his life *goals* (the principle of the practicality of knowledge).

(b) In reflecting on himself he can achieve knowledge of himself and recognize that such self-knowledge (called knowledge of one's nature) is essential for forming one's life-goals and achieving them together with his knowledge of the world (the principle of self-knowledge).

(c) In understanding the interrelationships between things relative to one's given situation and practical goals in life, one can decide what to do, not just for attaining one's practical goals, but what to do for cultivating and developing one's nature so that both practical good and ultimate good can be achieved (the principle of the efficacy of knowledge).

The above three analyses are essential for understanding the primordial relationships the philosopher of the *Yijing* experiences and articulates in formulating his metaphysical/holistic thinking about himself and the world. They are essential for understanding how theory and action are inseparable, just as they are essential for understanding how the world and man are inseparable. Furthermore, the understanding of the inseparability of knowledge and action is essential for understanding the inseparability of the world and man, and conversely. In fact, the inseparable interaction between knowledge and action presupposes the inseparability of the world and man and leads to the inseparability of man and the world. If man wants to change the relationships between man and the world either towards relative separation or relative closeness, he has to cultivate in himself a relative separation or relative closeness to knowledge and action.[2] This point is important for the development of epistemological thinking based on Chinese metaphysical philosophy.

This point is also closely related to the existential situation of man. Whenever man has to learn to know the world by his actual engagement with the world in his conduct and action, at the same time he has to learn to act according to his knowledge of the world. Knowledge is born out of the interaction between knowing and acting and always carries the practical intention of the human person, whether this intention is to *overcome* the world, or to overcome the self, or to reach a fulfilment of the individual in harmony with the world (the harmonization of man and world).

In the Chinese philosophical tradition, *knowledge* is centred on the harmonization of self and world, whereas in the mainstream of Western philosophy knowledge is for overcoming the world, and in the Buddhistic philosophical tradition knowledge is for overcoming the self. We shall make an epistemological analysis of this epistemological phase inherent in the practical analysis of the practical phase of Chinese philosophy. But we also should note that both the existential and cosmological phases of Chinese philosophy contribute to the development of the practical and epistemological phases of Chinese philosophical thinking, for both the existential sense of uncertainty and sense of cosmological totality enable the practical person to seek knowledge and make decisions in the light of the existential connection of man with the world and with the totalistic interrelationship of things. The existential experience of change and the cosmological perception of pervasive change by

man also urge man constantly and continuously to seek enlightenment about things and understanding of himself: knowledge is not
just a matter of understanding universal principles and forming
abstract concepts, but a matter of direct insight into the nature of
relationships and a grasp of the particularity of things.
With this understanding of the ontogenesis of knowledge, we
can formulate an epistemological analysis of the epistemological
phase centring on the practicality of knowledge motivated by
the existential urgency of self-reflection and enlightened by the
cosmological observation of *nature* (the totality of nature). We
may observe that, since, for the Chinese metaphysical tradition,
knowledge is a matter of practical self-fulfilment, this epistemological phase can be regarded as a sub-phase of the practical phase
in the development of metaphysical thinking as embodied in the
texts of the *Yijing*.

Epistemological Analysis of Epistemological Phases

(a) Human knowledge is based on the practical concerns of man
    and, no matter how abstract human knowledge becomes, it
    always has a practical relevance and represents a practical in-
    terest in man (the principle of knowledge of practicality).
(b) Human knowledge is always rooted in the existential insights
    of man, and may be projected on the objective world to con-
    stitute that form of human existence which is both revealing
    and obstructing, and also to a great extent self-fulfilling (the
    principle of knowledge of subjectivity).
(c) Human knowledge is derived from the interaction between
    human self-reflection and human long-term observation of the
    world and is in essence cosmological in the sense of being both
    holistic and dynamic. How to project this cosmological insight
    on to individual particularity requires both imagination and
    an objective decision-making procedure (the principles of
    knowledge of interactive balance).

Onto-cosmologization and Dipolaristic Analysis in *Yijing* Metaphysics

In Chinese philosophy, man not only develops a holistic outlook
on the universe and man in the universe, but comes to see the
dynamic unity of all things and experience the dynamic source of

all things. To use this term 'dynamic' is to accentuate the importance of movement and creativity not only as a universal phenomenon but as a universal nature-of-things. It implies getting
behind the phenomenon and identifying the ultimate reality of the
phenomenon without denying the reality of the phenomenon. It is,
so to speak, getting to the substance of things through the functions of things. It is due to this penetrating insight into the nature
of things that the cosmological understanding of the world becomes the ontological understanding of things. The *ontological*
pertains to *nature* rather than the manifestations of nature, substance rather than the functioning of substance, and ultimate principle rather than the application of the principle.

It must be noted that the *ontological* is intended to express the
notion of *original substance* (*benti*), not the notion of Being, so
the ontological refers to that which pertains to the *benti* which
unifies the meaning of origin (*ben*) and *base* or substance (*ti*). *Ti*
refers to both the bone frame of a human body which gives the
human body its shape and to the base and centre of human activity, that is, *ti* is the unchanging *base* and the framework for a system of activities on the one hand; it is also the *source* and *origin* of
the system of activities on the other. Hence the metaphysical use
of *ti* is a metaphysical projection of the experienced reality of
human existence.

As a verb *ti* means to personally experience something, and to
embody and assimilate a given reality into the given *framework*
of human existence. Hence, *ti* also implies comprehension/
absorption/embodiment. *Ti* as a verb indicates an intimate interaction and integration so that what is embodied (*ti*) becomes
part of what *embodies* without, however, necessarily changing the
identity of what is embodied. Therefore, *ti* also implies comprehension of integration and harmonization. It makes possible
the union of the object of *ti* and the subject of *ti*. Hence *ti* is not
simply a static concept, but a dynamic concept suggestive of
embodiment, integration, and harmonization in the expression
and consideration of reality.

It is with this *benti* understanding of the ontological that we can
speak of the ontologicalization of the cosmological in Chinese
philosophy. But in doing so, it is clear that the cosmological is not
put aside as a distinct and separate consideration of the world from
the ontological consideration of the world. On the other hand, the

ontological is revealed in the functioning of the cosmological, and the cosmological is embodied in the framework of the ontological. Hence, with regard to this Chinese philosophical reflection (a deeper cosmological reflection) we cannot speak of the ontological alone. We have to speak of the *onto-cosmological* or *cosmo-ontological* to indicate the cosmological, and the ontological togetherness of the cosmological and the ontological. From the cosmological point of view, cosmology leads into ontology and hence should be called *cosmo-ontology*. From the ontological point of view, ontology reveals itself in cosmology and hence should be called *onto-cosmology*. This idea of the dynamic unity of the cosmological and the ontological is well expressed in the notion of the *dao* (the Way) as presented in the Great Appendix of the *Yijing*. Thus the *dao* is in both the cosmo-ontological and the onto-cosmological.

As the cosmo-ontological reality, the *dao* is what is revealed as the dynamic force in the cosmological activities of things. It is the universe-presenting force. It is the *ti* (body) of the universe. It is things going back to their origin and source. As the onto-cosmological reality, *dao* is also the process of presenting things in the universe, and hence the process of presenting the universe. It is therefore the origin and source at work towards the differentiation of reality. *Dao* is not separable from the concrete and the visible at work, which is called the *qi* (utensil) in the *Dazhuan* of the *Yijing*, but it does not interfere with the *functioning* of things within shape. Thus when the *Dazhuan* says: 'What is above shape is called the *dao*, what is within shape is called the *qi*,' it does not mean that *dao* and *qi* are separated as two distinct entities. It means that the same entity is *dao* when seen as above shape, and is *qi* when seen as within shape.[3]

Dao is spoken of as the *ti* of things and *qi* is spoken of as the *yong* (functioning) of things. It may be said that, as the ontological entity, the *dao* explains both the origin of things, and the being and becoming of things. But as the cosmological entity, the *dao* is the origin of things and also constitutes the very being and becoming of things as a whole. This is how the *dao* is conceived as the *ti* of things when things are considered as a whole. For as the *ti* of things, the *dao* can be holistically and integratively conceived or explained when thought of in terms of and in reference to things. It *is* the whole world and it is what *makes* the whole world possible.

It is in this sense that the *dao* is radically different from *being* in the Western metaphysical tradition especially as represented by Parmenides. Whereas *being* separates itself absolutely from the changing phenomenon of nature, the *dao* never leaves things behind or aside but always embraces them in change. Whereas *being* denies reality to things in change and therefore condemns becoming to unreality, the *dao* imparts both being and becoming to things and as such becomes the essence of both being and becoming, thus making being and becoming equivalent. Whereas *being* transcends the world by being self-identical, the *dao* immerses itself in the world by producing difference and variety. Whereas *being* is the object of pure thinking, the *dao* is the effect of a process of profound experiencing, including feeling and perception. Thus *being* becomes the exclusive subject of ontology by excluding cosmology, whereas the *dao* bridges the gap between ontology and cosmology by including both.

The integration of being and becoming, the inclusion of cosmology and ontology, and the comprehension of both thinking and feeling are based on the comprehensive experience of things in the universe as a whole. This experience is one of unity in variety and variety in unity, and is specifically one of polarity of opposition and complementarity, unity of oneness and difference at the same time. This experience of polarity, however, should be understood primarily as a direct experience of change and transformation. In change and transformation, that which is becomes that which is not, and that which is not becomes that which is, as formulated in the Platonic language of being. As the Parmenidean analysis makes out, there is a contradiction of being and nonbeing in becoming, hence one must conclude that there is no becoming. But contrary to the Parmenidean analysis, the *Yijing* analysis concludes that, as there is both being and nonbeing in becoming, becoming must be a being which contains being and nonbeing as opposite and complementary parts of the whole. Hence experience of change and transformation leads to an understanding and experience of totality of inclusive being, as against the Parmenidean identity of exclusive being.

What is experienced in individual change is difference. Change is possible only when difference is possible. Any difference is opposite to the original identity of a thing, but as a thing is experienced as a whole in time and space (as time and space are also experienced as inseparable parts of the whole reality), so the difference which is opposite to the original identity is an inseparable complement to the original identity. Hence, the whole of a thing is always an integration of opposite and complementary entities or processes, whereby the individuality of a thing becomes realized. It is with regard to this inner logic of the individualized integration of identity and difference, opposites and complements, that the *Yijing* philosophy comes to the symbolic articulation of the polarities of *yin* and *yang*.

Yin and *yang*, comprising a whole class of complementary opposites or opposite complements, such as shade and light, rest and motion, softness and firmness, dividedness and unbrokenness, female and male, are symbolic of universal change and transformation as exemplified in the rotation of day and night, sun and moon, heaven and earth, water and fire. *Yin* is always the phase of difference, and *yang* always the phase of identity in the process of change (*yin*). Therefore *yin* represents the potentiality changing into the actual and *yang* the actuality changing into potentiality. Hence it is said in the *Dazhuan* of the *Yijing* that one *yin* and one *yang* in alteration is called the *dao*. This means that the *dao* is a process of change comprised of *yin* and *yang* and the totality of reality, or anything comprised of *yin* and *yang* is a process of change. From this it is easy to see that the alternation of *yin* and *yang* in unity is a creative process of differentiation. Hence the *dao* can be seen as a creative source of the world of differences of things.

We can also analyse and see all interrelationships among things in terms of opposites and complements. This is because any single relationship is founded on some difference which implies potential for change and which is capable of creating actual change. As change consists in either differentiating between or unifying opposites and complements, so a relationship which is presupposed by difference is accomplished by change and can lead to a change of related things. On the other hand, with change as a universal feature of reality, relationships also become an inevitable feature of reality.

Now we can formulate in the following our cosmo-ontological analysis of a cosmo-ontological experience in Chinese metaphysical thinking as derived from and based on the cosmological analysis of the cosmological phase.

Cosmo-ontological Analysis of the Cosmo-ontological Experience

(a) All changes reveal that they come from one single source and origin of reality which is not separable from all changes (the principle of the cosmo-ontological unity of things in change).

(b) The power of integrating and comprehending all things demonstrates itself in the differentiation of the manifold nature of things (the principle of the onto-cosmological unity of things).

(c) All differences come from changes which in turn come from the integration and unity of polarities of complementing opposites (the principle of the relative unities of polarities).

It is clear that the ontogenesis of things and their unities in terms of polaristic changes and relationships is important for the onto-cosmological and cosmo-ontological understanding of the world. Hence it is important for us to present the polaristic analysis of polaristic differences as an integral part of the metaphysical thinking in the *Yijing* tradition.

The Dipolaristic Analysis of Dipolaristic Experience

(a) All unities of things are to be found in unities of polarities of *yin* and *yang* in different relationships (the principle of reality as *yinyang* polarity).

(b) Unity gives rise to change in terms of *yin/yang* polarities and hence forms a dynamic whole with the *yin/yang* process (the principle of creativity as a *yin/yang* polarization).

(c) There is an ultimate reality of unities in all *yin/yang* reality and processes in an open hierarchy which can be said to give rise to all polarities (the principle of ultimate unity).

The existential experience of man places man in a position in the world in which he feels both stability and unstability, freedom and bondage, confidence and uncertainty. He is able to feel stability, freedom, and confidence because he can identify himself in a network of relationships with other people and things which are essential for his growth, satisfaction, and self-fulfilment. He can feel instability, bondage, and uncertainty because all relationships need appropriate strengthening, development, and substantiation, for which appropriate knowledge and action are required. Hence, if one can acquire appropriate knowledge and can also correctly act, one will be able to avoid the negative impact of instability, bondage, and uncertainty of a relationship.

It is in self-reflection and historical reflection that one can develop one's *virtue* for meeting the demands of stability, freedom, and confidence. Hence, cultivation of one's virtue, which is one's nature for self-discipline and self-restraint, becomes a crucial existential requirement for the well-being both of oneself and of all those related to one. Hence this existential prerequisite can be said to be the basis for ethical and axiological experience which leads to the establishment of firm ethical norms governing the human relationships of individuals. To be ethical is to be able to satisfy the needs of a relationship in establishing stability, harmony and well-being between oneself and others. To be ethical is also to be able to fulfil a demand on oneself toward freedom and effective participation society. To be ethical is to be able to follow certain principles in action for enriching the existential being of an individual together with other individuals in society. Existential needs also dictate the existence of degrees and grades of relationships. Hence ethical relationships such as the five basic relationships in Confucian ethics are developed.

Not only ethical values are found in, and founded on, the existential experience of man. Axiological values in general such as sincerity, vitality, and beauty, are all sometimes parts of the human existential experience in the form of potential values to be realized when men come to relate to the world in goal-directed activities. To be axiological is to see value in human effort towards fulfilling the goals of life, and to be able to participate in an open process of change and transformation of reality, as well as of the change and transformation of oneself. To be axiological is to bring what is potential in an individual entity into actuality for the development of the world. In this sense value and existence are inseparable. 'Value' is simply a term for the purpose-fulfilling power inherent in the order and nature of things. There cannot be existence without value nor value without the actuality of existence.

To separate fact from value, what is from what ought to be, is a matter of conceptual abstraction. In reality no separation of the two is possible. Therefore, the existential experience of life is in essence an axiological experience of life. Even anxiety and other negative emotions and feelings presuppose *values* for their relevance and significance. Needless to say, the existential experience of value is also inseparable from the practical essence of life for the individual, for it is through practicality and its union with understanding that one can realize value as value, and that value can become powerful because of its being rooted in the same source as existence.

Similarly, we may also say that man's cosmological experience together with an ultimate understanding of onto-cosmology and cosmo-ontology are relevant for defining and elaborating the existential experience of man. It is with regard to the cosmological knowledge of the world that values rooted in human existence can become better understood and that a cosmological understanding of the world will impart *value*, significance, and relevance to the existence of man. This no doubt provides a foundation for the value experience of existence as well as existential experience of value in human life. In the light of this, we can represent the development of the existential experience of man in an existential analysis of ontological value.

The Ethical/Axiological Analysis of the Ethical/Axiological Experience

(a) Human beings are related in an existential bond of natural feelings, and experience the self-fulfilling relationships of obligation and freedom (the principle of ethical ordering).

(b) Man can fulfil his experience of the cultivation of one's nature toward fulfilment of oneself and of others in society (the principle of ethical fulfilment).

(c) Value is the potential of existence for advancing existence in terms of harmonious relationships and creative change, whereas existence is the actuality of both obligation and freedom for a person to form harmonious relationships and creative changes (the principle of universal value).

We may now summarize the above analyses of the Chinese metaphysical thinking in the *Yijing* as follows. Firstly, we must note the basic mutual supportive relationship between the existential meaning and the cosmological meaning, and between existential meaning and practical meaning. This means that the existential meaning of the metaphysical thinking is derived from the existential situation of man and is projected into the cosmological meaning of the world as well as into the practical meaning of possible action.

$$existence\begin{cases} \rightarrow cosmos \\ \quad \downarrow \uparrow \\ \rightarrow action \end{cases}$$

This imparts a close relationship between the cosmos and the actions of man so that the cosmological can always carry a practical meaning for action and the action of man can have a cosmological significance. We may speak of the interpretation-supportive trinity of human existence, cosmos, and human action which are three dimensions of the same reality experienced as change and transformation.

Secondly, we have also noted the extended implication and actual growth of epistemology (knowledge) from practical action, of onto-cosmology/cosmo-ontology (being of becoming/becoming of Being) from cosmological observation (experience), and of ethics/axiology (good or right values) from the existential situation of man. Therefore, there rests a mutual interpretative (or interpretation-supportive) relationship between the two in each case. The practical can shed light on the theoretical, the cosmological on the cosmo-ontological or onto-cosmological, and the existential on the ethical/axiological. Thus we can speak of a mutuality of interpretation when the symbolism is applied to an individual situation.

Thirdly, we can see that the basic language of heaven, earth, and man (referring to the basic intimate relations of man to the visible material world, and to the invisible source of being, that is, to the near environment and to the large environment) can apply to the three-phase analysis of the symbolism of the *Yijing*. It is apparent that the existential represents the near environment of the earth; the cosmological represents the large environment of Heaven, and the practical represents man with his interests of life. Hence the interpretation-supportive trinity of human existence, cosmos, and practical action is simply that of earth, heaven, and man, and all the natural meanings associated with heaven, earth, and man can be imparted to the framework of human existence, cosmos, and practical action.

Fourthly, since the practical gives rise to the theoretical and knowledge, knowledge in turn can give rise to practical action in light of the cosmological and the existential experience of man. This is referred to as the unity of knowledge and practice in

Chinese philosophy. Then, with regard to the relationship between cosmology and cosmo-ontology, we can speak of the unity of substance and function. Similarly, with regard to the existential and the ethical/axiological, we note that the existential does not only simply refer to the existence of one's self, but the existence of one's self in the whole world of human relationships and hence the existence of the whole world of other persons. It does not only refer to things in actuality but also to things to be brought out in the future as objects of the aspirations of man, that is, as the ideal realization of values and life-goals. The latter in turn gives a meaning to the things in the present. Hence we can speak of reciprocal unity of fact (existence) and value, actuality and ideality.

Fifthly, in light of both the trinity of heaven, earth, and man, and the unities of knowledge/action, substance/function, and fact/value, we have thus an integrative unity of the trinity of unities. *This is the most enriched reality which Chinese metaphysical thinking has brought out and which embodies an infinite possibility of understanding and interpretation as well as an inexhaustible source of meaning and value.*

Now we can represent this unity of thinking of unities as follows:

polaristic unity	earth: existential	⟷	ethical/axiological: unity of knowledge and action
	heaven: cosmological	⟷	onto-cosmological/ cosmo-ontological: unity of *ti* and *yong*
	man: practical	⟷	epistemological/ doxalogical unity of fact and value

The Philosophy of the *Yijing* as Primordial Metaphysical Thinking

In what precedes, we have made a detailed analysis of all phases or dimensions in metaphysical thinking as presupposed and virtually present in the texts of the *Yijing* as well as in the practice of *Yijing* divination. *Yijing* divination uses the symbolism of the *Yijing* as a cosmic map for identifying the symbol representing the position or situation of an inquirer and making an interpretation or reading of the symbol representing the position/situation in light of the whole symbolic map. Without such a symbolic system functioning as a cosmic map, no divination is possible.[4] However, the development of such a symbolism cannot be initiated without thorough-going reflection on, and observation of, nature in terms of its patterned changes and transformations, nor can such a symbolism be accomplished without an understanding of the universe in the form of systematic organization.

Furthermore, if the symbolism is to be given a meaning, such a meaning has to reflect a co-ordination of meanings in a functional system applicable to reality as whole, and at the same time to present relevance to the actuality of a given situation. Thus, a generative system of meanings together with an interpretative mind informed of the cosmological is required for the interpretation of individual events, whether historical or social, for both understanding the symbolism and for understanding a given situation. In other words, the interpretative mind must interpret the whole symbolism for a single symbol, by which I mean it must identify the primordial meaning of the symbolism for the individual symbol in the light of an historical situation or an actual situation, as well as interpret the individual symbol for a historical situation or an actual situation in the light of the whole symbolism and its primordial meaning. The interpretation must be always bi-directional, and consists of the bi-directional processes in the following:

nature	the whole system of symbolism	situation
history		event
social reality	individual symbol	action

In the foregoing, I have explored the six dimensions of meaning as developed in the text and symbolism of the *Yijing*. The articulation of these dimensions of meaning may be a gradual process, but it is important to recognize that without a core meaning in the symbolism no such development would be possible. The core meaning is the primordial meaning contained in the core symbolism of the *Yijing* which is derived from the experience of existence by reflection and observation and also from our experience of nature as a cosmological process. As we also experience practical urgency in knowing the world and ourselves, we have also to recognize *practicality* as a central part of the core meaning of the primordial symbols of the *Yijing*. In this sense the core meaning of the primary symbols can be said to consist of the three original dimensions of meaning in terms of the existential, cosmological, and practical experiences of man. This rich ambiguity of meaning is creative, for it will lead to the development of the *Yijing* philosophy as a philosophy directly relevant and applicable to life and change.

Apart from interpreting the primordial symbols of the *Yijing* in terms of its core meanings of the existential/cosmological/practical experience, we may also extend the core meaning to domains of epistemology, cosmo-ontology, and axiology. Hence a total of six dimensions of meaning can be attributed to the primordial symbols of the *Yijing*: they need not be considered only as a matter of attribution, but rather as a matter of manifestation. For these meanings are inherent in the symbols in so far as the symbols form a generative base for capturing the primary meanings. When the primordial symbols generate secondary symbols, these secondary symbols inherit the core meanings of the primordial symbols and also generate new meanings in reference to new details of actualities. In the following we may list the three dimensions of meaning pertaining to the primordial symbols of the *Yijing*.

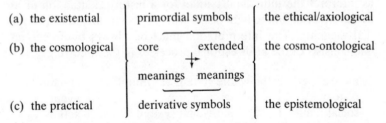

(a) the existential	primordial symbols	the ethical/axiological
(b) the cosmological	core extended	the cosmo-ontological
	meanings meanings	
(c) the practical	derivative symbols	the epistemological

The explicit primary symbols of the *Yijing* metaphysical thinking are the '——' for *yang*, and the '— —' for *yin*. There is no explicit symbol for the unity and integration of the two polarities of *yang* and *yin*, but this does not mean that there is no unity and integration of *yang* and *yin*. This unity and integration is clearly assumed and present in the whole symbolism of the *Yijing*, for not only in the original *Zhouyi* symbolism every two hexagrams (six-line diagrams formed from the *yang* and *yin*) form a unity of opposite complementarities, but the whole group of hexagrams also forms a unity of unities. It is on this basis that the Confucian commentaries (*Dazhuan, Duanzhuan, Xugua*) of the third century BC are able to explain the inner coherence of meaning and structure of the symbolism as a whole.

One may even see that in the original decisions and judgements attached to each hexagram (*gua*) and to each line (*yao*), a unity of opposite complementarities is followed as a principle of interpretation. This principle of unity of complementary opposites is of course derived from the unity of the primary symbols '——' and '— —' and is thus exemplified in pairs of trigrams and hexagrams as well as in the formulation of the whole system of trigrams and hexagrams. For example, we have in the following the diagram of the ontogenetic (the so-called 'prior-heaven') ordering of the trigrams and the diagram of cosmogenetic (the so-called 'posterior-heaven') ordering of the trigrams[5]:

Diagram A

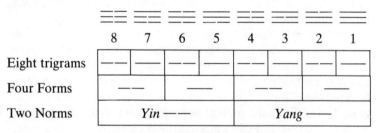

	8	7	6	5	4	3	2	1

Eight trigrams								
Four Forms								
Two Norms	*Yin* — —				*Yang* ——			

The Great Ultimate

Diagram B

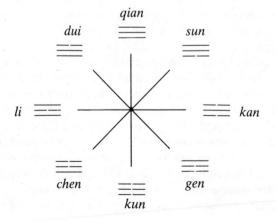

The Song *Yijing* philosopher Shao Yong constructed Diagram A to illustrate the *Dazhuan* cosmological statement: the *dao* has the *taiqi* (the great ultimate); this gives birth to two norms: two norms give birth to four forms; four forms give birth to eight trigrams. The *taiji* referred to in the *Dazhuan* is an explicit name for the unity of *yin* and *yang*. This unity is the creative source from which generate all the norms, forms, trigrams, and hexagrams, which are combinings and interactions of the primary symbols *yin* and *yang*. Thus, not only the unity of complementary opportunity is explicitly named and indicated in the diagrams, the creative and generative function of the unity is also clearly exhibited in a sequence of upward differentiation. Another important point in this diagram is that the primary symbols are always preserved in the creative process of differentiation and in the constitution of trigrams and hexagrams, and thus always play a significant role in determining the nature of the trigrams and hexagrams, giving them unique meanings.

Diagram B is based on the Confucian commentary the *Shuogua* which describes the ordering of the symbols in the *Zhouyi* as follows: 'Heaven and earth are mutually positioned, the mountain and lake exchange their vital forces; the thunder and wind mutually intertwine; water and fire are interacting in opposition.' Diagram B illustrates the mutual opposition and complementarity of all the trigrams and the unity of these opposite complementary unities as a whole, following the order of generation of the trigrams in Diagram A.[6] In Diagram B, the *taiji* was not even named. But the presence of *taiji* as the unity of complementary opposites which generates all differences and yet always preserves the unity is obvious from the diagram. *Taiji* is both the total system of the well-ordered trigrams as well as that which makes this system possible.

When we speak of the primary symbols of *yin* and *yang* in the above, we have already introduced a primary core meaning for the symbols '——'/'——', and their names *yin* and *yang*. It can be noted that '——' and '——' do not exist by themselves in the symbolism of *Zhouyi*. The *Zhouyi* symbolism presents itself as a system of 64 hexagrams which are ready to be used for practical divination. But this practical divination is premised on the fact that the world is a complex of complicated situations which requires a complex representation to the level of 64 hexagrams. Hence the hexagram system is practically, cosmologically, and existentially orientated. Furthermore, it is made relative to human needs and the experiences of human existence so that the hexagram representation makes totalistic and individualistic sense. In this light, the primary unity of the primary constituent symbols '——'/'——' is equivalent to the unity of the hexagrams ' ☷ ' and ' ☰ ', and by the same token, the unity of the trigram ' ☷ ' and ' ☰ '. Hence whatever meaning accrues to one unity applies to the other.

For the present purpose of illustrating the *Yijing* metaphysical thinking as the originating form of Chinese philosophy and Chinese metaphysics, we shall concentrate on explaining the primary unity of the polarities of *yin* and *yang* as the founding experience of existence, life, and reality in Chinese philosophy. The most important characteristic of this way of thinking is that nothing in the experience of reality is left out in understanding reality. In fact, the experience is that of total reality and reality is that of total experience. The basic motif in Chinese metaphysical thinking is to preserve and present this totality of experience of reality and this reality of total experience in a comprehensive system of symbols, language, and undertaking.

The demarcation line in this way of metaphysical thinking is the integration of change and transformation and unchanging order and permanence, and hence the integration of difference and identity, and the integration of cosmic generation and *ontic* being. In short, it is the integration of becoming and being without giving up either becoming or being. It is in this sense that I have labelled the Chinese way of metaphysical thinking as *seeking the way*, in contrast with the Western way of metaphysical thinking as the *quest for being* which amounts to the elimination of becoming from being from the Chinese metaphysical point of view. The *Yijing* symbolic way of thinking precisely inaugurated Chinese metaphysical thinking as seeking the way, and has succeeded in making the integration of being and becoming possible.

The meanings of the primary symbols *yin* and *yang* are derived from the existential situation of man in understanding and relating to the world. The *yin* is the dark, shady side of the hill, whereas the *yang* is the bright and lighted side of the hill. This experience of shade and light is one of nature, but is also one of relevance for life-survival and death. For light can signify the conditions of growth, activity, and life; shade can signify the conditions of decline, rest, and lack of life or cessation of life. But again the existential experience of light and shade need not be precisely defined or described, for it contains a rich ambiguity which is not absolutely positive nor absolutely negative, not necessarily good nor necessarily bad, where good and bad must also be seen as existentially *defined* in terms conducive to a continuing and fulfilling life, and conducive to bringing detriment to a continuing and fulfilling life. For light can be too harsh, and shade can be comforting when rest is needed in the existential process of human living. In other words, neither is light absolutely good nor is shade absolutely bad. The existential experience of man is that of his life as a process with its inner needs and its inner goals. Since light and shade are both needed for life, it is united in life as a process of completing one's life goals.

On the other hand, the phenomenological observation of light and shade, not only as the alternation of day and night but as a juxtaposition of sunshine and tree shade, enables us to see light and shade, *yin* and *yang* as forming a unity of complementary opposites and as such giving rise to growth and differentiation. Hence the existential meaning is mixed with the cosmological meaning and practical meaning in the phenomenological analysis of the experience of *yin* and *yang*.

The existential meaning of *yin* and *yang* is not only confined to light and shade (life and lack of life). It is linked and merged with other existential human experiences of world and self in connection with them: *yang* is linked to motion (*dong*) and firmness (*gang*), whereas *yin* is linked to rest (*jing*) and softness (*rou*). If this linking is not to be existentially understood in the light of a phenomenological description of human feelings and perceptions (or experience), how is it to be understood? *Light* is experienced as motion, and shade is experienced as *rest*, just as motion can be explained as causing light (and heat) and rest can be explained as causing darkness. This seems to be true of our observation of sunrise and sunset. Similarly, light is *firm* in the sense of penetrating and progressive advance, whereas shade is *soft* in the sense of receiving and recessive absorption; and conversely. All these indicate that *yin* and *yang* are not simply qualities independent of a context of human experience nor are they external to the human experience of the world. The unity of *yin* and *yang* represents a core of rich meanings which is the source for all other meanings in the formation of Chinese metaphysics.

The unity of *yin* and *yang* hence implies unity of light and shade, unity of motion and rest, and unity of firmness and softness. From this fundamental unity the unity of difference and identity and the unity of being and becoming will arise. First of all, we can see this extension of unity in terms of the analysis of levels of meaning. Second, we can see how it is actually expressed in the philosophy of the *Yijing* as formulated explicitly in its Confucian commentaries. As cosmological principles, the *yin* and *yang* are simply principles of heaven and earth. The heaven principle not only brings a real universe into being, it represents the actual framework of the real universe. It is both the creating power and the substantiating power. The earth on the other hand is the complementary substance for such creativity, for it is due to the earth that things become abundant and well nourished. Hence, in the *Dazhuan* it is said that the principle of heaven (called the *qian*) is that which produces life as a great event (*dasheng*), and that the principle of earth (called the *kun*) is that which produces life in its comprehensive scope (*guangsheng*). The cosmological meaning of the principles of heaven and earth naturally give rise to cosmo-ontological meanings. Thus we have the principle of heaven and earth conceived as the alternation of *yin* and *yang*, which is called the *dao* and also *taiji*. The *dao* or *taiji* is the creative unity of heaven and earth which integrates being and becoming, difference and identity. Overleaf we list the various qualities of complementary opposites which are integrated by *taiji* or *dao* in the form of various alternations of *yin* and *yang* or co-ordinations of heaven and earth.

This juxtaposition of *yin*/*yang* qualities shows that the polarities of *yin* and *yang* can be realized in an unlimited number of ways. It may be that all the categories of metaphysical thinking regarding reality are thus derived. For example, motion and rest, beginning and completion, source (*ben*) and ending (*mo*) are clearly formulated as qualities of the *taiji*. Oneness and multitude are indirectly suggested, for the principles of heaven and earth, *qian* and *kun* interact to give rise to all things characterized by enlarging life and broadening life, whereas *qian* and *kun* form a unity of oneness characterized by creativity of creativity (*shengsheng*). This suggests that one has to see metaphysical categories emerge from the cosmo-ontological productiveness of the *qian* and *kun*, as well as from their relating to the ultimate oneness as the great beginning (*dashi*) and as the *substance* (*ti*). Categories are normally conceived either horizontally or vertically. The *dong*/*jing* exemplifies horizontal categories, whereas 'one'/'many' exemplifies vertical

The *taiji* (the *dao*) = *ti*

yin (earth) moon	*yang* (heaven) sun
1. rest (*jing*)	movement (*dong*)
2. softness (*rou*)	firmness (*gang*)
3. within form (*qi*)	above form (*dao*)
4. femininity (*kun*)	masculinity (*qian*)
5. completion (*zheng*)	beginning (*shi*)
6. simplicity (jian)	easiness (*yi*)
7. progression (*jin*)	regression (*tui*)
8. darkness (*yu*)	brightness (*ming*)
9. ghosts (dissemination *gui*)	spirits (stretching *sheng*)
10. goodness (*shan*)	nature (*xing*)
11. wisdom (*zhi*)	benevolence (*ren*)
12. hiddenness (*cang*)	disclosure (*xian*)
13. following/closing the door (*bi*)	forming/opening the door (*xi*)
14. enlarging life (*dasheng*)	broadening life (*guangsheng*)

Change and transformation (*biandong*)
Creativity of creativity (*shengsheng*)
Supreme Power (*jide*)

categories. On the other hand, there could be metaphysical categories which can be both horizontally and vertically conceived, such as change (*bian*) and constancy or permanence (*chang*). One can see change as a source of many and constancy as a basis for oneness, but one can also see change as a source of motion and constancy as a basis of rest. Thus change and constancy have a double orientation.

We must be careful to distinguish a relative cosmological categorical use of change from an absolute onto-cosmological or cosmo-ontological use of change. In the former sense, change is relatively defined with regard to constancy; in the latter sense it is absolutely defined with regard to the source of both change and constancy. In this latter sense both the terms 'change' (*yi*) and 'transformation' (*bian*) are used. Thus, the *Dazhuan* speaks of change as 'having no substance' and the spirit as 'having no direction'. But change may generate all things without limit and hindrance. 'No substance' means 'no physical focus', but not 'no centrality'. In this sense change is compared to the spirit which has no set direction, but exists as pure freedom and pure creativity. The same can be said of change as the primordial being which is at the same time primordial becoming.

This unity of being and becoming is brought out also in the concept of change as *bian* and *dong* (transformation and development). *Bian* is said to be 'one closing and one opening', while *dong* is said to be 'infinite coming and going'. Notice that these existentially and practically formulated meanings and images of change carry subtle cosmological and onto-cosmological significances. This means simply that change (*bian*) is the nature of the *dao* which consists in the infinite productive transformations of things in the world. This is how reality is ultimately conceived: the infinite creative becoming in the being of the totality of things and the oneness of the great ultimate as the primordial source where being and becoming cannot be really separated. *Biandong* can be regarded as another term for *shengsheng*, the 'creativity of creativity' in change. Human beings can apply and follow the same nature of *biandong* for creating and developing society, civilization, and humanity. Hence it is said that 'to transform and shape is the *bian*, to promote and practice is called the *dong*.'[7]

Thus, we can see how the *Yijing* symbolism leads to a formulation of metaphysics from its well-formulated symbolic system of dynamic relationships. This means that the *Yijing* formulates a metaphysical system rooted in the existential/cosmological/practical experiences of man which can be extended into ethical/axiological/onto-cosmological/cosmo-ontological/epistemological *concepts* and categories. Here, we do not intend to bring out the full impact of the change-oriented metaphysics of the *Yijing*. We merely wish to indicate how this metaphysics presents a totally different orientation in metaphysical thinking from that of Western metaphysics: the seeking of the way, in contrast with the quest for being.

It is clear that the seeking of the way consists in conceiving reality as a unity of polarities engaged in creative interaction and an infinite process of transformation which is regarded as intrinsically valuable and self-fulfilling.

Introduction of Non-being (*wu*) in Metaphysical Thinking in Daoism

In the history of Chinese philosophy the *Yijing* tradition exists as the primordial orientating system of thinking providing both form and substance, direction and momentum for later cosmology and ontology (or, strictly speaking, cosmo-ontology), and other metaphysical ways of thinking. In so far as divination is part of the *Yijing* tradition, what is revealed in the symbolism of divination makes possible not only divination but also the explicit philosophy of the *Yijing*, as expounded in Confucian commentaries, and the development of Daoist metaphysics. Philosophically speaking, it seems quite natural that the polaristic principle in the *Yijing* leads to a polaristic metaphysics which should also culminate in the metaphysics of the *taiji* as the dynamic source of all things. But still we can see the Daoist philosophy of Laozi (Lao Tzu) and Zhuangzi (Chuang Tzu) as an innovative and yet continuous development from the *Yijing*. To see that, we have to understand implicit metaphysical thinking (as explained above) as the framework and base for the development of the Daoist philosophy of the *dao*. This framework is where the Daoist philosophy of *dao* has its continuity with the *Yijing*. But this framework also provides a basis for innovation and insight into reality which leads to the Daoist philosophy of the *dao*. This innovation and insight consist in introducing the notion of void or non-being (*wu*) into metaphysical thinking on reality and life. In the light of this innovation and insight, the *Yijing* philosophy of *dao* as *taiji* becomes the Daoist philosophy of *dao* and *wu*. Hence the metaphysical thinking initiated or presupposed by the *Yijing* (which is polaristic and yet integratively single-source oriented) developed into the metaphysical thinking of the *Laozi* which embraces polarities and yet transcends them in reformulating the concept of ultimate source.

If we can refer to the *Yijing* metaphysics as being- and becoming-oriented, we can refer to Laozi metaphysics as non-being- and being-oriented. In the *Yijing* metaphysics it is the *dao* which integrates being and becoming, and the *dao* is conceived or explained as the *taiji*, whereas in Daoist metaphysics it is also the *dao* which integrates non-being and becoming, but the *dao* is conceived and explained as non-being (*wu*). In fact when we speak of Daoist metaphysics as non-being- and becoming-oriented, the notion of non-being is introduced, in the first place as an innovation, as an essential *factor* in describing reality as a whole.

In order to understand the Daoist metaphysics of *wu* as both a continuity with and an innovation upon *Yijing* metaphysics, we may show how the Daoist metaphysics of Laozi can be explained as being inspired by the polaristic principle of the *Yijing* symbolic system and how the polaristic principle generates the notion of *wu*.

We have seen how the polaristic principle of the *Yijing* symbolism gives rise in a natural way to the explicit-metaphysical thinking of *yin/yang* and the *taiji* as formulated in the Confucian commentaries on the *Yijing*. Now, we can also see how in a natural way the polaristic principle gives rise to the Daoist philosophy of *wu*. Thus, we may say that the symbolistic system of the *Yijing* has given rise to two systems of metaphysical thinking in Chinese philosophy, the Confucian *Yizhuan* metaphysics, and the Daoist Laozi metaphysics.

It is important, however, to point out that the *Yijing* outlook on the world and man, together with its divinatory practice, was the oldest and the principal pre-philosophy and proto-philosophy in the Chinese history of philosophy. But there is no mention in the *Yijing* tradition of *wu* or the idea of *wu*. The polaristic principle certainly made no reference to *wu*. It is the totality of things together with the being and becoming of things that is explicitly assumed.

Among all the 64 hexagrams there is, for example, the hexagram called *dayou* which can be rendered as 'great having' or 'great being'. *Dayou* indicates the shining of the sun in the sky and hence suggests that great being, and thus being, is *yang* in essence by virtue of 'heaven' (as the principle of creative power) and 'fire' (as the principle of light and brightness). Hence when the *Yizhuan* comes to formulate explicitly the metaphysical thinking in the *Yijing*, it becomes basically a philosophy of *you* or `dayou` (great being). The concept of the *dao* and that of the *taiji* (being) suggest the creative flow of being and the creative beginning of being. Thus when we speak of the *Yizhuan* metaphysics of the *dao*, it is the *dao* in the sense of abundance of being that is referred to as the beginning and source of being, and it is the *dao* in the sense of continuous activity that is referred to as the process of change and transformation.[9] Here we identify *you* as 'having' with *you* as 'being'. Actually, *you* is 'having' without anyone or anything 'having' or being had. 'Having', thus described, is a state of self-sufficiency of 'being'. Perhaps a better description for *you* is 'three-beingness' or 'there-is-ness'. The opposite of *you* is *wu*, or *bu-you* (not-having)[10], which is the absence of *you*, and is translated as 'non-being', or 'emptiness', or 'void'.

It is significant to note that *you* as 'having' may be said to assume an implicit subject which has a 'being'; the implicit subject of 'having' should and can not be specified in any manner: it is an implicit, non-specificable 'being' or reality. Thus, *wu* as not-having is not absolute nothingness but a reality that is not to be specified in any manner. Hence we must carefully distinguish *wu* from *kong* (nothingness) in the Buddhistic tradition. This means that *Yizhuan* metaphysics is a natural unfolding of the polaristic principle and implicit metaphysics of *you* or *dayou* in the symbolic system of the *Yijing*. It is in this sense that Confucians can be said to continue in the *Yizhuan* the main tradition of metaphysical thinking from the antiquity represented by the *Yijing*.[11]

It is in the light of this Confucian *Yizhuan* metaphysics that we say that the Daoist metaphysics of the *dao* is an innovation in comparison with the Confucian metaphysics of the *dao* and thus an innovative divergence from the more articulate mainstream metaphysics expressed in the *Yizhuan*. But we may also say that it is from the *Yijing* symbolic system that the two types of metaphysical thinking emerge, one of which articulates the inherent metaphysics in terms of being (having), with the other innovating on the basis of the inherent metaphysics.

The question now is how the innovation of the Daoist metaphysics of non-thinking (non-being-thinking) takes place, with the *Yijing* metaphysical thinking preserving its characteristic feature, and yet introducing the innovative notion of *wu* (non-being). First of all, the metaphysical implication of the polaristic principle of the *Yijing* is that once a category of reality is defined or understood, then an opposing and complementary one must be identified. In metaphysical terms, one polar concept would not be possible without a corresponding polar concept. Hence reality is seen as the process of interacting between polar entities leading to and reaching polar entities. This understanding of the polar entities and hence polar concepts is well understood in the *Daodejing*. That is why Laozi says:

> Being and Nonbeing mutually generate each other
> The difficult and the easy mutually accomplish each other
> The long and the short mutually shape each other
> The high and the low mutually lean on each other
> The tone and sound mutually harmonize each other
> The before and the after mutually sequence each other.[12]

What Laozi says here clearly explains both how things relate to each other in reality and how our language comes to be used. Language is polaristic because *reality* is polaristic. But sometimes we forget the polaristic characteristic of reality, and make absolutes out of terms such as long and short, before and after. We forget that there is no fixed quality, but only relationships between different things. It is important to respond to concrete things but not to abstract qualities; on the other hand, it may be important to respond to relationships of polarity rather than to concrete things. Among the six polarities quoted above, it is clear that except for one, all are good examples of empirical relativity, either spatial or temporal, either auditory or evaluational.

All of these examples of empirical relativity are taken from the common experience of man, but the first is open to both empirical and non-empirical interpretations. Being and non-being as *you* and *wu* could be related to a person's experiences of having or not having, hence the polarity can be empirically verified. If one is to have something, he will have to not have something and vice versa. The one leads to and depends on the other, and therefore they mutually generate each other. But Laozi apparently intends this as an non-empirical cosmological/ontological statement. There is being and there is also non-being, and vice versa. Being and non-being are opposite and yet complementary and as such not only produce each other, but produce everything else in their mutual generation—as we shall see.

Metaphysically speaking, it is clear that, given being, there must be non-being. Being is a common name in common use. It refers to being, the totality of things, and the generality of existence of things. Hence non-being arises as the negation of being. But here the negation of being is to be understood as opposing and complementing being. Therefore non-being (*wu*) is considered the force or reality-transcending being, which forms a unity and totality with being. Hence if being is sayable, this non-being cannot be said; if being is nameable, this non-being cannot be named, that is, it cannot be said in the same way as being is said, and it cannot be named in the same way that being or any part of being is named. Laozi calls this non-being the *dao*, and intends the *dao*, as so called, to be not sayable or nameable in the same way in which being and things are talked about and named. Thus he says:

> The *Dao*, when it is sayable, is not the constant *Dao*
> The name when it is nameable, is not the constant name.[13]

Since all things are parts of being, therefore non-being is not a part of being, but is something opposing and complementing being and must be non-sayable and non-nameable. As there is always non-being which polaristically transcends being, the *dao* which is this non-being must be always opposing and complementing being. It is in this sense that the *dao* as the polarity *against* being is the *constant* unsayable *dao* and the constant unnameable name.

Given the *dao* as the non-sayable, non-nameable non-being, that is, given the *dao* as the opposite and complement of being, how does the *dao* generate being and all things in being? To answer this question, one must make a distinction between the logical meaning of polaristic relation and the onto-cosmological or cosmo-ontological meaning of the polaristic relation. We come to know the non-being or the *dao* by way of transcending being, but once we come to see the non-being or the *dao*, then we can also come to see, by way of the principle of polarity as an onto-cosmological principle of generation, that the non-being *dao* generates *being* just as we come to see that being generates non-being.

We may distinguish the two subtle senses of generating: the onto-cosmological generation of being from non-being *dao* and the cosmo-ontological generation of non-being from being. Non-being as the ontological source and ground of everything brings about being. This is onto-cosmo-genesis. Being as the cosmological movement of everything naturally evidences and presents non-being as its ground. This is cosmo-onto-genesis. It is in this sense that Laozi is able to explore the source and ground meaning of non-being from which he produces the metaphysics of *wu*, and it is in this sense that Laozi is innovative. He sees *wu* as more primary than *you* because it is unrestricted and unlimited in space, time, power, and creativity, and because it can bring out the *actuality* of things in a unique way in which any being or being in general cannot. For it is to be noted that, logically or cosmo-ontologically, being can bring out non-being, which is not the actuality of things. Hence, polaristically it requires non-being *dao* to generate everything.

In this sense the polaristic non-being polarity against being becomes the integrative non-being *dao* which integrates, unifies, and generates both being and non-being in a polaristic context. This understanding of *wu* immediately resolves the apparent difficulty in Laozi's referral to mutual generation of *you* and *wu* on one occasion, and his referring to *wu* generating *you* on another occasion. It also explains why he says:

Being not nameable, it is the beginning of heaven and earth,
Being named, it is the mother of the ten thousand things.[14]

Being non-nameable is the constant *dao* spoken of earlier. It is
wu which gives rise to the framework of existence (heaven and
earth) by being that which generates being, and hence the beginning of heaven and earth as the framework of existence. But when
naming takes place among things, then differentiation and distinction ensue. It is not naming itself, but that which makes naming
possible, that is, the differentiation of the *dao* into finite things,
which is the initiator of the world of ten thousand things. The unnamed and the named are again opposite and complementary, but
the unnamed which is the constant *dao* non-being can be also said
to integrate both being (the named) and non-being (the unnamed
not-being), for the unity of being and non-being as opposites and
complements cannot have a name, that is, cannot be named, and
cannot be identified as a thing or as the totality of things which is
being (*you*).

Laozi's statement about *wuming* (the unnamed) and *youming*
(the named) reminds one of Zhou Dunyi's (Chou Tun-i's) well-
known propositions on the diagram of the Great Ultimate in Neo-
Confucian philosophy. Zhou says: 'The ultimateless (*wuji*) and
then the Great Ultimate.'[15] The ultimateness is like the unnamed
undifferentiated and unlimited, and being such transcends differentiation and limitation. It is non-being. The Great Ultimate,
on the other hand, is like the named, the starting point of differentiation and limitation, hence the limit itself which generates
all limited things, and hence the being which brings about all
beings. Though it is difficult to prove that Zhou Dunyi is inspired
by the *wuming/youming* statement in the *Daodejing*, the essential
similarity and resonance between Laozi's statement and Zhou
Dunyi's statement makes the influence of the former upon the latter obvious. The relation of the ultimateless to the great ultimate is
again one of opposition and complementarity, yet at the same time
that of one going beyond the other and thus one generating the
other. The ultimateless generates the great ultimate in an onto-
cosmological sense, whereas the great ultimate generates in the
cosmo-ontological sense, hence the dialectical force of the preposi-
tion *er* (and then) linking the word *wuji* and the *taiji*. The
relation between the ultimateless and the great ultimate as well as
that between the unnamed and the named can be expressed in the
following fashion:

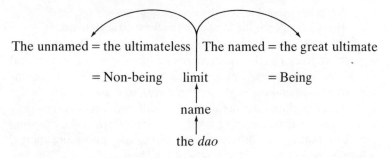

In this representation non-being and being are opposite and complementary, forming a unity on the one hand and effecting the process of creative generation on the other. The *dao* as both the unity and creative generative source of both non-being and being is a flow from the non-being into being and a return of the being into non-being, and in this sense the *dao* has achieved the ultimate metaphysical status in the Daoistic philosophy of Laozi. It is in this sense of the *dao* that the *dao* is the *wu par excellence*. Following this, the *dao*, in the sense of providing a unity for all things, being a source to originate from as well as a source to return to, is clearly developed in the *Daodejing*. We will briefly illuminate these three functions of the *dao* in the following paragraphs.

Dao *as the Unity or Oneness of All Things*

Laozi says: 'The *dao* produces one, one produces two; two produces three, and three produces the ten thousand things.'[16] 'One' is the original unity and the great ultimate for all things, for it is through this oneness that all things derive. But this cosmogenesis of all things must proceed from the unity of opposites and complements. Hence one produces two. But the two opposite and complementary forces generate a third, thus all individual things are the results of the interaction of the two opposite and complementary forces. The 'three' represents the creative fruits of the creative interaction of the two forces. Hence a whole world of things is produced from the process of unity (one)—complementary opposition (two)—creative fruits (three). The two is specifically identified as *yin* and *yang*. As all things come from the interaction of *yin* and *yang*, it is understandable for Laozi to say that all things contain the two as their essence. But in an individual thing, *yin* and *yang* harmonize and balance each other to give individuality to the individual thing.

Laozi's statement 'Each of the ten thousand things has *yin* in its back and holds *yang* in its front; and reaches harmony in the invisible vitality (*qi*) [of *yin* and *yang*]'[17] not only illustrates how individual things become individuated but how individual things have their *dao* in themselves in so far as the *dao* is the creative generative unity of *yin* and *yang* as two opposite complements. This of course leads Zhou Dunyi to say that every individual thing has its own great ultimate (*taiji*). This also illuminates Zheng Yi and Zhu Xi's statement that the principle is one and its manifestations (or distributions) are many (*li-yi-fen-shu*).[18] A deeper insight exhibited here is that the *dao* as the ultimate unity of all things is ever present in all things, and all things are interpenetrating with the *dao*. Therefore *Dao* is not an historical origin of things, but the ever present origin of things.

The unity or oneness of the *dao* which is the harmony of *yin* and *yang* is the principle of achieving full nature for any individual thing. Thus Laozi says:

Heaven acquires oneness so that it is pure.
Earth acquires oneness so that it is peaceful.
Spirit acquires oneness so that it is perceptive.
Valley acquires oneness so that it is full.
The ten thousand things acquire oneness so that they have life.
Kings acquire oneness so that they are leaders.[19]

Dao *as the Source of All Things*

Laozi makes it clear that the very unity or oneness of the *dao* is the creative source for generating all things in the world. In other words, the *dao* is the cosmological origin of things, yet it is not confined to being only an origin, for it is also the ever-present ground or background of things. However, two important things can be said about the *dao*'s being the cosmological origin of all things.

Firstly, *dao* is the production of things from no-things, hence *dao* is the *wu* we spoke of in connection with the transcending nature of the *dao*. The paradigm of unity of *yin* and *yang* leads to the paradigm of the unity of being and non-being, and leads to the conception of the *dao* as non-being creating being. It is in this sense of *wu* that Laozi says: 'All ten thousand things are born from being (*you*); and being is born from non-being (*wu*)'.[30] Non-being is here used as *wu* in the transcending and integrative sense, not in the opposite and complementary sense. But it is from the latter sense that the transcending and integrative sense arises. It is in this sense that *wu* becomes the *dao* and *dao* becomes the process of generating *you* from the *wu* and the everlasting source of such generation. Therefore, there is no inconsistency between the above statement in *Daodejing*, section 40, and the statement of mutual generation between *you* and *wu* which we find in the *Daodejing*, section 2.

The second thing to be pointed out is that even though *dao* is the ultimate source of all things and the ever-present support of all things, this does not mean that things have no individuality or independence of their own. On the contrary, Laozi stresses the principle and fact that they are all things on their *own*, without being dominated or *owned* by the *dao*, for it is in the nature of the *dao* that *dao* '. . . produces without possessing, doing without controlling, achieving without dominating.'[21] *Dao* in fact does nothing, and in doing nothing it produces all things, and all values of the *dao* for maintaining an orderly world become possible.

Dao *as the 'Home' of All Things*

Dao is not only the source of all things. It is also the 'home' for all things to return to. *Dao* in this sense explains not only the production and formation of things but the destruction and dissolution of things. To bring out this point of return to the *dao*, Laozi says: 'To move in the opposite direction (*fan*) is the movement of the *dao*.'[22] 'To move in the opposite direction' (*fan*) is to return to the origin, for if generation of a thing exhibits one direction of moving, then the dissolution of a thing must be the opposite direction, which is the return to the source of generation. In this sense Laozi clearly conceives death as both natural and spontaneous, a point which Zhuangzi elaborates. The return to the source which is the *dao* is a return to *wu*, where there is no form or formation of anything. Hence the view that *dao* as *wu* is the home of all things also illustrates the *dao* as the origin of all things where all things come from non-being into being. There is a level where Laozi exhorts man to hold to the principle of the *dao* in order not to overspend life before its time. Man should preserve life and reduce his desires in order to maintain his *being* and, therefore, his well-being in following the natural course of the *dao*.²³ On this level Laozi speaks of the '. . . return to the ultimateless (*wuji*)' or the '. . . return to the simplicity (*bu*)'. He says:

To become the lowly part of a carriage, one will not deviate from the constant virtue [which is the *dao*]. Then one will return to the ultimateless.

To become the valley of the world, one will hold the constant virtue in self-sufficiency, and then one will return to simplicity.²⁴

The constant virtue is the principle of the *dao* one cultivates in one's person and mind according to which one will follow the *dao* in order to achieve one's natural well-being and natural power as a leader. It is to be noted that the term *wuji* appears here for the first time, and it may not yet have the meaning of the cosmo-ontogenerative source which Zhou Dunyi introduces in his philosophy. But the analysis above of the unnamed and the named provides indisputable evidence of the influence of the *Daodejing* on Zhou Dunyi. *Wuji* in Laozi indicates the origin where no limitation or differentiation of being is initiated.

The essence of the Daoist metaphysics of *dao* and *wu* is in a sense fully displayed in the *Daodejing* of Laozi. But there are many subtle points to be worked out in reference to the transformation of things in the *dao*, and in reference to the application of the metaphysics of the *dao* to individual life. Although Laozi has much to say in favour of the embodiment of the *dao* and *wu* in one's life to achieve well-being, many implications are left unsaid. Zhuangzi develops the metaphysical insights of Laozi into a philosophy of life. What Zhuangzi continues in essence may be stated as follows. Our understanding of life and reality is en-cumbered by our knowledge of things, but it is capable of being enlightened by our knowledge of the *dao* as a liberating force by way of voiding and emptying. In doing so the creativity of the *dao* and *wu* will ensure a life of freedom and enjoyment.

The *dao*-metaphysical thinking of Laozi and Zhuangzi is further elaborated in the Neo-Daoist works of Wang Bi (Wang Pi) (AD 226–49). It is important to point out that Wang Bi concentrated on the *wu* concept of Laozi in his commentary on this work, and in his working out of a metaphysical system of the *dao* as *wu*. Wang Bi says: 'The ten thousand things and ten thousand forms all return to oneness. How do they need oneness? It is due to *wu*.'[25] Wang Bi regards *wu* as the origin of all things, by virtue of its not *having* or determining all things. In this sense *you* is inherent in *wu* by virtue of *wu*. It is a matter of self-transformation of *wu*. *Wu* is the liberation of any limitation of activity and power so that power and activity in creativity become free, unrestrained, infinite, and spontaneous, an insight also derived from Zhuangzi. Thus Wang Bi also uses *wu* to interpret *ziran* (natural spontaneity). He says: '*Ziran* is a term of no name and a limiting word.'[26] *Ziran* is thus the natural consequence of *wu* which is no consequence. It is 'do-nothing' so that everything can come into being by itself. Hence Wang Bi sees in *wu* all possibilities of existence as well as all possibilities for the explanation of nature.

In Daoist metaphysics, Wang Bi systematises *wu* by making *wu* the integrative unity for the following metaphysical categories which come basically from the *Yijing* texts and the *Yizhuan* philosophy:

$$
\begin{array}{rcl}
\text{root } (ben) & \longleftrightarrow & \text{branch } (mo) \\
\text{one } (yi) & \longleftrightarrow & \text{many } (duo) \\
\text{rest } (jing) & \longleftrightarrow & \text{motion } (dong) \\
\text{constancy } (chang) & \longleftrightarrow & \text{change } (bian)
\end{array}
$$

For Wang Bi, the categories on the left side are features of *wu*: *wu* is root, one, rest, and constancy, whereas the categories on the right side are features of *you*: *you* is branch, many, motion, and change. The main difference between Wang Bi and the *Yijing* metaphysics of the *dao* is that, for the *Yijing*, the *dao* is not only the source of activity, but is engaged in creative activity as its essence. Even Laozi would not see the *wu* as simply a matter of rest, for the *tao* which has *wu* as its characteristic does everything by doing nothing. *Dao* is above motion and rest. We may say that Wang Bi in a way obscures the distinction between *wu* as the *dao* integrating the *wu* and *you*, and *wu* as the polaristic correlate to *you*.

In the transcending sense of *wu*, not only may we say that the *dao* integrates the four categories above, we may also say that the *dao* should integrate the categories of *wu* and *you* themselves, as well as the categories of substance (*ti*) and function (*yong*), beginning (*shi*) and end (*zhong*), before (*xian*) after (*hou*). In other words, the *dao* as *wu* is not only *wu*, *ti*, *shi*, and *xian*, whereas the *you* is *you*, *yong*, *zhong*, and *hou*; it is the generative unity and totality of *wu/you*, *ti/yong*, *shi/zhong*, and *xian/hou*. With this understanding a full system of metaphysics of the *dao* and *wu* can be developed in the innovative spirit of Laozi as well as with the comprehensive scope of the *Yijing*.

Concluding Remarks and a Metaphysical Hypothesis

This chapter has analysed Western metaphysical thinking in terms of and in the light of Parmenides. Parmenides is shown to have paved the way and laid the foundation for the orientation of Western metaphysical thinking as a quest for being, where being is understood as a permanent object of intellectual thinking. It is pointed out that many Western philosophers tried to save the appearances and changes of the world. Most Western philosophers during the last 2400 years have been unable to get out of the Parmenidean paradigm of metaphysical thinking; neither of the two ways of escape—a metaphysical dualism between reality and appearance or a rejection of metaphysical thinking—is satisfactory. There is the perennial paradox and puzzle of metaphysical thinking. Whitehead and Heidegger continued the quest for being in different disguises, with eternal objects and being as time and appropriation exerting different pulls. The problem is that no adequate conception of *non-being* was ever developed and accepted. The abhorrence of non-being as a vacuum exists in both science and metaphysics as the quest for being. This is true of both Heidegger and Whitehead. In the Idealistic metaphysics of Fichte and Hegel, non-being becomes an abstraction as revealed by negation and hence is contradictory to being so that it needs to be 'uplifted' out of itself. Hence the negation of negation or the non-being of non-being, which still conforms to the Parmenidean dictum: 'What is, is, what is not, is not.'

In recent Western philosophy, Derrida has attempted to improve upon Heidegger by introducing the concept of *différence* as the indefinite and infinite action of deferring and differing all activities of thinking, speaking, and, perhaps, existing. Thus, as an ontological principle, it may approximate to the Daoist notion of *wu*.[27] But as such how much may it integrate all existing differences and yet transcend them, how much can it produce differences and yet preserve a unity of them, will remain an open question.

In the foregoing, we have contrasted the seeking of the way (the *dao*) as the main characteristic of Chinese metaphysical thinking, with the quest for being as the main characteristic of Western metaphysical thinking. We have pinpointed Chinese metaphysical thinking in this sense in the symbolic system of the *Yijing*, in the explicit Confucian metaphysical thinking of the *Yizhuan*, and finally in the innovative Daoist metaphysical thinking of Laozi. We have brought out the Confucian metaphysics of the *dao* in the *Yizhuan* as an integration of the polaristic principle implicit in the symbolism of the *Yijing*.

We have brought to light the metaphysics of the *dao* in Laozi as both an innovation and a continuation from the metaphysics of the *dao* in the *Yijing*. Both forms of metaphysical thinking wanted to conserve, and actually did conserve, the natural experience of change and transformation of things, and in doing so have achieved a naturalistic onto-cosmogenetic and cosmo-ontogenetic philosophy of being and becoming, which is vastly different from the Western tradition of metaphysical thinking. But in Laozi we also detect an innovation which may be compared to Parmenides' innovation in his metaphysical thinking of Being. The Daoist innovation did not change the course of the Chinese metaphysical tradition, which is presumably embodied in the experience of human existence and cosmological change of the world in a primordial form, whereas Parmenides' metaphysics of being did change the course of Western metaphysical thinking.

The Parmenidean metaphysics of being caused Western metaphysical thinking to seek for being in a closed system of concepts, and thus caused the loss of a natural sense of reality and open creativity. Being becomes the foundation of Western dualistic metaphysics, set against change and non-being. Being also becomes the origin of Western science. It brings out the human power of human thinking. It defines the rationality of knowledge and methodology. But it also impoverishes the life and lifeworld of man and nature, and hence traps man in an imbalance of metaphysical individualism with a solipsism and an agnosticism of pure reason which conflicts with and suppresses the natural cravings of original man, and force him to find rest and comfort in the form of transcendental religion.

The Laozi metaphysics of the *dao* as a continuation from the *Yijing* brings the *Yijing* philosophy of being of the *dao* to a natural maturation, and one can see in it the emerging of non-being from being and the consequent emerging of being from non-being, which, metaphysically speaking, exhibits the dynamic unity of both being and non-being. This is the fullest meaning of the *dao*, in the light of which man can fulfil his nature in the fold of being and fulfil the nature of being in the fold of non-being. Understanding change as well as embodying change is the very gate to wisdom in the metaphysical thinking of the *Yijing* and the *Daodejing* in Chinese philosophy.

In so far as Chinese metaphysical thinking, in the form of the *Yizhuan* and the *Laozi*, preserves the phenomenon of change and transformation as an essence of metaphysical thinking, we may rightly say that Chinese metaphysics is non-metaphysics in the sense of 'quest for being' in the Western metaphysical tradition. On the other hand, we ought also to say that Western metaphysics is non-metaphysics in the sense of 'seeking the way'. However, if we want to preserve metaphysical paradigms of both systems or traditions, it is necessary that we should enlarge our metaphysical vision to allow the interaction and interpenetration of the two ways of metaphysical thinking. Then it becomes clear that the Chinese paradigm of the polaristic unity of complementary opposites will have a valuable use. Chinese metaphysical thinking and Western metaphysical thinking should form a unity of complementary opposites so that metaphysics may exhibit a new unity and generate fruitful consequences. This, then, is the new challenge.

Whether it can be met is open to question. What seems less debatable are the reasons for the difference between the two traditions. On both historical and philosophical grounds, it seems clear that Parmenides represents a harsh and extraordinary break from the earlier Greek tradition of polaristic thinking which concentrates on the preservation of change and transformation. Chinese metaphysical thinking experienced no such break or radical turn. Even though Daoist metaphysics has made some innovation, they are still in the direction of polaristic thinking in preserving the reality of change. In fact, it has brought out the full impact of polaristic thinking in the notion of the *dao* as *wu*, a concept which the West has never succeeded in developing, despite considerable effort.

I should like to put forward the metaphysical hypothesis that Chinese metaphysical thinking is the primordial form of metaphysical thinking. It is primordial in at least two senses: historically—in the sense of existing before the initiation of the metaphysical quest for being; and philosophically—in the sense of being the natural beginning of human thinking, and thus being founded on the primordial human experience of existence and the world. To say this is to recognize not only that Chinese metaphysical thinking has a universal and primordial appeal, but also that Chinese metaphysical thinking provides a focus for a return to the origin of human metaphysical thinking. Now, one may ask how the Parmenidean split and deviation took place in the West and why such a turn was not made in the Chinese metaphysical tradition. Again, we need an explanation in the form of a metaphysical hypothesis.

I have already indicated above that the Greek language, being a phonetic language, produces an abstraction of thinking more easily than the visual language of Chinese. This tendency toward abstraction is conducive to transcendental thinking in extensive abstractions and thus leads to the crystallization of both thinking and the object of thinking in an enclosure of concepts. The Chinese language, however, being rooted in the concrete representation of the reality of experience oriented both visually and auditorily, always brings the image of the world to metaphysical contemplation. Hence the *change* paradigm of the *Yijing* becomes the guiding principle of metaphysical thinking. Metaphysical thinking is a matter of seeking the way, the comprehensive and integrative understanding of reality, with all its changes and transformations. Metaphysics is not to go beyond this reality, but to embrace it. If language is any clue, and if the use of language is to make any metaphysical sense, the choice and development of a language is already a metaphysical choice and a metaphysical reality, predisposing the consequent metaphysical thinking in the tradition, whether conscious or unconscious, whether reflective or nonreflective.

Notes

1. Compare with my articles 'Greek and Chinese Views of Time and Timeless' in *Philosophy East and West*, 1974, Vol. 24, No. 2, pp. 15–19; 'Categories of Creativity in Whitehead and Neo-Confucianism,' in *Journal of Chinese Philosophy*, 1979, Vol. 6, No. 3, pp. 251–74; and 'Confucius, Heidegger and the Philosophy of the I Ching,' in *Philosophy East and West*, 1987, Vol. 37, No. 1, pp. 50–70.

2. The more a man is to separate his knowledge from his action, the more he is separated from the world in which he finds himself. In the closeness of knowledge and action, there is closeness of man and the world, because action is a mediation for his self-transformation and the transformation of the world in the world. Hence unity or non-unity of knowledge and action is always a measure of the unity or non-unity of man and world.

3. This interpretation of the relation of *dao* to *ji* is explicitly put forward in the literature for the first time.

4. There may be many *ad hoc* types of divination, but as far as I can ascertain, there exists no divination similar to the *Yijing* divination with regard to a developed reference framework or system of reference as embodied in the *Yijing* symbolism.

5. See Zhu Xi's *Zhouyi benyi*, the authorized commentary on the text of *Zhouyi* or the *Yijing from the Zhou*.

6. By the same token a similar diagram for hexagrams can be constructed.

7. *Dazhuan*, part I, p. 12.

8. In the light of recent archaeological discoveries of both material culture and old texts of the *Yijing*, it is clear that China had developed a sophisticated culture which warranted the practice and understanding of *Yijing* divination as early as the Xia dynasty (*c.* BC 2000–1600).

9. See the *Xici*, *Duanzhuan*, *Xiangzhuan*, and *Shuogua* of the *Yizhuan*.

10. The term *buyou* appears in the *Daodejing*, Chapters 10 and 51. It also appears in the *Zhuangzi*, in the chapter on Autumn Floods and in the chapter on *Xu Wugui*.

11. See my monograph 'On Timeliness (*shih-chung*) in the Analects and the *I Ching*: An Inquiry into the Philosophical Relationship Between Confucius and the I Ching', in *Proceedings of the International Conference*, Academia Sinica, Taipei, Taiwan, 1982.

12. *Daodejing*, section 2.

13. *Daodejing*, section 1.

14. The original text could also be read as '*Wu* is the name of the beginning of heaven and earth. Being is the name of the mother of the ten thousand things.' This form of reading is not only awkward, because Laozi seemed to have already intended that the *wu* has no name and should not be named, but is also contradictory to another statement in the *Daodejing*, namely, 'The *dao* always has no name', section 32.

15. Compare with Wing-tsit Chan's translation of *Ching ssu lu*, *Reflections on Things at Hand* (New York, Columbia University Press, 1967), page 5.

16. *Daodejing*, section 42.

17. *Daodejing*, section 42.

18. See *Zhuzi Yulei*, *zhuan* 5.

19. *Daodejing*, section 39.

20. *Daodejing*, section 40.

21. See the *Daodejing*, sections 2, 10, 34, 51 and 77. The importance of this point cannot be overestimated. It is a point which Laozi stressed over and over again in the *Daodejing*. This point is an illustration of both an onto-cosmological principle for the possibility of things and the *dao* altogether, and a moral-political principle for happy survival and successful government. It is in essence the same principle

called 'non-action for all action' (*wuwei er wu buwei*) 無為而無不為 as is stated in section 37. It is also the principle of self-transformation (*zihua*) stated in section 37.

22. *Daodejing*, section 40.
23. Compare with *Daodejing*, sections 55, 19.
24. *Daodejing*, section 28.
25. See Wang Bi's annotation of the *Laozi*, section 42.
26. See Wang Bi's commentary on the *Laozi*, section 25.
27. See my unpublished paper on 'Derrida's difference and the Daoistic *void*'; presented at the International Society for Chinese Philosophy panel, in conjunction with the 1987 Annual Meeting of the American Philosophical Association, Eastern Division, New York, 27 December 1987 (forthcoming in *Journal of Chinese Philosophy*).

7 The Concept of *Li* in Confucian Moral Theory

Antonio S. Cua

Introduction

One main difficulty in understanding Confucian ethics lies in the absence of systematic exposition of its basic ideas, such as *ren* (humanity), *li* (propriety), and *yi* (rightness).[1] It has been justly observed that 'for the Chinese the idea is not so much to analyse and define concepts precisely as to expand them, to make them suggestive of the widest possible range of meaning. Generally, the more crucial or central the idea, the greater the ambiguity.'[2] This pervasive feature of Confucian discourse, from the point of view of contemporary moral philosophy, may appear to be an anomaly, given the classical emphasis on the right use of terms. Even in the works of Xunzi (Hsün Tzu), the philosopher most preoccupied with the problem of definition, it is difficult to locate adequate definitions of basic ethical terms. His essay on rectifying terms (*zhengming*)[3] contains relatively clear definitions of terms used in the formulation of his theses to human nature and the mind, but key ethical notions such as *ren*, *li*, and *yi* are not included. This fact is surprising in view of his recurrent employment of certain definitional locutions (e.g. *zhiwei* and *weizhi*), which suggest the requirements of necessary and/or sufficient conditions for proper use of terms.[4] In general, Xunzi has a pragmatic attitude to the use of language. Explanations of his terms are primarily addressed to a particular rather than a universal audience.[5]

Two different assumptions underlying this attitude toward language may account for the absence of Chinese interest in context-independent explanation of the use of ethical terms. First, there is an assumption of the primacy of practical reason implicit in the Confucian doctrine of the unity of knowledge and action (*zhixing heyi*).[6] Definition, in the sense of meaning-explanation, is a matter of practical rather than theoretical necessity. Since discourse is viewed as possessing normative import, implying a unity and harmony of knowledge, thought, speech, and action, it is not something one engages in for the sake of theory-construction, which has no necessary connection with conduct. The point does not depreciate the importance of theoretical inquiry, but focuses upon its relevance to the requirements of practice. Since such requirements may vary in time and place, any theory is finally tested in the light of changing human circumstances. In general, ethical requirements cannot be stated in terms of fixed principles. Even the ethical ideal of the good life, *dao* (Way), cannot be captured in formulae. As Wang Yangming put it, the rationale of *dao* (*dao-li*) '. . . has neither spatial restrictions nor physical form, and it cannot be pinned down to any particular. To seek it by confining ourselves to literal meanings would be far off the mark.'[7]

Related to the primacy of practical reason is the assumption that reasoned discourse may legitimately appeal to what may be called 'plausible presumptions',[8] that is, appeal to shared knowledge, belief, or experience, as well as to established or operative standards of competence.[9] These plausible presumptions are often suppressed, and in the main form the background of discourse. Thus Confucian argumentation appears to be highly inexplicit. From the Aristotelian point of view, Confucian reasoning is 'rhetorical', as it frequently involves enthymemes and arguments from example.[10] In the light of the legitimate use of plausible presumptions, it is readily intelligible that Confucian thinkers have not been preoccupied with the systematic explication of basic ethical terms. These terms, (*ren*, *li*, and *yi*) are much like 'adjuster words', that is, '. . . by the use of which other words are adjusted to meet the innumerable and unforseeable demands of the world upon language'.[11] Moreover, *ren*, *li*, and *yi* operate more like satellite notions revolving around the ideal of *dao*, the Confucian vision of human excellence. They all hang together, so to speak, and constitute a family of interdependent notions, adaptable to employment in varying contexts of human life. For a contemporary Confucian philosopher concerned with the development of an adequate moral theory, one major task pertains to a coherent and plausible explication of these fundamental notions in accord with the ethical sensibility of Confucian thought and tradition.[12] This task is not unlike Rawls' explication of the liberal tradition of justice, that is, '. . . a study of substantive moral conceptions and their relation to our sensibility'.[13]

Recently, in dealing with the problem of conceptual unity of basic Confucian notions, I suggested that they are best construed as focal notions used in conveying distinct, though not unconnected centers of ethical concern. *Ren* typically focuses on love and care of one's fellows, *li* on ritual code, *yi* on rightness.[14] All these notions may be considered as interdependent, fundamental specifications of the concrete significance of *dao*. Relative to current purposes of discourse, each of these notions, in turn, is amenable to further and more concrete specification, say, kindness, respectfulness, or personal integrity. More formally, adopting Xunzi's distinction, *dao* is a generic term (*gongming*) that has *ren*, *li*, and *yi* as specific terms (*bieming*).[15] This distinction between generic and specific terms is not a dichotomy but a functional distinction relative to a particular context of discourse.[16]

In this paper, I centre my attention on *li* as a generic term *open* to specification of its significance in response to certain critical questions concerning its subject matter, scope, purposes or functions, and justification.[17] Its connection with *ren* and *yi* is assumed to be unproblematic.[18] The principal aim is to shape the notion of *li* into a distinctive ethical conception by sketching a set of coherent and plausible answers to critical questions.[19] No claim to final adequacy is intended, since any of these answers may be further challenged or contested. While any reasonable question presupposes 'a right answer', as Collingwood reminds us, a right answer is '. . . an answer which enables us to get ahead with the process of questioning and answering'.[20] In this sense, *li* is an essentially contested concept.[21] For my task, I have drawn freely from the works of Xunzi, supplemented by contributions of other Confucian thinkers.[22] For Xunzi, to my knowledge, is sensitive to these critical questions, and offers us, perhaps, the best insights into the significance of *li* in Confucian ethics.[23]

Scope

As a generic term, *li* focuses on a traditional ritual code (*lixian*), which is essentially a set of formal prescriptions or procedures for proper behaviour (*Quanxue*, L15, W21, D38–39).[24] In the Confucian classic (*Liji*), the subject matter ranges from formal prescriptions (henceforth, ritual rules) concerning mourning, sacrifices, marriage, and communal festivities, to the more ordinary occasions relating to conduct toward ruler, superior, parent, elder, teacher, and guest. The first critical question is the issue of change of ritual rules. One may wonder whether these rules are amenable to modification in terms of quantity. Also, whether, in application, the rules are absolute or subject to qualification in the light of particular circumstances. To both queries, a Confucian theorist would give similar answers. As far as the number of rules is at issue, adapting to changing circumstances may reasonably call for either addition or subtraction, depending on the needs of the time (*shi*).[25] As one writer in the *Liji* remarks, 'Kings of the Three Dynasties did not copy the *li* of the preceding dynasty, because of differences in society.'[26] In other words, the subject matter of *li* cannot be determined wihout regard to the current needs and conditions of the society.

Fundamentally, *li* are the prescriptions of reason.[27] Any rule that is deemed right and reasonable can be accepted as an exemplary rule of conduct. 'The *li* are the embodied expression of what is right (*yi*). If an observance stands the test of being judged by the standard of what is right, although it may not have been among the usages of ancient kings, it may be adopted on the ground of its being right.'[28] The issue of change with respect to ritual rules is thus a practical rather than a mere theoretical issue. The governing consideration is the reasoned exercise of *yi* or the sense of appropriateness to the time and place of a particular society. More generally, one must use *yi* to cope with changing circumstances.[29] The traditional ritual code represents no more than a codification of ethical experiences based on *ren* and *yi*. Its relevance to the present, particularly in exigent situations, is a matter of reasoned judgment. In this light, the *li* are, in principle, subject to revision or even elimination. Notably, one must reject those rules that are unreasonably burdensome and superfluous, and retain those rules that are practicable and essential to the maintenance of the social order.[30] A respect for a living tradition is quite different from the attitude of the traditionalist. For '. . . tradition is the living faith of the dead, traditionalism is the dead faith of the living.'[31]

Similar consideration applies to the query whether the *li* are absolute or relative to particular circumstances. In normal stituations within a community, the *li* may be said to be absolute, in that they pose no serious moral perplexity; they have no exceptions. But in dealing with customary practices of other communities, one's sense of appropriateness must determine proper conduct. As it is said in the *Liji*, 'One must comply with *li* in accord with appropriateness, just as a person sent on a mission to another state follows her customs.'³² Of course, an ethically cultivated person (*junzi*), informed by the spirit of *ren* and *yi*, while exercising his art of accomodation (*jianshu*), will not sacrifice his integrity (*decao*). He can neither be subverted by his natural desire for personal gain, nor by the power of an established authority or the masses (*Quanxue*, L19, W23–24, D40–41). Most importantly, in any situation which he deems exigent, whether within or outside his own community, the *li* have to be declared irrelevant, while they may be 'absolute' as a first consideration in moral reflection. An exigent situation calls for immediate attention. The issue here has nothing to do with *building* an exception to the rule but one of *making an exception* to the rule. The rule retains its absolute character, but judged as irrelevant to the exigent situation.³³ When the judgment is challenged, the Confucian agent will engage in argumentation.³⁴

In ordinary life, the enforcement of the *li* of human relationships (*lun*), for example, calls for unquestioning compliance. In exigent situations, refusal to follow the *li* may well be necessary. In the case of a morally responsible minister, where the ruler has departed from *dao*, it is quite proper for the minister to follow *dao* rather than the ruler. So also, while filial piety requires obedience, there are situations where disobedience is morally justified. When, for example, one's compliance with parental wishes will bring them disgrace rather than honour; when one will endanger the lives of the parents rather than bring them peace; and when the parents' wishes are such as to compel one to behave like a dumb creature rather than like a man of moral cultivation. In all these cases, one must follow *yi* or one's sense of what is right (*Zidao*, L651).

Much in the spirit of the later Wittgenstein, Xunzi reminds his readers: 'Just as there are no laws that can stand by themselves [without men who carry them out], there are no classes (*lei*) that can by themselves be applied' (*Jundao*, L263).³⁵ I take this to mean that class terms and rules do not contain their own rules for application. The application of rules depends on the purpose and context of a particular discourse. More importantly, Xunzi explicitly cautions us: '. . . a clear system of rules and regulations, weights and measure, exist for the sake of proper employment; they are not conventions to be tied down to' (*Jundao*, L286).³⁶ In general, established rules must be diligently enforced. But in circumstances where they are deemed inapplicable, one must exercise reason in determining the kind of problem at hand and decide in accord with one's sense of rightness.[37]

Functions

If the change concerning expansion and contraction of the scope of *li* and their application to particular circumstances is a matter of reasoned judgment, an understanding of their basic purposes or functions is presupposed. Some explanation, and ultimately, justification of the existence of *li* is required in order to render *li* a viable and distinctive ethical notion. For Xunzi, explanation (*shuo*) and justification (*bian*) represent two different phases of argumentative discourse,[38] though in his own discussion of *li*, the distinction is not always clearly made. In some contexts, it may be difficult to maintain the distinction.[39] For purposes of analysis and evaluation, the distinction is important as it reflects two different kinds of support for a proffered thesis. The explanatory question is especially important, since for Xunzi, the *li*, as a set of formal prescriptions of proper conduct, are merely 'markers of *dao*';[40] they 'present us with models but no explanations' (*Guanxue*, L14, W20, D38). A person who has a mastery of rules without understanding their significance cannot properly respond to changing human affairs. Indeed, reliance upon the guidance of such a person will lead to nothing but confusion (*Jundao*, L263–64).

Xunzi's account of the existence of *li*, for the most part, was motivated by a concern for a good socio-political order informed by *dao*. In his view, no state can be considered just and upright without establishing and promulgating a set of clear and precise rules of proper conduct. 'If a state has no *li*, it cannot be said to possess rectitude (*zheng*). *Li* is like a plumb line for the crooked and the straight; like a T-square or compass for the square and the round. When such standards are properly established and enforced, no one can be deceived' (*Wangba*, L239).[41]

The primary function of *li* is to prevent human conflict.[42] It is a set of constraints that defines the negative limits of self-regarding activities. In addition, the *li* have also supportive and ennobling functions. This threefold function of *li* is fairly explicit in the following passage from the *Lilun* and is discussed further in the following paragraphs.

What is the origin of *li*? Humans are born with desires. When desires are not satisfied, they cannot but seek some means to satisfy them. When this seeking has no measure and limits, there will be contention. From contention comes social disorder; from social disorder comes poverty. The former kings hated such disorder, and hence they established *li* in accord with their sense of rightness (*yi*), in order to set limits (*fen*) to this confusion, to educate and nourish (*yang*) human desires, and to provide opportunity for this seeking of satisfaction (*geiren zhi qiu*). They saw to it that desires did not overextend the means for their satisfaction, and material goods did not fall short of what was desired. Thus both desires and goods were looked after and satisfied. This is the origin of *li* (*Lilun*, L417).[43]

Delimiting Function

Let us set aside for later consideration the justification of the necessity of *li* based on a conception of problematic human nature and the role of 'former kings' or sages in establishing the *li*.[44] I shall assume, then, that the problem of human conflict is one to be reckoned with in explaining the significance of *li*, or for that matter, of any kind of rules governing human conduct. Given this assumption, we can readily appreciate the primary function of *li* as a set of formal prescriptions, delineating the boundaries of pursuit of self-regarding needs and interests. The *li* purport to set forth orderly proceeding regulating such a pursuit, ultimately, to promote the unity and harmony of human association in a state ruled by an exemplary king or a sage in accord with the spirit of *ren* and *yi* (*Ruxiao*, L131, D96). The orderly proceeding consists of social distinctions or divisions (*fen*) in various kinds of human relationships (*lun*), namely, the distinction between ruler and minister, father and son, eminent and the humble, the elder and the younger, the rich and the poor, and the important and the unimportant members of society.[45] In addition, the *li* also serve as a basis for official appointment, promotion or demotion, and division of labour or occupations, for example, farmers, artisans, and merchants (*Wangba*, L242).

In Xunzi, what is envisaged is an ethical state with a hierarchical political structure, with positions clearly defined and occupied by men of merit and ability.[46] However, most human relationships cannot be properly subsumed under the political structure, since a person can, as is often the case, simultaneously play different roles in his or her community, say, a father and teacher, a poor and elderly, or humble and righteous person (*Zhenglun*, L410–11, D208).[47]

For Xunzi, the social distinctions circumscribed by *li* reflect differences among humans, owing to circumstances and natural endowment. No society or state can persist for long, in peace and security, without an organization (*qun*) in terms of distinctions invested in *li* (*Fuguo*, L202). When human desires are confined to the limits set by *li*, every person will be assigned a proper status and given his or her deserts. In this light, the *li* '. . . embody the rationale of the unity and harmony of human association' (*Lilun*, L447, W108*, D241).[48]

Supportive Function

Aside from regulating conflict that arises out of the pursuit of individual desires or interests, the *li* also have supportive and ennobling functions. In Xunzi, for the most part, these two functions are treated as one, with emphasis given to the ennobling function (*yang*). However, the distinction is crucial to understanding two different, though complementary, purposes of *li*.

As a point of departure for appreciating the supportive function of *li*, let us reflect further upon its delimiting function, in abstraction from connection with *ren* and *yi*. The delimiting function of *li*, as a set of formal prescriptions, may be compared to that of negative moral rules or criminal law. Like rules against killing, stealing, or lying, the *li* impose constraints upon conduct. They create, so to speak, paths of obstruction, thus blocking certain moves of agents in the pursuit of their respective individual interests or desires. The *li*, in effect, stipulate the conditions of eligibility or permissibility of actions, regardless of the substantive character or value of desires or interests. In this sense, the *li* have merely a negative function. They provide information on the limiting conditions of action but no positive guidance as to how one's desires may be properly satisfied. Put differently, they tell the agents what goals *not* to pursue, but not *how* one goes about pursuing those goals within the prescribed limits of action.

If we consider the *li* also as having a supportive function, again, the agent will not be apprised of what goals to pursue, but he will have positive guidance on the ways of pursuing whatever goals that are deemed admissible within the prescribed limits of action. In Xunzi's words, the *li* also provide opportunities for satisfaction (*geiren zhi qiu*). Instead of being merely constraints upon conduct, they also facilitate the satisfaction of desires, or provide the conditions of achievement. The focus on the supportive function of *li* is evident in Xunzi's critique of two prevailing theories of desires that have been offered as solutions to the problem of founding a well-ordered society. One theory advocates the elimination of desires; the other, the reduction of desires. Says Xunzi:

All those who maintain that desires must be got rid of before there can be orderly government fail to consider whether the desires can be guided, but merely deplore the fact that they exist at all. All those who maintain that desires must be lessened before there can be orderly government fail to consider whether desires can be controlled, but merely deplore the fact that they are so numerous. Beings that possess desires and those that do not belong to two different categories—the living and the dead. But the possession or non-possession of desires has nothing to do with good government or bad (*Zhengming*, L527, W150, D293–94).

Xunzi goes on to point out that the key issue lies in the direction of the mind, that '. . .it is the office of the intellect to guide the search for satisfaction' (*Zhengming*, L529, W152, D295).

In their natural occurrence, our desires are spontaneous responses to our feelings (*Zhengming*, L506, W139, D281). In this respect, all humans are alike: 'when hungry, we desire to eat; when cold, we desire to be warm; when toiling, we desire to rest; we prefer to seek what is beneficial and to avoid what is harmful' (*Rongru*, L64, D60*). In their supportive function, the *li* provide the acceptable channels for the fulfillment of desires. Instead of suppressing these desires the *li* offer an outlet for our search for satisfaction. In an important sense, the supportive function of *li* implicitly acknowledges, so to speak, the integrity of our natural desires. These desires are part of human nature. While we need to confine our pursuit within the boundaries of propriety, we accept them for what they are. We do not make any value judgment. Whether reasonable or unreasonable, wise or foolish, good or bad, the main concern of the supportive function of *li* is the redirection of the course of our self-seeking activities, not a suppression of the motivating desires. Indeed, what distinguishes an ethically superior person from a small-minded person lies not in the love of honour and the hate of shame, or in the love of what is beneficial and the hate of what is injurious, but in the contrary ways in which they seek their goals (*Rongru*, L60, D58).[49]

As earlier remarked, the delimiting function of *li* may be compared to that of criminal law. In this light, the *li* may be seen as *disabling* rules. If we follow another legal analogy for the supportive function of *li*, we may compare it to an aspect of procedural law that contains rules that *enable* us to carry out our desires and wishes. I have in mind the law of contracts and the law of wills. The *li*, like these procedural rules, are aids to the realization of desires. In Xunzi's words, they '. . . provide opportunity for this search for satisfaction'. In this manner, the supportive function of *li* furnishes us positive, though not substantive, guidance to conduct.

Ennobling Function

Focus on this function of *li* is widely acknowledged as a distinctive feature of Confucian ethics and traditional Chinese culture. Doing justice to this feature requires a complex characterization and evaluation, quite beyond the scope of the present paper. The general idea is aptly expressed by Thomé Fang: [*li* is] '. . . cultural refinement, bodying forth either the prudence of conduct, or the balance of emotion, or the rationality of knowledge, or the intelligent working of order. Especially, it is blended with the excellent spirit of fine arts such as poetry and music. In short, what is called 'Li' in Chinese is a standard of measurement for the general cultural values, according to which we can enjoy the beauties of life in the rational order of political societies.'[50] For present purposes, I shall concentrate on some salient aspects of *li* as cultural refinement in relation to their supportive and regulative functions.

The keynote of the ennobling function is the education and nourishment (*yang*) of desires, or the *transformation* (*hua*) of desires in accord with *dao* or the spirit of *ren* and *yi*. As Xunzi reminds the student, 'If a person does not comprehend the unifying significance of different kinds of human relationship and make himself one with *ren* and *yi*, he does not deserve to be called a good scholar' (*Quanxue*, L18, W22*, D40). Both acquisition of knowledge and critical reflection upon its actuating import in human life are indispensable, especially in coping with changing human affairs.[51] The characteristic concern with the *form* of proper conduct is still present, but the form stressed in the ennobling function of *li* is not just a matter of fitting into a structure of social and political organization, nor with the methodic procedure that assists the agents in carrying out their wishes or desires, but the *elegant form* (*wen*) of pursuing the satisfaction of desires. In other words, the ennobling function of *li* is primarily concerned with the development of beautiful virtues (*meide*),[52] or of goodness (*shan*), which is essentially the outcome of transformation (*hua*) of human nature (*xing*), our basic motivational structure (feelings and desires).[53] In this sense, the *li* represent '. . . the acme of *dao* and virtue (*de*)' (*Quanxue*, L10, W19*, D37).

Feelings and desires, being constitutive of human nature (*xing*), are thus the basic stuff for ethical transformation.[54] Through the exercise of creative ability (*wei*), involving imagination and reflective choice, this original nature can be transformed into something beautiful and noble (*mei*) (*Zhengming*, L506, D281–2, W130–40). As Xunzi points out, 'Human nature provides the basis and raw materials. The exercise of creative ability (*wei*) is responsible for its elegant pattern and glorification. Without human nature, there would be nothing for the ability to apply to and supplement human nature' (*Lilun*, L439). It is the exemplary or sagely exercise of this creative ability that accounts for the existence of *li*. 'The sage gathers his thoughts and ideas, experiments with various forms of creation; and so produces *li* in accord with his sense of rightness (*yi*) and sets forth laws and regulations.' His activity may be likened to that of a potter who makes a vessel out of clay or a carpenter who makes a utensil out of wood (*Xing'e*, L544, W160*, D305).

Likewise, the ethically committed person can beautify his character, through reflective choice of desires, that is, through the development of reflective desires in accord with the guidance of reason.[55] In abstraction from the guidance of reason, reflective desires are just the natural desires as we normally experience them. For example, our natural desire for food, when subjected to the direction of the mind by means of the *li* of civility, no longer appears as a natural drive, but a desire invested with a regard for the elegant form of satisfaction. In this way, our natural desires may be said to be transformed by the reasoned exercise of our creative ability. Every person can strive to become a sage, because of the inherent ability to understand and abide by *ren* and *yi*, to follow rules of proper conduct. 'If a man in the street applies himself to training and study, concentrates his mind and will, and considers and examines things carefully, continuing his efforts over a long period of time and accumulating good acts without stop, then he can achieve godlike understanding and form a triad with Heaven and Earth' (*Xing'e*, L552, W167, D313). In this light, the ennobling function of *li* directs the agents toward the achievement of goodness and human excellence (*shan*).

Being prescriptions of reason, it is justly said that it is the idea of rational rule that '. . . connects all shades of meaning of *li*.'[56] Each of the three functions of *li* admits of further elaboration in response to queries concerning its relevance to substantive issues of human conduct. The importance of *yi*, or reasoned judgment on what is right and appropriate, suggests that concrete issues cannot be settled in advance of a careful consideration of actual circumstances of human life (see above). The more difficult issue pertains to the justification of the three-fold function of *li*, the subject of our next section.

Justification

At the outset, let us observe that the three-fold function of *li* provides a basis for distinguishing two different kinds of rule of proper conduct. Following Searle, we may say that the rules that perform the delimiting and supportive functions are *regulative* rules, in that they '. . . regulate antecedently existing forms of behaviour'. The rules that perform the ennobling function, on the other hand, are *constitutive* rules, in that '. . . they do not merely regulate, but create or define new forms of behaviour'.[57] In terms of this distinction, the justification of the Confucian conception of *li* calls for two different sorts of consideration. The justification for the necessity of regulative rules, on the whole, seems unproblematic, as it involves plausible presumptions. The justification for the necessity of constitutive rules, however, is extremely difficult. My discussion will be largely confined to raising some questions that are worthy of further exploration.

Human Predicament[58]

For appreciating the necessity of regulative rules, we may recall and elaborate the sort of consideration involved in a passage cited earlier. Reflection on human nature (*xing*) in terms of its motivational aspect discloses a self-seeking propensity to satisfy desires. Conjoined with the observation of the scarcity of resources to satisfy everyone's desires, it is plausible to maintain that, in the absence of regulation, conflict or contention, social disorder, and eventually poverty will result. As Xunzi succinctly put it, 'people have desires and aversions for the same things. Their desires are many, while things are few. This scarcity will inevitably lead to contention' (*Fuguo*, L195, D152*).

This natural tendency to seek satisfaction of desires, however, need not be construed as selfish, as excluding any concern for other people's feelings and desires. Rather, it is a tendency to be partial (*bian*), to favour things and persons of one's own relation and affection.[59] This natural partiality is in some way 'bad' (*e*), for without regulation, it is liable to produce conflict and strife, which is undesirable from the point of view of a good social order. Were humans intrinsically good, that is, 'upright, reasonable, and orderly,' Xunzi asks, 'what need would there be for sage-kings and *li*?' (*Xing'e*, L547, W162, D307). Imagine the situation in which all regulative rules were removed, the respect for *li* and *yi* gone, along with laws and punishment, how would the people in the world deal with one another? In this situation, it is reasonable to think that 'the strong would injure the weak and rob them, and many would do violence to the few and shout them down. The whole world would be in violence and disorder' (*Xing'e*, L547, W163*, D307).[60] Without regulative rules, in particular the *li* that perform the delimiting function, it is a plausible presumption that social disorder or chaos would result.

Apart from the prevention of human conflict, the regulative *li* with the delimiting function, in focusing upon the division of labour or distinction of occupations, promotes social existence. 'Humans cannot live without society or social organization (*qun*)' (*Fuguo*, L202). Given the scarcity of resources to satisfy all of their wants, there is a special need of co-operation. 'For the fruits of the hundred crafts contribute to the sustenance of one man whose capacities cannot be directed towards all the crafts and who cannot attend to all tasks, with the result that if he cuts himself off from society, he would find himself in an impossible situation' (*Fuguo*, L196).[61]

Similar consideration would justify the acceptance of *li* that perform the supportive function. In providing the appropriate outlet for the satisfaction of desires within the prescribed limits of action, these regulative rules may be viewed as a guiding standard for weighing desires and aversions, thus averting the individual agents from untoward and unwanted consequences. For humans are partial (*bian*), not only in the sense of being biased toward their objects of affection, but also partial in the sense of limited foresight. According to Xunzi, humans generally suffer because of this sort of partiality.

> When they see something that they want, they do not carefully consider whether it will lead to something that they detest; when they see something beneficial, they do not carefully consider whether it will lead to something harmful. In this way, any action that they perform is bound to entrap them and bring about harm. This is the predicament that besets us all—the harm that ensues from partiality (*bian*) (*Bugou*, L53).[62]

The foregoing considerations offer a defense of the necessity of regulative rules, invoking some familiar plausible presumptions concerning the human predicament. Taken together, they may be viewed as an informal, coordinative argument, in that each standing alone, is quite weak in supporting the thesis. Each factor, (scarcity of resources, partially or limited benevolence and foresight, and vulnerability), independently, does not provide sufficient warrant for the thesis of the necessity of regulative rules.[63] Moreover, each factor is also open to further query. The scarcity factor, for example, may give rise to a further question of diagnosis. On this question, Xunzi thought that the situation of scarcity in his own time (third century BC) was brought about by a failure in managing natural resources. He believed that if there were men in authority who possessed the skill in managing available resources, there would be more than sufficient goods, if not surplus, to satisfy human needs and desires (*Fuguo*, L208). So long as there are *li* that perform both the delimiting and supportive functions, and effective, uniform compliance, human desires and goods can be attended to and satisfied without strife or social disorder (*Lilun*, L417).

Regulative rules are essential to remedy the ills that befall all humans. Whether they are sufficient to resolve this predicament remains an important question to explore. At any rate, the *li* of regulation, are an antidote to the plight that afflicts common humanity. It is an artifice (*wei*) designed '. . . to enable people to reap the benefit of living in society while avoiding the accompanying evils'.[64] This insight of Xunzi, however, must be dissociated from his problematic claim that it is the 'former kings', sage-kings, or the sages who established the *li* in accord with their sense of rightness (*yi*). This historical claim is highly implausible, for apart from the difficulty of identification and authentication, there are problems in accepting his thesis. However, there are passages in his works that suggest a different claim, that is, that sages are *ideal* persons who embody *ren*, *li*, and *yi*.[65] At any rate, the historical claim has no contribution to the justification of *li* as a set of regulative rules.

Human Excellence

When we turn to constitutive rules or the *li* that perform the ennobling function, we are concerned not merely with regulation of conduct, but more fundamentally with the realization of *dao*, the Confucian vision of human excellence. In this vision, the good human life as a whole comprises *ren*, *yi*, and *li*. The special role of *li* lies in their being the constitutive, rather than instrumental, means to the attainment of *ren* and *yi*, for ultimately the good life is also an elegant and beautiful *form* of life.[66]

For several reasons, the justification of *li* as a set of constitutive rules, for a Confucian moral theorist, is an onerous task. To begin with, while agreeing to the general thesis that *ren*, *yi*, and *li* are basic notions, the Confucianists hold different views on their relation to one another. Also, the notion of *ren* has a divergence of interpretation throughout the history of Chinese philosophy and in contemporary Chinese and Western scholarship.[67] More generally, there is the question of vindicating the adoption of the Confucian vision, even granting that a coherent characterization is possible and sufficiently significant to command attention in moral philosophy.[68]

My own limited study and examination of competing views regarding Xunzi suggests the viability of what I called the completion thesis.[69] In this view, *ren*, *yi*, and *li* are distinct, but interdependent, notions of virtue (*de*).[70] *Ren* is the virtue of extensive affection or benevolence; *yi* is the virtue of reasoned judgment of rightness or appropriateness; *li* is the virtue of compliance or rule-responsibility. The exercise of *ren* depends on *yi*, that is, the expression of affection must pay heed to what is right and reasonable in a particular situation. Likewise, the exercise of *yi* must be imbued with the spirit of *ren*. *Li* is the constitutive means to the realization of *ren* and *yi*. In the ideal case, these three virtues are present in conduct.

An adequate development of the completion thesis, however,

must deal with the following problems. Firstly, there is the question of the role and conflict of specific virtues, such as filiality, loyalty, trustworthiness, courage, friendliness, integrity, and so on. From the practical point of view, ren, yi, and li represent 'thin' rather than 'thick' ethical concepts. Even if a completion thesis can be developed in overcoming the problem of conflict of virtues, it can offer only a theoretical solution. It is presently unclear to me how such a theory may be tested against the Confucian doctrine of the primacy of practical reason, alluded to in the Introduction. Perhaps, even more important, with li that expresses a concern for a living tradition or cultural refinement, some account is needed of the role of principles, particularly transcultural principles, in such an ethics of virtue. Put differently, if the li are the prescriptions of reason (see 'Scope' above), what rational or reasonable principles must be acknowledged to distinguish a critically sanctioned ritual code from one that persists merely because of inertia. The appeal to the exercise of yi, to the sense of reasoned judgment of rightness, may in part ease this query, but it cannot be viewed as a satisfactory solution to our problem without an effort to articulate a set of transcultural principles that provide a basis for distinguishing customary from reflective morality.[71]

In stressing the beauty of elegant form (mei) in the expression of feelings and transformation of desires, justifying the ennobling function of li today is an arduous task. For, aside from the difficulty of rendering intelligible the notion of beauty (mei) in ethical discourse, it seems a heroic undertaking to incorporate this notion in an ethical theory that has any promise of attracting serious attention from contemporary moral philosophers. For the ennobling function of li points to the significance of an aesthetic dimension of ethical experience.[72] In this conception, an ethically good character transformed by li, imbued with the concern for ren and yi, will express his concern in a graceful and joyful manner, displaying a harmony of inward feelings and attitudes with outward circumstances. For a philosopher who has a critical appreciation of the Greek notion of kalokagathos (where grace, rhythm, and harmony are the hallmarks of moral character) or the propriety of the language of 'the beauty of virtue and the deformity of vice', as was prevalent in the major writings of the eighteenth century British Moralists, the problem may not appear insurmountable.[73]

A Confucian theorist will acknowlege the distinction between

form and content of ethical conduct. The real difficulty lies in articulating their connection, more especially in establishing the connection between ritual rules and moral rules as standardly understood in moral philosophy. A general line of response is to invoke
the notion of functional equivalence. It may be said, for example,
that since ritual rules are the prescriptions of reason, any so-called
moral, or for that matter, legal rules that perform the same function as ritual rules can be properly considered parts of *li*. In this
view, acceptable moral rules will be seen as ideally embedded
rules informed by a concern for *ren* and *yi*. Perhaps, what is at
issue is the relation between substantive and procedural rules of
conduct, much akin to the issue between substantive and procedural due process theories in American constitutional law.[74] It may
be worthwhile for a Confucian theorist to pursue this affinity in
dealing with the problem of form and content in Confucian ethics.
But this general line of response is not very helpful, for conceding
the distinction between ritual and morality carries the burden of
showing their connection. In the concluding section, I shall make
some tentative suggestions on this topic.

Conclusion

In this chapter, I have endeavored to present the Confucian *li* as
a distinctive, yet complex, ethical conception by way of sketching
some answers in response to queries concerning its scope, functions, and justification. These answers, as amenable to further elaboration and questions, are best construed in the spirit of critical
self-understanding of Confucian ethics. Some of these answers,
especially the ones on justifying the ennobling function of *li*, represent no more than intimations for the sake of further inquiry into
the role of *li* in a systematic Confucian moral theory. From the
point of view external to Confucian ethics, there is one major difficulty in appraising the significance of *li* for moral philosophy. For
the utility of *li* in understanding contemporary moral discourse is
open to doubt. No major meta-ethical theory, for example, makes
use of any notion that is functionally equivalent to *li* in its stress on
ritual forming character or conduct.[75] Moreover, in the analysis of
moral issues today, a notion like *li* seems entirely out of place. If a
Confucian theorist is to respond to this external challenge, he must
at least make clear the desired connection between ritual and

morality. In these closing remarks, I shall make some suggestions on how this challenge may be met, intended solely as an indication of a possible approach to this complex and difficult problem.

Except as an uninteresting stipulation, a Confucian theorist cannot maintain the thesis of a necessary connection between ritual and morality. What is wanted is a thesis on non-contingent connection, much in the sense in which intention is non-contingently related to action. Though not every intention need be followed by relevant action, '. . . the concept of intention could hardly have arisen unless intentions were usually followed by the relevant action.'[76] Similarly, we may say that the concept of morality is non-contingently related to ritual, in that it is ritual, as comprising customs, conventions, or formal rules of proper conduct, that provides the starting point of individual morality. Even if we distinguish customary or positive from reflective or critical morality, the distinction is relative rather than absolute. For as Dewey points out, 'Some degree of reflective thought must have entered occasionally into systems which in the main were founded on social wont and use, while in contemporary morals, even when the need of critical judgment is most recognized, there is an immense amount of conduct that is merely accommodated to social usage.'[77]

Even if a member of a society develops an autonomous and rational set of moral beliefs and attitudes, the possibility of successfully communicating his standards or rules of conduct depends on deploying a conventional or ritual language. One need not espouse the extreme thesis that moral values are '. . . the ceremonial treatment of a wide variety of natural facts and situations.'[78] It is a plausible presumption that compliance with a common ritual language, say, something like the *li* that perform the delimiting and supportive functions, is more than just a matter of personal convenience. For it is doubtful that intelligible communication of personal moral beliefs and feelings, however well-founded, and reasonable a response to others' moral beliefs and feelings, is possible without a commitment to the value of an established set of conventions. As Hampshire reminds us, 'If a person disclaimed any commitment to any set of conventions, he would lack the normal means of conveying his feelings, and of responding to the feelings of others through shared discrimination and evaluations.'[79] Recalling also the importance of the *li* that perform the ennobling function, in the extensive concern for the well-being of one's fellows (*ren*) informed by the reasoned exercise of the sense of what is right and appropriate (*yi*), we may quite properly say with Hampshire, that '. . . customs and rituals that govern, in different societies, the relations between the sexes, marriage, property rights, family relationships, and the celebration of the dead, are *primary moral customs*; they always disclose the peculiar kind of respect for human life, and occasions for disrespect, which a particular people or society recognizes, and therefore their more fundamental moral beliefs and attitudes.'[80] These rituals and customs are subject to critical modification or diminishing significance in developing nations such as China and India, owing to modern industrialization.[81] But even in today's modern societies, there appears a large overlapping between '. . . the claims of good manners and moral claims.'[82] For the Confucian, so long as some customs and manners survive in modern industrial societies, something like the *li* that performs the ennobling function will be present, embodying a diversity of *forms* for the concern for common humanity (*ren*). In the words of Wang Yangming, '. . . the practical significance of *dao* cannot be exhausted with any claim to finality.'[83]

Notes

1. The parenthetical terms are not intended as translations, but as convenient indicators of one of the basic meanings.

2. William Theodore de Bary (ed.), *Self and Society in Ming Thought* (New York, Columbia University Press, 1970), p. v.

3. Textual references to *Xunzi* in this essay pertain to the following: Li Tisheng, *Xunzi zhishi* (Taibei, Xuesheng, 1979), H.H. Dubs (tr.), *The Works of Hsüntze* (Taibei, Chengwen, 1966), and Burton Watson, trans., *Hsün Tzu: Basic Writings*. Abbreviated references are used, for example, 'L377,' 'D183,' and 'W87' for the works of Li, Dubs, and Watson with their page numbers. The second occurrence of the reference indicates the translation adopted. Whenever available, a third reference is given for comparative purpose only. Emendations are marked by asterisks. When only Li is cited, this indicates my own translation or reference to a passage not found in both Dubs' and Watson's works. Emendation of translation is indicated by asterisk. For convenience of readers who have other editions, all references are preceded by the titles of the essays.

4. For an extensive discussion of Xunzi's uses of quasi-definitional locutions involving *wei*, see A.S. Cua, *Ethical Argumentation: A Study in Hsün Tzu's Moral Epistemology* (Honolulu, University of Hawaii Press, 1985), pp. 101–37. Hereafter cited as *Ethical Argumentation*.

5. For the distinction between particular and universal audience, see Chaim Perelman and Anna Olbrechts-Tyteca, *The New Rhetoric: A Treatise in Argumentation* (Notre Dame, University of Notre Dame Press, 1969), p. 30.

6. For a detailed examination of this doctrine, see A.S. Cua, *The Unity of Knowledge and Action: A Study in Wang Yang-ming's Moral Psychology* (Honolu-

lu, University of Hawaii Press, 1982), hereafter cited as *The Unity of Knowledge and Action*.

7. Wing-tsit Chan (tr.), *Instructions for Practical Living and Other Neo-Confucian Writings by Wang Yang-ming* (New York, Columbia University Press, 1963), sec. 66.

8. See Nicholas Rescher, *Dialectics* (Albany, State University of New York Press, 1977), p. 38. For the role of plausible presumptions in the Confucian appeal to historical personages and events, see A.S. Cua, 'The Ethical Uses of the Past in Early Confucianism: The Case of Hsün Tzu,' *Philosophy East and West*, 32, No. 2 (1985).

9. See my *Ethical Argumentation*, chapters 1–2.

10. Aristotle, *Rhetorica*, Book I.

11. J.L. Austin, *Sense and Sensibilia* (Oxford, Clarendon Press, 1962), p. 73.

12. For further elaboration, see my 'Tasks of Confucian Ethics,' *Journal of Chinese Philosophy*, 6, no. 1 (1979). Compare with Xie Fuya, *Lunlixue xinlun* (Taibei, Commercial Press, 1973), p. 285.

13. John Rawls, 'The Independence of Moral Theory,' *Proceedings and Addresses of the American Philosophical Association*, Vol. XLVIII, 1974–5, p. 6.

14. For a detailed discussion, see my 'The Problem of Conceptual Unity in Hsün Tzu and Li Kou's Solution,' *Bulletin of Chinese Philosophical Association*, Vol. 3 (1985); and 'Hsün Tzu and the Unity of Virtues', *Journal of Chinese Philosophy*, 14, no. 4 (1987), [Chinese translation by Xu Han appeared in *Zhexue yu wenhua* 12, no. 12 (1985)]. A brief general discussion may be found in my 'Confucian Ethics' in James F. Childress and John Macquarrie (eds.), *The Westminster Dictionary of Christian Ethics* (Philadelphia, Westminster Press, 1986), pp. 113–16; and my *Ethical Argumention*, pp. 160–3.

15. *Zhengming*, L515–6, W143–4, D286. For further discussion, see *Ethical Argumentation*, pp. 44–5, 76–9, 160–3; and 'The Problem of Conceptual Unity,' pp. 476–9.

16. Chen, *Xunzi xueshuo*, p.125.

17. Arguably, ethical notions, particularly the open ones, act as challenges to our moral thinking in hard cases. More generally, from the point of view of moral ideals as ideal themes, for example, *dao* or *agape*, they act as challenges to specification of their concrete significance. For the former point, see J. Kovesi, *Moral Notions* (London, Routledge & Kegan Paul, 1967). For the latter, see my *Dimensions of Moral Creativity: Paradigms, Principles, and Ideals* (University Park, Pennsylvania State University Press, 1978), chapter 8; and the *The Unity of Knowledge and Action*, pp. 56–70.

18. See the papers cited in note 14.

19. This paper complements my earlier studies in 'Some Reflections on the Structure of Confucian Ethics', 'Dimensions of *Li* (Propriety): Reflections on an Aspect of Hsün Tzu's Ethics', and '*Li* and Moral Justification' in *Philosophy East and West*, 21, no. 2 (1971); 29, no. 4 (1979); and 33, no. 1 (1983). The first paper was reprinted with minor revision in my *Dimensions of Moral Creativity*, chapter 4.

20. R.G. Collingwood, *An Autobiography* (Oxford, Oxford University Press, 1939), p. 37.

21. W.G. Gallie, *Philosophy and Historical Understanding* (London, Chatto & Windus, 1964), chapter 8.

22. The present chapter pretends to no novelty in explication of *li*, for its merits, if any, owe to the reading and reflection on some of the Confucian classics. Apart from Xunzi, who offers us the best conception of *li*, perhaps inspired by Kongzi (*The Analects*), I am greatly indebted to the writers of the *Li Chi*, Li Gou, Zhu Xi, and to contemporary Confucians, particularly Chen Daqi and Kao Ming (Gao Ming). See Chen Daqi, *Kongzi xueshuo* (Taibei, Zhengzhong, 1977) and *Xunzi*

xueshuo (Taibei, Zhonghua wenhua, 1954); Kao Ming, *Lixue xintan* (Taibei, Xuesheng, 1980); Li Yekang, and others, *Sanli yanjiu lunji* (Taibei, Liming, 1981). For a translation of Kao Ming's recent paper, see 'Chu Hsi and the Discipline of Propriety' in Wing-tsit Chan (ed.), *Chu Hsi and Neo-Confucianism* (Honolulu, University of Hawaii Press, 1986). For a comparative-historical approach to *li*, see N.E. Fehl, *Rites and Propriety in Literature and Life: A Perspective for a Cultural History of Ancient China* (Hong Kong, Chinese University of Hong Kong Press, 1971).

23. While I was preparing this chapter, Dworkin's new book appeared. His distinction between concept and conception in some way parallels my reconstruction of Xunzi's distinction between generic and specific terms. In a way my task of shaping the notion of *li* may thus be properly considered as a development of a conception of *li*. Also in consonance with Dworkin's thesis on the nature of law, the task may be characterized as one of creative interpretation of a social institution, especially in view of his imaginary example of the institution of courtesy. This task, in his words, is '. . . to impose meaning on an institution—to see it in its best light—and then to restructure it in the light of that meaning.' However, on the whole, I refrained from appealing to the distinction between concept and conception, partly because of a desire to preserve consistency of usage with my previous writings on Confucian ethics; and partly because of my uncertainty concerning the logical propriety of assimilating two parallel distinctions, though Dworkin's distinction, construed in a non-dichotomous way, is useful in elucidating the force of Xunzi's distinction. As noted earlier the distinction between generic and specific terms is a functional one, not a logical dichotomy as seems to be the case in Dworkin's distinction between concept and conception. I am not certain about this construal of Dworkin's thesis. If we, one the contrary, take Dworkin's distinction in the non-dichotomous, functional sense, then we may also say that a conception, as distinct from a simple concept, is a complex concept as it embodies a conception that is developed in response to reasonable questions regarding the significance of the simple concept. Perhaps, in the final analysis, the choice of distinction is a matter of terminological preference. See R. Dworkin, *Law's Empire* (Cambridge, Harvard University Press, 1986), chapter 2. Also R. Dworkin, *Taking Rights Seriously* (Cambridge, Harvard University Press, 1978), pp. 134–6; *A Matter of Principle* (Cambridge, Harvard University Press 1986), pp. 70–3. For similar distinctions, see H.L.A. Hart, *The Concept of Law* (Oxford, Clarendon Press, 1961), pp. 156–60; J. Rawls, *A Theory of Justice* (Cambridge, Harvard University Press, 1971), pp. 5 and 9.

24. Alternatively, in the words of Li Gou, *li* is '. . . an abstract label (*xucheng*), a collective term for all laws and institutions.' See *Li Taibo xiansheng quanji* (Taibei: Wenhai, 1971), vol. 1, p. 192. For a brief but informative discussion of the content of the three classics of *li* (*Zhouli, Yili* and *Liji*), see Kao Ming, 'Chu Hsi's Discipline of Propriety.' A more detailed discussion of the *Liji* is found in Kao Ming, *Lixue xintan*, pp. 13–95. See also Joken Kato, 'The Meaning of *Li*,' *Philosophical Studies of Japan*, 4 (1963). It may be noted that the question of classification of ritual rules has no intrinsic philosophical significance, though of importance to *li*-scholarship.

25. See *The Analects* (*Lunyu*), 2:23. Compare with T. Aquinas, 'Treatise on Law', *Summa Theologica*, Question 94, Fifth Article. Compare with Henry Rosemont, 'Notes from a Confucian Perspective: Which Human Acts are Moral Acts', *International Philosophical Quarterly*, 16 (1976), p. 60.

26. See Wang Meng'ou, *Liji jinzhu jinyi* (Taibei, Commercial Press, 1977), vol. 2, p. 498. The translation is adopted from Kao Ming, 'Chu Hsi's Discipline of Propriety,' p. 322. See also J. Legge (tr.), *Li Ki or Collection of Treatises on the Role of Propriety or Ceremonial Usage* (Delhi, Motilal Banarsidass, 1966), vol. 2,

UNDERSTANDING THE CHINESE MIND

p. 102. Throughout the quotation, I retain the transcription of key notions rather than adopt the proposed translation of different writers.
27. Legge, *Li Ki*, vol. 2, p. 275; Wang, *Liji*, vol. 2, p. 663
28. Legge, *Li Ki*, vol. 1, p. 390; Wang, *Liji*, vol. 1, p. 308.
29. See *Bugou*, L43; *Zhishi*, L306. See also *The Analects*, 15 : 17; 18 : 8.
30. See Kao Ming, 'Chu Hsi's Discipline of Propriety,' p. 324. (Chu Hsi's Preface to *Chia-li*.)
31. Jaroslav Pelikan, *The Vindication of Tradition* (New York, Yale University Press, 1984), p. 65. A contemporary Confucian theorist would concur with Pelikan that the critical examination of a living tradition is '. . . made obligatory, not only by the inner dynamic of the tradition itself, but by outsiders who have raised questions about the unexamined assumptions of the tradition' (p. 72).
32. My translation. Compare with Legge, *Li Ki*, vol. 1, pp. 62–3; Wang, *Liji*, p. 2.
33. See *Dimensions of Moral Creativity*, pp. 72–106.
34. See *zhishi*, L307.
35. L. Wittgenstein, *Philosophical Investigations* (New York, Macmillan, 1958), Part I, secs. 85–7 and 201.
36. 'If there are laws, but in actual practice they do not prove to be of general applicability, then points not specifically covered by the laws are bound to be left undecided . . . Where laws exist, to carry them out, where they do not exist, to act in the spirit of precedent and analogy' (*Wangzhi*, L163, W35 and D123). For further discussion, see *Ethical Argumentation*, pp. 65–73.
37. This concern is particularly evident in the occasional tendency of early Confucians in associating *li* with its homophone, meaning 'reason' or 'rationale'. The ritual theorists of the third century were mainly concerned with the reasoned defense of the established ritual code. As Waley points out, their task 'was to detrivialize ritual, to arrest its lapse into a domain of mere etiquette or good manners by reintegrating it into the current system of thought'. A. Waley, *The Analects of Confucius* (New York, Random House, 1938), p. 59. For the evolution of *li* in early Confucianism, see Hu Shi, *Zhongguo zhexue shi dagang* (1918), Part I (Taibei, Shangwu yinshuju, 1947), pp. 134–43. Compare with Herbert Fingarette, *Confucius—The Secular as Sacred* (New York, Harper Torchbooks, 1972).
38. See *Ethical Argumentation*, pp. 55–100.
39. Note 38, especially pp. 51–5. Also, Stephen Nalor Thomas, *Practical Reasoning in Natural Language* (Englewood Cliffs, Prentice Hall, 1976), second edition. In philosophy of law or legal theory, the distinction between explanation and justification is especially difficult to maintain in a clear-cut fashion if we adopt Dworkin's recent thesis that '. . . legal reasoning is an exercise in constructive interpretation' (Dworkin, *Law's Empire*, Preface). Indeed, in recent American Constitutional Theory, the issue between interpretivism and non-interpretivism (or textualism and non-textualism) seems largely an issue in adequate explanation of the nature and function of the U.S. Constitution. The justificatory question, if distinguished, seems parasitic upon the explanatory theory. See, for example, John Hart Ely, *Democracy and Distrust: A Theory of Judicial Review* (Cambridge, Harvard University Press, 1980); Michael Perry, *The Constitution, the Courts, and Human Rights* (New Haven, Yale University Press, 1982); and the Interpretation Symposium, *Southern California Law Review*, vol. 58, nos. 1 and 2 (1985), especially articles by Michael Perry, D.A.J. Richards, Larry Simon, and Frederick Schauer.
40. *Tianlun*, L379, W87; *Dalü*, L603.
41. See also *Lilun*, L428–9, D224, and W95; *Zhishi*, L307.
42. In an earlier study ('Dimensions of *Li*'), I adopted an axiological approach to elucidating the functions of *li* in terms of the interconnection of moral, aesthetic,

THE CONCEPT OF *LI*231

and religious values. The focus there was on the value-significance of ritual performance. A later paper ('Li and Moral Justification') elaborates the moral dimension with reference to some contemporary justificatory questions on human rights and the role of music in dealing with the problem of moral emotions. In what follows, to avoid repetition, I focus on the functions of *li* mainly for the purpose of providing a background for dealing with the justificatory issue in the next section.

43. Compare with W89 and D213. This translation is a modification of the one given by Dubs and Watson. The major emendation pertains to *yi*. This reading is based on Xunzi's claim that *fen* (established limits of action or social distinctions) owe their existence to *yi* construed as sense of rightness, the exercise of which is in accord with reason. See *Dalü*, L605–6; *Wangzhi*, L180, D136, and D45. An extensive analysis of *yi* is given in my 'Hsün Tzu and the Unity of Virtue.'

44. A detailed discussion of Xunzi's conception of human nature and arguments is given in my 'The Conceptual Aspect of Hsün Tzu's Philosophy of Human Nature' and 'The Qusai-Empirical Aspect of Hsün Tzu's Philosophy of Human Nature,' *Philosophy East and West*, 27, no. 4 (1977) and 28, no. 1 (1978).

45. *Zhishi*, L307; *Lilun*, L419, W90, and D214.

46. 'Merit (*de*) is the criterion for promotion or demotion within the hierarchy; ability the criterion for conferring official appointment' (*Zhishi*, L307). 'Although a man may be the descendent of kings, dukes, or high court ministers, if he cannot adhere to *li* and *yi* he should be ranked among the commoners. Although a man may be the descendent of commoners, if he has acquired learning, and can adhere to *li* and *yi* he should be promoted to the post of prime minister or high court official' (*Wangzhi*, L161, W33*, and D121). For an instructive account of Xunzi's political thought, see Y.P. Mei, 'Hsün Tzu's Theory of Government', *Tsing Hua Journal of Chinese Studies*, NS 8, no. 1–2 (1970). See also Henry Rosemont, Jr., 'State and Society in the Hsün Tzu', *Monumenta Serica*, vol. 29 (1970–1). For Chinese sources, see valuable discussions in Chen, *Xunzi xueshuo*, pp. 161–81, and Cai Renhou, *Kong Meng Xun zhexue* (Taibei, Xuesheng, 1984; pp. 479–515; and Wei Zhengtong, *Xunzi yu gudai zhexue* (Taibei, Shangwu yinshuju, 1974), pp. 80–124.

47. For further discussion, see '*Li* and Moral Justification', pp. 3–6.

48. See also *Rongru*, L69, D65–6.

49. 'People have both a sense of rightness (*yi*) and a sense of benefit. Even a Yao or Shun cannot destroy people's love of what is beneficial, but he can see to it that their love of what is beneficial will not prevail over their love of rightness' (*Dalü*, L619). Perhaps, it is this view that renders intelligible the saying. 'The *li* have their foundation in compliance with [the demands of] human mind' (*Dalü*, L605).

50. Thomé H. Fang, *The Chinese View of Life: The Philosophy of Comprehensive Harmony* (Taibei, Linjing, 1980). (First published in 1956). Along with this incisive book, one must also take note of Herbert Fingarette, *Confucius: The Secular as Sacred*; and Tu Wei-ming, 'The Creative Tension between *Jen* and *Li*', and '*Li* as Humanization', *Philosophy East and West*, 18 (1968) and 22 (1972). For my own work, see papers citied in note 17. For the anthropological significance of *li*, see A.R. Radcliff-Brown, 'Taboo', in W.A. Lassa and E.Z. Vogt (eds.) *Reader in Comparative Religion* (New York, Harper & Row, 1965); and Victor Turner, *Dramas, Fields, and Metaphors* (Ithaca, Cornell University Press, 1974), pp. 283–5.

51. For a discussion of Xunzi's theory of moral education, see my 'The Ethical Uses of the Past in Early Confucianism', pp. 135–9. Compare with Y.P. Mei, 'Hsün Tzu's Theory of Education', *Tsing Hua Journal of Chinese Studies*, NS 2, no. 2 (1961).

52. In Confucian ethics, as Chen points out, it is important to contrast *meide*, literally 'beautiful virtue', from *ede*, literally 'ugly virtue', for *de* has also a value-neutral sense. In most Confucian literature, when *de* is used alone, there is implicit

the evaluative sense of possession of laudable traits of character. As one recent comprehensive Chinese dictionary put it, *de* is the nature that is formed after personal cultivation. Arguably, it is *yi* that distinguishes *meide* from *ede*. See the insightful discussion in Chen Daqi, *Bingfan de daode guan* (Taibei, Zhonghua, 1977), ch. 9; and *Zhongwen da cidian*, vol. 3 (Taibei, Zhonghua xueshuyuan, 1979).

53. For Xunzi, transformation (*hua*) of things consists in the change in appearance (*zhuang*), rather than the basic stuff or actuality (*shi*). See *Zhengming*, L516, D287, and W144.

54. For extensive discussion, see my 'The Conceptual Aspect of Hsün Tzu's Philosophy of Human Nature'.

55. 'A single desire which one receives from nature (*tian*) is regulated and directed by the mind in many different ways, consequently, it may be diffcult to identify and distinguish it in terms of its original appearance . . . If the guidance of the mind is in accord with reason, although desires are many, what harm will this be to good government' (*Zhengming*, L527, W151*, and D294). This interpretation in terms of the distinction between natural and reflective desires is discussed in 'Dimensions of *Li*', pp. 380–1. After publication, I discovered the same interpretation of this problematic passage in Liang Qixiong's annotated text. Liang remarks that the contrast lies in the distinction between *tianxing yu* (desires as endowed by nature or natural desires) and *lixing yu* (desires as guided by reason or reflective desires). Because of this distinction, it is difficult to classify all desires in the same way. See Liang Qixiong, *Xunzi jianshi* (Taibei, Shangwu yinshuju, 1978), p. 323.

56. Joken Kato, 'The Meaning of *Li*', p. 82.

57. As an example of regulative rules, Searle cites the 'rules of polite table behavior'. For a Confucian, however, rules of etiquette are constitutive rather than regulative rules in Searle's sense. Rules of etiquette are part of the *li* of civility that perform the ennobling function. Serving guests at the table, for example, is quite distinct from placing food at the table. Negative moral rules or precepts are better examples of regulative rules. Unlike rules of chess (Searle's example of constitutive rules), these precepts do not define the nature of the antecedent forms of behavior. See John R. Searle, 'How to Derive "Ought" from "Is"', *Philosophical Review*, 73 (1964). Reprinted in W.D. Hudson (ed.), *The Is/Ought Question* (London, Macmillan, 1969), p. 131. For distinction in the same terminology but used with different purpose, see J.D. Mabbott, *An Introduction to Ethics* (London, Hutchinson University Library, 1966), pp. 43–5.

58. The following set of observations on the human predicament are fairly familiar in the history of Western ethical theory, for example, Protagoras, Hobbes, Hume, Hart, Rawls, and Warnock. However, this set of observations has been used for establishing quite different theses. Xunzi's view of human nature is closest to Hume and Hart. It must also be noted that this set of observations may be recast in the form of arguments from thought-experiments, as I have done in my 'The Quasi-Empirical Aspect of Hsün Tzu's Philosophy of Human Nature'. For a survey and critical discussion, see J.L. Mackie, *Ethics: Inventing Right and Wrong* (New York, Penguin Books, 1977), ch. 5. A comparative critique may be found in my 'Morality and Human Nature', *Philosophy East and West*, 32, no. 3 (1982); Chinese translation by Li Dengxin in *Zhexue yu wenhua*, vol. 13, no. 7, 1986. For an incisive exposition of Xunzi's theory of human nature, see D.C. Lau, 'Theories of Human Nature in *Mencius* and *Shyuntzyy*', *Bulletin of the School of Oriental and African Studies*, 15 (1953).

59. 'Yao asked Shun, "What are man's passions like?" Shun replied, "Man's passions are very unlovely things indeed! What need is there to ask any further? Once a man acquires a wife and children, he no longer treats his parents as a filial son should. Once he succeeds in satisfying his cravings and desires, he neglects his duty to his friends. Once he has won a high position and a good stipend, he ceases

to serve his sovereign with a loyal heart"' (*Xing'e*, L555, W168, DL314). Compare Hume's similar, but more perspicuous observation on the confined generosity of man: 'Now it appears, that in the original frame of our mind, our strongest attention is confined to ourselves; our next is extended to our relations and acquaintance; and 'tis only the weakest which reaches to strangers and indifferent persons. This partiality, then, and unequal affection, must not only have an influence on our behavior and conduct in society, but even on our ideas of vice and virtue.' D. Hume, *A Treatise on Human Nature* (Oxford, Clarendon Press, 1951), Book 3, Pt. 2, Sec. 2.

60. Of special concern for Xunzi is the suffering of the aged and the weak, who are particularly vulnerable to exploitation of the strong. Moreover, the situation without regulative rules would not be beneficial even to the strong, since they will 'suffer the calamity of division and strife' (*Fuguo*, L196 and D152).

61. This translation is Lau's. I have not, however, followed his manner of exposition. The original context of the passage deals with the problem of scarcity. See Lau, 'Theories of Human Nature in *Mencius* and *Shyuntzyy*,' p. 552. For Dubs' translation, see D152.

62. Professor Dahlstrom has justly pointed out that the connection between these two senses of partiality was unclear in my *Ethical Argumentation*. See Daniel Dahlstrom. 'The *Tao* of Ethical Argumentation' and my response in 'Some Aspects of Ethical Argumentation: A Reply to Daniel Dahlstrom and John Marshall', *Journal of Chinese Philosophy*, 14, no. 4, (1987). For an account of Xunzi's notion of partiality in the sense of limited foresight, see *Ethical Argumentation*, pp. 138–45.

63. For the importance of this sort of reasoning in Xunzi, see *Ethical Argumentation*, pp. 91–5. For a general discussion, see Thomas, *Practical Reasoning in Natural Language*, ch. I. This argument has close affinity to Hume and Hart, and to some extent, to Warnock and Rawls. See Hume, *A Treatise of Human Nature*, Book 3, Pt. 2, Section 2; Hart, *Concept of Law*, pp. 189–91; G.J. Warnock, *The Object of Morality* (London, Methuen, 1971), ch. 1; J. Rawls, *A Theory of Justice* (Cambridge, Harvard University Press, 1971), pp. 126–30. See also R.S. Downie, *Roles and Values* (London, Methuen, 1971), ch. 2; and Mackie, *Ethics: Inventing Right and Wrong*, ch. 5.

64. Lau, 'Theories of Human Nature in *Mencius* and *Shyuntzyy*', p. 556.

65. For a discussion of this textual issue and my reconstruction, see *Ethical Argumentation*, pp. 61–5. Recently, Professor Marshall plausibly suggested that Xunzi's notion of sage may be construed as an ideal legislator. On this reconstruction, '. . . ritual and moral rules have the authority of sage-kings, conceived as ideal legislators, this authority deriving in turn from the principle their legislation expresses. For Hsün Tzu, this principle is *ren*—roughly benevolence'. See John Marshall, 'Hsün Tzu's Moral Epistemology', *Journal of Chinese Philosophy*, 14, no 4 (1987). For a forceful critique of Xunzi's historical claim, see Lau, 'Theories of Human Nature in *Mencius* and *Shyuntzyy*', p. 562; and Liang Ch'i-hsiung (Liang Qixiong), 'A Descriptive Review of Hsün Tzu's Thought', *Chinese Studies in Philosophy*, 6, no. 1 (1974), pp. 20–3.

66. 'If one wants to inquire [into the *dao* of] the former kings, the foundation of *ren* and *yi*, then *li* is the proper road you must travel' (*Quanxue*, L15, W21*, and D38). See also *Quanxue*, D40 and W22; and *Dalü*, L605–6 given in note 70 below.

67. See Wing-tsit Chan, 'The Evolution of the Confucian Concept of *Jen*', *Philosophy East and West*, 4, no. 4 (1955); and 'Chinese and Western Interpretations of *Jen* (Humanity)', *Journal of Chinese Philosophy*, 2, no. 2 (1975).

68. For a suggestion of an answer in terms of the notion of reasonableness, see my *The Unity of Knowledge and Action*, ch. 4.

69. See my 'The Problem of Conceptual Unity in Hsün Tzu and Li Kou's Solution' and 'Hsün Tzu and the Unity of Virtues.'

70. The following passage provides the basis of my brief summary of the completion thesis. 'Expressing affection toward parents and relatives, respecting and loving old friends, and rewarding meritorious deeds are the different degrees of *ren*. Honouring and reverencing the eminent and the worthy are reasonable requirements of *yi*. Acting in accord with rules and regulations [on matters pertaining to *ren* and *yi*] in proper order is the requirement of *li*. *Ren* is expressed in love . . . *yi* is accord with reason . . . *Li* is regulation . . . If one extends benevolent affection without regard to reason, one cannot realize the objective of *ren*. If one acts in accord with reason without paying heed to the *li*, one cannot realize the objective of *yi*. If one has a clear understanding of rules and regulations, but is unable to live in harmony with others, one cannot realize the objective of *li* . . . Hence, it is said, 'although *ren*, *li*, and *yi* . . . are distinct virtues, their ultimate destination constitutes a unity . . When a person has a clear comprehension of the interconnection of these three things (that is, *ren*, *yi*, and *li*), and acts accordingly, he may be said to be a man of *dao*' (*Dalü*, L605).

71. For this distinction between customary and reflective morality, see J. Dewey, *Theory of the Moral Life* (New York, Holt, Rinehart & Winston, 1960), pp. 3–8. See also the distinction between positive and critical morality in H.L.A. Hart, *Law, Liberty and Morality* (Stanford, Stanford University Press, 1963), pp. 17–24. For a tentative exploration of this problem of transcultural principles, see my 'The Status of Principles in Confucian Ethics', *Proceedings*, the International Symposium on Confucianism and the Modern World, Taibei, Taiwan, 12–18 November 1987.

72. For a detailed discussion, see my 'Dimensions of *Li* (Propriety)'.

73. Notably Kant, with his unqualified insistence on the autonomy of ethics or 'pure moral philosophy', acknowledges the notion of beauty as '. . . the symbol of morality'. See J.H. Bernard's translation of Kant's *Critique of Judgment* (New York, Hafner, 1951), pp. 196–200. For a rare defense of the notion of moral beauty, see Guy Sircello, *A New Theory of Beauty* (Princeton, Princeton University Press, 1975), pp. 81–97.

74. See note 39.

75. There are some rare exceptions to the standard lines of meta-ethics. I have in mind some remarks of Austin, MacDonald, and Hampshire. Austin, for example, once claimed that ethics cannot be adequately studied without paying attention to 'conventional or ritual acts.' MacDonald, perhaps inspired by Austin's notion of performatives, maintains that when philosophers attend to the analogy between moral judgments and 'performatory and ritual speech', they can derive some insight into '. . . the impersonal, authoritative, and practical features unaccounted for or distorted in other analyses'. She suggests that closer study may disclose more than just an analogy, for '. . . moral judgments are . . . , as it were, impersonal verdicts of a common moral ritual'. Among contemporary philosophers, Hampshire is singular in drawing attention to the importance of seeing the connection between ritual and morality. I shall cite some of his suggestions shortly. Hampshire's recent collection of essays, in my view, repays careful study, especially for its contribution to moral philosophy. See J.L. Austin, *How to Do Things with Words* (Cambridge, Harvard University Press, 1962), pp. 19–20; Margaret MacDonald, 'Ethics and the Ceremonial Use of Language', in Max Black (ed.), *Philosophical Analysis: A Collection of Essays* (Ithaca, Cornell University Press, 1950), pp. 227–29; Stuart Hampshire, *Morality and Conflict* (Cambridge, Harvard University Press, 1983).

76. A.R. Lacey, *A Dictionary of Philosophy* (New York, Charles Scribner's Sons, 1976), p. 135.

77. Dewey, *Theory of the Moral Life*, p. 3.

78. MacDonald, 'Ethics and the Ceremonial Use of Language', p. 228.

79. Hampshire continues, 'Mathematics and the natural sciences do cross frontiers and unite humanity. But we also need to enter into, and to share, the conventions of significant behaviour and of speech and of expressions which hold a community together as a community, in part thereby creating the frontier which is crossed by mathematics and the natural sciences.' (See Hampshire, *Morality and Conflict*, p. 162.)

80. Hampshire, p. 97, see note 79. (Italics mine). See also pp. 91 and 131.

81. See Gluckman, 'Les Rites de Passage' in Max Gluckman (ed.), *Essays on the Ritual of Social Relations* (Manchester, Manchester University Press, 1962), pp. 25–6.

82. Hampshire, *Morality and Conflict*, pp. 102–3.

83. See Chan, *Instructions on Practical Living*, sec. 64.

Glossary

bian　辨, 偏

bieming　別名

Bugou pian　不苟篇

Cai Renhou　蔡仁厚

Chen Daqi　陳大齊

dao　道

daoli　道理

de　德

decao　德操

e　惡

ede　惡德

fen　分

Fuguo Pian　富國篇

geiren zhi qiu　給人之求

gongming　共名

Hu Shi　胡適

hua　化

Jundao Pian　君道篇

junzi　君子

lei　類

li　禮

Liji　禮記

Lilun Pian　禮論篇

lixian　禮憲

lixingyu　理性欲

Liang Qixiong　梁啓雄

lun　倫

meide　美德

meishen　美身

qianshu　兼術

Quanxue Pian　勸学篇

qun　群

ren　仁

Rongru Pian　榮辱篇

Ruxiao Pian　儒效篇

shan　善

shi　實

shuo　說

Tianlun Pian　天論篇

tianxing yu　天性欲

Wangba Pian　王霸篇

Wang Yangming　王陽明

wei　偽

weizhi　謂之

wen　文

Xie Fuya　謝扶雅

xing　性

Xing'e Pian　性惡篇

Xunzi　荀子

yang　養

yi　義

zheng　正

Zhenglun Pian　正論篇

Zhengming Pian　正名篇

zhiwei　之謂

zhixing heyi　知行合一

zhuang　狀

Zidao Pian　子道篇

8   Chinese Aesthetics

KUANG-MING WU

THIS chapter treats beauty from a Chinese perspective, benefiting from the clarity of Western philosophical analysis.

For the Chinese, beauty is the constitutive inter-involvement of many into one, and one with many, until the entire unison becomes both concrete-particular and cosmic-universal, both in scale and in substance. Here is a twofold characteristic—distinction and interchange, even on the level of the subject. As a result, beauty is less of a subject to be independently discussed than a pervasive attitude and atmosphere in which one moves and has one's being.

The original aesthetic experience is a continuum whose integrity is later found to be interpenetrated by various elements. Thus, *pace* Filmer S. Northrop, the Chinese experience is a *differentiated* aesthetic continuum. This is shown by Zhuangzi (Chuang Tzu) who single-handedly influenced the Chinese aesthetic experience more than anyone else. He told us a famous story which clinched the philosophical parody of his Second Chapter:

In earlier times,
Zhuang Zhou dreamed, taking himself to be a butterfly.
Flitting, flitting, he *was* a butterfly.
Convincing himself of what he was, he went as he pleased.
He did not understand 'Zhou.'
Suddenly, he awoke.
Then—thoroughly, thoroughly, it was Zhou.
But then he did not understand—did Zhou's dream make the butterfly?
Did the butterfly's dream make Zhou?
Zhou and the butterfly—there must be, then, a division.
This it is which people call 'things interchanging' (my translation).

Two points are entwined here: (a) Zhuangzi is not butterfly, dreaming is not awakening, knowing is not ignorance, neither of which is uncertainty; yet (b) these distinct situations so interfuse, interdepend, interchange, that we are uncertain of where we are. These two moments in Zhuangzi's dream experience correspond with the twin pillars of the Confucian Utopia, *li*, 'decorum', and *yue*, 'music'. The essence of *li* is *jie*, 'control'; that of *yue* is *he*, 'harmony'. Control restrains, harmony blends. *Li* holds to distinct integrity; *yue* flows in mutual interchange. They answer Zhuangzi's two moments in his dream experience. These two points— distinction and interchange, many interacting into a whole, and the whole promoting the many—pervade our life. It is this twofold life-experience, both Daoist and Confucian, which art reflects.

In literature, the entire world comes to us, yet stamped with the author's perspective. Here, on the one hand, many scenes, events and people interact, opening up an entire tapestry of the life-world. The author is not to be seen. Yet, on the other hand, the entire work is toned and hued with the author's peculiar sentiment. The same holds for calligraphy, painting, music. The universal and the particular are there, both intact, both infused, informed by the other. One is one and not the other, thanks to the other.

This Chinese world of beauty differs from Western philosophy which tends to analyse, that is, exclusively dichotomize and isolate elements from the whole. The separation-mentality takes 'characterization' as isolation of characteristics from a coherent whole. Socrates' quest for definitional essence (abstracted from its concrete embodiments) of piety (or courage, love, the Real, and the like) led to the famous platonic doctrine of Forms, eternally separate from our world; their relation must be maintained by another doctrine of Participation and Recollection.

The trend continued. Descartes isolated the *cogito* and split existence into two—thinking and extension, the subjective and the objective. The Copernican revolutions of the critical Kant and the phenomenological Husserl operated in this mode—Kant in the subjective categories over against the unknowable Noumena, Husserl in his noetic-noematic distinction, transcendental Ego, subjective intentionality, *Wesensschau*, and his mighty fight against 'psychologism'.

Sartre's subjective For-Itself constructs the objective world; Heidegger's truth is objectively Revealed (Uncovered) to the subject. Merleau-Ponty's 'perception' is a network of relations connecting the subjective and the objective, the former (the invisible) responding to the call of the latter (the visible). In Mikel Dufrenne, an aesthetic object (the work of art) is synthesized with its aesthetic perception by the subject in the affective *a priori*, which is both cosmological-metaphysical (objective) and existential-anthropological (subjective).

Similarly, Santayana's beauty is in the beholder's eyes; Dewey's beauty is the subject's meaningful experience making the intended difference. In analytic philosophers the subjective aspect of experience is one of the *objects* of their investigations. All in all, characterization is isolation and split before putting-together.

But of course distinction is one thing; isolation is another. Western aesthetics distinguishes by isolation; it characterizes beauty, for instance, by setting it apart from all other considerations— isolating beauty as objective quality, subjective attitude, or both, but never quite as pervasive togetherness of things and persons, interdependent and interconstitutive. Yet ingenious isolation makes for clarity of understanding, and can be much utilized to organize Chinese insights on art and beauty. The following pages are such an attempt to benefit from both traditions in understanding beauty.[1]

Yin-yang Constitutive Involvement

Beauty is something poetic, which is *yin-yang* constitutive involvement. Originally meaning the shaded and the sunny, the *yin* and the *yang* are reciprocals, that is, counterparts and counterpoints. Counterpoints are contraries and contrasts such as yes and no, can and cannot, dark and bright, good and evil, comic and tragic, construction and destruction, and so on. Counterparts are mutuals such as this and that, form and content, will and desires, feeling and reason, body and mind, subject and object, husband and wife, writer and reader, composer, player, and audience, the Five Elements (elementary ways of things), and so on.

When these reciprocals are constitutively involved one with another, the situation is 'beautiful'. It is mutual constitution, in which the one is so much a constituent of the other that when the one is taken away the other disappears. Positively put, these elements—counterpoints and counterparts—constitute together a self-involved unity, presenting a self-recursive integrity.

Since this is a unity of *counterpoints*, it is always a unity in polar motion; here dwell such phrases as 'use of no use', 'breath-bone', 'the Way that is no way', 'self-forgetting', and the like, describing the inscrutable vitality of beauty. Being creative constitution, it is called *poetic*. The entire world comes alive; things dwell therein without attachment, accommodated without being overwhelmed.

By the same token, as *counterparts* are constitutively involved, the form and the content, the natal and the actualized, and the like, realize their self-referential unity and consistency. It is then dispersed, and then realized again, in a dancing rhythm. This is the world of beauty.

In this atmosphere of poetic beauty, the 'affective quality', 'atmosphere of feeling', the subjective answer to the objective call, and the like, are included and transcended. We need no dichotomy here.[2]

Here each element of the counterpoints-and-counterparts (a) is mutually distinguished from each other, and (b) interchanges with and constitutes the other. And since they are mutually 'counter', their togetherness is radically dynamic. Here doing is not doing; in aesthetic creativity not-doing is involved in doing, and doing is involved in not-doing, as Daoist 'non-doing' aptly describes. Here is that 'bone (—structure of) breath (—thrust)', the vitality that forms the inevitable reasonable concord of beauty. Here the self forgets itself in ennobling the integrities of individual wholes.[3]

'You are doing metaphysics', someone may object, 'for "all things interrelated" is metaphysics, not aesthetics. Aesthetics concerns feelings, sensibility, perceptiveness, not cognitive comprehensive interpretation.' My response is as follows.

Metaphysics produces an abstractive scheme as a principle for the interpretation of all things. Aesthetic comprehension is not abstractive but both symbolic (that at which things are thrown together) and metaphoric (ferrying us from one concrete meaning/shore to another). Here there is no inference but transference and mutuality. Chinese aesthetics is never an abstraction but is concrete, never particular *or* abstractive universal but always intersubjective and interobjective, interfused and interdependent. If Chinese people have metaphysics it is aesthetic (metaphoric, co-implicative), and if they have aesthetics it is metaphysical (comprehensive, structural).

Now we can go into concrete characterizations of Chinese beauty. The traditional topics in beauty—poeticity, calligraphy, music, dance, painting—will be treated to show how Chinese beauty is a comprehensive interpenetration of parts and wholes. Unsuspected topics such as cooking, martial arts, medicine, and even politics will be treated to show how beauty is more of a pervasive attitude than a specific subject matter.

Being Poetic

To be poetic is to be self-involved. A writing is poetic when:
  (i) its content (what is says) involves its *form* (how it says it);
  (ii) one *place* in the writing explicates what is said in other places. Such structural involvement may use literary devices such as rhythm (metre) and versification (parallelism, alliteration, and so on), but the reverse is not true. Writing in verse (which is called 'poetry') may or may not be poetic writing; verse is neither needed nor enough to make a writing poetic. Some verses are not poetic; some poetic writings are not in verse.

Furthermore, a writing is poetic when:
  (iii) its *thought* progresses self-reflexively; its beginning, middle and concluding thoughts mutually enhance, entwine, and entertain, and thereby
  (iv) involve the *reader* in an open-ended quest for more implications, sometimes mutually reinforcing, sometimes mutually contrasting. Thus:
  (v) to be poetic is to be *open*-ended, unfinished, ever ready for future involvement, devolvement, development.

Such various involvements render the reader one with the poetic writing, involving the poetic writing with the reader. This is 'self-ing' involvement, self-involvement, *creating* a new self; it is 'poetic'.

Many say, for instance, that the *Zhuangzi* is poetic; few look into its meaning. The *Zhuangzi* is poetic in that its *thoughts* weave into clusters—a thought points to another which explains it, then the pair points to another, and the movement goes on—and goes *back*. Clusters of thought co-mirror, co-imply into layer after layer of meaning. A spiral of thought loops, twisting back to itself only to start over again a new direction, from a fresh perspective. 'Loop' sounds linear.[4] It is rather a co-deepening co-resonance; to enter its pulsing rhythm is to enjoy life.[5]

How does such looping resonance work? As our (author's, reader's) eyes thus move back and forth with our minds, our very perspectives change. Such multi-linear movements form spiral loops, and the loops overlap, leapfrog, criss-cross. This is an art of spatial looping and temporal echoing. A logical architectonic—analytical scrutiny, systematic synthesis—builds itself while the same perspective stays at the same spot. When many perspectives bounce off each other, the scenes change and resonance and history happen. This is movement in time, recursive and resonating.

In such co-echoing, *thoughts* themselves have a poetic cadence which renders them intelligible. Often stories are told, for the story is coherent in its layers of recursive meaning. Besides, stories can be freely cut into bits and mixed into a montage, co-implicating, co-explicating. All this describes 'poetic writing', with or without a traditional literary pattern of poetry.

But *can* such writing be called 'poetic'? Well, what is the so-called 'poetry' like? Besides (a) co-responding rhythm, it (b) conforms to the established rule of versification—metre (rhyme) and cadence. And Chinese poetry (c) *opens* out to the Beyond, 'the Landscape beyond landscape' with 'radiant transparency', 'touching many things with few words'.[6] Thus poetry is poeticity, (a) and (c); (b) reinforces them.

Every expression has its rhythm: '[A]ll literatures are, in their infancy, metrical, . . . based on. . . regularly recurring rhythm.'[7] Later, our literary style was codified into 'rules of versification'; they fixed, standardized, and stranded our expressive rhythm.[8]

Now Owen Barfield must say that 'prosaic' and 'poetic' are irrelevant to literature. 'On the roof/ Of an itinerant vehicale I sat/ With vulgar men about me . . . ' is *verse*, and *prosaic*. ' . . . Behold now this vast city, a city of refuge. . . ' is *prose*, and *poetic*.[9] Zhuangzi, for instance, writes in poetic prose.

All this agrees with the 'poetic' in China. *Shi* has two meanings. In a narrow sense *shi* is poetry rigidly rhymed and metred, as distinguished from non-metred writing, *wen*. In a wide sense, *shi* is literature that expresses intention (*zhi*), that is, inner thoughts and feelings that chant, as distinguished from a descriptive report of external affairs (*shu*). Poeticity is used here in the latter wide sense,[10] which has its own inevitable natural cadence, rhyme, and metre, as the wind of our feeling brings up patterns of ripples in the waters of literary expression. But the wind has little to do with human convention; such natural ripples may or may not conform to the traditional canon of metre.[11]

Such *shi* in the wide sense naturally came to include the best of literature, even the description of acts, external or internal. If the Grand Historian Sima Qian (Ssu-ma Ch'ien) wrote poetic descriptive literature of external affairs, then the grand man Zhuangzi wrote poetic literature of internal affairs.

But what about metre? *Chinese* poetry is, for Wen Yiduo, something worth remembering, recording, and cherishing.[12] Here words are used in such a *way* as to 'arouse aesthetic imagination', that is, 'felt change of consciousness'[13]—the way of wedding rhythm and music to sense. One such wedding is performed by metre, the rhythmic recurrence of words and notions. The usual metric rules are only one variant among many such rhythmic patterns.

Prose describes meaning; poetry sings it. Poetic meaning happens when the reader co-resonates rhythmically; the strict convention of metre is spontaneous co-resonance in folk songs and folklore adopted and codified by recognized poets and institutional ritualists.

We cannot, then, judge non-metric poetic sentences as 'not poetic'. Zhuangzi's sentences whose sentiment pervades almost every Chinese poetic diction cannot be branded 'not poetic', just because they do not conform to the versification rules. Not to see poeticity in Zhuangzi's writing because of its overall lack of metre, makes as much sense as not to see rationality in Socrates' speech because of its overall lack of syllogistic jargon.

Literature, Music, Dance, and Painting

Logical principles are valid among poets, essayists and philosophers alike, yet used differently among them. What legitimizes their respective styles of usage is something contextual—the actual context of subjects, subject matters, precedents.

If logical principles are the rules and grammar of writing, then context is their being-woven-together with the actuality of subjects and subject matters, to form an under woven-pattern (*wen*, commonly translated as 'literature') for subtle deep literary revelation. This is the contextual legitimation of a great writer. The contextual interweaving extends throughout culture, precedents, etymology, pronunciation, rhythm, convention and taste—all woven into what is real and compelling.

And so great literature gathers two legitimations into one—logical and contextual. The Western thinking tends toward abstraction into logical universality; the Chinese tends toward discernment of contextual diversity.

Such difference in emphasis explains the difference of approach and of topics in aesthetics. Western aesthetics pursues the essence of beauty and the definition to creative novelty. Chinese aesthetic considerations look into what counts as vital, profound, structural, expansive, and interpenetrative. The West analyzes and argues; the Chinese rhymes in homophones, etymologies, and precedents. The literary rhyming comes to us as naturally as music and dance. In fact literature came from, and forms a unity with, music and dance; literature is a linguistic extension of sympathetic bodily rhythm with that of nature. Confucius was very intent on music and its educative value.[14] Zhuangzi characterized the Utopic situation in musical terms (as in Chapter Eight), and when he attacked music and literary eminence his sentences soared up to the heights of musical literary beauty (as in Chapter Ten).

Chinese characters are ideograms, patterned after what we see. Chinese literature is a composition (collection of these ideograms) patterned after music and dance; it is something rhythmic and auditory, in sympathy with natural rhythm inside our body and outside it. 'Good' sentences read well, that is, chant well. Good literature is poetic, good poetry is musical, and good music is danceable. There is, then, a felt unity of seeing and hearing in Chinese literature.

As visible literature is auditory, so are visible painting and calligraphy, in which rhythms of our nature and nature of things breathe as they live. The cosmic breathings-in and -out must correspond with the shades and lustre of the painting. And the pulsation of cosmic vitality must go through the slow and the fast, the vibrant and the subtle, in calligraphy. At the lifting of the brush, the cosmos sighs in anticipation. Calligraphy is poetic painting, painting is pictorial poetry, and both pulsate in musical rhythm.

What does all this—poetry, dance, music, literature, painting, and calligraphy—have to do with actuality?

Zhuangzi used the word 'piping' (Chapter Two). Piping comes about when two non-beings meet—hollows in things and the blowing wind. 'Gentle wind, then a small chorus (*he*); whirling wind, then a huge chorus', said he (Chapter Two; my translation). Selflessly listening, he discerned three pipings—the piping of humans, of earth, and of heaven; so can we. As the dead ashes blow up sounds of the hollow dry wood, so do *we* selflessly take part in the cosmic fugues, mutually sounding forth, mutually shading in.

Blowing thus over the hollows, the wind (nothing-power) calls forth the piping of the earth. It inspires the piping of humans which interacts with it. And both pipings reveal their root, the piping of heaven, manifesting itself in them, stirring up nature into musical resonance. Humans respond by singing with it in their daily goings-on and by sometimes composing music (artworks, thinkings). If human piping is music, then earthly piping is musical (yet-to-be music), and heavenly piping is what evokes both. Human piping is resonance with thing-resonances (earthly piping). Heavenly piping is 'yet-to-begin to yet-to-begin all these'. These are the three levels of the cosmic polyphonic fugue, produced in the meeting of the wind with hollows, resonating among nothings.

What does all this mean? The wind is vibration, which is nothing in itself, but a thing vibrating; yet that thing is not in itself its vibration. But is it really all right to say that something is not in itself vibration? Where is that something that vibrates, if not in its peculiar vibration?

Furthermore, without the wind of vibration, can something vibrate as itself? It stays quiet and hidden (a hollow, a nothing) until vibrated, to resonate to the wind of sympathetic resonance. Thus something is as it is when it vibrates to the wind, vibrating itself forth.

Likewise, the wind is an initiator of vibrations in many things as they respectively are, and yet it is nothing but a sympathetic resonance *of* something. The wind is itself and not itself. Thus, with the wind in sympathetic resonance, activity and passivity, subject and object, existence and nothing, make sense in terms of one another.

Resonating vibration is sound with particular structural interrelation—among the sound, the wind, and the peculiar characteristic of each thing. If the wind is a world force of resonance, then each existential sound is a manifestation of the world in the manner of a particular thing, being as much of that sounding thing as the world sounds/sings forth in that thing. It is not right, then, just to say wind, resonance, and vibration, as if they are not related.

And so Zhuangzi used 'piping' (chorus) to characterize the situation. Music is an organized group of sounds, a structured nonbeing that is not nothing. And piping is of three levels, each closely interrelated to the other two; we see in one the other two. The world is such a mutuality of pipings of cosmic-and-individual life. To discern and live it is joy and beauty.

The heavenly piping behind all this cannot be directly heard but can only be tacitly felt in our daily interactions with things and thinkings. The disappearance of antagonism between the subject and the object enables the self to hear hollows in the universe piping out knowledge and talks. All of them are equal, arranging themselves into pipings of humans, of earth, and of heaven. Now we can make 'our own kind of music' together. When each of us makes his or her own kind of piping, it is our own yet not ours. It is the piping of humans to blend in with the polyphonic pipings of earth, reflecting resonating with them. All this is the piping of life, of heaven, to be lived.

To resonate and sing together is to mingle and touch each other inside out. Atoms collide and produce molecules; events collide and form history. Colours, sounds, and tastes merge and come out in new configurations. Chains of new creations and changes in previous entities take place. It is a mutual echoing, a sounding forth and shading into each other, even a dreaming of each other. Literature describes this world, where things and events co-touch to co-arise out of their commonly originative piping. And this is where literature begins.

Things have their own birth of meanings, 'wild' when found— their peculiar 'wild meanings' (Merleau-Ponty) chanting their own ontological vibrations. Things have their waves of voices, their hollows that sing. As we hollow ourselves we can overhear and then become part of their voices; we call it language. Our utterances can 'sing the world' (Don Ihde) with trees, hollows, birds, insects, subatomic systems of energy; we call such singing literature. Vibrations of our souls resonate with those of monkeys, butterflies, brooks, and mountains. We become they as they become us, and we are one, one in all our differences. For without distinction there would have been no resonance which chants the world. We can feel with Su Dongpo (Su Tung-p'o) (1036–1101), in his poem on the wall of a friend,

> Receiving the moisture of wind,
> My intestines sprout and fork out, .
> And from out my liver and lungs
> Shoot rocks and bamboos.
> Surging through my breast, irresistible,
> They find expression on your snow-white wall.[15]

As Su's intestines are at one with rocks and bamboos, so the selfsame mountain has as many mountains as there are perspectives. Guo Xi (Kuo Hsi) (c. 1020–90) said:

A mountain looks this way close by, another way a few miles away, and yet another way from a distance of a dozen miles. Its shape changes at every step, . . . Its aspect changes from every angle, as many times as the point of view. . . It looks this way in spring and summer, another way in autumn and winter, . . . another . . . at sunset, . . . Thus . . . a mountain contains in itself . . . a hundred mountains.[16]

And so the 'walking perspective' of Chinese painting has no fixed privileged perspective but constantly invites the viewer to go everywhere in the painting, to penetrate everywhere into the presented and the hidden; Chinese poetry is a world of presences in which one travels, dwells, encounters, discovers. All Chinese artworks pulsate with 'rhythmic breath'. For all artworks on paper (painting, calligraphy, poetry, novel) are done with the same brush which opens the blank space/time into a new dimension of cosmic dynamism, into lived time and space. It is no accident that, in his book *Chinese Poetic Writing*, François Cheng has to include discussions and illustrations of paintings and calligraphy.[17] One brush stroke says it all.

Inevitably, there is a peculiar cosmic thrust in a single brush stroke, with rhythms of mutual relations more than techniques of representation through contour and light. This is natural if we remember that the brush is an extension of the hand, which is an extension of the spirit extending-throughout, as indeed *shen* (commonly translated as 'spirit') means 'cosmic extension'. The great Wu '. . . concentrated his spirit and harmonized it with the working of nature, rendering the things through the power of his brush'; nothing should impede the spirit flowing through it. All the traditional three faults of the stiff (*ban*), carved (*ke*), and knotted (*jie*) brushes concern the impediments of the spirit-flow, killing effortlessness of the flow.[18]

Such flow of the brush describes nature. Traditionally the Chinese learn to paint nature (bamboo, willow, mountain) before painting human figures; in the West the learning process is reversed. As a result, the Western rhythm is centred, plastic, sensuous, organically poised, and can move in any way; the Chinese rhythm is flowing, growing, responding to the wind and sometimes the storm. And of course all these things painted are symbolic of, that is, thrown-together-with, skies and fields; they are metaphors ferrying us to the dynamic flow of the heaven-and-earth, the cosmic piping, re-presentable only in a nestling, moving space in the painting.[19]

Such painterly re-presentation also occurs in literature. The Chinese language has no grammar that irrevocably fixes and categorizes; that is, it has no parts of speech, number, gender, tense, declension, and so on. The Chinese language does not define but presents. Taking advantage of the inchoate character of the language, Chinese sentences tend to poetry. A poem usually says *a*, then *b*, then *c*; it is a montage-painting, criss-crossing, literary-weaving *wen*. The montage is skillfully woven so as to intimate flowing rhythms and echoing implications.

Such a poem paints such a painting, and a painting is such a poem, never categorized in a fixed perspective. The painting represents our visual response to the call of things. Vision and response are typically confrontational, looking *at* the things to be painted. In this spectator's perspective, the more comprehensive and penetrating a painting is made to be, the more jagged it becomes, as Picasso's paintings show.

Suppose the painter changes his perspective by entering things, and paints things in the same gaze as that of those things, looking out in the same direction as the things he paints, standing with them, experiencing *their* experience, living their lives, dwelling in their world. Such seems to describe months of accommodating silence in which the Chinese painter steeps himself, roaming in the mountain and the brook—without a thought of picking up his brush.

As the painter enters the world of mountains, brooks, and birds, so does the viewer. There both the painter and the viewer see with the eyes of mountains, brooks, and birds, breathe their breaths, world their worlds, thing their things. Herein is the poetic truth of the legend that the painter *enters* the painting.[20]

To see with the eyes of mountains, brooks, and birds is to see with none of the eyes of the outsiders. The painter and the viewer themselves must disappear, as it were, in the perspective of a dry roadside skull.[21] Hence, again, the poetic truth of the legend that the painter *disappears* in the painting. Far from being the confronting spectator, the painter is the clearing, the open horizon, in which things dwell and spread their breaths of life.

Here the freshness of an apple exudes the breathing energies of the skies and the fields, of the mountains and the brooks and the birds, of the smell and the colors and the air. And still the apple-freshness is all its own, glowing in its own aura and energies and smell. The fresh apple and the mountain-aura enhance each other as they dwell in and point to each other. The cosmos is the apple whose freshness is cosmic, and the fresh is fresh, the cosmic, cosmic. And here the painter becomes the fresh, the cosmic, while remaining self, glowing with the apple-freshness in the sunny hills of autumn, *that* day. They enter each other, and are entered.

In this manner the painter lives in a mountain for several months, even years. Many days and scenes give many perspectives; many perspectives give many mountains for *that* mountain. A Chinese painting re-presents (re-lives) such a set of many mountains, not by superimposing many *definite* perspectives onto one scene, as Picasso did, but by avoiding definite perspectives altogether. The painter simply 'worlds' forth the world of the mountain, ever fresh, ever changing, ever alive. As a result, the viewer can freely roam about *in* the painting to live in many mountains. This is the 'walking perspective' mentioned a few pages earlier.

Such painting-effect is fully manifest in literature. The common poetic phrase 'pine wind' is a twofold thing-event ('pine-wind') which impresses the poet. It is not a categorized (fixed, arranged) scene, 'pines in the winds', 'pine-scented winds', 'winds through the pines'. It is all of these and none of them; it is a raw bumping into the 'pine wind'. Such is the concrete, the rich actual, overflowing all grammatical fixing, all conceptual arranging.

'Brook noon, not hear gong', says Li Bo (Li Po). The resonance in this simple line is staggering. The inexhaustible cleanliness of the gong is enhanced by its silence. The silence in turn reflects on the brook. And it is noon. Such peace.

On hearing this description, however, Li Bo would just shrug his shoulders and go away. We have inadvertently fixated that moving montage—brook, noon, not-hearing, gong. Particularly 'brook noon' is a surprise, defying description. It is a concord of two salient features (spatial, temporal) mutually nodding, together-presenting the actuality of that scene—'brook noon'. Because the phrase is grammatically loose, we can *freely* go in and out of it, walk and sit around in it, each time feeling differently, seeing different implications. The phrase sets us free as it nonchalantly invites us in.

In some such manner, the poet/painter criss-crosses many counterpoints and counterparts; we come in, see different unities, hear different echoes. Here the poet/painter is the painter/poet; counterpoints and counterparts are such parts and points; we the

viewers/audience are ourselves. Yet all of us come together, forming a living unity. And the unity changes each time the com-posing
happens.[22] In sum, the poeticity of the brush reveals concrete reality. If
the concrete is a complex of concresced components (to borrow
Whitehead), then the components mutually compose one another,
as well as mutually composing with the whole. A complex comprises its constitutive elements. What is complicated is that the
elements so co-implicate that they themselves are complexes; they
interfuse and interdepend. Even the contraries are constitutive
complementaries.

Whitehead's concrescence is one-directional; the prehender
always prehends the prehended. In China the prehended is also
the prehender; co-implication is everywhere. Zhuangzi's Umbra
and Penumbra conversing, Zhuang Zhou and the butterfly co-
dreaming, bring out this point. Various brush shades of black intimate shapes, things, and atmosphere. One dimensional lines are
part and parcel of two-dimensional shapes, three-dimensional
things, and four-dimensional historical dialogues, participations
between the poet-painter and the viewer-audience—*and vice versa*, that is, shapes, things, and histories are also part and parcel of
lines, and we the later comers enrich the implications of the old
texts and paintings, intimating the rhythm of history, implicating
the trans-empirical meanings. Furthermore, painting and poetry
interfuse; as poetry is painting and painting poetry, so calligraphy
and painting are one in two, and two in one.

Dance and Music

Civilization came from religion and the arts. The arts came from
play, which produced singing and dancing in nature. Singing and
dancing were used both for molding our feelings, attitudes, and
behaviour (for education), *and* for resonating with animals, men,
nature, and gods (for religion). All this is because singing and
dancing tune the resonance of things; they smooth our inner resonance, sublimate and unify our thinking, feeling, and willing, and
tune them in with nature. It is no accident that in China the
phrase 'ritual and music' (*li yue*) appears routinely in literature.[23]

Singing and dancing meet in music, the human music (words,
tunes, rhythm, musical instruments), in which the human and the
natural, the subjective and the objective, sing and dance together.

Music the time/art pervades and vitalizes painting the space/art. In this manner art re-presents nature, both in us and in things. The time-space-art vibrates, spreads and re-emerges all *with* all; all this nourishes life.

Since the dawn of time, humankind has been dancing sympathetically with and to the heaven and earth—at first with hearts, souls, feathers and sticks, then with hands, mathematics, technics and instruments. Nature is rhythmic, and so are our dances—the *yin* and the *yang* alternating, coalescing. Francis Bacon's adage, 'Nature can be conquered on our knees' has captured such dance—the *yin* of our knees (science and technics), the *yang* of our conquest. Science is as much of our dance to nature as the so-called 'primitive dances' are, and the so-called correspondence, coherence, and revealment theories of truth express the sympathetic modes of our dance. Why does '2 + 2 = 4' apply to counting things? Only magical sympathy can describe it.

Medicine as Art

Medicine is our self-understanding informed by external discernment. Fascinatingly, two medical traditions gave us two differing kinds of external discernment. In Western medicine distinct entities (organs, structures, performances) are measured quantitatively and analyzed linearly/causally, typical of separation-mentality; precision is possible here.

Chinese medicine is pattern-thinking, phenomena-discerning, and takes things as interpenetrative.

First, in Chinese medicine a 'thing' (Organ, Meridian, Basic Substance) is recognizable not by anatomy but only by a network of functions with others; the network is called 'the human body'. One of the Basic Substances, *qi* (*ch'i*), is bodily vital energy, similar to so-called 'electricity'. Electricity goes into a phonograph, say, and activates it to produce sound. As raw electricity makes no sound, so *qi* itself does nothing. Yet without electricity a phonograph can do nothing. If our Organs put together are a phonograph, *qi* is its electricity.

We can look at the phonograph in two ways—looking at *it* producing music (the Western way, a substance-language), or looking at electricity (phonograph-*qi*) activating it to produce music (the Chinese way, a function/language). To repair a phonograph is to let the phonograph-*qi* travel without interruption or irregular routing. As electricity can be regulated, so *qi* can be cultivated and re-routed. Chinese medicine is *pattern-thinking* in such a way.

Secondly, Chinese medicine *discerns the appearance* of waves of bodily tendencies with the help of commonsense notions—'Heat', 'Pulse', 'Rapid', and the like. A sign means nothing by itself until it is related to other signs of *this* patient. As musical notations of *forte* and *pianissimo* mean little until applied in a concrete musical performance, so Chinese medical terms mean little until used in a particular clinical situation. Chinese medicine discerns a set of phenomena with everyday language as metaphor. Phenomena are perceived together to see 'what is going on', as either in tune or needing re-attunement.

Finally, things *interpenetrate* in Chinese medicine. Signs and tendencies, the external and the internal, mirror, produce, and imply one another. As a Chinese word can be a noun, an adjective, or a verb, depending on the context, so 'heat' can mean the body's normal situation, a Pernicious Influence, a quality of disharmony, depending on the patient's situation.

Technical terms in the West are independently and precisely defined; words in China are adumbrative and contextual. Western notions refer to specific entities and quantities; Chinese notions are paradigms for phenomena-configurations and -treatment. Western 'health' is a fixed somatic structure with a list of precise measurements in various technical categories. Chinese 'health' is a comfortable attunement ('at-one-ment'?) with one's somatic stages and environment—seasonal, cultural, social.

For Chinese medicine, human health is a landscape in which various functions come together into a fine weather of concord within the body and with the body's environment. The patterns of bodily weather vary, depending on integration or dis-integration of relations among *qi* the material energy (the breath-energy), Blood the nourisher, *Jing* the essence, *Shen* the vital awareness, and Fluids the bodily liquids.

Names of these five fundamental Substances are capitalized because they are technical terms *taken from common words*. As common words pervade our life, so common meanings constantly com-prehend our Organs (five *yin* organs, six *yang* organs)— locations of dynamic functional activity rather than fixed somatic structures. The Organs are intersected by twelve regular Meridians and eight extra-Meridians—an invisible network of channels that carry *qi* and Blood through the body, regulate *yin* and *yang*, moisten and benefit bones and joints, and tune the bodily interior with its exterior.

Health is thus not a collection of good parts, theoretical or physiological, but a concord of functions; ill health is judged less by an etiological approach than by an aesthetic discernment of physiological disharmony (Eight Principal 'ill'-Patterns of bodily landscape) by Four Examinations of signs and symptoms—Looking, Listen-and-Smelling, Asking, and Touching, especially feeling the pulse in three positions to discern thirty basic types of pulses. Eight Principal Patterns of bodily landscape are four pairs of polar opposites: *yin/yang*, Interior/Exterior, Deficiency/Excess, and Cold/Hot.

All in all, if to understand something in Western medicine is to grasp bodily parts and causes linearly and quantitatively, then to understand a phenomenon in Chinese medicine is to discern patterns of bodily dynamism in the environment uniquely and coordinately. Such discernment has a touch of the painter going from a simple drawing to a fine painting.

Instead of deciphering organic dysfunctions and infections, Chinese medicine discerns patterns of discord, out of which it coaxes the patient. Chinese medicine has aesthetic sensitivity to personal 'trivia' that may be of clinical significance, and treats each client in his/her own terms, in terms of his/her unique social environment.

It is up to Chinese medicine to weave its subtle flexibility with Western precision, its recursive configurations with Western causal lines. Medicine truly so called is a unity of Western and Chinese medicines, a subtle web 'underwoven' (as its etymology suggests) in the 'con-text' of living situations, body-and-environment.[24]

Culinary, Martial, and Political Arts

The rhythm of Ding (Ting) the cook in Zhuangzi's Third Chapter makes the story a beautiful classic that delights every reader. It is the story of the rhymed dance in the undoing of an ox, in order to feed:

> The hands touch,
> The shoulders lean,
> The knees press;
> So swoosh! So swing!—the meat is whisked from the bone,
> So swish!—the knife performs through the ox,

Hitting the tune of the Dance of Mulberry Forest,
The symphonic tune of the Neck and the Head (or Passing
through the Head). [author's translation]

All this is joy and expertise; and it is natural. To be an expert
is to be experienced, trailing nature, becoming natural. Nature is
rhythmical—in space and in season, at the right spot and time. To
find and dwell in the spatio-temporal rightness is to be natural, to
be an expert. No wonder the cook's lord is fascinated with the
dancing expertise of loosening up an ox.[25] The beautiful movement of the cook's knife reminds his lord of two tunes, the dance
of the Mulberry Forest and the symphonic music of Jing Shou.

'The Mulberry Forest' is a legendary piece of dance music
named after a place called Mulberry Forest (in Song territory),
where the legendary Emperor Tang cut short his hair and finger
nails, presented himself as a sacrifice, and prayed for rain to re-
lieve seven years of drought. The music is that with which to dance
and pray for rain (for crops). 'Mulberry' also symbolized home,
peace, native soil, culture. 'The Jing Shou' is another legendary
piece of music that is part of an orchestral suite called *Xianchi* (the
Universal Pond), the mythological Eastern Ocean where the sun
rises. The *Xianchi* music is the music as vivacious and auspicious as
the sunrise, to be played in the mid-spring month (March/April).
Spring is the season of things sprouting in life, not at all the season
of butchery.

And so there seems to be an ironic truth here. Those tunes belong to the Spring of life. The cook's knife is that of Autumnal
butchery. The cook's expertise joins life and death, the Spring and
the Autumn, in the dance that rises with the rain and the sun.

'Nature red in tooth and claw' describes the bare necessity of
eating in the animal kingdom. Animals eat, but only humans raise
eating to the culinary *art*. How life is cooked and eaten dictates
how we are nourished, and this 'how' is the art that synthesizes
nature and culture, death and life, the animal and the human, distinguishing and uniting them at the same time. Zhuangzi made the
preparation of life into food into a cosmic dance—slithering,
quivering with the ox of our food, with the treasured knife that
nourishes. The butcher-and-his-knife dance(s) through the ox,
turning killing into a feast, as long as we stay on our life-line pulsation (*yuandu*). Such a cosmic aesthetic attitude enables us to
feast on suffering, and grow.[26]

The cook-butcher's knife is the epitome of the martial arts, which are not far from culinary art. Both are the arts of death and of health. They go along with the breathing pulses of the life-force that pervades space and time, skies and fields, animals and enemies. Both go to the highest peak of artistic sublimity. For the martial arts are also the art of dance, of resonance, of concord. They dance to the rhythm of things (including the enemy), then dance things' rhythms. They resonate and resound with the body-pulses which spread to the heart-mind; then the performer realizes that those pulses are none other than those of nature, the outer and the inner nature, the swingings back and forth between the past and the present, the present and the future, and back to the past. And the art is the art of concord (inter-dependence, interfusion)—of goings-forth and comings-back, be-ginnings and endings, spreading and convergings. It is the art at once individual and cosmic-communal, empty-accommodating and dynamic-attacking, moving without moving, the art of life and of death, exactly what the Cook Ding did—dancing the art of death which begins the art of cooking/nourishing.[27]

Cooking is a process of mixing ingredients. Ingredients enter one another, change one another, composing a coherent whole which comes out differently each time. Such coming-together is the end of some lives and the nourishing of some others. Such art of death and life, and of many into one, one in many, has long fascinated Chinese intellectuals. Food is one of the traditional themes of literature, and since the legendary Emperor Fu Xi invented the art of cooking several thousand years ago, Chinese Thackerays and Dickenses have always composed recipes, written treatises, and compiled encyclopaedias on the culinary arts.[28]

Many surprising philosophical implications have been garnered from cooking. A pre-Confucian scholar-minister Yen Ying de-scribed concord (*he*) in terms of cooking, and applied it to politics. As cooking which nourishes and purifies requires a coming-together of many different, sometimes contrary, ingredients (water/fire, sauce/vinegar), so must political concord comprise dif-fering talents, functions, and positions.[29] Laozi (Lao Tzu) said, 'As you cook a small fish, so you rule a big country' (*Daodejing*, Chap-ter Sixty), for too much handling spoils both. Mengzi (Mencius) learned from the Royal Chef to Duke Huan, Yi Ya, our *common* taste for food (otherwise why should the entire world follow him?), which indicates our common propensity (for good) (6A7), our root-affinity. This is the solid base on which to build the government of universal benevolence.

Aesthetics as Cosmic Attitude

The above considerations demonstrate that whatever thinking that went into beauty has been in connection with a *specific* topic, say, literature, painting, calligraphy, and the like. In fact, what immediately strikes one, on mentioning 'Chinese aesthetics', is that there is no such formal discipline in China. The Chinese neither raised theoretical problems (say, whether there is beauty in nature without the artist) and pursued them rigourously, nor erected metaphysical systems about the structure of beauty itself, nor even produced principles of aesthetic activities as a whole.[30] Chinese thinking about beauty is always on the specific and the concrete, never abstract theorization.

Suppose we have a sketch of an apple. We can either stay there and enjoy the freshness of the apple, or leave it for the eternal form of Beauty of which it is a mere pointer and participant, or consider the relation among actuality, the art work and the subjects (the artist's feeling, intuition, sensuality; the viewer's reception through its revealment; adequacy to the apple-actuality), or, finally, classify all such considerations as exclusively in the realm of aesthetics, as the job of the philosopher of art, not of the artist himself or of the philosopher of politics.

In all this what is assumed are the separate entities—the artist, the idea, the art work, the intuition, the revealment or adequacy, the audience, the relation, the harmony, the event, the thing in itself, and all this as separate from other branches of philosophy.

In China such barriers break down. When considering the freshness of an apple, we see how the freshness emanates the breathing energies of the skies and the fields, of the breeze and the sun, of the smell and the colours and the atmosphere. The apple-freshness, glowing in such aura, energies, and smell, enhances the universe, and is enhanced by the universe; the apple and the universe dwell in each other and point to each other. The heaven-and-earth is the fresh apple and the freshness is cosmic, and the fresh is fresh, the cosmic, cosmic.

Without Dürer's sensuous colours and lines or Picasso's jagged abstractions and juxtapositions, the Chinese painting lures us on with rhythm-like natural dynamism, ebbing and flowing through the skies and fields, the cosmic joys and sorrows, the feelings and discernings, and all that amid daily hustle and bustle. The Chinese concrete universality unobtrusively nestles us in our world that is both ordinary and mysterious. The Chinese painterly accuracy is not exactly Italian; it is somehow transparent. In the painting shapes and colours invite us to *their* compellingly actual dynamism that pulses *throughout* the world. There is a diffusion which enhances the concrete. There in diffusion and enhancement is a cosmic significance in the particular. The poet/painter raises the brush, and the heaven-and-earth echo in anticipation. The cosmos-breath flows through the brush's beautiful execution into letters, calligraphy, and paintings, composing the very tapestry (*wen*) of the universe.

And in all this the artist and the viewer are involved. They in turn become the cosmic, while they remain themselves, glowing with the apple-fresh in the sunny Autumn hills. They enter and are entered, while they engage in the activities of medicine, cooking, martial arts, politics. Thus every human activity is artistic, and every aesthetic act is cosmic; in everything we do, we utter the 'language of ocean, language of sky' which cultivates our cosmic sense of justice, of truth.[31]

All this is to say that we cannot define beauty, because its very definition depends on our attitude. Aesthetics is reflective sensibility, primarily attitude. We can think about aesthetic objects, and we can think about everything aesthetically. In the former our attitude is often that of objective analysis; in the latter, our attitude is not, and cannot be. We can have two attitudes in aesthetics, then: objective analysis and pervasive concord.

Analysis is divisive and sequential; things are arranged in sequence, and synthesized into harmony. Thus synthesis and harmony assume analysis. In contrast, concord is many in one, one in many, mutually enhancing—between the one and the many, and among the many.

Objective analysis is the world of dichotomy of subject matters and methods—metaphysics, ethics, rhetoric, poetics. Such analysis is discriminatory and classificatory—aesthetics is not psychology, politics, ethics, cooking, or martial arts. Such an attitude also sets the subject against the object, with priority given to objectivity, even the objectivity of subjecthood. Western aesthetics tends toward such a frame of reference. 'Imitation' makes little sense unless a beautiful object exists there to be imitated by a separate subject here. Similarly separation of entities is assumed in standard aesthetic analyses—representation, communication, revealment, attainment of the unity of many separate entities, reduction of their clashes, promotion of their balance, adequacy, correspondence.

In contrast, pervasive concord describes the Chinese world of interdependent and inter-changing autonomies; here subjectivity is objectivity and objectivity, subjectivity. Each subjectivity (originative individuality) is distinct without separation. Sound is said to break silence. Yet birds chirp and waves come to make silence; nature has sound-silence. Chinese aesthetics belongs to such a pervasive concord of naturalness.

Such a pervasive stance, such a distinct *way* of life ('aesthetic spirit'), not only allows us, but regards it as natural, to consider and enhance all aspects of life in its light—in its treatment of the self (in the moral, medical 'heart-mind'), in its outlook on things (in Chinese music and painting), in its self-expressions (in calligraphy and literature), in its dealings with things (in the Chinese approach to technology, socio-politics, and the *yin-yang* cosmology).

It is a mistake to say that *xin* is a unity of both emotion and cognition, as if to say that here is the heart, there is the mind, and those two are pulled together to make up a whole called *xin*. For *xin* is just that, the core and soul of one's being. It is the self's marrow-centre, *zhongxin*, literally the central heart-mind which goes through the self. Such 'heart of the self' happens to exhibit (why does it need to 'express'?) various functions, such as those of emotion and intellection. Those functions may inter-act, inter-influence, inter-mingle, to shade into each other. They are in attunement when the person is integral, full and authentic—'sagely' and healthy. When the person is abandoned to desires, he or she is 'self-abandoned', 'laid waste' (*Mengzi*). Such loss of inner concord is as immoral as it can be physically unhealthy; the person is then 'sick'. Chinese medicine is designed to restore such pervasive dynamics of bodily and psychic wholeness. Chinese medicine is literally an art-as-science of bodily landscaping.

If Chinese music is spatial, lingering on in the flow of rhythm that tarries in silence, then Chinese painting lives in time, a spatial music, painting the fish as Schubert's trout in his 'Trout Quintet', ever moving on in nature.

Kongzi (Confucius) regarded music as one of the Six Arts to cultivate personality, as Plato regarded music as one of the powerful means of harmonizing personality. But whereas Plato wanted to inundate the soul with music in a planned geometric manner, Confucius wanted music to 'perfume' the soul-chamber with its vapour, tuning the soul into a vital flexible whole.

Such natural oneness of the soul with the cosmic rhythm is apparent in painting. People usually say of a Chinese painter that the painter expresses himself, not the mountain, as he paints the mountain; after living in the mountain for months, absorbing it into himself, he goes home and paints.

Not so; the painter is instead at home in self-mountain. He paints as he moves and has his being in the world of the mountain; he neither paints the mountain nor expresses himself. He just is and behaves—he in the mountain and the mountain in him. He goes home because he goes home; have you seen anyone not going home? He neither purposely absorbs the mountain nor is he absorbed by it and disappears in it. He just is; the mountain just is. He paints as naturally as the mountain is there, naturally. He paints as naturally as he eats, sleeps, and dies. To paint is part of himself as he is, in the world as it is, in front of the mountain as it is.

To repeat: this is not mystical absorption of the self into the world in which the self and the mountain are abolished, or a pre-established harmony of the two, or their mutual reflection. All these descriptions are too fixated, too much categorized, missing that simple naturalness of the painter painting the world, rejoicing and singing the world as he lives at home in it. This is why the painter walks into his own painting; the painting is part of himself and the world. He can go into it because he is it; it is his world in which he lives.

Such a situation is encapsulated in calligraphy. Highly compressed from sensual shapes and colors, the brush just moves as it 'paints' the flow of things with the calligrapher's hand, the hand in the world introducing itself into the world, and the world going into the mind-heart moving as the hand moves—in simple naturalness, yet according to the social conventions governing the calligraphic condensation of images, ideas, and imaginations in specified patterns.

As the brush (one of the most ingenious inventions of Chinese culture) moves to build a paragraph, then another one, and so on, until an essay is produced, we see Chinese characters patterning themselves forth into a tapestry of literature (*wen*) that reflects and pervades the world, through that nodal point of the writer's brush-and-mind-heart. Literature *is* the world seen and sung from the 'heart' of the writer. It is a moving painting, a spread-out music, a structural vitality, of the world gathered up in that particular brush.

Often poetry and essays arise out of suffering in life. Demotion from office occasions repeated gazings at nature; cries of pain create poetry, poverty opens the literary eye to principles of living—so much so that poets are called 'vexed persons' and poetry, 'vexed rhymes'. Literature is fed by life, enriched by life negativities; to write is to live pathetically and sympathetically.

Such close intertwining of life with arts is nowhere more apparent than in technology and socio-politics. As the apprentice matures, his skill disappears into the divine breaths of things and of himself. The artisan, engineer, and skilled professional are artists-and-'sages'. They are concentrated, becoming 'one-with' things. They *are* the knack of how to live things. Their art is the art of living, living itself.

The 'thickless' knife enters the interstices of an ox, and the ox loosens itself, says Zhuangzi in his story of Cook Ding. The butcher is nowhere; he *is* the knife-and-the-ox. And so are all other artisans—the wheelwright, the buckle maker, the bellstand maker, even the cicada catcher, the swimmer, the archer, and so on. There is no gap between the thing and the man. The gap initiates the separation of the subject who machinates, from the object which is manipulated. This is that famous 'machinating mind' with which Zhuangzi (in Chapter Twelve) condemned the senior disciple of Confucius who was so intent on inculcating sincerity. What irony!

Similarly, there should be no gap between the emperor and his people; the sagely emperor pains as he sees his people in pain (Mengzi, Lü Donglai).[32] Such 'no-gap' is in fact an application of the *yin-yang* view of the world, in which both the yes and the no, the this and the that, intertwine, inter-depend, and inter-change in pervasive dynamic concord, ever moving, ever staying. No wonder life negativities produce exquisite literature and great heroes.

This is the Utopia lived here and now, where we have no sickness or immortality, no violence or 'justice'. This Utopia is alive yet attracts no one. As paintings and essays suggest different things to different people, this Utopia aesthetically expands life ripples on the pond of the universe, as natural and bland as those ripples.

Every Chinese aesthetic production (the *xin*, the painting, the poem, the calligraphy, the essay, the society) is the dragonfly dotting the pond with its tail, touching without touching, to initiate the ever-expanding, ever-overlapping ripples. A final remark. This chapter began by announcing that it treats beauty from a Chinese perspective, benefiting from the clarity of Western philosophical analysis. We now see why; in beauty method bites into content. As Chinese beauty is inter-involvement, so its presentation is inevitably to be infused with Western analysis, gaining clarity and expressiveness thereby.

Notes

1. To put in Zhuangzi's terms such benefitting from both traditions, in Chapter Twenty-Two Knowledge asks three people about *Dao* (*Tao*): Do-Nothing-Say-Nothing, Wild-and-Witless, and the Yellow Emperor. Only the last can answer his query, albeit in cryptic terms. The Yellow Emperor is analytic-interpretive (separation-isolation) mentality; knowledge is aesthetic togetherness expressing itself. Their conversation is their coming-together for a description of beauty. And then the Yellow Emperor said that those two who did not know how to answer are truly right; for those who speak do not know. (Burton Watson, tr., *The Complete Works of Chuang Tzu* (New York, Columbia University Press, 1968), pp. 234–5) Description requires saying, yet saying requires separation; to say and then to erase the saying characterize togetherness.

2. These phrases are cited because in my opinion they are the least dichotomous notions in Western aesthetics. Even here their force depends on the subject/object dichotomy. The phrases occur in the subtle systematic context of Mikel Dufrenne's *The Phenomenology of Aesthetic Experience* (Evanston, Northwestern University Press, 1973), which enamoured even such sensitive literary critics as James J.Y. Liu (in his *Chinese Theories of Literature* (Chicago, The University of Chicago Press, 1975)). Dufrenne is influenced by Maurice Merleau-Ponty, especially his *The Visible and the Invisible* (Evanston, Northwestern University Press, 1968), in which the phrase 'call and answer' appears.

For more citations from both Chinese and Western literati and literary critics see Liu's student, Pauline Yu's *The Poetry of Wang Wei: New Translation and Commentary* (Bloomington, Indiana University Press, 1980), pp. 1–42. For the reason listed here and in the main text, I depart from her when she said: 'Yet these very notions do reappear in the writings of nineteenth- and twentieth-century Western poets, suggesting that the poetry of Wang Wei may be regarded as an illuminating embodiment of their poetics as well. Furthermore, I believe that a methodology drawing on twentieth-century phenomenological criticism, with its possible affinities to both Chinese and Symbolist conceptions of literature, may be the most appropriate and least foreign approach to his poetry' (p. 1).

3. Lin Yutang is only partially justified in castigating Osvald Siren for going tediously into the meaning of each component word in a Chinese phrase, rather than idiomatically translating the usage of the phrase as a whole (Lin Yutang, *The Chinese Theory of Art* (New York, G.P. Putnam's Sons, 1967), pp. 3–4, 36–7). Within the 'definite' meaning of a Chinese compound word, such as the notorious 'bone(-structure) of breath(-power)', the original meanings do form its implicit connotation which a straightforward rendering as 'force of personality' misses.

4. If not 'begging the question', then 'going in a vicious circle', and the like.

5. Martin Buber and Gabriel Marcel in the modern West perhaps come closest to Zhuangzi in this regard. Plato is of course here, too.

6. François Cheng, *Chinese Poetic Writing* (Bloomington, Indiana University Press, 1982), pp. xiii–xiv. Compare with James J.Y. Liu, *The Art of Chinese Poetry* (Chicago, The University of Chicago Press, 1962), pp. 91–130, *Chinese Theories of Literature* (the same press, 1975), pp. 16–105.

7. Owen Barfield, *Poetic Diction*, Middletown, Wesleyan University Press, 1973, p. 146. Compare with Note 8 below.

8. On this point and the points raised in Notes 7 and 9, see one of the leading literary critics of our time, Wang Meng'ou's *General Introduction to Literature*, pp. 95–107.

9. Barfield, pp. 145–6, note 7 above.

10. See Wang Meng'ou, *Researches in Theories of Chinese Classical Literature*, 1984, pp. 3–6, 156–9, 163–8, 280–5, 323–4, and elsewhere throughout (this book predominantly discusses Chinese poetry with sensitivity and erudition). His view agrees with Chou Tse-tsung's (ed.) *Wen-lin* (Madison, The University of Wisconsin Press, 1968), pp. 155–66, and with Zhuangzi's view in Chapter Thirty-three.

11. See Wang Meng'ou, *Researches*, pp. 11–13, 22 (note 3). See also Note 5 above.

12. Wen Yiduo, *Mythologies and Poetry*, 1975 (reprinted in Taiwan), pp. 181–92. His view was quoted approvingly by both Chou Tse-tsung, note 10, pp. 164–5, and Liu, *Literature*, pp. 67–68.

13. Barfield, pp. 41, 48.

14. See especially Xu Fuguan's *The Chinese Aesthetic Spirit* (Taipei, The Students Press, 1966), ch. 1.

15. Lin Yutang's translation in his *Chinese Theory of Art*, p.92.

16. See note 15, p. 75.

17. Bloomington, Indiana University Press, 1982. So do George Rowley, Lin Yutang, Wing-tsit Chan, Osvald Siren, and others who discuss Chinese paintings.

18. See Fu Baoshi's *The Chinese Theories of Art* , ch. 6 (no publisher, no publication date).

19. Here I am indebted to George Rowley's exquisite description in his *Principles of Chinese Painting* (Princeton, Princeton University Press, 1959), pp. 40–7. My departures from him would be obvious, however, to anyone who compares my text with his. Omitted are notions like 'ideational', 'abstract', 'servant', 'one-way'.

20. Paralleling this famous legend, we have stories on the enchanting power of paintings (to draw the viewer in) in, for instance, 'Mural' and 'Painterly Skin', in the early chapters of *Strange Stories from a Chinese Studio* by Pu Song-ling of the Qing Dynasty. I failed to secure a copy of the English translation by Herbert A. Giles.

21. See Zhuangzi's story of the conversation with a roadside skull in his Chapter Eighteen titled 'Ultimate Happiness'. Compare with Watson, *Chuang Tzu*, 193–4, and my meditations on it in my *The Butterfly as Companion: Meditations on the First Three Chapters of the Chuang Tzu* (Albany, NY, The State University of New York Press, forthcoming), in Prologue C.

22. I am happily indebted to William Yeh in his excellent though slightly repetitive 'Activities of Communication and Hermeneutics in Chinese Classical Poetry', *UNITAS: A Literary Monthly*, Taipei, June 1985, pp. 168–81. Sadly, I depart from him when he describes such poetic expressions as 'between signifying and not signifying', as if poetic phrases were vague. They are not; they are pointedly concrete.

23. Since the Book of Poetry (*Shijing*), life, writing, dance, and music have been entwined in China, as eloquently expressed in the *Wenxin Diaolong* (Dragon Carvings of a Literary Heart-Mind) by Liu Xie (Chapters 6–10, 33, 48–9), Han Yu's (AD

768–824) 'To Meng Dongye', Ouyang Xiu's (1007–72) 'Autumn', 'To Yang Zhi', and so on. For contemporary thinkers, see Wen Yiduo, *Mythologies and Poetry* (Taiwan, Landeng Publishers, 1975, reprint), pp. 181–200, and Xu Fuguan, *The Aesthetic Spirit in China* (Taiwan, Xuesheng Shuju, 1966), pp. 1–143. Compare with my *Companion*, ch. 3, n. 94.

The stories were told of how music so tunes up the cosmic continuum that performing some tunes brought drought, spring, or (to an unworthy emperor) defeat in battle, as narrated in the *Han Feizi* (Chapter 10), *Liezi* (Chapter Five, see A.C. Graham's translation, *The Book of Lieh-tzu* (London, John Murray, 1960), pp. 107–10), *Wen Xuan* and the like. Their poetic licenses carry more than poetic truths.

24. I am indebted to Ted J. Kaptchuk's *The Web That Has No Weaver: Understanding Chinese Medicine* (New York: Congdon & Weed, 1983). I depart from him toward the end of the book where he rails at Chinese medicine. See my review in *Philosophy East and West*, January 1986.

25. The Chinese character, *wu*, meaning 'thing', depicts an ox being loosened with a knife.

26. For a detailed description of all this see my *Companion*, ch. 3.

27. Sophia Delza's excellent *T'ai-Chi Ch'uan* (Albany, State University of New York Press, 1985, revised edition), is marred by suppression of the lethal aspect of that martial art.

28. Compare with Dr Lee Su Jan, *The Fine Art of Chinese Cooking* (New York, The Bobbs-Merrill Company, Inc., 1962), published by Crown Publishers, Inc.

29. Compare with Chung Ying Cheng, 'On Harmony as Transformation: Paradigms from the I Ching,' in Shu-hsien Liu and Robert E. Allinson (eds.), *Harmony and Strife: Contemporary Perspectives, East and West* (Hong Kong, Chinese University Press, 1988), pp. 225–47.

30. Mary Mothersill said that there are no principles of aesthetic taste, although there are valid judgments of taste in her *Beauty Restored* (New York, Oxford University Press, 1985). But she is in the minority in the West.

31. 'Language of ocean, language of sky' is Conrad Aiken's and was quoted approvingly by Irving Yucheng Lo to conclude his beautiful introduction to Wu-chi Liu & Irving Yucheng Lo, (eds.), *Sunflower Splendor: Three Thousand Years of Chinese Poetry* (Garden City, Anchor Press, 1975), p. xxiii. For the link between poetry and cosmology see Zhong Hong's words in his *Shi Pin* as quoted by François Cheng in his *Chinese Poetic Writing*, Bloomington (Indiana University Press, 1982), pp. x–xi.

32. *Mengzi*, 1A7, 1B5. *Comprehensive Disputations by Tung-Lai* (Hong Kong, and Kuang Chih Publishers), pp. 165, 180, 199, 203, 238, 242, 245, 269, and 271.

Glossary

ban 版 stiff
Chou Tse-tsung 周策縱
Daodejing 道德經
Donglai Boyi 東萊博議 *Comprehensive Disputations by Donglai*
Fu Baoshi 傅抱石
Gudian Wenxue Tansuo 古典文學探索 Researchers in Theories of Chinese Classical Literature
Guo Xi 郭熙
Han Feizi 韓非子
Han Yu 韓愈
he 和 harmony
huabi 畫壁 'Mural'

Ye Weilian 葉維廉 William Yeh

Yen Ying 晏嬰

Yi Ya 易牙

yuandu 緣督 to stay on the life-line pulsation (or follow along the spine artery of energy)

yue 樂 music

zhengjing 正經 regular Meridians

zhi 志 inner thoughts and feelings

zhi 知 knowledge

Zhong Hong 鐘嶸

Zhongguo Huihua Lilun 中國繪畫理論 *The Chinese Theories of Art*

Zhongguo Gutianshi Zhong de Chuanshi huodong 中國古典詩中的傳釋活動 'Activities of Communication and Hermeneutics in Chinese Classical Literature'

Zhongguo Yishu Jingshen 中國藝術精神 *The Chinese Aesthetic Spirit*

Cheng Zhongying 成中英

zhongxin 中心 marrow-center

Zhuangzi 莊子

zibao 自暴 to lay waste oneself (to dissipate oneself)

ziqi 自棄 to abandon oneself (to throw oneself away)

9 On Understanding Chinese Philosophy: An Inquiry and a Proposal

LAO SZE-KWANG (LAO YUNG-WEI)

Preliminary Remarks

Even if it sounds a little presumptuous to declare that I want to help Western thinkers and academic researchers to understand Chinese philosophy, I do think it would be quite acceptable to say that the purpose of this chapter is to show both Chinese and non-Chinese philosophers some of my reflections upon the basic problems concerning our understanding of Chinese philosophy, as well as some possible solutions to them.

What is Chinese philosophy? Or, what are the characteristics of Chinese philosophy as a branch of learning? In answering such a question, we will find serious difficulties from the very beginning, since, even to talk about a 'Chinese philosophy' at all, requires justification and clarification. In modern Chinese, the equivalent of the English term 'philosophy' is *zhexue* (哲學), but this is not a conventional term and was completely unknown to Chinese scholars, including those who are now called 'classical Chinese philosophers', *until translators of the last century created this term as a Chinese equivalent of 'philosophy'.*[1] Is there any good reason for us to single out certain Chinese writings as representing Chinese philosophy? 'By their content, they are works of Chinese philosophy', perhaps somebody would suggest. But it is here that the real difficulty arises. In representative works of Chinese philosophy, such as the teachings of Mengzi (Mencius) or Wang Yangming, for example, we find almost nothing in common with philosophical writings of the European or American traditions. The basic interest, the way of formulation, and the criterion of significance in such classical Chinese works are all quite different.

Of course, in daily life, few people are even aware of the existence of such a problem. Going to libraries or bookshops, we always find books on certain shelves classified as 'Philosophy', and books of Chinese philosophy are somewhere among them. There seems to be no difficulty in identification. However, this is only a matter of labelling or name-giving, which is purely conventional. Labelling theory might explain proper names in Frege's sense, but has nothing to do with characteristic description.[2]

Since no established theory can help us, and it is obviously futile to appeal to ordinary experience, we must regard this problem as a preliminary point to be clarified in any discourse on our understanding of Chinese philosophy. It appears to me that a solution to such a problem calls for our reconsideration of the concept of philosophy itself. Only under an amplified concept could an undistorted understanding of Chinese philosophy become possible.

In the following sections, I shall, in the first place, mention certain views held by well-known Western schools on what philosophy can do. Secondly, I shall offer a proposal of my own, concerning the functions of philosophy with theoretical and pragmatic justifications. Finally, I shall give a brief characterization of Chinese philosophy with examples, and show that, with the proposed new concept of philosophy, there will be no real obstacles to people understanding Chinese philosophy.

The Concept of Philosophy

I choose to talk about the concept of philosophy, instead of the definition of philosophy. This is because, in this case, an essential definition in the Aristotelian sense is, according to my understanding, impossible. However, an explanation of this impossibility can still provide some clue for us to grasp the basic features of philosophical thinking. Let us begin with the following question:

Question A: Why is a Definition of Philosophy Impossible?

The answer is: we cannot find the logical differentia capable of covering the subject matter of all kinds of philosophical thought which are informative at the same time. For example, let us take the popular view that philosophy is the discipline which seeks to discover ultimate principles. While this sounds plausible to some people, closer examination will show immediately that this definition cannot tell us much about what philosophy is. Neither can it cover all inquiries that have been called philosophical. First of all, 'ultimate principles' belong to general descriptions. One may ask: 'principle of what?'. Until this question is answered, the definition does not give us a concept of philosophy. However, from a glance at the history of even Western philosophy, it is evident that the object of philosophical inquiries has varied widely through the centuries. Cosmologists in ancient Greece thought they were trying to discover the ultimate principles of the structure of the world, but, in the view of Immanuel Kant, they had only made grave mistakes; Kant insisted that philosophy should be the search for principles of knowledge and morals in a transcendental sense, but the Empiricists of British tradition would say that the Kantian project is impossible. All these scholars have been called philosophers and they did claim to search for some ultimate principles, but the objects of those principles belong to different realms or dimensions. Secondly, if we turn to the contemporary philosophers, we will find that such high-sounding terms as 'ultimate principles' or 'ultimate reality' are completely excluded from their vocabulary. Carnap held that philosophy should engage itself with the moderate job of offering systematic analysis of scientific language. Later Wittgenstein advocated that philosophy is only a therapeutic activity. For all these analysts, the concept of an ultimate principle makes little sense to their inquiries.

The futility of the efforts to determine an essential definition for philosophy can be shown in further detail. But let it suffice. For the present purpose, let us turn to another question.

Question B: Is there Some Other Way to Define or Explain Philosophy?

Here, the first alternative which occurs would be the idea of an ostensive definition. Actually, this is almost the customary way of explaining philosophy in our daily discourse. Imagine that a child asks us what philosophy is. On such an occasion, we would usually point to the philosophical books on our table or bookshelf and say: 'Well, philosophy means such books.' Or, when you find your younger brother reading Plato's dialogues or a book by Carnap, you would say: 'You are doing philosophy.' All such evidence shows that we feel quite at home with an ostensive definition of philosophy. But whether this is really the final answer to the problem of defining philosophy remains to be decided. Obviously, to explain philosophy by pointing to the books that have been called works of philosophy is only to use the term 'philosophy' as a label for a group of writings. We have already said that labelling theory cannot answer our problem. Of course, an ostensive definition, if supplemented by some additional strategy, can be quite useful for certain purposes, but it cannot do much for the purpose of the present chapter, which is to help promote the understanding of Chinese philosophy.[3]

However, taking it from another angle, some clues to a solution might be revealed. When we point to a group of books or writings to explain the meaning of philosophy, we might be simply following a convention; in other words, it is probably only because those writings have been regarded as works of philosophy by people, past and present. However, the reason why just these writings are labelled as 'philosophy' can become an object of exploration. Are there some common elements to be found? If there are, we will find where the justification lies.

On this point, I must take a risk and make the following assertions: firstly, philosophy, even though understood through an ostensive definition, cannot have been used by people in an arbitrary way. I might think that I call certain books 'philosophical' only to follow a linguistic convention; but that convention is a result of accrued understanding, instead of a label-choosing act. When people called a treatise by Aristotle or Descartes a work of philosophy, they were referring to some aspects of its content in order to make such a decision. Although it is not clear what elements played the central part in such decisions, and even whether the same elements appeared in each case, a decision of this kind is impossible without having such essential elements as its basis. Convention only came after such decisions had been made.

Moreover, if we consider the fact that there are always new writings to be categorized as writings of philosophy, we cannot appeal to linguistic convention to explain how this is done. A convention concerning existing writings cannot automatically expand its own application to writings in the future. At least, we have to compare the content of these writings with writings already conventionally called philosophy before putting the former beside the latter as writings of the same category. It would inevitably involve a recognition of some common features of different philosophies. The real problem is how we should understand such features, rather than whether they exist. This leads to my second assertion.

Philosophy can be characterized by the special feature of philosophical thinking (which distinguishes itself from other kinds of thinking), while not defined by a subject-matter.

Why are there always unsurmountable difficulties facing us in determining an essential definition of philosophy? Briefly speaking, it is because, in the first place, an essential definition always involves the subject-matter and, secondly, because the subject-matter of philosophical studies is constantly shifting. This is especially true in European philosophies. Ranging from the search for the 'world-stuff' to the inquiries of knowledge, meaning and language, the subject-matter of philosophical studies has changed drastically. If we have only this tradition in mind and, at the same time, want to explain how we can still use the word 'philosophy' in a clear sense, we will naturally appeal to Wittgenstein's idea of 'Family Resemblance'.[4] But this is not what I am about when I try to characterize the common feature of philosophical thinking. In my opinion, the only promising way to clarify the concept of philosophy is to consider philosophical thinking instead of the results of philosophical studies. While philosophical studies may deal with widely different topics, philosophical thinking always bears its special mark, namely, a reflective character. Let me explain these two points with a few words.

To say that philosophical thinking is primarily reflective is nothing new. When Socrates used the Delphic maxim 'Know thyself' as a watchword, he was already suggesting this idea. However, the Empiricist trend in modern and contemporary philosophy has been so strong that most philosophers have tried to avoid talking about reflective thinking completely. I believe, on this point, that perhaps we have to be a little old-fashioned in order to get started on our new attempt.

Initially, let us ask: 'When are we engaging in philosophical thinking?' It is not when we report some facts in the external world or try to frame some empirical explanation of what we have observed. We engage in philosophical thinking only when we reflect upon our own activities. This is obvious in epistemological and ethical studies. Metaphysics and cosmology are also reflective in the sense that what is attempted is the imposition of some unity upon the empirical image of the world. Even analysts, when they examine language and meaning, are also engaged in reflective thinking, although they do not like this term. People who are dubious of this characterization of philosophy may have two objections. The first one is: whether reflective thinking belongs exclusively to philosophy. They might point out the fact that mathematicians and scientists usually to reflective thinking in a similar way. But this is not a difficult problem. When we say that philosophical thinking is reflective, or reflective thinking is an essentially philosophical activity, we do not refer to professional philosophers only. Everybody can do some reflective thinking sometimes, and, at that moment, he is entering the realm of philosophical thinking. It is not surprising for a mathematician to think reflectively about the foundation of mathematics and thus to engage himself with an inquiry of mathematical philosophy. This also applies to scientists and ordinary people. Only engagement with reflective thinking as a career distinguishes philosophers from other people. Reflective thinking, hence philosophical thinking, can be found in everybody, although it is not always mature enough to produce a philosophical theory. The second objection is: since many branches of empirical learning have their origin in some ancient philosophy, empirical thinking must have been included in philosophy at least in ancient times; therefore it is questionable whether philosophical thinking must be reflective. This problem involves a general distinction between historical facts and intrinsic nature. When we assert that philosophical thinking is reflective by nature, we do not mean that philosophers in history actually keep their thinking purely reflective. The ancient philosophers, who did get the two types of thinking mixed up, might be unaware of the difference. However, the fact that certain philosophers made a mistake in calling empirical thinking philosophical does not contradict the view that philosophical thinking, in a strict sense, is reflective. History is a process of growth and it is simply natural for philosophy to develop from an impure state to a purer one.

It might also be argued that such a characterization is not informative and actually similar to an empty definition such as 'Philosophy is the study of ultimate principles'. This constitutes a critical problem. To clarify it, I must move to my third assertion.

The characterization of philosophy I have made can lead to an open concept of philosophy and thus enable people of different philosophical traditions to communicate with each other.

To characterize philosophical thinking as reflective thinking is not meant to give a definition to philosophy. Instead it serves the double purpose of fixing the general scope of philosophical discourse on the one hand, and, on the other, leaving room to an open dimension of philosophical thinking. This characterization must be supplemented by an enumeration of the functions of philosophy in order to make the concept of philosophy particular. For greater clarity, let me express my thesis in the following form:

Philosophical thinking is reflective thinking upon (a, b, c, . . .).

Here, a, b, c, . . . stand for functions of philosophy. Since philosophy in different periods of history possesses different functions (supposed to do different jobs), the (a, b, c, . . .) has a variable character. However, in a particular period, they can be assigned with particular values and thus make the concept of philosophy also particular. It is important to note that such particular philosophies are in no sense equivalent to Philosophy in General or Philosophy *per se*, but are no more than the results of philosophical thinking operating in certain specific fields. People in every historical period are confronted with a specific field of philosophical studies and thus get a particular concept of philosophy, which possesses definite contents. They tend to hold this particular concept to be the only acceptable one and forget Philosophy in General. A particular philosophy can have an informative definition but that always implies a closed concept of philosophy which would give rise to misunderstanding and conflict between both the modern and the classical, and between one tradition and the other. For every period, a definite and closed concept of philosophy naturally comes into being. We cannot escape it. It will do no harm if we understand its particular character and, at the same time, achieve an awareness of the general and open concept of philosophy, which not only enlarges our vision of philosophy but also helps facilitate philosophical communication.

So much for the explanation of my three assertions and my basic idea of a new concept of philosophy. Let it suffice. Now, I am going to offer a proposal and discuss its implications, whereby it will be shown how we can achieve a sound understanding of Chinese philosophy—which is actually the real theme of the present chapter.

My Proposal and its Implications

This proposal is intended to put forth a view of philosophy. As a proposal, it cannot, of course, claim any truth, but only a kind of utility in the sense that it can help improve communication between different philosophical traditions and secure a better understanding of the history of philosophical thought. Moreover, it also helps retain our sense of continuity in philosophical thinking together with our demand for the development of philosophical studies. For brevity and clarity, I would like to formulate this proposal in the following points, and then give some explanations:

(a) Philosophical thinking is characterized as reflective thinking, which means thinking about our own activities.

(b) The subject matter of reflective thinking can change drastically from one period to another. Different branches of philosophical learning thus arise. The variety in subject matter does not contradict the original characteristic of philosophical thinking but simply means that there are particular philosophies. Each particular philosophy represents the operation of reflective thinking upon a certain field of our own activities.

(c) At a certain point in time, we can always enumerate the fields upon which reflective thinking has operated, and tell what kinds of studies have been subsumed under the general name, 'Philosophy'. However, with the development of history, new fields are always possible. In other words, there is no complete list of the subject matters of philosophical thinking and no need to ask for it. Hence, this proposed concept of philosophy is an open concept.

(d) When reflective thinking operates over a certain kind of subject matter, it strives to solve certain problems and thus gives rise to philosophical theories or particular philosophies. The significance of such effort is completely dependent upon the significance or importance of those problems. If we want to examine whether a certain problem is significant enough to make reflective thinking worthwhile, we must return to real life. In such cases, the answer might be positive or negative and would thus determine our attitude towards a particular philosophy. But this does not apply to Philosophy in General, or reflective thinking in itself. It makes no sense to inquire whether reflective thinking is significant or not, just as we cannot question the need for understanding or knowledge itself.[5]

(e) To understand a particular philosophy we must begin with the problems it deals with. The only justification for denying a particular philosophy is the evidence that the problems it deals with have no relevance to real life. If no such evidence is found, this fact must be taken into account as a part of our philosophy.

Now, let me explain some points mentioned above. The first and foremost thing in need of clarification is the open-ended character of the proposed concept of philosophy.

In the history of philosophy, we have found great philosophers who are said to have made epoch-making contributions to philosophical thinking or studies. By 'epoch-making', we really mean that the philosopher has selected a new subject matter, offered a new method, constructed a new system, for example, and, all in all, has given us a new concept of philosophy. But, if we look upon such matters more closely, we always find that, in each case, the philosopher tends to hold that the kind of philosophy he is doing is the only justifiable one. Other philosophies are regarded as insignificant or off the mark. Although he might admit that there will be development of philosophical thinking in the future, he would see such a development as studies of details under his principle. In brief, the philosopher offers a closed concept of philosophy which claims some final truth. However, the simple fact that such cases are plural in number is sufficient to show that history is not answerable to their claims. Closed concepts of philosophical thinking or studies appeared on the stage one after another, but none of them represented anything final.

Ample evidence is available in the history of philosophy. Needless to say, metaphysical systems, such as Platonic or Aristotelian Doctrines, which claimed 'true knowledge' of 'Reality', always carried a closed concept of philosophy or philosophical thinking. Such models had been followed through the medieval age and extended to the early stage of modern European philosophy. The real change came only when there arose the critical philosophy of Immanuel Kant. Theoretically speaking, there might be some special interpretation of Kantian methodology which would confer upon the critical philosophy an open character. However, for Kant himself, that was not his intention. This is clearly shown in his 'Open Letter on Fichte's *Wissenschaftslehre*'. He said:

I must remark here that the assumption that I have intended to publish only a propaedeutic to transcendental philosophy and not the actual system of this philosophy is incomprehensible to me. Such an intention could never have occurred to me, since I took the completeness of pure philosophy within the *Critique of Pure Reason* to be the best indication of the truth of my work.[6]

So, Kant did not intend to give us a view or a method only, but a complete system. This system, as presented in the *Critique of Pure Reason*, really became a closed one in his 'Analytic of Principles'.[7]

According to the criterion I have adopted in this chapter, anyone who has declared that philosophy can do only this or that job is regarded as giving us a closed concept of philosophy. To apply this criterion to twentieth-century philosophies, we will find that, while certain great renowned philosophers have spoken against systematic philosophy or classical patterns of philosophical thinking, they have also given us some closed concepts of philosophy. Take Wittgenstein and Heidegger as concrete examples.

Wittgenstein, even in his *Tractatus* period, tended to see philosophical thinking as a therapeutic discipline.[8] In his *Philosophical Investigations* period, this view became a dominating idea. Whether this means a 'miserable failure' in his philosophical career, as Gustav Bergmann put it, is not our concern here.[9] The point I want to make now is that this concept of philosophical thinking or philosophy is also closed in the sense that it excluded all other functions of philosophical thinking, although it seems to be extremely dissimilar to any classical concepts. Since Wittgenstein's view has been so well known in our time, I believe no quotation is necessary.

The case with Heidegger is more delicate. His philosophical writings are so notoriously difficult that all interpreters of this philosophy would appear unreliable on some points, but his concept of philosophy *per se* is not so remote from our understanding. In 'What is Philosophy?', he expressed his basic view rather clearly. He held that 'philosophy is Greek in nature' and 'philosophy is the philosophia'. Putting aside the part involving the 'Being of being', his emphasis on the Greek nature of philosophy is sufficient to show that his concept of philosophy is closed in the European tradition.[11]

Here, I must make an additional remark to prevent possible misunderstanding; that is, I do not mean that creating closed concepts should be faulted, but only that the proposed open concept of philosophy is basically a different thing and is not found in established theories.

Again, let this suffice for an explanation of the open concept. Now, let me turn to my second point.

This is concerned with the notion of the function of philosophy. As the proposed concept of philosophy goes, there is the universal characterization of philosophical thinking in general and there are particular philosophies as the result of the operation of reflective thinking upon special subject matters. These two parts combine to constitute this open concept of philosophy. If we only have particular philosophies, we will always have closed concepts of philosophy which always involve difficulties in communication. However, so far as the function of philosophy is concerned, only in each particular philosophy could we find an answer to such questions as 'What should philosophy do?', 'What is philosophy supposed to do?' or 'How should we do philosophy?' and so on. Actually, each particular philosophy deals with a set of special problems and thereby exhibits a special function. This function always implies a special view of philosophy as the guiding principle of the studies within this particular philosophy. I used to call such principles 'quasi-paradigms', allusive to Thomas Kuhn's 'Paradigms' in scientific studies. They are at least similar in that they both bear a closed character. Such quasi-paradigms, when becoming dominant in a certain period of history, would be regarded as the *right view of philosophy*, although with our understanding described above, we are sure that every quasi-paradigm only represents a closed concept in a particular philosophy. But particular philosophies, as well as their closed concepts of philosophy-in-itself, are in no sense condemnable. In the evolutional process of philosophical thinking, one particular philosophy follows another. They constitute the contents of philosophical studies. The only undesirable consequence is in the problem of communication between such different particulars.

To achieve good understanding of a certain philosophy requires that we get into the closed conceptual world and see its function, its problems, and its theoretical interest clearly and fair-mindedly. This is hardly possible if we are already preoccupied with some other closed concept of philosophy. On the other hand, it is also extremely unlikely that a person without any philosophical training can understand a particular philosophy at all. Here is a dilemma. This problem is a specially conspicuous when we study the history of philosophy. In such a case, we are always liable to impose one particular philosophy with which we are familiar upon another philosophy and thus seriously distort the latter or even reduce it to truism or queer belief. It is a tragic fact of philosophical communication.

If we have this communication problem in mind, the appeal of the open concept of philosophy will become apparent. In the first place, it enables us to realize the important fact that a particular philosophy can only manifest an aspect of reality and can offer no more than a closed concept of philosophy. Such a concept cannot become a criterion for some other particular philosophy. It thus removes the obstacle in our way to understanding philosophies of other traditions. In other words, it helps get rid of the above-mentioned dilemma in a quite natural way. In the second place, we have the universal characterization of Philosophy in General and have no difficulty in deciding whether what we are confronted with belongs to the realm of philosophy or not. For instance, if we look at some empirical studies about external objects, we will not hesitate to judge that this is not philosophy. In the third place, in an effort to understand some particular philosophy, we have the notion of the function of philosophy as a guideline. Since every particular philosophy becomes what it is only because it possesses a certain function (in dealing with its special subject matter or problems), the key to understanding is always its function. Of course, in such efforts, the researcher always needs some training in analytic techniques and documentary studies, but on that level there is no real problem.

The final point I have to mention is that philosophical thinking, as reflective thinking, can play a cognitive or an orientative role in the world of cultural activities. This distinction in function entails a separation of two kinds of philosophy. A philosophical tradition is often one-sided. In other words, particular philosophies in a certain tradition, although mutually different on another meaning-level, tend to be cognitive or orientative in principle. In case two different philosophical traditions, each taking a different side, face each other, the communication problem usually appears unsurmountable. If we want a concrete example, the problem concerning the understanding of Chinese philosophy by people of other traditions would be the best choice. Now, I shall move to the last section of this last chapter, in which I shall try to present my view of this problem.

Understanding Chinese Philosophy

The difficulty is obvious. Attempts and failures are numerous. Up to this day, genuine understanding of Chinese philosophy among Western philosophers is, frankly speaking, very rare. Even Chinese philosophers are also haunted by this difficulty, when they want to communicate with Western students or a Western audience about Confucianism or Daoism. However, since technology has brought all parts of the world closer, it is almost imperative

that we should find out some way to overcome such communication problems. For me, as a Chinese philosopher, my attention
must be concentrated on philosophical communication.

With my proposal of the open concept of philosophy in mind, I
hope to help to improve the situation by making the following
points:

Chinese philosophy as a whole is primarily orientative in character. There have been many philosophical schools in the Chinese
tradition. But, with very few exceptions, they are all orientative
philosophies. To make it clearer, let me try to give an explanation
of the term 'orientative' in this usage, and then cite some examples
from history as testimonies.

When we say that some philosophy is orientative, we mean that
this philosophy intends to effect some change in the self or in the
world. For convenience, we may suggest two terms, namely, 'self-
transformation' and 'transformation of the world'. These two
terms cover the basic function of philosophy in Chinese tradition.

The root of a philosophical theory or doctrine lies in the concern
or the interest of the philosopher. With a special concern or interest, the philosopher selects a primary problem and roughly fixes
his subject matter. Then he will take an approach and work out
some points as the solution and interpretation of his primary problem. These points constitute his philosophical theory. This is the
general order of the formation of philosophical theories. But when
we try to understand a theory, we must move in the reverse order.
The theory is before our eyes. We have to abstract its main points
first and then trace back to the primary problem and its subject
matter. This sometimes involves a painstaking inquiry. Only after
these things are clear can we reach an understanding of the function of this particular philosophy. When we are sure what this philosophy intends to do and how much has been done, our understanding is almost complete.

Now, let me take two examples from Chinese Daoism and Confucianism as typical cases of the orientative philosophy of Chinese
tradition: Zhuangzi (Chuang Tzu) and Mengzi (Mencius).

The Original Doctrine of Zhuangzi

The *Zhuangzi* as we know it today was formed in the early years of
the Han Dynasty. It is composed of three parts. Only the first part
or the *neipian* (內篇) represents the original doctrine.

At first sight, the *Zhuangzi* is simply confusing, and not like a theoretical work at all. There are only fragmentary fictions in a mythological style and isolated paragraphs containing some points or arguments. However, if we understand his intention, this particular philosophy is by no means unintelligible, in spite of the fact that the language is comparatively difficult.

The main theme of Zhuangzi's philosophy is to show people what they should do and should not do. In other words, he gives us a purpose with some arguments against other purposes. But the verb 'do' and the noun 'purpose' must be understood in his special sense. As for the concrete contents of this purpose, it is more distantly removed from common sense and is especially in need of accurate interpretation. To clarify all these things, we have to analyse the essential structure of this doctrine.

Let us begin with the general character of a purpose-theory. To advocate a purpose always requires three steps. They are:
(a) Selecting a purpose and establishing it as the right goal of wisdom.
(b) Giving some justification to the above decision.
(c) Offering practical maxims to show how this purpose can be achieved.

Therefore, the purport of a purpose-theory can always be found through the ideas expressed on three problems; namely, 'what is the purpose?' 'How is it justified?' 'What are the maxims for achieving this purpose?' To apply this approach to Zhuangzi's philosophy, I provide a corresponding exposition as follows.

The Purpose   This is given in the first chapter of Zhuangzi's book, which is, in general, composed of legendary anecdotes with fragmentary comments. There are no clear statements or arguments. However, the title of this chapter gives the original idea in a straightforward way. It is *Xiaoyaoyou* (逍遙遊). *Xiaoyao* means absolutely unburdened and unbound freedom and *you*, in ordinary language, means 'wandering', but is here used to refer to the natural operation or movement of mind. The purpose Zhuangzi gave us is to achieve *Xiaoyao* for the mind or the self. To put it in a more philosophical way, I suggest to call it 'transcendent freedom'. It is transcendent because this freedom is not supposed to exert any influence upon objects or the objective world in any active way.

This idea actually represents the principle or basic standpoint of primary Daoism (as distinguished from later Daoist doctrines), and must be understood through the whole perspective. For convenience of our explanation, let me take the concept of *wuwei* from the teachings of Laozi (Lao Tzu) to help shed light on it. *Wuwei* literally means 'not doing' or 'inaction', but in the context of Laozi's thought, it also points to freedom in the transcendent sense, but more straightforwardly. Laozi actually said: *wei wu wei* (為無為), which means 'try to achieve *wu wei*'. This shows clearly that freedom from doing is regarded as a purpose and should be achieved by conscious efforts. This corrobates our interpretation of *Xiaoyao*.

However, the real difficulty in understanding Zhuangzi just begins to emerge here. The interpretation of *Xiaoyao* naturally gives rise to the following questions: What is the exact meaning of 'doing nothing'? Why should we regard this transcendent freedom as a purpose? Why should the freedom of which he speaks be transcendent? All in all, this is a problem of justification. This leads us to the next section in which the bulk of Zhuangzi's doctrine of Self and Freedom will be examined.

The Justification of the Purpose of Daoist Philosophy   The Justification, especially that of the philosophy of Zhuangzi, must begin with an accurate description of the Daoist view of the world. There are two possible interpretations of a view of the world. In the first place, there is a world-view before the fixation of purpose. In the second place, there is a world-view after the achievement of the purpose. In other words, Zhuangzi must have seen or understood the world in such a way that he had some good reason to advocate *Xiaoyao* or transcendent freedom; while after achieving this freedom, he would present a picture of the world from the perspective of his enlightened mind. Now, only the world-view in the former sense is relevant to the justification problem. The way Zhuangzi saw the world is found described in different parts of the text, but the focus point is his concept of change or *hua* (化), which was specially emphasized in the Sixth Chapter. The concept of change has a very special denotation in Zhuangzi's language. It does not refer to the events in the phenomenal world but denotes the essential ontological principle of all beings. He also had another term derived from *hua*; that is *zao hua*, which literally means 'making change' but actually is used as a noun, namely the 'Change-making Principle'.[13] This principle is also a power in itself. It governs all beings, ranging from physical things to psychological and even cultural entities. Such a view of change is nothing special, and was actually advocated by Heraclitus of ancient Greece and in scriptures of primitive Buddhism. However, this view of the world leads to an important philosophical point in Zhuangzi's teachings when it is applied to determine the ontological status of the human body or the Physical Self. Here, a quotation seems appropriate. In the Sixth Chapter, we have the following famous paragraph:

Zi Si, Zi Yu, Zi Li, and Zi Lei talked together, saying: 'Whoever has the wisdom to see Nothingness as the head, Living Process as the spine, and Death as the rump, knowing the internal unity of Life and Death, will be qualified as our friends. The four persons smiled at each other and felt well-communicated in their minds. They became friends. Then, Zi Yu was seriously sick. Zi Si went to see him. . . . Zi Si asked: 'Do you worry about it (death)?' 'No!' Zi Yu said: 'Why should I worry? If it happens to change my left arm into a chicken, I (my mind) will let it be used as poultry; if it happens to change my right arm into a pellet, I will let it be used for birds; if it happens to change my rump into a wheel and my sensations into a horse, I will let it be used for riding. . . .'. Then Zi Lei was ill and about to die, and his wife and children stood around him and wept. Zi Li went to see him. Zi Li said (to Zi Lei's wife and children): 'Oh, Keep away! Don't interrupt *hua* ('the change'). And then he, leaning against the door, said to Zi Lei: 'Oh! What is the great Change-Making doing with you and where is it carrying you? Is it making you the liver of a rat, or a limb of an insect?' Zi Lei said: 'The parents tell the children where to go, and the children follow suit. The *yinyang* principle (cosmic power) stands in a similar position to the human body. . . The cosmic power gives me the body, makes me burdened with living process, reduces the burden by giving me old years and gives me death to make me rest. One who sees life rightly sees death also rightly.'[14]

The main theme of this paragraph is to show the important truth that the physical self is only illusory. And this is also the most important point that is derived from the concept of change in Zhuangzi's doctrine. From the understanding of *hua*, we must be able to see the simple truth that every empirical existence is in a relation of transformation with other existences. The elements that constitute my body did constitute, and will constitute, other things in the same time/space structure, or empirical world. Therefore, the body is no more than a congregation of physical elements, which happened to be formed by the cosmic power, or Change-making Principle, and which will disintegrate when the elements move to form other physical things. Then, there is obviously no reason to regard the body as the self, which is, by definition, distinguished from outer things.

The ordinary idea to regard the body as the self is thus repudiated as a foolish illusion. Then, what is the real self? It is not an object or an existence on a particular level. It cannot be described with any empirical predicate. We can only say that the self is 'free', because the self is not only beyond the body, but also beyond all beings. It is not burdened or bound unless it limits itself and falls into the realm of beings, and becomes an empirical mind. However, an empirical mind can return to selfhood, if it strives, by conscious efforts, to get rid of self-limiting inclinations.

Following Zhuangzi's view of self to this point, it suddenly appears clear that freedom as the only purpose has a justification in its own right. A purpose is always a purpose of a self; if the self is not acting to contradict itself, it must move towards freedom.[15] But this can only be manifested in reflective thinking, and cannot be described or demonstrated in any language of objects.

Now, clarification of why the self must stay in transcendent freedom is still required. A handy clue is the term 'self-limiting' mentioned above. For convenience, we may take Fichte's Ego to make a contrast. According to Fichte, Ego is also free in itself, but has to pass through a self-limitation in order to develop. In other words, Fichte thought that it is a proper activity of the Ego to move to Non-ego because it has to develop itself in order that a world of spiritual values could be created. However, his thesis depends upon the optimistic supposition that creating values in the phenomenal world is basically possible. Now, Zhuangzi took just the opposite view. Zhuangzi never accepted this possibility. He rather thought that there is really nothing valuable to be done in the physical world, in which the cosmic principle operates eternally and all beings follow their courses. So-called cultural values only make sense to prejudicial minds. To see the matter in a reversed way, we can also point out that the mind, when trying to engage itself with cognitive and moral efforts, is only seeking the impossible and creating all kinds of trouble for itself and the world. This is also the basic attitude towards human culture and knowledge, held both by Laozi and Zhuangzi. Zhuangzi, in his book, tried to establish this point by giving arguments and metaphors against the authenticity of knowledge and the function of moral norms. The following quotations may serve to demonstrate this view:

How does the Principle get covered and the true/false bifurcation arise? How does language (the genuine function of language) get covered and the affirmation/denial bifurcation arise? How is it that the Principle is moving away and not staying (within the human mind)? How is it that language is right here but loses its proper function? The Principle is covered at the moment when there are petty achievements; language is covered where extravagance prevails.[16] Therefore, the Confucians and Mohists both have advocated their criteria of right and wrong, to affirm the right in their own sense, and deny the wrong in their own sense. In order to see the limitation of such affirmations and denials, we must appeal to the enlightened mind. Everything can be seen in That (way, system). Everything can also be seen in This (way, system). The limitation is not seen there (in the systems), but is known by wisdom. Thus, we may say that from This there arises That and on That does This depend. Here we have the theory of the co-existence of This and That. However, when there is a process of emerging, there is, in the same time, a process of decaying. And vice versa. When an affirmation is being made, a denial is, at the same time, being made. And vice versa. The right and the wrong depend upon each other. Therefore, the sage (the enlightened mind) never follows this path (the relative and limited way of thinking) but mirrors the reality with original wisdom. That is also true for right (in a higher order). This and That possess the same status. That represents one kind of right-and-wrong; This also represents one kind of right-and-wrong. Is the opposition of This and That really a necessity or not? To release That and This from opposition, we get the Pivot Principle. As a pivot, the Principle stands in the centre and responds to infinite processes. The views of right constitute an infinite series, and the views of wrong constitute an infinite series, too. Therefore, I say, there is only the enlightened mind (to be affirmed).[17]

This long paragraph from the Second Chapter represents the bulk of Zhuangzi's arguments against the significance of knowledge and value standards. The contention is not as difficult as the language. He pointed out that every theory or system of knowledge is inevitably closed, and, thereupon, it never touches reality. The criterion of truth is always relative to the system. For every system, there is always an opposite one. They exclude each other but, at the same time, depend upon each other. Disputes based upon such 'petty achievements' go on indefinitely. We cannot say the truth is now reached, no matter how long we study and argue. In other words, the efforts to reach knowledge and value criteria are bound to be fruitless. In brief, his view was also expressed in a metaphor found in his followers' remark on another contemporary philosopher, Hui Shi. It runs:

Hui Shi failed to rest with this (principle), but consumed his energy in external things without feeling bored; in the end, he was known as an orator-sophist. What a pity it is! With his talent, he wandered without rest and pursued external things without return. That is like seeking echoes by making more sounds, or running after his shadow with his body! How sad it is![18]

This metaphor shows exactly what Zhuangzi would say about cognitive activities and empirical knowledge. The writer of this paragraph must have been a very faithful follower of Zhuangzi's teachings.

Now, putting the arguments and this metaphor together, we find the conclusion in sight. If there is no significance to seek knowledge or to establish value norms for the outer world, or the empirical world, then the Self of Zhuangzi must only stand in its own freedom. Unlike Fichte's Ego that must enter the external world to achieve values, the Self would only maintain its transcendent freedom. In Zhuangzi's philosophy, this is also the only value to be pursued by people. His teachings thus become orientative in character. What he really wanted to do is to lead people to this freedom or enlightenment.

Before we turn to Confucianism as the other example of the orientative philosophy of Chinese tradition, a few words must be added to make Zhuangzi's philosophy less incomprehensible. The first point to be supplemented is concerned with the question of how one would act after achieving the transcendent freedom of self. This is also the view of the world after enlightenment. Of course, a man of wisdom will still live in the world. Then what is his attitude towards the world? A brief answer is that he will not seek any goal in the world but will only see events in change and enjoy a kind of aesthetic observation. Things or beings come and go in their natural course, including one's own body, and the mind need not do anything for there is nothing worthwhile to be done. This view points to the artistic dimension of spiritual activities and has actually exerted influence upon Chinese arts in the subsequent centuries. The second point is about the change of Daoist tradition in later history. Actually, not long after the time of Zhuangzi, different ways to interpret the philosophy of Laozi and Zhuangzi appeared in various areas of ancient China. Some of them took several side points from these teachings and combined them into a special religious faith, and thereby gave rise to Daoist Religion. Others distorted the whole doctrine and took certain ideas out of the original context to form another political philosophy. In the Han-Wei period, The title 'Daoists' was used by three different groups of people, each claiming to be followers of Laozi and Zhuangzi but none of them inheriting the genuine spiritual tradition. Therefore, one must be careful to distinguish the later so-called Daoist writings from the original teachings of Laozi and Zhuangzi. More details cannot be discussed in the present chapter.

Practical Maxims On practical maxims corresponding to (c) Zhuangzi offered nothing. By becoming enlightened, one achieves freedom of the self, but how to become enlightened remains an unanswered question. Zhuangzi seemed to rely on the right view of the world and the self as a necessary condition, but did not show us that it is also sufficient. Thus, this is almost a blank in this philosophy of purpose.

Mengzi: an Example of Confucian Orientative Philosophy

Mengzi had a philosophy, clear and clean. It is clean in the sense that it is not dependent upon metaphysical speculation to establish its theme. It is clear in the sense that it does not involve unnecessary sophistication in language. However, the significance of Mengzi's philosophy cannot be exaggerated, especially in view of its influence upon the shaping of Chinese mentality and the formation of intellectual tradition in later centuries.

Mengzi's philosophy is also a philosophy of purpose. Let us make our exposition in three steps, in accordance with the order of the three questions proposed above.

The Purpose of this Philosophy Mengzi, while ready to take up his special historical mission, was a dedicated follower of Kongzi.[19] Therefore, the purpose of his philosophy is basically contained in Kongzi's teachings. As is well known to many people, Kongzi intended to establish proper order both for individual life and for society. He developed his philosophy until a doctrine was completed in his later years. In this doctrine, found in the *Analects*, he set up the three seminal concepts, *li*, *yi*, and *ren*. *Li* refers to the order, *yi* refers to the right, and *ren* refers to the 'will-to-right'. In striking contrast with Daoism, Confucianism primarily held that it is the constant goal of human life to create a cultural order in the world; this really means a transformation of the natural world.

And this transformation must depend upon human efforts. Therefore, transformation of personality by education becomes the starting point. In this way, he was known as a teacher of moral life, but the true central point of his teachings is the principle of transformation. As any primordial figure in a philosophical tradition, Kongzi taught more about the principle and the orientation than details. It was left to later followers to provide systematic explanation and theoretical justification. Now, Mengzi is the man. Mengzi inherited the Confucian idea that the most important thing is to achieve transformation, not to talk about it. However, he believed that his historical mission was to construct a philosophical system because there were evil ideas and misguided doctrines to be cleared up.[20] As a result, he became the first system-maker in the Confucian tradition. Speaking from this angle, we may also say that the philosophy of Mengzi is mainly a justification of the purpose of Confucianism. Thus, a summary of this philosophy should belong to the next section.

The Justification   Mengzi's philosophy is quite complicated, but the main points essentially relevant to the present purpose can be subsumed under three topics, namely, transformation of mind, transformation of society, and instructions on practice. Now, let us give a brief account of each part.

The first part is known as Mengzi's philosophy of mind. In the Chinese language, it is called *xinxinglun*, or 'Doctrines of Mind and Essence'. And these two terms actually provide the key to this part of his philosophy. Here, it is advisable to begin with an explanation and then give the necessary quotations. Mengzi primarily intended to solve such basic problems in Kongzi's teachings on moral transformation as: 'How can human beings achieve a moral order?', 'Why should we pursue the right or be moral?', 'Why should we create a cultural order for society?' and so on. His solution is to present a doctrine of the essential nature of the human mind. In the first place, he pointed out that the real root of all moral values, and even cultural values, lies in the special capacity of the human mind. It belongs to human nature because it is not learned from experience. It is essential in the sense that this capacity distinguishes human beings from other biological beings. In other words, if human beings are to live as human beings, they must follow and develop this innate capacity. If it does not make sense to doubt why human beings should live as human beings, then here is a justification in its own right. In the second place, this capacity, or essential nature of mind, operates automatically. It ceases to operate only when it is hindered by animal desires which have roots in the body. Therefore, we need not worry about how we can follow the moral course in life; the only thing to do is to maintain the mastery of mind over the body. On this point, it is easy to see that Mengzi's concept of mind is quite similar to Zhuangzi's concept of self in status, although quite different in function. Mengzi, like Zhuangzi, also held that the body is not the real self, and that the moral mind is not transcendent to the world. The moral mind is, on the contrary, the origin of the proper order of the world. Mengzi's concept of *xing*, or essential nature, is comparable to Aristotle's concept of essence in the sense that both refer to the property which is possessed by all members of the species and, at the same time, not possessed by other beings. However, the context is different. The concept of *xing* is not based on an ontological theory, as in Aristotelian philosophy, but directly established through reflective thinking on mind itself. As for the concept of innate capacity, *xing* is furthermore comparable to the concept of language capacity advocated by Noam Chomsky, while, once more, there is the important difference that Mengzi would never give any biological interpretation to *xing*, as Chomsky gave to his language capacity.

Such a comparison can help to show that Mengzi's doctrine of *xin* and *xing* is by no means especially difficult to accept. To cover the points given above, we now make the following quotations:

There is only a minute difference between human beings and animals. Ordinary people lose it while men of wisdom keep it.[21]

This refers to the special capacity of the human mind.

For (human) mouths, there is the common form of taste; for the ears, there is the common form of sound; for the eyes, there is the common form of colour. Is there nothing common to the mind? What is common to the mind is the *logos*, the right. The sage only achieves what is common to all of our minds. Therefore, the *logos* and the right satisfy the mind just as good food satisfies the mouth.[22]

This paragraph shows that the moral capacity or *xing* is universal to all members of the human race.

More important and well known is the paragraph about 'the four beginnings'. Mengzi said:

Every human being has a sense of commiseration in his mind. . . . . What I mean can be illustrated in this way: when a man suddenly sees a child about to fall into a well, he immediately feels alarmed and worried; this is not because he wants to make friends with the parents, nor because he wants to get a good reputation among his acquaintances, nor because he dislikes the crying. (This response to human suffering belongs to his *xing*.) Seeing it in this way, a human being who has no sense of commiseration is not a human being at all. Similarly, a human being without the sense of shame and abhorrence (of evils), or without the sense of unacceptability (of improper things), or without the sense of right and wrong, ceases to be a human being. The sense of commiseration is the beginning of *ren*, the sense of shame and abhorrence is the beginning of *yi*, the sense of unacceptablity is the beginning of *li*, and the sense of right and wrong is the beginning of wisdom. Every human being has the four beginnings in his mind, just as he has the four limbs in his body. One, possessing these four beginnings but saying that he cannot achieve these virtues, is self-destroying.[23]

Here, Mengzi pointed out the four *a priori* modes of moral consciousness, or four concrete manifestations of the innate moral capacity.

Following this view, the incentive to achieving moral and cultural values, both for the person and human society, is simply natural. Evils arise only because human beings sometimes follow animal desires and fail to maintain their *xing*. To develop the innate capacity, we need education. But such details are not to be discussed here. Now we can move to Mengzi's political thought, to show his ideas of moral order for society.

Although Mengzi seemed to put little emphasis on the human body, this does not imply that he did not care for actual society. On the contrary, it is the primary goal of Confucian philosophy to create a cultural and moral order for the actual world. Unlike the Daoists who taught about 'not-doing', when they advocated their social and political philosophy, Kongzi and Mengzi placed all the emphasis upon the concept of duty, namely, the things we must try to do. Now, let us pick out two important points from Mengzi's doctrine to illustrate the basic view of his orientative philosophy in this aspect.

The first point is his theory of the 'right' government. As already shown above, Confucian philosophy demands that people must do the right thing, or follow a criterion of right, in every case. Political affairs cannot be exceptional. But in early societies, this problem seemed to be rather distant from common sense. In ancient times, human beings also followed the 'law of the forest'. Rulers got their power by force or violence, and then governed with this power. People lived and worked under the ruler's government and accepted it as a fact. They rarely felt that the status and the power of the rulers would need some justification. Rulers, on the other hand, usually appealed to some mystic authority to justify their rulership. Kongzi was the first man in Chinese history to set forth clear moral requirements for rulers, as a derivative of his theory of duties. The famous maxim that a ruler should be a ruler means that the ruler also has to fulfill his duties. Mengzi developed this doctrine by declaring that the real basis for a government lies in the people, instead of by virtue of the Mandate of Heaven (*Tian-ming*). He gave a new interpretation of ancient historical stories about the transition of power and rulership.[24] This material is mainly found in the fifth chapter of the *Mengzi*. Then he went further to say that:

What is of foremost importance (for a state) is the people. Next is sovereignty. Rulers (as individuals) are not important.[25]

Why do the people represent the most important thing for a state? It is only because the will of the people determines the rise and fall of rulers. Mengzi said:

Jie and *Zhou* (defeated rulers) lost the world (the rulership) because they lost the people; losing the people means losing the support of people's will. There is the right way to get the world. Getting the people, one will get the world. There is also the right way to get the people. Getting the support of people's will, one will get the people.[26]

Holding this view about the justification of rulership, Mengzi considered political revolution against a ruler who has failed to fulfil his duties as completely unobjectionable. This is directly counter to the current idea of loyalty in his time. But this is really a natural consequence of his theory of government. Mengzi did not advocate democracy in a modern or Western sense, but he did apply the concept of right to political life and thus brought morality and rationality to a new dimension. His doctrine typifies Confucian political theory.

Of less theoretical importance, but of more pragmatic significance, is the second point to be discussed now. This is Mengzi's view about policies.

A government depends upon the people's will for its existence, therefore the principle of policies must be one for the people. Mengzi emphasized two things, namely, economic welfare and education. The priority was given to economic policy because, if people do not live without worrying about daily needs, they cannot be expected to achieve cultural values. On this point, it is clear that Mengzi had different standards for self-transformation and social transformation. For self transformation, we can teach every individual to achieve sagehood, but we cannot have a society of sages. Materials concerning these points are abundant but we cannot quote too much in the present chapter. After all, this chapter is not an introduction to Mengzi's philosophy. We only take Mengzi and Zhuangzi as concrete examples for our understanding of Chinese orientative philosophies. Let us be satisfied with this outlined account. As for the arguments and metaphors given by Mengzi in his teachings, interested readers should refer to special essays and the original texts.

Practical Maxims   For these, Mengzi also had a complicated doctrine. We can only give a brief description of his main ideas in this connection. The first thing we must point out is that Mengzi's teachings on practice had a complete emphasis upon self-transformation. The transformation of society must depend on leadership. The reason is obvious. He cannot, as we said in the last paragraph, expect that all of the people would become sages, therefore he can only place his hope in great leaders who can achieve a certain degree of self-transformation and know the right thing to do for the people. Hence, he entertained a concept of the sage-ruler. However, in practice, he only emphasized moral education for the ruler, which would enable him to fulfil his duties, instead of making him a real sage.

While the transformation of society can only be achieved through good rulers, self-transformation can be achieved through a process of enlightenment. Since he held that moral capacities are innate, he did not see formidable difficulties in this process. He taught that, with the innate capacities, everybody can achieve self-transformation simply by developing what he already possesses. The only impediment arises when there is a problem of misplacement; namely, if you place the physical desire or emotional impulse in the leading position, your moral capacities will fail to play the orientative function. If you do not allow the desire or the impulse to encroach upon the mastery of moral capacities, these capacities will develop naturally. Therefore, at bottom, his maxim is simple; that is the purification of the will, although he presented his ideas in quite complicated ways. If we understand what Immanuel Kant meant when he said, in his discussion of Practical Reason, that the pure will is the rational will, Mengzi's contention will not be difficult to understand.

Now, it is time to conclude this section. As Chinese orientative philosophies, the teachings of Mengzi and of Zhuangzi make a very interesting contrast, but their common traits are also clear. To understand a philosophy of this kind is not difficult in itself. But it will become difficult or even incomprehensible, if we put it in the category of cognitive philosophy, which it is not. From the examples given above, we have treated such Chinese philosophies as the results of Reflective Thinking upon their special subject matter, namely, the problems of 'where should we go', instead of that of 'what it is', and we can see quite clearly what Zhuangzi and Mengzi were doing. If, on the contrary, we put these doctrines under the criteria of cognitive philosophies, we will find such orientative doctrines failing to meet the basic requirements of those closed concepts of philosophy from the very beginning.

Conclusion

In concluding, I will turn to the basic purpose of this chapter and say a few more words in explanation.

For years, I have been concerned with the problem of communication between philosophical societies with different traditions. I had been puzzled and disappointed before I realized that the obstacle is not in language or ideology but in the concept of philosophy. Following the Cartesian tradition, Western philosophers have, for centuries, taken it for granted that philosophy should provide compulsory knowledge, like mathematics or the sciences in general. To fix the realm for philosophical knowledge has become the focus point of their attention. Only in the latest generation can we find some exceptions. According to this concept of philosophy, the functions of philosophical thinking are bound to be cognitive, no matter what kind of cognitive activities one would prefer. When one applies this criterion to the Chinese or Indian doctrines, it is natural for one to conclude that these doctrines cannot be regarded as philosophy at all. The main function of such doctrines is not cognitive, even though they contain some minor points concerning cognitive problems. In this way, Chinese philosophy is excluded from the realm of philosophical studies in a serious sense. I actually have no objection to this view in itself. After all, who does not think and speak in a traditional context? What is wrong with using a word such as 'philosophy' in a certain conventional way? However, if one is to achieve understanding of other philosophical traditions, this is an obstacle. To remove this obstacle requires that the concept of philosophy be modified or broadened. Here, we do not have a real theoretical difficulty. Just as a conventional use of a word is not objectionable in principle, it is equally unobjectionable to offer another way of using the word, in order that some important purpose might be fulfilled. This is the basis of the thesis of the present paper; that is: it is advisable to adopt the open concept of philosophy if we want to help people of different philosophical traditions communicate better with each other.

My proposal does not involve sophisticated arguments or profound scholarship. It is not far beyond common sense. But, so far as we agree that philosophical communication is significant for the contemporary world, I am quite sure that this proposal makes good sense as an orientative idea.

Notes

1. Although it is impossible to identify who first introduced this Japanese translation of 'philosophy' into China, it is quite certain that when the Capital University (京師大学堂) in Peking, in the first decade of the twentieth century, did adopt this term '哲学' as a title for courses, this should indicate official acceptance of this translation.

2. Frege, of course, did not use a labelling theory to explain 'Proper Names', but what he meant by this term is really very close to the concept of an individual thing. Labelling theory only applies to the naming of individual things.

3. In one of my early writings, *Basics of Philosophy*, (哲学淺說), I actually gave an ostensive definition for philosophy. My strategy was to make a list of the branches of learning and then try to describe every branch, while keeping 'philosophy' as the common name of all these branches. I chose to do so because I was writing that small book for beginners only and just wanted to help readers get rid of this troublesome definition problem as early as possible. That purpose is far different from what I want to do here.

4. 'Family Resemblance' (FR) only means a 'common feature in a special relational sense.' Thus, objects of FR form an ordered series and only between a member in this series and the one imediately before or behind it can there be some common feature. This does not guarantee any common feature between the first member and the last member in such a series. Obviously, this idea cannot help to characterize philosophy as we would want.

5. Sceptics or Chinese Daoist philosophers who seemed to repudiate knowledge actually advocated their theory as a kind of higher-order knowledge.

6. See: I. Kant, *Philosophical Correspondence, 1759–99*, edited and translated by Arnulf Zweig (Chicago, The University of Chicago Press), p. 254.

7. See: B 188 *Critique of Pure Reason*: when Kant advocated to 'exhibit completely and systematically all the transcendental principles of the use of understanding', his system is clearly closed.

8. When Wittgenstein advised people to be silent on metaphysical problems, he was under the belief that, with his picture-theory of meaning, 'metaphysical disease' would be avoided. Although, in *Tractatus*, he still retained the constructive function of philosophical thinking.

9. See: Gustav Bergmann, 'The Glory and the Misery of Ludwig Wittgenstein,' *Essays on Wittgenstein's Tractatus*, edited by I.M. Copi and R.W. Beard.

10. Martin Heidegger: *What is Philosophy?* translated by William Kluback and Jean T. Wilde (New York, Twayne Publishers, Inc., 1958).

11. Rumours have it that Heidegger once expressed his appreciation for Chinese Daoist ideas, but I do not think we can take these rumours seriously.

12. *Wei wu wei* (為無為) appears in Chapter Three of *Daodejing* (道德經). Since *different versions* have been discovered during the centuries after Wang Bi (王弼), these three characters were in some cases not found in certain versions, (although they were found in Wang Bi's) some commentators (such as Gao Heng 高亨 and D.C. Lau), raised doubts that this short phrase might be the result of some mistake in the copying process, but I do not see any strong ground for this view. After all, the phrase does not cause any real difficulty in interpretation and there are stronger theoretical grounds for retaining this phrase than deleting it.

13. *Zaohua* (造化) originally a philosophical term, afterwards became a term of ordinary Chinese language 'to designate cosmic power' (personal or impersonal). In Chinese literature after the Han Dynasty, this term frequently appeared as an alias for the universe. Most people forget its Daoist origin.

14. See: *Da Zong Shi* (大宗師), *Zhuangzi*, Chapter 6.

15. Here, the theoretical supposition is that a purpose cannot exist apart from a mind or consciousness. This is of course different from the Aristotelian concept of *Entelechy* immanent in concrete things. Zhuangzi also had a concept of natural order, but that order has its root in the 'Change-making Power', and is only manifested in things, not existing in things.

16. In these sentences, the Chinese Character 隱 (*yin*) has been translated as 'covered'. Some Chinese scholars once thought that '*Yin*' might mean 'dependent', or 憑 *ping*, but that interpretation is not consistent with the whole context. I still believe the present translation is correct.

17. See: *Qi wu lun* (齊物論) *Zhuangzi*, Chapter 2.

18. See: *Tianxia* (天下), the last chapter of the *Zhuangzi*. This chapter was actually an afterword, written by his disciples. In ancient China it was customary to put such a last chapter in every book, with a short biography of the author or comments on the contents.

19. Mengzi actually said: 'As for my own wish, I follow Kongzi as the example'. (乃所願，則学孔子也). See: Chapter 2, Part I, (公孫丑上). (In the *Mengzi*, every chapter is divided into two parts)

20. See: *Mengzi*, Chapter 3, Part II (滕文公下). In this section, Mengzi responded to a student's question about why Mengzi was known as especially 'interested in debating' (好辯) by telling him that it is his historical mission to fight against erroneous theories and evil ideas.

21. See: *Mengzi*, Chapter 4, Part II (離婁下).

22. See: *Mengzi*, Chapter 6, Part I (告子上).

23. See: *Mengzi*, Chapter 2, Part I (公孫丑上).

24. Part of such stories are actually legendary in character. Mengzi just used such stories to show his points, not to make objective historical statements.

25. See: *Mengzi*, Chapter 7, Part II (盡心下). Here, I have translated *sheji* (社稷) as 'sovereignty'. The original meaning of these two characters is the deity of agriculture, but it is used to symbolize sovereignty. I have made a paraphrase in accordance with the context.

26. See: *Mengzi*, Chapter 4, Part I (離婁上).

Bibliography

Western Language Sources

Allinson, Robert E., 'The Negative Formulation of the Golden Rule in Confucius,' *Journal of Chinese Philosophy*, Vol. 2, No. 3, September, 1985, pp. 305–315.

——'Having Your Cake and Eating it, Too: Evaluation and Trans-Evaluation in Chuang Tzu and Nietzsche,' *Journal of Chinese Philosophy*, Vol. 13, No. 4, December, 1986, pp. 429–443.

——'The Confucian Golden Rule in Negative Sentential Formulation,' (in Chinese translation), *History and Theory*, Chinese Academy of Social Science, Beijing, September, 1988.

——'The Golden Rule in Confucianism,' (in Chinese translation), *Universitas*, Vol. XV, No. 11, Taipei, November, 1988.

——'Taoism in the Light of Zen: An Exercise in Inter-Cultural Hermeneutics,' *Zen Buddhism Today*, No. 6, Kyoto, November, 1988, pp. 23–38.

——'The Concept of Harmony in Chuang Tzu," in Liu Shu-hsien and Allinson, Robert E. (eds.), *Harmony and Strife Contemporary Perspectives, East and West* (Hong Kong, The Chinese University Press, 1988), pp. 169–183.

——and Liu Shu-hsien (eds.), *Harmony and Strife: Contemporary Perspectives, East and West* (Hong Kong, The Chinese University Press, 1988).

——*Chuang-Tzu for Spiritual Transformation: An Analysis of the Inner Chapters* (Albany, State University of New York Press, 1989).

Aquinas, Thomas, *Treatise of Law* (Chicago, Gateway, 1967).

Aristotle, *Ethica Nichomachae*, first edition (Bywater, Oxford, Oxford Classical Texts, 1962).

Austin, J.L., *Sense and Sensibilia* (Oxford, Clarendon Press, 1962).

——*How to Do Things with Words* (Cambridge, Harvard University Press, 1962).

Bergmann, Gustav, 'The Glory and the Misery of Ludwig Wittgenstein', in I.M. Copi and R.W. Beard (eds.), *Essays on Wittgenstein's Tractatus* (London, Routledge & Kegan Paul, 1966).

Carus, Paul, *The Canon of Reason and its Virtue* (Chicago, Open Court, 1913).

Chan, Wing-tsit, 'The Evolution of the Confucian Concept of Jen', *Philosophy East and West*, Vol. 4, No. 4, 1955.

——(tr.), *Instructions for Practical Living and Other Neo-Confucian Writ-*

ings by Wang Yang-ming (New York, Columbia University Press, 1963a).

—(ed., tr.), *A Source Book in Chinese Philosophy* (Princeton, Princeton University Press, 1963b).

—'Chinese and Western Interpretations of Jen (Humanity)', *Journal of Chinese Philosophy*, Vol. 2, No. 2, 1975.

—*Chu Hsi and Neo-Confucianism* (Honolulu, University of Hawaii Press, 1986).

Chang, K.C. (ed.), *Food in Chinese Culture* (New Haven, Yale University Press, 1977).

Chen, Annie, *The What and How of Chinese Painting* (Taibei, Art Book Co., Ltd., 1978).

Ch'en, Chih-mai, *Chinese Calligraphers and Their Art* (Melbourne, Melbourne University Press, 1966).

Cheng, François, *Chinese Poetic Writing* (Bloomington, Indiana University Press, 1977).

Childress, James F. and Macquarrie, John (eds.), *The Westminster Dictionary of Christian Ethics* (Philadelphia, Westminster Press, Second edition, 1986).

Ching, Julia, *To Acquire Wisdom: The Way of Wang Yang-Ming* (New York, Columbia University Press, 1976).

Cikoski, J.S., *Classical Chinese Word-Classes*, unpublished Ph.D. dissertation, Yale University, 1970.

Coates, J.R. (tr., ed.) *Bible Key Words from Gerhard Kittel's Theologisches Wörterbuch zum Neuen Testament* (London, Adam and Charles Black, 1951).

Collingwood, R.G., *An Autobiography* (Oxford, Oxford University Press, 1939).

—*The Idea of History* (New York, Oxford University Press, 1956).

Copi, I.M. and Beard, R.W. (eds.), *Essays on Wittgenstein's Tractatus* (London, Routledge & Kegan Paul, 1966).

Cornford, Francis MacDonald (tr.), *The Republic of Plato* (New York, Oxford University Press, 1967).

Couvreur, S. (tr.), *Li Ki*, 2 Vols. (Ho Kien Fu, Imprimerie de la Mission Catholique, 1913).

— *Tch'ouen Ts'iu et Tso Tchouan* (Paris, Cathasia, 1951).

Crump, J. (tr.), *Chan-kuo Ts'e* (Oxford, Clarendon Press, 1970).

Cua, Antonio S., 'Some Reflections on the Structure of Confucian Ethics', *Philosophy East and West*, Vol. 21, No. 2, 1971.

—'The Conceptual Aspect of Hsün Tzu's Philosophy of Human Nature', *Philosophy East and West*, Vol. 27, No. 4, 1977.

—'The Quasi-Empirical Aspect of Hsün Tzu's Philosophy of Human Nature', *Philosophy East and West*, Vol. 28, No. 1, 1978.

—*Dimensions of Moral Creativity* (University Park, Pennsylvania State

University Press, 1978).
——'Dimensions of Li (Propriety): Reflections on an Aspect of Hsün Tzu's Ethics', *Philosophy East and West*, Vol. 29, No. 4, 1979.
——'Tasks of Confucian Ethics', *Journal of Chinese Philosophy*, Vol. 6, No. 1, 1979.
——*The Unity of Knowledge and Action: A Study in Wang Yang-ming's Moral Psychology* (Honolulu, University of Hawaii Press, 1982).
——'Morality and Human Nature', *Philosophy East and West*, Vol. 32, No. 3, 1982.
——'Li and Moral Justification: A study in the *Li Chi*', *Philosophy East and West*, Vol. 33, No. 1, 1983.
——*Ethical Argumentation: A Study in Hsün Tzu's Moral Epistemology* (Honolulu, University of Hawaii Press, 1985).
——'The Ethical Uses of the Past in Early Confucianism: The Case of Hsün Tzu', *Philosophy East and West*, Vol. 32, No. 2, 1985.
——'The Problem of Conceptual Unity in Hsün Tzu and Li Kou's Solution', *Bulletin of Chinese Philosophical Association*, Vol. 3, 1985.
——'Hsün Tzu and the Unity of Virtues', *Journal of Chinese Philosophy*, Vol. 14, No. 4, 1987.
Dahlstrom, Daniel, 'The Tao of Ethical Argumentation', *Journal of Chinese Philosophy*, Vol. 14, No. 4, 1987.
Dawson, Raymond, *Confucius* (New York, Hill and Wang, 1981).
de Bary, William Theodore (ed.), *Sources of the Chinese Tradition* (New York, Columbia University Press, 1960).
——*Self and Society in Ming Thought* (New York, Columbia University Press, 1970).
Delza, Sophia, *T'ai-Chi Ch'uan* (Albany, State University of New York Press, 1985).
Dennett, Daniel C., *Brainstorms: Philosophical Essays on Mind and Psychology* (Cambridge, MIT Press, 1981).
Deutsch, Eliot, *Studies in Comparative Aesthetics* (Honolulu, The University Press of Hawaii, 1975).
Dewey, J., *A Common Faith* (New Haven, Yale University Press, 1934).
——*Theory of the Moral Life* (New York, Holt, Rinehart and Winston, 1960).
Dickie, George, *Aesthetics: An Introduction* (Los Angeles, Pegasus, 1971).
Downie, R.S., *Roles and Values* (London, Methuen, 1971).
Dubs, H.H. (tr.), *The Works of Hsüntze* (Taibei, Chengwen, 1966).
Dufrenne, Mikel (Don Ihde and others, trs.), *The Phenomenology of Aesthetic Experience* (Evanston, Northwestern University Press, 1973).
Dworkin, R., *Taking Rights Seriously* (Cambridge, Harvard University Press, 1978).

——*A Matter of Principle* (Cambridge, Harvard University Press, 1985).

——*Law's Empire* (Cambridge, Harvard University Press, 1986).

Ely, John Hart, *Democracy and Distrust: A Theory of Judicial Review* (Cambridge, Harvard University Press, 1980).

Erkes, E., *Ho-shang-kung's Commentary on Lao Tse* (Ascona, Artibus Asiae Publishers, 1958).

Fang, Thomé H., *The Chinese View of Life: The Philosophy of Comprehensive Harmony* (Taibei, Linking, 1980).

——*Chinese Philosophy: Its Spirit and Development* (Taibei, Linking, 1981).

Fehl, N.E., *Rites and Propriety in Literature and Life: A Perspective for a Cultural History of Ancient China* (Hong Kong, Chinese University Press, 1971).

Fenollosa, Ernest F., *Epochs of Chinese and Japanese Art*, two vols. (New York, Dover Publications, 1913, 1963).

Fingarette, Herbert, *Confucius: The Secular as Sacred* (New York, Harper and Row, 1972).

Forke, A. (tr.), *Lun Heng* (New York, Paragon, 1962).

Gallie, W.G., *Philosophy and Historical Understanding* (London, Chatto & Windus, 1964).

Girardot, Norman, *Myth and Meaning in Early Taoism: The Theme of Chaos (hun-tun)* (Berkeley, University of California Press, 1983).

Gluckman, Max (ed.), *Essays on the Ritual of Social Relations* (Manchester, Manchester University Press, 1962).

Graham, A.C., 'The Background of the Mencian Theory of Human Nature', *Tsing Hua Journal of Chinese Studies*, Vol. 6, No. 1, 2, 1967, pp. 215–74.

——*Later Mohist Logic, Ethics and Science* (Hong Kong and London, Chinese University Press, 1978).

——*Chuang Tzu: The Inner Chapters* (London, George Allen & Unwin, 1981).

Grousset, René, *Chinese Art and Culture* (New York, Grove Press, 1961).

Hall, David and Ames, Roger, *Thinking Through Confucius* (Albany, State University of New York Press, 1987).

Hampshire, Stuart, *Morality and Conflict* (Cambridge, Harvard University Press, 1983).

Hansen, Chad, *Language and Logic in Ancient China* (Ann Arbor, University of Michigan Press, 1983).

——'A Tao of Tao in Chuang Tzu', in Mair (ed.), *Experimental Essays on Chuang Tzu* (Honolulu, University of Hawaii Press, 1983), pp. 24–55.

——'Chinese Language, Chinese Philosophy, and "Truth"' *Journal of Asian Studies*, Vol. XLIV, No. 3, May 1985, pp. 491–520.

——'Individualism in Chinese Thought', in Munro (ed.), *Individualism and Holism: Studies in Confucian and Taoist Values* (Ann Arbor, University of Michigan Press, 1985), pp. 35–56.

——'Punishment and Dignity in China', in Munro, (ed.), *Individualism and Holism: Studies in Confucian and Taoist Values* (Ann Arbor, University of Michigan Press, 1985), pp. 359–82.

Harbsmeier, C., 'The grammatical particle *i* in Classical Chinese', paper presented at the Second International Conference of Sinology, 28–30 December 1986.

——'Language and Logic' in Joseph Needham, *Science and Civilisation in China*, Vol. 7, Part 3 (Cambridge, Cambridge University Press, forthcoming).

Hart, H.L.A., *The Concept of Law* (Oxford, Clarendon Press, 1961).

——*Law, Liberty, and Morality* (Stanford, Stanford University Press, 1963).

Havelock, Eric A., *Preface to Plato* (Cambridge, Harvard University Press, 1963).

Hayakawa, S.I., *Language in Thought and Action* (New York, Harcourt, Brace and World, 1939).

Hegel, G.W.F. (E.B. Speir and J.B. Sanderson, trs.), *Lectures on the Philosophy of Religion, Together with a Work on the Proofs of the Existence of God* (London, Routledge & Kegan Paul, 1895).

Heidegger, Martin (William Kluback and Jean T. Wilde, trs.) *What is Philosophy?* (New York, Twayne Publishers Inc., 1958).

——(John Macquarrie and Edward Robinson, trs.), *Being and Time* (London, SCM Press, 1962).

Henke, F.G., (tr.), *The Philosophy of Wang Yang-Ming* (Chicago, Open Court, 1916, repr. New York, 1964).

Hicks, R.D. (ed.), *Diogenes Laertius, Vitae philosophorum* (Cambridge, Harvard University Press, 1965).

Hofstadter, Albert, *Truth and Art* (New York, Columbia University Press, 1965).

——and Kuhns, Richard (eds.), *Philosophies of Art and Beauty: Selected Readings from Plato to Heidegger* (New York, The Modern Library, 1964).

Hsiao Kung-chuan (F.W. Mote, tr.), *A History of Chinese Political Thought, Volume I: From the beginnings to the Sixth Century A.D.* (Princeton, Princeton University Press, 1979).

Huang, Al Chung-Liang, *Embrace Tiger, Return to Mountain* (Moab, Real People Press, 1973).

Hudson, W.D. (ed.), *The Is/Ought Question* (London, Macmillan, 1969).

Hume, D., *A Treatise on Human Nature* (Oxford, Clarendon Press, 1951).

——*Dialogues Concerning Natural Religion* (New York, Social Sciences Publishers, 1948).

Ingarden, Roman, *The Cognition of the Literary Work of Art* (Evanston, Northwestern University Press, 1973).

——(George G. Grabowicz, tr.), *The Literary Work of Art* (Evanston, Northwestern University Press, 1973).

Jenyns, Soame, *Chinese Painting* (New York, Schocken Books, 1966).

Kant, Immanuel, *Critique of Judgment*, translated by J.H. Bernard (New York, Hafner, 1951).

——(T.M. Greene and H.H. Hudson, trs.), *Religion within the Limits of Reason Alone* (New York, Harper, 1960).

——(Arnulf Zweig, ed., tr.), *Philosophical Correspondence 1759–99* (Chicago, University of Chicago Press, 1967 and 1970).

——*Critique of Pure Reason* (London, MacMillan Press Ltd).

Kao Ming, 'Chu Hsi's Discipline of Propriety' in Wing-tsit Chan (1986).

Kaptchuk, Ted. J., O.M.D., *The Web That Has No Weaver* (New York, Congdon & Weed, 1983).

Kato, Joken, 'The Meaning of Li', *Philosophical Studies of Japan*, Vol. 4, 1963.

Köster, H., *Hsün Tzu, Ins Deutsche Übertragen* (Kaldenkirchen, Steyler Verlag, 1967).

Kovesi, J., *Moral Notions* (London, Routledge & Kegan Paul, 1967).

Kripke, Saul A., *Wittgenstein On Rules and Private Language* (Cambridge, Harvard University Press, 1982).

Lacey, A.R., *A Dictionary of Philosophy* (New York, Charles Scribner's Sons, 1976).

Larson, Gerald J. and Deutsch, Eliot (eds.), *Interpreting Across Boundaries: New Essays in Comparative Philosophy* (Princeton, Princeton University Press, 1988).

Lassa, W.A. and Vogt, E.Z. (eds.), *Reader in Comparative Religion* (New York, Harper & Row, 1965).

Lau, D.C., 'Theories of Human Nature in Mencius and Shyuntzyy', *Bulletin of the School of Oriental and African Studies*, Vol. 15, 1953.

——*Tao Te Ching* (Hong Kong, Chinese University Press, 1982).

——(tr.), *Confucius: The Analects* (New York, Penguin Books, 1979).

——(tr.), *Mencius* (Baltimore, Penguin Books, 1970).

Legge, J. (tr.), *Li Ki or Collection of Treatises on the Role of Propriety or Ceremonial Usages* (Delhi, Motilal Banarsidass, 1966).

Lewis, David, 'General Semantics', in Davidson and Hasman (eds.), *Semantics of Natural Language* (Dordrecht, Reidel, 1972), pp. 169–218.

Liang Ch'i-hsiung, 'A Descriptive Review of Hsün Tzu's Thought', *Chinese Studies in Philosophy*, Vol. 6, No. 1, 1974.

Liao, W.K. (tr.), *Han Fei Tzu, Works Translated from the Chinese* (London, A. Probsthain, 1939, 1959).

Lin Yutang (tr., ed.), *The Chinese Theory of Art* (New York, G.P. Putnam's Sons, 1967).

Liu, James J.Y., *The Art of Chinese Poetry* (Chicago, The University of Chicago Press, 1962).

——*Chinese Theories of Literature* (Chicago, The University of Chicago Press, 1975).

——*The Interlingual Critic* (Bloomington, Indiana University Press, 1982).

Liu Wu-chi, *An Introduction to Chinese Literature* (Bloomington, Indiana University Press, 1966).

——and Lo, Irving Yucheng (eds.), *Sunflower Splendor: Three Thousand Years of Chinese Poetry* (Garden City, Anchor Press, 1975).

Lloyd, G.E.R., *Polarity and Analogy* (Cambridge, Cambridge University Press, 1966).

Locke, John, *Reasonableness of Christianity* (London, A. & C. Black, 1958).

Luschei, E.C., *The Logical Systems of Lesniewski* (The Hague, Reidel, 1962).

Mabbott, J.D., *An Introduction to Ethics* (London, Hutchinson University Library, 1966).

MacDonald, Margaret, 'Ethics and the Ceremonial Use of Language' in Max Black (ed.), *Philosophical Analysis: A Collection of Essays* (Ithaca, Cornell University Press, 1950).

Mackie, J.L., *Ethics: Inventing Right and Wrong* (New York, Penguin Books, 1977).

McLeod, M.D. (ed.), *Lucian, Works* (Cambridge, Harvard University Press, 1967).

Manaka, Yoshio and Urquhart, Ian A., *The Layman's Guide to Acupuncture* (New York, Weatherhill, 1972).

Marshall, John, 'Hsün Tzu's Moral Epistemology', *Journal of Chinese Philosophy*, Vol. 14, No. 4, 1987.

Mates, B., *Stoic Logic* (Berkeley, University of California Press, 1961).

Mei, Y.P., 'Hsün Tzu's Theory of Education', *Tsing Hua Journal of Chinese Studies*, Vol. 2, No. 2, 1961.

——'Hsün Tzu's Theory of Government', *Tsing Hua Journal of Chinese Studies*, Vol. 8, Nos. 1–2, 1970.

——(tr.), *The Ethical and Political Works of Mo Tzu* (London, Arthur Probsthain, 1929).

Merleau-Ponty, Maurice (Alphonso Lingis, tr.), *The Visible and the Invisible* (Evanston, Northwestern University Press, 1968).

Metzger, Thomas A., *Escape from Predicament, Neo-confucianism and*

China's Evolving Political Culture (New York, Columbia University Press, 1977).

Moore, Charles A. (ed.), *The Chinese Mind: Essentials of Chinese Philosophy and Culture* (Honolulu, University of Hawaii Press, 1967).

Munro, Donald J., *The Concept of Man in Ancient China* (Stanford, Stanford University Press, 1969).

Munro, Thomas, *Oriental Aesthetics* (Cleveland, The Press of Western Reserve University, 1965).

Naess, Aren and Hannay, Alastair (eds.), *Invitation to Chinese Philosophy* (Oslo, Scandinavian University Books, 1972).

Neville, Robert C., *God the Creator* (Chicago, University of Chicago Press, 1968).

——, *Soldier, Sage, Saint* (New York, Fordham University Press, 1978).

——'From Nothing to Being: The Notion of Creation in Chinese and Western Thought', *Philosophy East and West*, Vol. 30, No. 1, 1980.

——*Reconstruction of Thinking* (Albany, State University of New York Press, 1981).

——*The Tao and the Daimon* (Albany, State University of New York Press, 1982).

——*The Puritan Smile* (Albany, State University of New York Press, 1987).

Nishida, Kitaro (David A. Dilworth and Valdo H. Vigliegmo, trs.), *Art and Morality* (Honolulu, The University Press of Hawaii, 1973).

Nussbaum, N., 'Iris Murdoch: Acastos', in *Times Literary Supplement*, 15 August 1985, p. 881.

Ong, Walter J., *Orality and Literacy: The Technologizing of the Word* (London, Methuen, 1982).

Ortega y Gasset, *Velazquez, Goya and the Dehumanization of Art* (New York, W.W. Norton & Co., 1972).

Osborne, Harold, *Aesthetics and Art Theory* (New York, E.P. Dutton & Co., 1970).

——(ed.), *Aesthetics* (London, Oxford University Press, 1972).

Palmer, Richard E., *Hermeneutics* (Evanston, Northwestern University Press, 1969).

Patzig, G., *Die aristotelische Syllogistik* (Göttingen, Vandenhock und Ruprecht, 1963).

Peirce, Charles, 'The fixation of Belief' in *Collected Papers of Charles Saunders Peirce*, Vol. 2.

Pelikan, Jaroslav, *The Vindication of Tradition* (New York, Yale University Press, 1984).

Perelman, Chaim and Olbrechts-Tyteca, Anna, *The New Rhetoric: A Treatise in Argumentation* (Notre Dame, University of Notre Dame Press, 1969).

302   BIBLIOGRAPHY

Perry, Michael, *The Constitution, the Courts, and Human Rights* (New Haven, Yale University Press, 1982).

Picard, Max, *The World of Silence* (South Bend, Regnery/Gateway, Inc., 1952).

Piovesana, Gino K., *Recent Japanese Philosophical Thought 1862–1962: A Survey* (Tokyo, Enderle, 1963).

Prémare, J.H. de, *Notitia linguae Sinicae* (Hong Kong, Imprimerie de la Société des Missions Etrangeres, 1893).

Priest, Alan, *Aspects of Chinese Painting* (New York, The Macmillan Co., 1954).

Quine, W.V.O., *Word and Object* (Cambridge, MIT Press, 1960).

Radhakrishnan, S. (ed.), *The Upanishads* (London, Allen & Unwin, 1962).

Rawls, John, *A Theory of Justice* (Cambridge, Harvard University Press, 1971).

——'The Independence of Moral Theory', *Proceedings and Addresses of the American Philosophical Association*, Vol. XLVIII, 1974–5.

Rescher, Nicholas, *Dialectics* (Albany, State University of New York Press, 1977).

Rosemont, Jr., Henry, 'State and Society in the Hsün Tzu', *Monumenta Serica*, Vol. 29, 1970–1971.

——'Notes from a Confucian Perspective: Which Human Acts are Moral Acts?', *International Philosophical Quarterly*, Vol. 16, (1976).

Rowland, Benjamin, Jr., *Art in East and West: An Introduction through Comparison* (Cambridge, Harvard University Press, 1954).

Rowley, George, *Principles of Chinese Painting* (Princeton, Princeton University Press, 1959).

Royce, Josiah, *The Problem of Christianity*, (Oxford, Archon Books, 1967).

Schwartz, Stephen P. (ed.), *Naming, Necessity, and Natural Kinds* (Ithaca, Cornell University Press, 1977).

Scott, A.C., *Literature and the Arts in Twentieth Century China* (New York, Doubleday & Co., Inc., 1963).

Searle, John R., 'How to Derive "Ought" from "Is"', *Philosophical Review*, Vol. LXXIII, 1964.

Shaner, David Edward, 'Interpreting Across Boundaries: A Conference of the Society for Asian and Comparative Philosophy', *Philosophy East and West*, Vol. 36, No. 2, 1986.

Shih, Vincent Yu-cheng (tr.), *The Literary Mind and the Carving of Dragons (Wen Hsin Tiao Lung)* (Hong Kong, The Chinese University Press, 1983).

Silbergeld, Jerome, *Chinese Painting Style* (Seattle, University of Washington Press, 1982).

Simons, P.M., 'On Understanding Lesniewski', *History and Philosophy of Logic*, Vol. 3, No. 2, 1982, pp. 165–92.

Sircello, Guy, *A New Theory of Beauty* (Princeton, Princeton University Press, 1975).

Siren, Osvald, *The Chinese on the Art of Painting* (New York, Schocken Books, and Hong Kong, Hong Kong University Press, 1963).

Smith, John E., *Experience and God* (New York, Oxford University Press, 1968).

Smullyan, Raymond M., *The Tao is Silent* (New York, Harper and Row, 1977).

Southern California Law Review, Vol. 58, No. 182, 1985.

Spinoza, Benedictus de, *Ethica Ordine Geometrico Demonstrata* (Heidelberg, Carl Winters, 1925).

——(R.H.M. Elwes, tr.), *Theologico-Political Treatise* (New York, Dover, 1955).

Stitch, Stephen, *From Folk Psychology to Cognitive Science: The Case against Belief* (Cambridge, MIT Press, 1983).

Tarski, A., 'Der Wahrheitsbegriff in den formalisierten Sprachen', *Studia Philosophica*, No. 1, 1935, pp. 261–405.

Teng, Ssu-Yü (tr.), *Family Instructions for the Yen Clan* (Leiden, Brill, 1968).

Thomas, Stephen Nalor, *Practical Reasoning in Natural Language*, 3rd ed. (Englewood Cliffs, Prentice Hall, 1976).

Tu Wei-ming, 'The Creative Tension between Jen and Li', *Philosophy East and West*, Vol. 18, 1968.

——'Li as Humanization', *Philosophy East and West*, Vol. 22, 1972.

Turner, Victor, *Dramas, Fields, and Metaphors* (Ithaca, Cornell University Press, 1974).

Veith, Ilza (tr.), *The Yellow Emperor's Classic of Internal Medicine* (Berkeley, University of California Press, 1949, 1972).

Waley, Arthur, *Three Ways of Thought in Ancient China* (London, Allen & Unwin, 1969).

——(tr.), *The Book of Songs* (New York, Grove Press, Inc., 1937, 1960).

——(tr.), *The Analects of Confucius* (New York, Random House, 1938).

Warnock, G.J., *The Object of Morality* (London, Methuen, 1971).

Watson, Burton, *Chinese Lyricism* (New York, Columbia University Press, 1971).

——(tr.), *Hsün Tzu: Basic Writings* (New York, Columbia University Press, 1963).

Weber, Max (Hans H. Gerth, tr.), *The Religion of China, Confucianism and Taoism* (Glencoe, The Free Press, 1951).

Wilhelm, R. (tr.), *Frühling und Herbst des Lü Bu-We* (Jena, 1928).

Wittgenstein, L., *Philosophical Investigations* (New York, MacMillan, 1958).
——*Tractatus Logico-Philosophicus* (Frankfurt am Main, Suhrkamp, 1963).
Wu Kuang-ming, *Chuang Tzu: World Philosopher at Play* (New York, Crossroad, 1982).
Yang, C.K., *Religion in Chinese Society* (Berkeley, University of California Press, 1970).

Oriental Language Sources

Allinson, Robert E., 'Rujia zhi jinlü: yizhong fouding de jushi' 儒家之金律:一種否定的句式, *Zhexue yu Wenhua* 哲學與文化, vol. 15, no. 11, 1988, pp. 734–7.
Beijing Zhongyixueyuan 北京中醫學院 (ed.), *Neijing Zeyi* 內經釋義 (*A Commentary on the Nei Jing*) (Shanghai, Kexue Jishu Chubanshe, 1964).
Chen Daqi 陳大齊, *Xunzi Xueshuo* 荀子學說 (*The Doctrine of Xunzi*) (Taibei, Zhonghua wenhua, 1954).
——*Kongzi Xueshuo* 孔子學說 (*The Doctrine of Kongzi*) (Taibei, Zhengzhong, 1977).
——*Pingfan de daode guan* 平凡的道德觀 (*Common Conceptions of Morality*) (Taibei, Zhengzhong, 1977).
Chen Puqing 陳蒲清 et al. (eds.), *Zhongguo gudai yuyanxuan* 中国古代寓言選 (*A Selected Anthology of Ancient Chinese Allegories*) (Hunan, Jiaoyu chubanshe, 1981, 1982).
Chen Qiyou 陳奇猷 (ed.), *Lu Shi Chun Qiu jiaoshi* 呂氏春秋校釋 (*A Commentary on the Lüshi Chunqiu*) (Jinan, Xuelin, 1984).
Chengdu Zhongyixueyuan 成都中醫學院 (ed.), *Zhongyixue jichu* 中醫學基礎 (*Fundamentals of Chinese Medicine*) (Sichuan, Renmin chubanshe, 1973).
Duan Yishan 段逸山 (ed.), *Yi guwen zixiu bidu* 醫古文自修必讀 (*Essentials for Self-Study of Ancient Texts on Chinese Medicine*) (Shanghai, Zhongyi Xueyuan chubanshe, 1986).
Feng Yaoming 冯耀明 *Baimalun de luoji jiegou ji qi zhexue yihan* 白馬論的逻輯結構及其哲學意含 (The Logical Structure of the Baimalun and its Philosophical Implications), in *Ehu Yuekan* 鵝湖月刊, No. 117, 1985, pp. 34–43.
Fu Baoshi 傅抱石, *Zhongguo Huihua Lilun* 中國绘畫理論 (*Theories on Chinese Painting*, 1934).
Fudan xuebao shehuikexueban bianjibu 復旦學報社會科學版編輯部 (ed.), *Zhongguo gudai meixueshi yanjiu* 中國古代美學史研究 (*Study of Ancient Chinese Aesthetics*) (Shanghai, Fudan daxue chubanshe, 1983).

Gao Ming 高明, *Lixue xintan* 禮學新探 (*New Explorations of Li*) (Taibei, Shangwu, 1980).

——(ed.), *Da Dai Li Ji jinzhu jinshi* 大戴礼記今註今譯 (*New Commentaries and Translations of the Da Dai Li Ji*) (Taibei, Commercial Press, 1981).

Gu Fang 谷方, 'Heshang Gong "Lao Zi shang ju" kaozheng' 河上公老子章句考證, (Heshang Gong's Commentary on Laozi: a Study) *Zhongguo Zhexue* 中国哲学 Vol. 7, 1982, pp. 41–57.

Han Feizi suoyin 韓非子索引 (*Index to Han Feizi*) (Beijing, Zhonghua, 1982).

Hayashi, Tatsuo 林达夫 et al., *Tetsugaku jiten* 哲学事典 (Tokyo, Heibonsha, 1971).

Hu Daojing 胡道靜, *Gongsun Long Zi kao* 公孫龍子考 (an examination of *Gongsun Long*) (Shanghai, Shangwu, 1934).

Hu Shi 胡適, *Zhongguo Zhexueshi dagang (1918), part I* 中国哲學史大綱, 卷一 (*Outline of History of Chinese Philosophy, Part I*) (Taibei, Shangwu yinshuju, 1947).

Hua Zhengren 華正人 (ed.), *Lidai shufalun wenxuan* 歷代書法論文選 (*Selected Essays on Calligraphy in Chinese History*) (Taibei, huazheng shuju, 1984).

Huang Jinhong 黃錦鋐, *Zhuangzi ji qi wenxue* 莊子及其文學 (*Zhuangzi and his Literature*) (Taibei, Dongda tushu gongsi, 1977).

Jiang Kongyang 蔣孔陽 (ed.), *Zhongguo gudai meixue yishu lunwenji* 中國古代美學藝術論文集 (*Essays on Aesthetics and the Arts in Ancient China*) (Shanghai, Guji chunbanshe, 1981).

Jin Chunfeng 金春峰, 'Ye tan "Lao Zi Heshang Gong zhangji" zhi shidai ji qi yu "Bao Pu Zi" zhi guanxi' 也談老子河上公之時代章句及其與抱朴子之関係 (The Dating of Heshang Gong's Commentary on Laozi and its relation to Bao Puzi) *Zhongguo Zhexue* 中國哲學 Vol. 9, 1983, pp. 137–168.

Jing Fa 經法 (*Ordering the Laws*) (Beijing, Wenwu chubanshe, 1976).

Li Disheng 李滌生, *Xunzi zhishi* 荀子集釋 (*Xunzi: Collected Commentaries*) (Taibei, Xuesheng, 1979).

Li Shixi 厉時熙 (ed.), *Yinwenzi jianzhu* 尹文子簡注 (*annotated Yin Wenzi*) (Shanghai, 1977).

Li Xuanshen 李玄深, *Gudian shige changshi* 古典詩歌常識 (*Introduction to the Classical Poetry and Songs*) (Xianggang, Zhongliu chubanshe, 1974).

Li Yuegang 李日剛 et al., *Sanli yanjiu lunji* 三禮研究論集 (*Collected Essays on the Three Li*) (Taibei, Liming, 1981).

Li Zhongpu 李鍾樸 et al. (eds.), *Zhongxiyi jiehe yanjiu silu ji fangfaxue* 中西醫結合研究思路及方法學 (*Methodologies of Research into Combined Chinese–Western Medicine*) (Shanghai, Kexue jishu chubanshe, 1985).

Liang Qixiong 梁啓雄, *Xunzi Jianshi* 荀子柬釋 (*Xunzi: Selected Interpretations*) (Taibei, Shangwu yinshuju, 1978).

Liu Dajie 劉大杰, *Zhongguo wenxue fadashi* 中國文學發達史 (*History of the Development of Chinese Literature*) (Taibei, Zhonghua shuju, 1968).

Liu Duzhou 劉渡舟 et al. (eds.), *Shanghanlun zhujie* 傷寒論註解 (*A Commentary on Shang Han Lun*) (Tianjin, Kexue jishu chubanshe, 1983).

Liu Si 劉勰 (ed. by Huang Shulin 黃叔琳), *Wenxin diaolong jizhu* 文心雕龍輯注 (*Collected Commentaries on the Wenxin Diaolong*) (Xianggang, Shangwu yinshuguan, 1960).

Lo Genze 羅根澤, *Zhongguo wenxue pipingshi* 中國文學批評史 (*A History of Literary Criticism in China*) (Shanghai, Guji chubanshe, 1957, 1958, 1984).

Lu Ji 陸機, *Wenfu jishi* 文賦集釋 (*A Poemprose on Literature: Collected Commentaries*) (Shanghai, Guji chubanshe, 1984).

Lu Kanru 陸侃如 and Mou Shijin 牟世金, *Wenxin Diaolong Shizhu* 文心雕龍譯註 (*A Commentary on Wenxin Diaolong*) (Jinan, Qilu shushe, 1982, 1985).

Lu Xun 魯迅, *Lu Xun lun qiangzuo* 魯迅論創作 (*Lu Xün on Creative Writing*) (Xianggang, Jiulong hongtu chubanshe).

Luan Xing 欒星 (ed.), *Gongsun Long Zi changjian* 公孫龍子長箋 (Detailed Commentary on Gongsun Long) (Zhongshou, Zhongshoushuhuashe, 1982).

Mi Wenkai 糜文開 and Pei Puxian 裴普賢, *Shijing xinshang yu yanjiu* 詩經欣賞與研究 (*Appreciations of the Shijing*) (Taibei, Sanmin shuju, 1964, 1969).

Mou Shijin 牟世金 and Lu Kanru 陸侃如 (eds.), *Wenxin Diaolong yi zhu* 文心雕龍譯注 (*Commentaries on the Wenxin Diaolong*) (Jinan, Qilushushe, 1981).

Ohama, Akira 大濱晧, *Chugokuteki shii no dento* 中国的思惟の伝統 (*The Tradition of the Chinese Way of Thinking*) (Tokyo, Keiso shobo, 1969).

Peng Fang 彭放 (ed.), *Guo Moruo tan chuangzuo* 郭沫若談創作 (*Guo Moruo on Creative Writing*) (Heilongjiang, Renmin chubanshe, 1982, 1983).

Qi Yuzhang 祁玉章 (ed.), *Jia Yi Xin Shu* 賈誼新書 (*The New Book by Jia Yi*) (Taibei, Zhongguo Wenhua Zazhishe, 1974).

Qiu Peiran 裘沛然 et al. (eds.), *Zhongyi lidai gejia xueshuo* 中醫歷代各家學說 (*A Historical Anthology on Theories of Chinese Medicine*) (Shanghai, Kexue jishu chubanshe, 1984).

Renmin wenxue chubanshe bianjibu 人民文學出版社編輯部 (ed.), *Tangshi jianshangji* 唐詩鑒賞集 (*Collected Essays on Appreciations of Tang Poetry*) (Beijing, Renmin chubanshe, 1981, 1987).

Shiba, Rokuro 斯波六郎, *Chugokubungaku niokeru kodokukan* 中国文学

における孤独感 (*'Loneliness' in Chinese Literature*) (Tokyo, Iwanami shoten, 1958, 1968).

Suzuki, Shuji 鈴木修次, *Nihon Kango to Chûgoku: Kanji-bunkaken no kindaika* 日本汉语と中国: 汉字文化圈の近代化, (Tokyo, Chuokoron-sha, 1981).

Tang Guizhang 唐圭璋 (ed.), *Tangsongci jianshang cidian* 唐宋詞鑒賞辭典 (*A Dictionary for the Appreciation of Tang and Song Lyrics*) (Jiang-su, Guji chubanshe, 1986).

Tu Guangshe 涂光社, *Wenxin shilun* 文心十論 (*Ten Essays on Wenxin Diaolong*) (Shenyang, Xinhua shusian, 1986).

Wang Li 王力 *Hanyu Shigao* 汉语史稿 (History of Chinese) (Beijing, Zhonghua, 1980).

——(ed.), *Gudai hanyu* 古代漢語 (*Classical Chinese*) (Beijing, Zhonghua shuju, 1981).

Wang Meng'ou 王夢鷗, *Wenxue gailun* 文學概論 (*General Theories on Literature*) (Taibei, Yiwen yinshuguan, 1976).

——*Gudian wenxuelun tansuo* 古典文学論探索 (*Researches on Theories of Classical Literature*) (Taibei, Zhengzhong shuju, 1984).

Wang Yao 王瑶, *Zhongguo wenxue sixiang* 中古文學思想 (*Thought in Ancient Chinese Literature*) (Xianggang, Zhongliu chubanshe, 1973).

Wang Yunxi 王運熙 et al. (eds.), *Zhongguo wenxue pipingshi* 中國文學批評史 (*A History of Literary Criticism in China*) (Shanghai, Guji chubanshe, 1964, 1979, 1985).

Wei Zhengtong 韋政通, *Xunzi yu gudai zhexue* 荀子與古代哲学 (*Xunzi and Ancient Philosophy*) (Taibei, Shangwu yinshuju, 1974).

Weng Xianliang 翁顯良, *Gushi yingyi* 古詩英譯 (*An English Translation of Chinese Ancient Poems*) (Beijing, Beijing chubanshe, 1985).

Wu Xuantao 吳玄濤, *Gudian shige rumen* 古典詩歌入門 (*An Introduction to Classical Poetry and Lyrics*) (Xianggang, Wanli shudian, 1963).

Wu Yunpeng 吳雲鵬, *Zhongguo wenxueshi* 中國文學史 (*A History of Chinese Literature*) (Tainan, Jinghui shuju, 1967).

Wu Zeyu 吳則虞 (ed.), *Yanzi Chunqiu jishi* 晏子春秋集釋 (Beijing, Zhonghua, 1962).

Xiang Tuijie 項退結, *Zhongguo minzuxing yanjiu* 中國民族性研究 (*Characteristics of the Chinese People*) (Taiwan, Shangwu yinshuguan, 1966).

Xiao Difei 蕭滌非 et al., *Tangshi jianshang cidian* 唐詩鑒賞辭典 (*A Dictionary for the Appreciation of Tang Poetry*) (Shanghai, Cishu chubanshe, 1983, 1987).

Xie Fuya 謝扶雅, *Lunli xue xinlun* 論理學新論 (*A New Inquiry Concerning Ethics*) (Taibei, Shangwu yinshuju, 1973).

Xu Fuguan 徐復觀, *Zhongguo Yishu Jingshen* 中國言藝術精神 (*The Aesthetic Spirit in China*) (Taibei, Xuesheng shuju, 1966).

——*Zhongguo wenxue lunji* 中國文學論集 (*Collected Essays on Chinese Literature*) (Taibei, Xuesheng shuju, 1976).

Xu Jingsheng 許敬生 et al. (eds.), *Yiguwen xuandu* 醫古文選讀 (*Selected Readings on Ancient Chinese Medicine*) (Henan, Kexue jishu chubanshe, 1983).

Xu Li 徐立 and Chen Xin 陳新, *Guren tan wenzhang xiezuo* 古人談文章寫作 (*Ancient Writers on How to Write Well*) (Guangdong, Renmin chubanshe, 1985).

Yan Yu 嚴羽, *Canglang shihua xiaoshi* 滄浪詩話校釋 (*A Critical Commentary on Canglang Shihua*) (Taibei, Liren shuju, 1983).

Yang Bojun 楊伯峻, *Chunqiu Zuozhuan zhu* 春秋左傳注 (*Commentary on the Chunqiu and Zuo Zhuan*) (Beijing, Zhonghua, 1981).

Yao Zhi'an 姚止庵, *Suwenjing zhujiejie* 素問經注節解 (*Selected Commentaries on the Suwenjing*) (Beijing, Renmin weisheng chubanshe, 1963, 1983).

Zai Renhou 蔡仁厚, *Kong Meng Xun zhexue* 孔孟荀哲學 (*Philosophy of Kongzi, Mengzi, and Xunzi*) (Taibei, Xuesheng, 1984).

Zhan Ying 詹鍈, *Wenxin Diaolong de fenggexue* 文心雕龍的風格學 (*On 'Style' in the Wenxin Diaolong*) (Taibei, Muduo chubanshe, 1983).

Zhang Shizhao 章士釗, *Zhongdeng guowen dian* 中等國文典 (Shanghai, Commercial Press, 1907).

Zhao Ming Wenxuan 昭明文選 (*The Wenxuan of Emperor Zhao Ming*) (Tainan, Tainan xinshiji chubanshe, 1975).

Zhao Shanyi 趙善詒 (ed.), *Shuoyuan shuzheng* 說苑疏證 (*Commentary on the Shuoyuan*) (Shanghai, Huadongshifandaxue, 1985).

Zhao Zecheng 趙則誠 et al. (eds.), *Zhongguo gudai wenxue lilun cidian* 中国古代文学理論辭典 (*A Dictionary of Theories on Ancient Chinese Literature*) (Jilin, Jilin wenshi chubanshe, 1985).

Zhongguo wenshiciliao bianji weiyuanhui 中國文史資料編輯委員會, *Zhongguo meixueshi ciliao xuanbian* 中國美學史資料選編 (*Anthology of Materials on Chinese Aesthetics*) (Taibei, Guangmei shuju, 1984).

Zhongwen Da Zidian 中文大辭典 (*The Encyclopedic Dictionary of the Chinese Language*) (Taibei, Zhonghua Xueyuan, 1979).

Zhou Zhenfu 周振甫 (ann., tr.), *Wenxin diaolong xuanyi* 文心雕龍選譯 (*Selected Translations of Wenxin Diaolong*) (Beijing, Zhonghua Shuju, 1980, 1982).

Zhu Dongrun 朱東潤, *Zhongguo wenxue lunji* 中國文学論集 (*Collected Essays on Chinese Literature*) (Beijing, Zhonghua shuju, 1983).

Zhu Guangqian 朱光潛, *Zhu Guangqian Meixue Wenji* 朱光潛美学文集 (*Collected Works on Aesthetics by Zhu Guangqian*) (Shanghai, Wenyi chubanshe, 1982).

Zhu Ziqing 朱自清, *Jingdian Changtan* 經典常談 (*Introduction to the Classics in China*) (Xianggang, Taiping Shuju, 1965, 1981).

——*Zhu Ziqing Quanji* 朱自清全集 (*Complete Works of Zhu Ziqing*) (Tainan, Dadong shuju, 1967).

——*Zhongguo Geyao* 中國歌謠 (*Songs and Lyrics in China*) (Xianggang, Zhonghua shuju, 1976).

——*Shiyan Zhibian* 詩言志辨 (*On 'Poetry Expresses Heart's Intentions'*) (Taibei, Hanjing wenhua, 1983).

Zhu Zugeng 諸祖耿 (ed.), *Zhangguoce jizhu huikao* 戰國策集注彙考 (*Collected Commentaries on the Zhanguoce*) (Yangzhou, Jiangzhouguji, 1985).

Zhuang Zhong 莊中, *Zhongguo huashi yanjiu* 中國畫史研究 (*Researches into Chinese Painting*) (Taibei, Zhengzhong shuju, 1956).

Index